The Dambusters Raid

also by John Sweetman

Balaclava 1854
The Charge of the Light Brigade
Tirpitz: Hunting the Beast
The Crimean War
Tannenberg 1914

The Dambusters Raid

John Sweetman

CASSELL

Cassell Military Paperbacks

Cassell
Wellington House, 125 Strand
London WC2R 0BB

First published by Jane's Publishing Company Limited 1982
as *The Dams Raid: Epic or Myth*
Revised edition published by Arms and Armour 1990
as *The Dambusters Raid*
This Cassell Military Paperbacks edition 2002
Reprinted 2003

British Library Cataloguing-in-Publication Data
A catalogue record for this book is available from the British
Library

Printed and bound in Great Britain by
Cox & Wyman Ltd., Reading, Berks.

CONTENTS

ACKNOWLEDGEMENTS

A large number of people in the United Kingdom and abroad gave me invaluable assistance during the preparation of the first edition of this book, and to them I express my sincere appreciation for all their efforts on my behalf. I am deeply indebted to Sir Barnes and Lady Wallis for their overwhelming kindness during countless visits to White Hill House, Effingham, where I benefited immeasurably from their friendship, hospitality and unfettered access to a vast collection of private and official papers whose nature and significance Sir Barnes continued to discuss until shortly before his death. Dr A. R. Collins, who as a Scientific Officer at the Road Research Laboratory carried out experiments in connection with the destruction of gravity dams prior to Operation Chastise, has been both a valuable source of information and a painstaking critic. I cannot underline too heavily my gratitude to him. And I am also extremely grateful to Air Cdre H. A. Probert and Sqn Ldr J. P. McDonald of the Air Historical Branch, Ministry of Defence, for their many helpful suggestions and ready assistance.

The staff of the following libraries and archives have supplied me with material and patiently answered a multitude of questions:

Albert F. Simpson Historical Research Center, Maxwell Air Force Base, USA
Bundesarchiv-Militärarchiv, Freiburg, Federal Republic of Germany
Canadian Forces Records Centre, Ottawa, Canada
City of Birmingham Public Libraries
Commonwealth War Graves Commission, Maidenhead, Berks.
Department of Aviation Records, RAF Museum, Hendon
Department of Defence (Air Force Office), Canberra, Australia
Doncaster Metropolitan Borough Council Archives

Ennepe-Wasserverband, Gevelsberg, Federal Republic of Germany
Essex County Record Office
Exeter City Library
Gemeente Harlingen, The Netherlands
Imperial War Museum: Department of Documents and Department of
 Photographs
Institution of Civil Engineers
Leicestershire Record Office
Lincoln Public Library
Ministry of Defence, London, Air Historical Branch
Ministry of Defence, London, Department AR8b(RAF)
Portsmouth City Library
Public Record Office, Kew, London
RAF Staff College, Bracknell
Rhayader Public Library
Royal Aircraft Establishment
Royal Air Force Museum, Hendon
Royal Military Academy, Sandhurst
Royal Ordnance Museum, Priddy's Hard, Gosport
Ruhrverband und Ruhrtalsperrenverein, Essen, Federal Republic of Germany
Severn-Trent Water Authority
Sheffield City Libraries
South Yorkshire County Record Office
Transport and Road Research Laboratory, Crowthorne, Berks.
Wupperverband, Wuppertal, Federal Republic of Germany
617 Squadron Museum, RAF Scampton, Lincs.

I readily acknowledge permission to use the information which they have produced, and I particularly thank the Controller of Her Majesty's Stationery Office for permission to reproduce photographs and to quote from records under Crown copyright; the Imperial War Museum for allowing reproduction of photographs held there; the Ruhrverband und Ruhrtalsperrenverein, the Ennepe-Wasserverband and the Bundesarchiv-Militärarchiv in the Federal Republic of Germany; British Aircraft Corporation, Weybridge; Vickers Ltd, London; and the Officer Commanding No 617 Squadron RAF for similar permission. I am grateful also to the following for supplying photographs, illustrations, sketches and written material for reproduction: R. Burton, Dr A. R. Collins, E. C. Johnson, S. Oancia, Mrs A. Shannon, L. J. Sumpter, F. Tees and Sir Barnes Wallis.

Many of those directly involved in Operation Chastise gave, and many continue to give, freely of their time to meet me and/or correspond with me:

Marshal of the Royal Air Force Sir Arthur Harris, then Air Officer Commanding-in-Chief Bomber Command

Lord Louis Mountbatten, then Chief of Combined Operations

Air Chief Marshal the Honourable Sir Ralph Cochrane, then Air Officer Commanding No 5 Group

Air Vice-Marshal S. O. Bufton, then Director of Bomber Operations

Air Vice-Marshal H. V. Satterly, then Senior Air Staff Officer, No 5 Group

Members of 617 Squadron who flew on the operation: K. W. Brown, G. A. Chalmers, J. H. Clay, H. B. Feneron, D. P. Heal, H. S. Hobday, C. L. Howard, W. Howarth, E. C. Johnson, G. L. Johnson, R. G. T. Kellow, D. A. MacLean, S. Oancia, H. E. O'Brien, G. Rice, D. Rodger, D. J. Shannon, T. D. Simpson, L. J. Sumpter, F. Tees, W. C. Townsend, D. R. Walker, D. E. Webb, Gp Capt I. Whittaker

Other Service personnel connected with RAF Scampton or 617 Squadron, 16 May, 1943: Dr M. W. Arthurton, Mrs E. Bark (née Broxholme), J. A. Bryden, A. Drury, Mrs F. Gillan, Rev C. D. Hulbert, H. K. Munro, G. E. Powell, Mrs A. Shannon (née Fowler)

Ministry of Aircraft Production personnel: Sir Benjamin Lockspeiser, N. E. Rowe.

Vickers-Armstrongs employees: A. D. Grant, H. Jeffree, R. C. Handasyde, W. E. Startup

Royal Aircraft Establishment employees: C. W. Shaw, S. Wright

Others directly or indirectly concerned: H. C. Bergel, Mrs E. Gibson, Mrs H. V. Satterly, Gp Capt F. W. Winterbotham

The undermentioned have also provided considerable assistance, often of an important technical nature (ranks and all Service and civilian posts are those held at the time of assistance):

Herr G. Aders, H. Archer, G. Allen, M. Allison (Ruston-Bucyrus Ltd.), Gp Capt Sir Douglas Bader, J. V. D. Banham (Severn-Trent Water Authority), N. Barfield (Public Relations Manager, British Aircraft Corporation Ltd, Weybridge), D. R. Barraclough (Institute of Geological Sciences), D. M. Bennett (Severn-Trent Water Authority), T. Bennett (617 Squadron Association), N. W. Boorer, R. Burton, E. (Roy) Callow, Gp Capt G. L. Cheshire, Mrs Z. K. L. Chojecki (née Rowett), J. G. de Coninck (Manager and Head of BAC Film Unit), Gp Capt M. M. Dalston (British High Commission, Canberra), Oberstleutnant J. Damm (who undertook valuable research in the archives of Wasser-und-Schiffahrtsamt, Hannover-Münden), Herr H. Diener, Heer H. B. van den Dool, Flt Lt J. B. Dyson, P. Emmerson (Manager, Records Services,

British Steel Corporation, East Midlands Region), Mevr H. van Els-Theunissen, Herr H. Euler, J. A. Fielding (Building Research Advisory Service), Mrs M. E. Fish (Managing Editor, *Sixth Sense*), Maj M. Foster RE, R. Friedel, Miss J. Fulbrook (Transport and Road Research Laboratory), Cdr N. C. Glen (Hydrographic Department, Ministry of Defence), R. B. Goodall (Art Department, National Army Museum, for photographic assistance), Lt Col D. C. Goodban RAEC, P. Gordon Spencer (Director and General Manager, Essex Water Company), H. Hamer, Herr E. Handke, Sqn Ldr P. C. J. Herbert (British Defence Liaison Staff, Ottawa), Miss J. C. Hill (Technical Information Officer, National Physical Laboratory), Heer L. J. H. Hoesen, M. Hughes (Press and Information Officer, Severn-Trent Water Authority), M. B. Illott, D. Irving, T. C. Iveson (617 Squadron Association), K. W. Jones (formerly of Woolwich Arsenal), L. B. Jones (Factory Secretary, Royal Ordnance Factory, Chorley), Professor R. V. Jones, General Josef Kammhuber (former Commander of German night fighters), Herr P. Keiser, Flt Lt D. T. Lingard, A. A. Lowes, R. S. McLaren (British Steel Corporation), M. Meredith, Lt Col (Retd) J. A. Moore, Lt Cdr N. St J. Morley-Hall (British Defence Liaison Staff, Wellington, New Zealand), Wg Cdr R. F. Mudge (Air Attaché, The Hague), Mrs K. Newby-Grant, A. J. (Bill) Newman (formerly of Building Research Station), Dr P. Norris, G. C. S. Oliver (former Manager, Corby [Northants] & District Water Company), Mrs P. Podmore (former secretary to Sir Barnes Wallis), Mrs E. Priestley, F. Rayment (formerly of National Physical Laboratory), G. Raymond-Barker (Royal Greenwich Observatory), S. A. Richmond, J. Robertson, Lt Col B. A. Ruddy RAEC, A. J. W. Scopes (Manager, Corby [Northants] & District Water Company), H. E. Scrope (Company Secretary, Vickers Ltd), Flt Lt P. Shepherd (who plotted surviving logs of Chastise), Herr Albert Speer (former German Minister for Armament and War Production), Venerable H. J. Stuart (Chaplain-in-Chief RAF), J. R. Tate (St Edwards School, Oxford), R. Turnill, Wg Cdr J. C. Weller, B. Wexham (Photographic Manager, Vickers Ltd), J. Wickens (former member of Wg Cdr Gibson's crew on 106 Squadron).

I am most grateful to colleagues of the academic staff at the Royal Military Academy Sandhurst for their advice and encouragement, notably E. A. Brett-James, Dr A. H. le Q. Clayton, Dr E. R. Holmes, J. D. P. Keegan, Lt Col (Retd) J. P. Lawford, A. J. Newman, P. A. Warner and Dr S. J. Wright; to J. R. F. de Klerk for translating Dutch correspondence and to W. R. Newby-Grant and D. B. White of the Languages Section for dealing with a mountain of German letters and documents. Other colleagues have kindly checked draft chapters and suggested helpful amendments: Capt A. Danchev RAEC, Maj E. MacIntosh RAEC, M. Midlane, W. R. Newby-Grant (once more), K. R. Simpson, G. R. Snailham, Lt Cdr (Retd) G. S. Stavert and Gp Capt

(Retd) J. Walsh. My thanks are due also to student officers of CM Class 6, RCC 27, who were dragooned into assisting with photographic captions.

Dr A. R. Collins, A. D. Grant and N. E. Rowe carefully read the opening chapters of the typescript; D. P. Heal, H. S. Hobday, G. Rice and L. J. Sumpter (who all flew on Operation Chastise) similarly looked at chapters directly connected with 617 Squadron. All provided valuable comments and prevented unnecessary errors, and I am very much in their debt as a result.

At times, to protect my correspondents from acute eyestrain, Mrs M. Boyle, Mrs M. Lever and Mrs K. Rumbold have given typing assistance. My sincere thanks are due to them and to Mrs D. Fox for struggling through a literary maze to produce the final typescript.

I am further indebted to the following, who have kindly assisted me with additional information since publication of the first edition of this book: G. Barnes, Herr K. Bischof, Wg Cdr G. A. Bone, B. Broad, Mrs M. J. Brooks, P. S. J. Buller, C. E. Burgess, W. Carter, M. Chester, I. Davies, Mrs M. Dove (Roy Chadwick's daughter), P. J. V. Elliott, L. R. Fox, V. Gill, H. Goldstraw, L. Goldstraw, G. E. Hunton, B. King, Dr D. J. Littler, Dr J. McCormick, Dr R. McCormick, C. E. MacKay, R. Marshall, R. Owen (official historian, 617 Squadron), N. Parker, L. J. Pearce, H. J. Penrose, Miss D. Shepherd, R. F. Thoen, Dr. M. R. Stopes-Roe (née Wallis), B. W. Wallis and C. Wallis (Sir Barnes' children), Sqn Ldr E. A. Wass, (hon. sec, 617 Squadron Association), Dr D. W. Yalden, Dr N. Young.

PREFACE

'The Dambusters Raid', visually so dramatic in its execution and achievement, is possibly the best-known single operation in the history of aerial warfare.

The spectacular success of British, Canadian, Australian and New Zealander airmen, together with a lone American, from 617 Squadron RAF in breaching two of Germany's massive gravity dams to release torrents of water from their reservoirs during the early hours of Monday 17 May 1943 was rapidly publicised by the press and radio in neutral and Allied countries. By Tuesday 18 May, details had been flashed quite literally round the world. Photographs of the shattered dam walls, empty lakes and devastation in the path of the ensuing floods (brought back by reconnaissance aircraft within hours of the last Lancaster's return) sensationally illustrated the accuracy and effectiveness of the raid. Public, political and military opinion reacted swiftly and enthusiastically. Joseph Stalin signalled congratulations from the Soviet Union. In the United States the British Prime Minister, Winston Churchill, was loudly acclaimed when he referred to the operation in his address to a joint session of Congress on 19 May.

Yet, for security reasons, the story that emerged then was necessarily incomplete and even, in some respects, deliberately misleading. With official records also closed to the public for another thirty years, further inaccuracies and embellishments gradually became an integral part of the legend. So a book by Wg Cdr G. P. (Guy) Gibson, who led 617 Squadron to the dams, published in 1946 perforce concealed full details of the operational plan and the special weapon used, disguising their codenames and the identity of the civilian engineer principally involved. Gibson's book also wrongly conveyed the impression that all of those who flew to the dams were already highly decorated and experienced, extremely exuberant and personally selected to join the Squadron. It unfortunately contained, too, passages of confusion and error, which have since misled uncritical readers and authors: for instance, in the spelling of names, sequence of pre-operational events and distribution of aircraft among the different waves of the attacking force.

Still frequently shown on cinema and television screens with its attraction heightened by stirring theme music, a commercial film released in 1955 has further distorted the true course of events. Its producer admitted to Wallis a 'somewhat simplified treatment of highly complicated issues', pleading need for 'oversimplification, because we have so little time in which to make clear to an uninstructed audience . . . our film cannot hold interest unless we present "living" people whose feelings an audience can share', hence 'the many personal touches (by tacit admission, fictional) introduced to this end'. With a minimum of characters, the script concentrated on two dams, instead of the four actually attacked and six listed for attack. Gibson was shown discovering a method to ensure that aircraft maintained their precise, required height during the attack run, while watching theatre spotlights focus on a row of chorus girls. Less romantically, in reality a civilian scientist (Benjamin Lockspeiser) remembered an experiment with beams from aircraft to assist the inshore hunting of U-boats and thought, with modification, the idea worth trying for Chastise. All bomb-aimers supposedly used a triangular wooden contraption as a sight for gauging the exact point at which to release the special weapon over the water in front of the dam. In fact, during practice most crews found this device impracticable and worked out their own system involving marks on the clear vision panel in the nose of the aircraft. 'Mutt' Summers was shown inaccurately as the only test pilot and Gibson to have brought his own crew from 106 Squadron. Simplicity did, indeed, override accuracy.

The film has also popularised the claim that Barnes Wallis developed single-handed the special weapon used against the dams, in the face of reluctant (in his view 'singularly stupid') senior officers and obstructive civil servants. Undoubtedly, he did have an uphill struggle to convince responsible authorities that he had the means to breach the dams. But the Air Staff had long recognised their importance (especially the Möhne and Sorpe). Since 1937, it had been vainly seeking a way of destroying them; and these efforts intensified once war broke out. Special Operations Executive and Combined Operations staffs were among the many who strove to breach the Möhne Dam, at various times advancing proposals to use rockets, torpedoes, paratroopers, a pilotless aircraft or flying boat packed with explosives. Wg Cdr C. R. Finch-Noyes outlined a means of attacking this target, which had many of the features seen in the 1943 operation. In 1940, Air Chief Marshal Sir Charles Portal (three years later Chief of the Air Staff and a firm supporter of Chastise) advanced the concept of using a squadron of modified Hampdens as a long-range torpedo force against the Möhne. And it is clear that, certainly from mid-1940 onwards, Wallis did have access to official files and received considerable assistance from civilian and Service authorities. However, in turn, they had sound reasons for caution. Many hair-brained schemes passed across their desks (one of the more bizarre being the dropping of rats by parachute with incendiaries tied to their tails), and in 1940 by his own later admission Wallis persisted with a proposal for destroying the Möhne Dam which had no realistic hope of success at that time.

Acknowledging that Wallis did have valuable official help during his three-year quest for the wherewithal to destroy the German dams, and access to previous schemes for doing so, should not in any sense detract from his unique achievement in designing the ultimate weapon and refining the technique for its delivery. Nonetheless, it is a fact that a wide range of organisations throughout the length and breadth of Britain did contribute expertise, advice and invaluable effort to the project: the Road Research Laboratory; Building Research Station; National Physical Laboratory; Royal Ordnance factories at Chorley and Woolwich; Vickers-Armstrongs facilities at Newcastle, Barrow, Weybridge, Burhill and Crayford; A. V. Roe & Co Ltd at Manchester; the Royal Aircraft Establishment at Farnborough; the Armament and Aeronautical Experimental Establishment at Boscombe Down; and smaller manufacturing concerns like the Oxley Engineering Company at Leeds and the Limmer and Trinidad Lake Asphalt Company in London, among others.

Even more critically, as policy and operational decisions in the military sphere lay very much with them, the Air Ministry and Admiralty were closely involved. So, too, were the Ministries of Supply, Production, Economic Warfare and Aircraft Production. Few accounts of Operation Chastise even mention Admiralty association with the special weapon or recognise that three versions of it were under trial at the same time. They fail to explain that two types of dam (masonry and earth-supported concrete), built in quite different ways, were listed for attack. Thus, at the Sorpe Dam the bombers were briefed to fly along the crest not at right angles to it, and to drop their weapons on top not bounce them across the reservoir.

Opening official records to public scrutiny has not entirely dispelled misunderstanding about the operation – for example, in the speed and height of the attacking aircraft, shape and size of the special weapon and type of explosive in it. Statements, summaries and maps drawn up after the event – some, inevitably, reproduced in official publications – describe near-perfect execution of the Operation Order. Battles on land, at sea or in the air rarely follow the path optimistically traced in staff conferences or briefing sessions. Notwithstanding nearly two months of concentrated preparation and training, in this respect Operation Chastise proved no exception. On the night, crews experienced unexpected crises of navigation, uncharted flak, mist-filled valleys to hamper target identification and complications stemming from mechanical failure and human error. None of the first four aircraft to take off reached its objective. As one survivor has concluded, it was not 'a beautifully planned operation: all of it was very much fit and make fit, despite what has been said afterwards'.

There is, as well, a disturbing tendency by the unscrupulous or careless to make selective use of documents later to undermine operations. Chastise has not escaped this unwelcome attention. In the immediate aftermath of the raid, Air Chief Marshal Sir Arthur Harris, Air Officer Commanding-in-Chief (AOC-in-C) Bomber Command, declared the results of Chastise to be a 'major disaster' for the enemy, and Sir Archibald Sinclair, the Secretary of State for Air, described the operation as 'an epic feat of arms'. After the war, however, various British and German sources have dismissed such claims as extravagant and gone on to advance specific, often swingeing, criticisms of the entire enterprise. An example of such unreasonable bias has been concentration on one section of a report by a Ministry of Economic Warfare official in April 1943 to suggest that the Air Ministry did not recognise the significance of the Sorpe Dam, thus ignoring active interest in its destruction for the previous six years.

A number of interesting facts do emerge from a study of relevant papers, however – for example, the fact that the Germans recovered one of the special weapons from a crashed Lancaster during the morning of 17 May (shortly after the raid) and, in little over a month, had compiled full details of its construction and how it operated. Hence Allied obsession with secrecy for twenty years afterwards was utterly futile. More interestingly, only the Germans described Wallis's special weapon accurately. It was not a 'mine' (the contemporary description, which has been retained throughout this text), nor a 'bouncing bomb', despite that romantic and universally accepted definition. Wallis used a depth-charge to demolish the dam walls, after it had been back-spun across the surface of the reservoirs. The Germans correctly identified Upkeep (the codename), therefore, as a 'revolving depth charge'.

It now appears clear that one of the crews attacked the wrong dam without realising its error; however, back in England, staff officers most probably did realise and thereafter referred to an attack on a dam (the Schwelme) that did not exist. However, most definitely no blame should be attached to the crew in question, which made strenuous efforts in utter isolation to locate the target as daylight fast approached and mist began to fill the valleys. Its experience underscores the paucity of visual aids provided at briefings for other than the Möhne and Sorpe dams, and the skill of all 617 Squadron crews who pressed their attacks carrying a 'five ton lump of iron' suspended beneath their aircraft, while flying across enemy territory at a maximum of 100 feet without the protection of a mid-upper gunner.

In short, the story that has become accepted over the years, based upon original misleading cover stories and enhanced in a variety of ways down the years, is neither accurate nor complete. Much still needs to be told. The nineteen Lancasters that lifted so laboriously off the grass runway of RAF Scampton in May 1943 represented the point of an enormous technological pencil, which had taken six years to sharpen. Barnes Wallis became actively involved during the last three years of that process, 617 Squadron during the final seven weeks. Wg Cdr Gibson's leadership, his training of the new squadron up to the high level of competence required of it in that short period and his courage on the night cannot and should not be disputed. He thoroughly deserved his Victoria Cross.

Incredibly, when the decision to mount Operation Chastise was confirmed on 26 February 1943, no full-scale drawings of the special weapon even existed. The first (and only) test with a fully armed weapon, released and propelled across the water, took place on 13 May – just three days before the operation. Relief at that success was short-lived. When trials on the smaller version of the weapon (Highball), destined for use by Mosquitoes against the German battleship *Tirpitz*, failed, the Royal Navy attempted to stop Upkeep from being launched against the dams for fear of compromising the whole revolutionary technique. This inter-Service deadlock was broken not in London, but 3,000 miles away in Washington, where the British and American Chiefs of Staff were meeting. On 14 May, the Air Ministry received a welcome signal: 'Chiefs of Staff agree to immediate use of Upkeep without waiting for Highball.' The latest date for doing so was 19 May. Precious little time remained.

1

Theory

Aimed at the heart of Germany's armament industry in the Ruhr and her movement of war *matériel* through the Weser Valley and Mittelland Canal, Chastise was by no means unique as a concept. Before the Second World War operations of this nature had been planned as the nub of the RAF effort, and they had their roots in the First World War, when rapid technical advances led to long-range bombing by both sides. Then the twin prongs of 'strategic bombing' theory, which held that bombing of enemy factories and centres of population beyond the battlefield would cause collapse of production capacity and civilian morale, were forged. After the First World War, Maj Gen Sir Hugh Trenchard concluded that the moral effect of bombing outweighed the physical by twenty to one and, on becoming Chief of the Air Staff (CAS) for the second time, pointed to the relevance of this conclusion for the future: 'There can be no doubt that we must be prepared for long-distance aerial operations against an enemy's main source of supply.'

Less than twenty years later, needing to prepare for a second European conflict, the Air Staff turned to strategic bombing, in which it had come explicitly to believe. German industry became a particular focus of attention, and as war loomed closer the Director of Plans sought to co-ordinate intelligence on targets from inside and outside the Service. One such source was the Industrial Intelligence in Foreign Countries Committee, chaired by the experienced bureaucrat Sir Maurice (later Lord) Hankey, which with the aid of a full-time staff under Maj Desmond Morton at its subordinate

Industrial Intelligence Centre evaluated the war potential of possible enemies. Responsible to the Committee of Imperial Defence (CID), it soon acquired a satellite Air Targets Sub-Committee, also chaired by Hankey. The interests of this body, and its parent Industrial Intelligence Committee, soon extended to strategic air policy and inevitably progressed to identification of targets for Bomber Command to attack.

In October 1937 a list of 16 plans (known as the Western Air [WA] Plans) for use in the event of war was drawn up by the Air Staff. One was WA5, 'to attack the German War Industry including the supply of oil with priority to that in the Ruhr, Rhineland and Saar'. Bomber Command, responsible for its tactical implementation, decided to concentrate on 19 power plants and 26 coking plants in the Ruhr which had been identified as vital to the German war machine. It argued that the enemy's war production could be brought to a virtual standstill by 3,000 aircraft sorties over a fortnight for an estimated loss of 176 bombers.

The Air Targets Sub-Committee then put up another plan, which contained the germ of a project that came to fruition as Operation Chastise on 16–17 May, 1943. Agreeing with Air Ministry critics that neutralisation of these 45 industrial plants would prove difficult to achieve but that an assault on the enemy's war potential could bring rich reward, it proposed as an alternative just two targets: the Möhne and Sorpe dams. Damage equivalent to that foreseen under Bomber Command's proposal could be wrought with possibly less than 3,000 sorties by destroying these targets alone. Disruption of the Ruhr industry and widespread flooding would be inevitable through the release of water from the associated reservoirs and loss of their capacity for electricity generation and other industrial needs. Bomber Command replied by drawing the Sub-Committee's attention to the massive construction of German dams, against which existing bombs would be inadequate. But Hankey pressed his case and added another consideration, which later provided the theoretical basis for attacking the Eder Dam: locks, aqueducts and canals, so necessary to Germany's system of inland transportation, were vulnerable to aerial attack and successful operations against them too would disrupt enemy industry.

Dams, reservoirs and aqueducts were thus studied in some depth as potential targets pre-war. In September 1937, AI1(b) at the Air Ministry, which provided the secretary for Hankey's Air Targets Sub-Committee, identified three types of dam as possible targets, giving examples of each, including their dimensions and the water capacity of their reservoirs. A minute by the Director of Armament Development (D Arm D) on 11 October 1937, further examined the gravity, single-arch and multiple-arch types of concrete dam, doubting that a gravity-type dam (of which the Möhne was one) could be successfully attacked, even if 'fissures' were made in it. A month later, while agreeing that gravity dams could not be effectively attacked with existing bombs and that netting could protect them against torpedoes, the Chief Superintendent of the Research Department (CSRD) at Woolwich advised the secretary to a committee of the Ordnance Board that if a minimum of fifteen 500lb semi-armour piercing (SAP) bombs hit a circular area approximately 50 yards in diameter 'on the lower part of the dam on the water side . . . the strength of the structure would be seriously reduced and partial collapse might ensue'. However, in basing his opinion to D Arm D on this advice, the secretary to the Ordnance committee proved very cautious: 'If the policy to attack dams is accepted, the committee are of the opinion that the development of a propelled piercing bomb of high capacity would be essential to ensure the requisite velocity and flight approximating to the horizontal. Even then its success would be highly problematical.'

The difficulties of acquiring both a suitable weapon and the means of delivering it accurately would baulk all efforts to destroy gravity dams for a long time to come, and D Arm D recognised this in a paper of March 1938. He held that a 'normal' high-explosive (HE) attack would have little chance of success, recommending instead a stick of bombs. Calculating that a bomb would not ricochet when the angle of impact to the surface exceeded 30°, he concluded that the best dropping height would be 10–15,000ft. Bombing trials that year at this height showed an average error of 102–113 yards, meaning that if a 50-yard-long portion of the dam were attacked only a six per cent chance of hitting it existed. Gloomily, he added that in war conditions this could be reduced to two per cent. Applying his argument to breaking the toe of a 'typical gravity dam' 146ft high and 140ft thick at its base, which would 'probably' cause total failure of the structure, he argued that pattern bombing would be even more expensive, with 750 bombs required for a two per cent chance of success, assuming an average error of 200 yards.

On 19 March 1938, the Director of Staff Duties at the Air Ministry returned Bomber Command Paper No 16, *Air Attacks on Reservoirs and Dams*, to the AOC-in-C with a note that its contents had been recently discussed 'departmentally'. Although hitherto any attack had been considered 'uneconomical', a re-examination of possible destruction 'with existing bombs or torpedoes, or with newly developed weapons' seemed justified. Three weeks later, Gp Capt F. P. Don suggested that bombs be dropped to smash the protective nets before torpedoes were launched against the dam. But from Bomber Command Gp Capt N. H. Bottomley argued that neither torpedoes nor 500lb bombs could succeed against a gravity dam: 1,000lb bombs might have a 'small chance', although even this tactic would involve 'heavy expenditure'.

On 26 July 1938, the Bombing Committee of the Air Ministry considered Bomber Command Paper No 16 at its 18th Meeting in the knowledge that the Air Targets Sub-Committee wanted attacks on dams and reservoirs 'treated as urgent and of pressing importance'. Members of the Bombing Committee were asked to remember that attacks on these targets would deprive the enemy of 'the source of a large proportion of their power', and that they would be easily identified and almost certainly undefended: 'not only would power stations be automatically put out of action, but considerable damage would also be caused by the release of floodwater.' It was acknowledged that 'a not inconsiderable body of opinion' thought the chances of causing 'sufficient damage . . . remote'. However, 'the destruction of one dam may have the same result as the destruction of a considerable number of targets further down the chain of the industrial energy system, and it is therefore considered that, as targets, reservoirs and dams are worth the expenditure of a considerable effort'. This was the very kernel of strategic bombing theory.

Air Vice-Marshal W. Sholto Douglas, Assistant Chief of the Air Staff, chaired this important meeting, which was attended by representatives from the different RAF Commands, Air Ministry (including Sqn Ldr [retd] C. G. Burge of AI1[b], Secretary to the Air Targets Sub-Committee), Research Department Woolwich, Royal Aircraft Establishment Farnborough, Admiralty and War Office. The chairman opened by stating that 'investigations' suggested that certain reservoirs in Germany and Italy represented the potential enemy's 'Achilles' heel' as industrial power was 'derived almost entirely from these sources.' This contention was at least in part fallacious. Germany, and in particular the Ruhr, did not rely exclusively or even mainly upon water to generate electricity and, in any event, an efficient grid system could compensate for the loss of generating stations affected by the breaching of a major dam. But this was not recognised by the Air Ministry in July 1938, and Burge supported Douglas's thesis, emphasising that this type of target was 'of very great intrinsic importance'. Furthermore, the Ruhr consumed 25 per cent of Germany's water 'and the bulk of it was obtained from one large reservoir contained by a single-arch dam [sic] known as the Möhne Dam'. This appears to be the first official reference to the Möhne, which thereafter became central to all discussions about dams and gradually acquired the nature of a primary target. Burge had been informed that its destruction would cause 'enormous damage', with important hydroelectricity generating stations affected, and that the 'low-lying Ruhr valley would be flooded, so that railways, important bridges, pumping stations and industrial chemical plants would be destroyed or rendered inoperative'. Normally the Ruhr river flowed practically up to the top of its banks and therefore 'very little' would be needed to make it overflow. Breaching of 'four or five' other dams, whose reservoirs fed inland waterways, would dislocate water transport and produce 'chaotic conditions' by road and rail. Burge noted that Mr Hawkins of the Air Ministry's Transportation Targets Committee had strongly recommended an attack on the lower face of a dam so that water pressure would make it collapse, as described in D Arm D's paper in March.

Douglas pointed out that a low-level attack would be necessary to attain such accuracy and Dr R. Ferguson from Woolwich doubted whether even then sufficient velocity could be achieved. SAP bombs would penetrate only five feet, yet 40 ft below its crown a typical gravity dam was about 42ft thick. He thought that a propelled weapon would achieve greater penetration. Col I. Simson from the War Office inclined towards a series of missiles directed at a specific point of impact and suggested attacking downstream to avoid the inevitable eddies encountered in flying up a valley. Ferguson said that a short-delay fuse on the water side of the dam was most likely to succeed. Wg Cdr H. V. Rowley of the Air Ministry preferred a torpedo attack, and Douglas rejected Bottomley's argument for high-level 'stick' bombing as 'uneconomical'. Maj R. Purves from the RAE suggested that a standard 18in torpedo with a 400lb warhead despatched 3–400 yards from the target and equipped with a 'net cutter' might succeed, although Lt Cdr V. W. L. Proctor felt that a number of these torpedoes would be necessary. Douglas then expressed preference for the torpedo rather than the 500lb bomb, while conceding that a 'propelled bomb' might be developed in due course.

Burge raised the question of earth dams, noting that a number of general-purpose (GP) bombs dropped on top of such a structure seemed the most appropriate tactic but admitting that 'the prospect of success did not appear very favourable'. At this point on AOC-in-C Bomber Command's copy of the minutes was scribbled in the margin: 'What about the Sorpetal, one of the most important in Ruhr area?' The committee looked at the possibility of destroying outfall works downstream or intake towers upstream without seeing any better prospect of success than through Burge's plan. Thus the committee's conclusions concentrated on gravity dams, destruction of which it considered 'feasible', recommending an attack on the water side at high-water level with a number of 18in torpedoes or 1–2,000lb GP bombs; 500lb GP or anti-submarine bombs had less chance of success. The committee noted that the Admiralty was developing 'a new technique', which might be useful against dams, and that investigations should be carried out, too, into a propelled bomb and wire-cutters for standard torpedoes.

The Bombing Committee had in fact drawn specific attention to the difficulty of breaching gravity and earth dams (the Möhne and Sorpe respectively), which would continue to cause problems up to and during Operation Chastise. To hold back water in their reservoirs, earth dams have a vertical concrete or clay core (effectively a wall), stabilised by banks of earth on both sides. Excess water is taken away through a sluice, so as not to allow spillage over the top and erosion of earth on the air side. Minor cracks inevitably occur at joins in any core, so the loam and other material mixed with the supporting earth on the water side are not totally sealed: water can then trickle through the cracks in the core and make them virtually self-sealing. On the air side the supporting substance must be porous to permit this water to seep away quickly. The earth dam, often used in earthquake areas, is not readily susceptible to shock waves. Cratering on top, to allow water to wash over rapidly and erode both supporting material and the core, requires a very sharp indentation on the crown: a shallow depression would be unlikely to cause collapse of the structure. With an earth-type dam, water supplies are normally extracted from the reservoir upstream of it through an intake tower; thus no major machinery exists at the dam itself.

Gravity dams create different problems, while presenting a wider range of

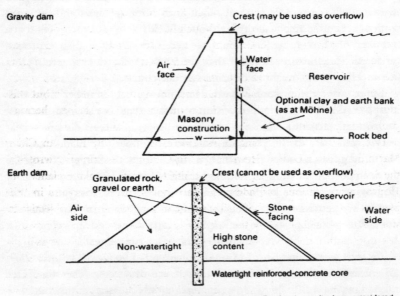

The two types of dam involved in Operation Chastise. For the six gravity dams considered, $\frac{w}{h}$ was about $\frac{2}{3}$; the single earth dam had a 1:2.25 incline.

options, for an attacker. Large masonry or reinforced concrete structures, with a broad base and in cross-section roughly triangular, they are essentially held in position by their own weight. They are either straight or, like the Möhne, curved towards the reservoir, although the curvature gives no significant additional strength. With no vulnerable earth support, spillage over the top of the wall or through outlets just below the crest is normal, with emergency sluices about half-way up the face of the dam to allow rapid drainage of the reservoir. Water is usually drawn off through sluice towers at different heights to prevent sludge at the bottom from being taken up, and it may be used for various purposes, including the driving of turbines to produce electricity. To knock out the emergency sluices or spillway would achieve little, and simply causing a breach in the wall need not be decisive. Water could still be drawn off below the breach, as more water would continue to reach the reservoir, and time to repair the breach would not necessarily be long, being a proportion of the length of time taken to build the dam (the Möhne took four years, including the foundations). Ideally, therefore, any attack should aim to damage the machinery controlling the sluices and the pipes through which the water flows, for a breach alone would not necessarily knock the dam out permanently. Sabotage after seizure of the dam, through the placing of explosives in the pipes on the air side, or a rocket attack to hit the lower part of the wall and damage these vital components, offers perhaps the best hope of success. Immediately before the Second World War, Dr R. G. Harris of the RAE Armaments Department conducted experiments aimed at the development of a pilotless aircraft, on the lines of the radio-controlled Queen Bee anti-aircraft target drone, which could be packed with explosives and launched against the Möhne; but this idea lapsed when the fall of France meant that the targets became prohibitively distant.

Two days after the Bombing Committee met, on 28 July 1938, Air Chief Marshal Sir Edgar Ludlow-Hewitt (AOC-in-C Bomber Command) wrote to the Secretary of State for Air noting the aim to attack 26 coking plants and 19 generating stations and adding: 'I have not included reservoirs in this plan, as I understand that the feasibility of attacking this form of objective is still under consideration by the Air Ministry Bombing Committee and is dependent upon the availability of a 1,000lb bomb.' He appended an analysis of electricity power stations in Germany, noting 33 in the Ruhr (including several such as those at Herdecke, Hengstey and Baldeney, which were later affected by Operation Chastise), and several in the Kassel area, including two stations at the Eder Dam and a central pump-storage works at Waldeck, served by the Eder reservoir, which ensured temporary cover in an emergency. Thus the Eder and Möhne dams figured prominently in Bomber Command's thinking as early as mid-1938.

Shortly before war broke out, on 29 August 1939, Justus Dillgardt (chairman of the organisation responsible for them – Ruhrtalsperrenverein) drew the attention of military authorities in Münster to vulnerability of the 'large dams in southern Westphalia'. He argued that 'the problem was not so much one of demolition due to direct hits by bombs on the wall, but of several bombs dropped twenty to thirty metres away from the dam which explode below the water-line. The compressed effect of the water caused by the explosion might cause the wall to collapse.' As a result of a 'vast outflow' of water from the Möhne, for example, 'this entire industrial area . . . would be completely paralysed . . . not only would the population of four to five millions be without water, but all mines and coking plants would suddenly cease work owing to lack of industrial water supply.' Dillgardt unknowingly echoed British thoughts.

Although the Air Ministry Bombing Committee in London showed a healthy degree of scepticism about the prospect of destroying the German dams, the subject was never entirely discarded. Nor could it be, so long as the Ruhr remained a major bombing target. In June 1940 Bottomley, then Senior Air Staff Officer (SASO) Bomber Command and later to chair an important committee during the lead up to Chastise, reopened with Burge the question of attacking reservoirs and dams. As a result, on 3 July his chief, Air Marshal Sir Charles Portal, wrote a strong plea to the Under-Secretary of State for Air for an attack on the Möhne, which was doubly significant for Operation Chastise: by 1943 Portal would be CAS and the plan that he now advanced bore a strong resemblance to features of the one used then. Portal referred to the conclusions of the 18th Meeting of the Bombing Committee in July 1938 and suggested 'that the time has arrived when we should make arrangements for the destruction of the Möhne Dam'. Incidentally showing how the enthusiasm of junior officers may mislead commanders into over-estimating the worth of a particular target, he explained: 'I am given to understand that almost all the industrial activity of the Ruhr depends upon the water contained in and supplied by this dam, and that if it were destroyed not only would most of the industry in the Ruhr be brought to a standstill but very great havoc would be wrought throughout the length of water course.' Portal believed success 'by no means impossible provided the correct weapons are available' and recommended either a torpedo attack from the water side or bombing attack on the 'dry side'. The Ordnance Board would no doubt advise as to the 'best time, relation between the [bombing] attacks and as to the precise position of the most vulnerable points of attack'. Long-delay-fuse bombs should be dropped with others, so as to impair restoration work: 'In the event of a main attack weakening but not completely breaking down the single-arched, highly-stressed structure of the dam, leakage and the weight and subsequent flow of water might well complete the destruction of the dam.' He therefore saw bombing as a practical possibility, but did not discount torpedoes, and it is in this respect that his thoughts foreshadowed Chastise. No torpedo-carrying aircraft had the necessary range to attack 'this most vital target', and he called most urgently for the necessary modifications to existing torpedo aircraft to give them the required endurance, and/or modifications to 'at least twelve' Hampdens, taken directly from the production line so as not to deplete operational squadrons, to carry torpedoes. The modified Hampdens would constitute a long-range torpedo force, which could then attack other dams, lock gates and inland waterways generally: a monumental task for a dozen aircraft, assuming that no losses nor other factors depleted their number. Portal wanted the attack on the Möhne to be mounted as soon as possible, provided the Air Ministry agreed. The following day he revealed that the letter had been drafted by Bottomley, and that personally he doubted whether 'any existing torpedo could be made to run in a canal 9 or 10ft deep'.

Ten days later Douglas, now Deputy CAS, answered Portal: 'Attacks on dams in general and of the Möhne dam in particular have been the subject of exhaustive study since July 1938.' But 'thousands of pounds of explosives' fired with one detonation would be required to damage a mass of concrete 'effectively'. Messrs Nobel had used 'an elaborate series of tests' with 3,435lb of 'specially prepared blasting gelignite' inserted into 134 holes (10–35ft deep) to blast out 3,000 cubic feet of rock with one detonation. Furthermore, the pressure of water against the face of an 'arch dam' tended to support and close cracks rather than break the structure; unlike an earth dam, a concrete structure would not be eroded by leaking water; and torpedoes fired at masonry jetties in tests caused only surface damage. Douglas concluded, with utter pessimism, that the only way of breaching 'a masonry arch dam' by air attack was to drop 100 or more 'M' mines against the water face of the dam and countermine with an HE bomb. 'The practical difficulties of this method are considered to be insuperable at present.' Commenting on Douglas's reply, Bottomley wrote: 'It reiterates the decisions already arrived at by the Bombing Committee in July 1938.'

At this time, however, other relevant investigations were being carried out at the instigation of the Chief Superintendent of the Research Department at Woolwich, who on 2 May 1940, instructed Wg Cdr C. R. Finch-Noyes, an assistant superintendent of the Research Department at Shrewsbury, to re-examine all previous papers connected with attacking enemy dams. This led Finch-Noyes to consider another way of destroying gravity dams, which he summarised to the Deputy Chief Superintendent of the Research Department (DCSRD) on 2 September. He held that if 20,000lb of explosive were detonated 40ft below the crest of a dam and against it 'there seems a probability that the dam would go', even if 2,000lb units were exploded 'at reasonably short intervals'. One of the dams under consideration, which later in his paper he identified as the Möhne, was 40ft thick at a distance of 40ft below the highest level of water in its reservoir and previous calculations noted at the 1938 Bombing Committee meeting suggested that forty torpedoes, each with 400lb of explosive, would bring about its destruction. Finch-Noyes believed that 'using existing appliances' a missile could be launched from an aircraft flying at 80 mph 'very low over the surface of the water' and propel itself to the wall of the dam. There it could be made 'to destroy its buoyancy' on impact, sink to forty feet and be detonated by standard hydrostatic fuses, 'the proposed charges being Service depth charges.'

To avoid wasting time in the Research Department, Finch-Noyes had enlisted the aid of Noel Pemberton-Billing, who had been a squadron leader on his staff in 1915 when Finch-Noyes was in charge of Aircraft Armament Development and Supply at the Admiralty. Suggesting to Pemberton-Billing that the targets would be installations in enemy harbours but insisting that he used 'Service stores as far as possible', he asked him to devise a container to run on the surface of the water as a 'hydroplane-skimmer' or, alternatively, to travel below the water as a torpedo. Either weapon would be carried by an aircraft, launched onto the water from it and be capable of travelling about a mile thereafter 'at reasonable speed'. Pemberton-Billing suggested a hydroplane-skimmer, self-propelled and 'directionally stable', which would jump over buoyed net defences, or a torpedo 'partly or wholly submerged' to attack boom defences or breakwaters in such harbours as Boulogne or Calais. Both weapons would have a total weight of 3,000lb (including 2,000lb of explosive), and Pemberton-Billing had made half-scale models of each. 'A well-known hydroplane and aeroplane expert', whose active involvement in aviation had prompted his resignation from the Royal Naval Air Service during the First World War to enter Parliament and campaign there on its behalf, Pemberton-Billing suggested for either weapon 'rocket-underwater plus steam jet propulsion,' in which he had been interested for a long time. Alternatively, Finch-Noyes advanced the idea of an automatic gun, 'say 20mm', firing blanks astern in a tube running longitudinally through the centre of the explosive container with a suitable cooling jacket. To test all of these ideas Pemberton-Billing put his works at Kingston, Surrey, at Finch-Noyes' disposal and gave 'generously' of his time and money towards the project, which Finch-Noyes stressed again was entirely private. He and Pemberton-Billing had laboured 'almost invariably' at night to avoid detriment to the normal work of either.

However, 'last week' Air Cdre P. Huskinson, Vice-President of the Ordnance Board, had told Finch-Noyes that 'a sudden demand has arisen for this operation [against the Möhne] to be carried out and a means evolved of carrying it out.' It is likely that despite Douglas's tepid encouragement, this stemmed from Bottomley's initiative transmitted through Portal a month earlier. Finch-Noyes explained his thoughts to Huskinson, who said that he 'could count on his support, but he emphasised again that the greatest speed was necessary otherwise the attempt would be made with existing weapons'. Finch-Noyes revealed that, as yet, neither of the proposed weapons had been developed beyond the experimental stage, but he had discussed the scheme with DCSRD, Dr Ferguson, Mr Dick and Dr Clemmow, and had met a favourable response. If approval to proceed further were given, Clemmow, Superintendent of Ballistic Research at Woolwich, could 'at once' provide an existing cordite-charge container and Finch-Noyes could have the necessary nozzle for it made at Pemberton-Billing's works. Wellingtons could carry two 3,000lb missiles, one slung under each wing, and ten bombers would thus carry 20,000lb of explosive, which would be detonated against the face of the dam at short intervals.

To his paper Finch-Noyes appended another, 'Specification of proposed missile for attack of Breakwaters etc.'. Repeating that the missile would weigh 3,000lb, including 2,000lb of explosive, and be capable of entering the water one mile from the target and travelling straight to it, he noted that it would be 18ft long and 2ft 6in in diameter. If the design did not enable it inherently to do so, he had 'in reserve' a device to ensure straight travel on a compass course. Either variation of the weapon, skimmer or torpedo, would destroy its buoyancy chambers on impact 'even at low speed', sink nose-first down the face of the wall to a given depth and be detonated by a hydrostatic fuse. A device in the form of a cup or weight would be trailed on a wire of suitable length from the aircraft, so that when the cup struck the water as the aircraft was 'say 20ft' above it, a tug on the wire would release the missile, ignite or start the propulsion and open wide the throttle of the aircraft. The missile had to be strong enough to withstand striking the water 'at 80 mph from 50 feet'. Alternatively, the skimmer or torpedo could glide down from the aircraft. Finch-Noyes explained that his proposals had been discussed at a meeting in the Admiralty on 21 August 1940. Although those present, including an RAE representative, supported the idea of a 'rocket torpedo' on which the Admiralty was already working, an underwater or airborne launch was rejected and use of the 'skimming torpedo' (an apparent confusion of the two proposals) by 'auxiliary patrol vessels' preferred. So keen was the Admiralty on attaining such a device that it wanted development by April 1941 in time for 'the next campaigning season'. Finch-Noyes may well have hoped that his experiments on the weapon would succeed, while the Admiralty's failed.

The latter did in fact occur. A meeting at the Admiralty Mine Design Department at Leigh Park, chaired by Capt Lane, noted experiments at Haslar Experimental Establishment; but further meetings on 15 January and 15 February 1941, underlined that little progress had been made. On 26 March tests were still in progress at HMS Vernon. Meanwhile Finch-Noyes continued his work and on 2 April 1941, produced a paper, 'The High Capacity Short Range Torpedo and Skimmer for Conveyance by Air and Other Craft'. Again noting CSRD's approval since May 1940 for his work on developing a high-capacity, self-propelled weapon for use on or under water, Finch-Noyes summarised the two types of weapon he proposed: a cylindrical, torpedo-shaped body and a skimmer in the form of a hydroplane. Both would be directionally stable with buoyancy jackets which would flood on striking the object, causing the weapon to sink to the desired depth and function by hydrostatic or other fuses. He thus gave more details than those outlined in his previous paper, but did not now confine the detonating fuse to a hydrostatic device. If either were used as a glide weapon from an aircraft, on touching the water it would shed its 'air-bearing surfaces and thereafter [be] driven by cordite propulsion from the stern'. Pemberton-Billing's method had therefore been discarded. The modified torpedo could be used against a dam or large ship; the 1938 Bombing Committee's report suggested that eight torpedoes would destroy the Möhne Dam. Finch-Noyes saw the skimmer as suitable for use against objectives protected by buoyed nets such as dam walls or boom defences, and emphasised that, lacking propellers, both weapons should break through nets. The skimmer might also retain its wings, fitted primarily for gliding purposes, after striking the water to bounce over obstructions such as barges or booms laid parallel to a dam wall or other objects for protection.

For the operation Finch-Noyes envisaged moonlight, calm conditions and good visibility; and he now changed the number of aircraft required: 16, each carrying one torpedo or skimmer (that is, a total of 32,000lb of explosive), which allowed generously for mechanical failure, aircraft losses or missing the target. The attacking aircraft would glide from 20,000 to 5,500ft at right angles to the dam wall and reach the lower height 5½ miles from it, releasing the weapon so as to strike the water half a mile from the target. Finch-Noyes explained that the gliding weapon would travel a horizontal mile for each 1,000ft it dropped and that successful tests had led him to modify the figures concerning distance and release contained in his original paper. When the weapon hit the water, cordite propulsion charges would ignite and the weapon would travel towards the wall, strike it, sink to a depth of 40 ft and detonate. He argued that any aircraft releasing such a weapon would be too far away from the dam for anti-aircraft defences to endanger it. Listing the dimensions of the Möhne Dam, he made clear that he very much had this target in mind, and called for a committee of Air Staff representatives, D Arm D from the Ministry of Aircraft Production (whence that department had been transferred from the Air Ministry), Superintendent of Ballistic Research, representatives of the Torpedo Development Unit at Gosport, CSRD and the RAE Farnborough fully to investigate this scheme. If its findings were favourable, then a small working committee could 'pursue the matter to a conclusion and envisage the operation involved.'

That same day, 2 April 1941, Finch-Noyes despatched a copy of this paper and all the preceding papers in a folder, 'Memorandum of Proposed Methods of Attack of Special Enemy Targets by Wg Cdr C. R. Finch-Noyes DSO AFC RAFVR', to Air Marshal Sir Richard Peirse, AOC-in-C Bomber Command at High Wycombe, informing him that he had sent copies also to D Arm D and Air Marshal Sir Philip Joubert de la Ferté, Assistant Chief of the Air Staff (Radio). He emphasised in a covering letter that 'the attack of dams in enemy country', of which the 'principal' one was the Möhne, had been the subject of 'a great deal of study' in the Research Department: 'The destruction of the Möhne Dam would flood the Ruhr valley and disorganise its industry. It is probably very heavily defended, so it is desirable to attack it from a distance and from a height.' 'By the scheme proposed this is possible, namely by the combination of gliding weapon attack and high explosive-capacity, self-propelled, water-borne torpedoes or skimmers, which weapons are under actual development by the Navy and have reached the stage of full-size trials.' Finch-Noyes thus suggested that the whole enterprise now rested upon success of the trials at HMS Vernon: whatever the validity of the arguments, the means of propulsion remained crucial. He held that the Möhne would be 'probably' screened by nets and/or barges, which would not stop these weapons. And he therefore proposed that a special unit of Bomber Command be formed (rather in keeping with Portal's suggestion of July 1940) to develop the method of attack, prepare the aircraft and train the crews: 'In determined hands with singleness of purpose and freedom from disturbance, such a unit should in six months from the word "go" have effected its objects given the necessary priority.'

On 4 April, revealing that he had asked Finch-Noyes to see him 'the week after next', Peirse asked his SASO, Air Vice-Marshal R. H. M. S. Saundby, and his Group Captain Operations, Mills, to examine the proposals and comment on them. Admitting that the scheme 'attracts me', he nevertheless felt that a torpedo travelling at 40 knots would bounce off the dam 'before sinking in a docile manner alongside the wall.' Evidently Peirse was not convinced by Finch-Noyes when they met, for on 2 June Mills wrote a discouraging final minute to Saundby. Agreeing that destruction of the Möhne Dam, which fed the Ruhr, 'would paralyse its industry', he noted that this had been 'considered on many occasions' and been abandoned due to the 'enormous quantity of explosive' required. He therefore doubted whether the skimmer or torpedo, with such limited explosive content, could succeed. Mills thought that 'big blast bombs' dropped against the water or air sides of the dam 'might be possibilities'. Finch-Noyes' weapons looked better prospects for attacking ships, and the Admiralty was pursuing this. 'Once we use a gliding weapon all sorts of errors in ranging and in line arise immediately, and are added to enormously when wind has to be taken into account.' Mills wanted to see the result of Coastal Command's 'Toraplane' ('a gyro-controlled Gliding Torpedo' proposed by Sir Dennis Burney) before Bomber Command committed itself 'to a gliding skimmer'. Effectively Finch-Noyes' plan had been rejected.

Thus by mid-1941 several of those who would play important roles in the planning and development of Operation Chastise (including Portal, Bottomley and Saundby) were aware of the alleged critical importance of the Möhne Dam to the industrial Ruhr, the difficulty of breaching its wall and a variety of plans to do so, of which Finch-Noyes' was only the latest and possibly most ingenious. How to deliver the necessary weight of explosive accurately and detonate it so as to achieve success remained conundra to be solved. When the idea had been orginally mooted in 1937, the RAF's heavy bomber squadrons were equipped with Heyford biplanes, and the standard available weapon was the 500lb GP bomb, whose indifferent explosive, Amatol, comprised only 25 per cent of its weight, which made it relatively ineffective. When Deputy Director of Plans in October 1938, Gp Capt J. C. Slessor summarised the primary considerations for target selection, which were relevant for the Möhne: '(i) Is it recognisable? (ii) Is it big enough to give us a reasonable chance of hitting it? (iii) Have we got the right sort of bomb to send it sky-high if we do hit it?'

In fact, the Germans soon showed themselves aware of the vulnerability of dams. In 1940 they considered attacking the Derwent and Howden dams near Sheffield, which were later used by 617 Squadron in training for Operation Chastise; and two years later they carried out a series of incomplete tests in the Obernach Programme on methods of breaking earth dykes and masonry dams with TNT. From an early stage in the war they posted police to protect their dams against sabotage and flak detachments to defend them against air attack. But in Britain it soon became clear to the RAF that it did not have the ability to execute any such accurate attack. Even before the war, an Air Staff circular argued that 'there has been a tendency in the past to overstate the case that "the bomber will *always* get through"', and before the close of 1939 the tactic of using Wellingtons and Hampdens (which had superseded the pedestrian Heyfords) in self-defending formations during daylight had been literally shot to pieces: during the 'phoney war' the average loss rate of bombers engaged in daylight sorties was a fearful 11.5 per cent. Then large numbers of Battles and Blenheims were lost when attacking enemy communications during the German advances in western Europe in May 1940. Later that year at RAF Scampton Flt Lt Gibson glanced round the pilots of 83 Squadron and saw that he was the only survivor from August 1937.

However, evasion of enemy defences did not necessarily mean accurate attacks on a target. Gibson once found himself over Denmark instead of Norway through a faulty compass, and in August 1941 the Air Ministry's Butt Report, based upon study of raid photographs, showed that in the Ruhr only one in ten of the bombers was getting within five miles of their target. It was a far cry from the expectations raised in 1932 when an official committee on coastal defence reported: 'We are informed by the Chief of Air Staff that accuracy of aim has improved so much that on the North-West Frontier of India aircraft are able to bomb the house of a particular sheik.'

Despite Bomber Command's proven shortcomings, however, the Ruhr industry continued to figure prominently in the minds of British planners, although due to its intrinsic strength the Möhne Dam, and other such desirable targets, came low on the list of priorities. Meanwhile, initially unknown to the Chiefs of Staff or the Air Ministry, a civilian engineer, Barnes Wallis, had begun the process which would ultimately bear fruit in Chastise. Later the Honourable Sir Ralph Cochrane, Air Officer Commanding (AOC) 5 Group during the operation, emphasised that the weapon involved was 'all Wally's idea'. But the premise for this operation and attacks on two of its main targets had been the subject of Air Staff speculation and activity for three years. Ironically, it would take Wallis almost precisely that length of time to perfect his method of destruction. Arguably, much of the psychological groundwork had already been done for him: reservoirs and dams, in particular the Möhne Dam and to a lesser extent the Sorpe, were familiar targets to many of those involved at various levels in the Air Ministry, Ministry of Aircraft Production, Admiralty and research establishments like Farnborough and Woolwich. Crucially perhaps, Portal, who had become and would remain CAS until 1945, was familiar with many of the arguments. In 1940 he had shown himself keen to destroy the Möhne Dam as a matter of urgency.

2

Frustration

As the second World War opened, Wallis, assistant chief designer of Vickers-Armstrongs' Aviation Section at Weybridge, was approaching his fifty-second birthday. An aeronautical engineer of established reputation, who had used geodetic construction in the design of the R100 airship and the Wellesley and Wellington aeroplanes, he was concerned primarily with structures, officially responsible to the chief designer, R. K. Pierson, and through him the works manager, Maj Hew Kilner. In practice he had a relatively free hand to make use of experimental, production and repair facilities on the main site and in three hangars at nearby Foxwarren. When camouflage nets spread overhead failed to protect the works from enemy bombers, Wallis and his staff were evacuated two miles east to the requisitioned offices of Burhill Golf Club. There, quite independent of the Air Ministry, Wallis began to examine means of destroying natural sources of energy, which led him to look at reservoirs and dams among other things.

He started to gather data from past and present, British and foreign journals through libraries, personal contacts and official records. 'Autumn 1939 to Autumn 1940 [I] spent learning about bombs, the behaviour, chemistry and elementary physics of High Explosives; the construction of the Winding Shafts of German collieries; the Construction of Gravity, Multiple Arch and Earth Dams,' he recalled later. Specifically, he sought information about the Möhne Dam some 30 miles east of the main Ruhr industries. On 25 October 1940, he asked the Ministry of Aircraft Production (MAP) for a copy of a report by a civil engineer, W. T. Halcrow, to the Air

Staff in December 1939, which concluded that its strong construction precluded successful attack, and shortly afterwards learnt from Halcrow himself that he doubted whether details other than the plain dimensions of the dam were available 'in this country'. Undeterred, Wallis informed Sqn Ldr F. C. Cole at the Air Ministry that he had a scholar 'combing through German text-books', and he pressed C. J. Inglis, librarian to the Institution of Civil Engineers, to join in the quest, while enlisting the support of his own sister-in-law to translate documents. Inglis did produce articles, which he discovered in a 'less accessible' library, but within three weeks of Wallis's request feared that he had reached 'the end of our resources'. In November, however, F. W. R. Leistikow, a representative of patent agents in Chancery Lane, produced some useful leads from the Patent Library, referring to articles in *Zeitschrift für Bauwesen* in 1919 and *Zeitschrift für Die Gesamte Wasserwirtschaft* of April 1906, and Wallis himself mentioned construction details in editions of *Schweizerische Wasserwirtschaft* during 1910 and 1912–13.

As yet Wallis had by no means committed himself exclusively to attacking dams, though he had come to believe that a peppering of small bombs against any target achieved scant effect. Painstaking calculations convinced him that the shape and composition of standard 1,000lb GP bombs then in use with the RAF led to inefficient performance, and he therefore produced the sketch of a 22,400lb bomb 19.85ft long, with a diameter of 3.72ft and in an 'R100 shape'. Benjamin Lockspeiser, Deputy Director of Scientific Research (D/DSR) at the MAP, argued that 'to get the highest supersonic speeds the bomb should have a sharply pointed nose,' but Ernest Relf of the National Physical Laboratory at Teddington found Wallis's plans for his 'super peardrop . . . quite sensible', assuming that it would achieve 1,340ft/sec, yet advised exhaustive tests in the Engineering Department's tunnel to examine the problem of drag. In August 1940 the Aeronautical Research Committee agreed to Wallis using the wind tunnel at Teddington, provided that scale drawings were made for its staff to construct the required models.

Shortly afterwards, a different series of experiments began at the Road Research Laboratory, Harmondsworth. During October 1940 the director, Dr W. H. Glanville, and one of his assistant directors, Dr A. H. Davis, agreed to carry out tests connected with destruction of the Möhne Dam. The task devolved on A. R. Collins, a scientific officer in the Concrete Section, with a team of four. Glanville, Davis and Collins met Wallis at Harmondsworth, where he explained that he had in mind the Möhne and Eder dams in Germany and Tirso in Italy as targets for a bombing attack. Wallis thought that if a squadron of aircraft dropped ten-ton bombs in the reservoir above a dam, 'a reasonable chance' existed of getting one bomb within 150ft of it. The Tirso Dam was considered as a separate proposition, and as the other two were similar in construction, the informal meeting decided to use 1/50-scale models of the Möhne for experimental purposes. Wallis said that he envisaged seven tons (15,680lb) of explosive in his bomb, which meant scaled-down charges of 2oz for the model tests. Wallis left a copy of a German publication, G. Kelen's *Gewichtsstaumauern und Massive Wehre*, which included dimensions of the Möhne Dam, with Collins, who thus knew that this dam and the Eder were potential targets from the outset.

The authority for undertaking these experiments is unclear. Glanville may have acted on his own initiative, but it is more likely that he persuaded Dr R. E. Stradling, Chief Scientific Adviser to the Ministry of Home Security and a former director of the Building Research Station with whom Glanville had worked closely for many years, to sponsor the work. It is possible, too, that Stradling had been approached by A. J. Sutton Pippard, a relative of his and professor of civil engineering at Imperial College, London, with whom Wallis had discussed his ideas, and that he used the need to identify danger to British dams as an excuse for financial cover. This is speculation, however, because relevant documents have not survived. Nor is there corroboration for the much later claim of a scientist stationed at Harmondsworth at that time: 'He [Wallis] approached the Laboratory through the Director of Scientific Research, Ministry of Aircraft Production', although it is noteworthy that from the beginning Collins' reports were addressed to the MAP.

In November 1940 Collins produced the first of many reports for that ministry on the results of his tests. This one, on the effect of underwater explosions on concrete pipes used to simulate the arches of the Tirso Dam and in no way connected with the Möhne, was swiftly followed in the same month by one concerning 'a model gravity dam'. Noting that 'preliminary tests' had been conducted on a 'roughly constructed' 1/50-scale model of a masonry gravity dam, he reported that 'promising' results suggested that 'severe damage' to a dam 140ft high and 100ft thick at the base would occur if a 15,600lb charge exploded 150ft upstream, but that further tests were necessary 'on a more carefully prepared model'. Collins' fifth report, in February of the following year, was less encouraging: it was now clear that 'severe damage' would not happen unless the 15,600lb charge were exploded 50ft from the dam face. Then, in March 1941, Collins reported that experiments involving the destruction of a small disused dam in Wales (the Nant-y-Gro near Rhayader, 35ft high and 180ft long) and a 1/10-scale model of it at Harmondsworth were to be carried out. In the event this work did not go ahead that year and no other detailed reports were produced for the

MAP before May, by which time the Air Staff had shelved the big-bomb concept.

As part of the Möhne experiments, in November 1940–January 1941 another series of tests was conducted on Glanville's request at the Building Research Station, Garston, near Watford, on the 'more carefully prepared model' mentioned by Collins in his report of November 1940. Dr Norman Davey, Head of Structural Development, and his subordinate Head of Concrete Section, A. J. (Bill) Newman, designed and constructed their own 1/50-scale model of the Möhne Dam from information in journals and from Kelen. Unfortunately, they used an equation for curvature expressed in yards, not metres, and the painstaking result was actually inaccurate, although this had very little effect on test data. Simulated towers were cast in the concrete laboratory and secretly carried on a wheelbarrow one Sunday morning down a slope to a silver-birch wood. Once dammed, the small stream there would simulate the Möhne reservoir. Exhausted by their efforts, the following day Davey and Newman delegated preparation of the foundations to Station labourers. In half a day they managed to excise only a minute area of turf, and so the job was entrusted to one stalwart, Amos Blackwell. The entire model measured 42ft long by about 3ft high and 2ft thick at the base, with 15 ft between the two mock towers. The section in between the towers comprised some three million blocks, each measuring $0.45 \times 0.35 \times 0.25$in and individually bedded in mortar in less than seven weeks by Davey, Newman, A. B. Stapleton and A. Smith, working in absolute secrecy and bitterly cold conditions; the extension outwards beyond the towers was normal concrete. Davey and Newman were annoyed at the stealth with which they had to work, arguing to no avail that this created an unnecessary atmosphere of suspicion. Less secrecy would have attracted less attention. Once completed, the structure was exposed by Collins to ten separate explosions of 2oz charges at distances of 1–3ft, but, although cracked, the dam held. Experiments connected with Möhne models were thereafter carried out at Harmondsworth, where, as at Garston, Collins dealt with the explosion of charges and another scientific officer, G. Charlesworth, with the measurement of the effect on models.

The models at Harmondsworth were also 1/50-scale replicas of the Möhne, and early in 1941 Collins used similar charges against them even though there were serious doubts as to the validity of scaling up the results. A model test would indicate with accuracy the direct damage caused by an explosion but not necessarily its effect on the target as a whole. With most structures this could be forecast using first principles or by calculation. However, a gravity dam created special problems, because its stability depended on its own weight, which was in turn due to the force of gravity. Wallis in no way directed these tests nor exercised responsibility for them. During one of his frequent visits to Harmondsworth he told Collins: 'You're the experts. I can't tell you what to do, you're telling me.' And curiously, in view of the tag later applied to 617 Squadron, as their work at Harmondsworth so obviously involved firing charges against a dam, at this time Collins' team acquired the local nickname 'Dam Blasters'.

During the winter of 1940–1, too, Stradling negotiated on behalf of the Ministry of Home Security with the Birmingham City Corporation for authority to carry out tests on the Nant-y-Gro dam, which was owned by the Water Department. On 27 December he visited Birmingham and secured permission to use the dam 'for experimental purposes', which might result in its destruction, with no requirement for 'reinstatement'. Early in the new year, on 18 February 1941, Stradling wrote to Dr D. R. Pye, Director of Scientific Research (DSR) at the MAP, pointing out that, if experiments were to be carried out on his behalf at Nant-y-Gro, Pye must cover the costs; this was agreed four days later. Thus the MAP may not have become involved until tests connected with the Welsh dam came under consideration.

Despite Collins' discouraging reports, Wallis remained convinced that a large bomb dropped from 40,000 ft could cause titanic destruction to selected, vital installations by penetrating the earth and creating shock waves to undermine the foundations of a target. He realised, however, that neither the Manchester, Stirling nor Halifax bombers would be capable of carrying a ten-ton bomb. Possibly in response to an Air Staff search for 'the ideal bomber for the RAF' initiated in March 1938, pre-war he had set out his ideas for a six-engined bomber in a document, 'Bomber Aircraft: Determination of the Most Economical Size', which was widely circulated among Service and civilian personnel including Sir Henry Tizard, Norbert Rowe and Gp Capt the Hon R. A. Cochrane, who had first met Wallis on a windswept tarmac at Walney Island, Barrow, during the First World War and who would be intimately concerned with the execution of Chastise. In the paper Wallis argued that his calculations 'show clearly how very much cheaper, in terms of man hours per pound of weight or per unit of Offensive Power, it is to build large machines'. With hostilities fast approaching, R. K. Pierson then proposed a six-engined bomber with a 235ft wing span and 20-ton bomb-load, based upon Wallis's ideas and an abortive Vickers-Armstrongs scheme of 1937 for 'a super-heavy civil aircraft operating at normal altitudes', arguing that one would carry more offensive power than an entire squadron of Wellingtons and be 55 mph faster. As four-engined bombers were not yet in service, the Air Staff quite reasonably rejected this more advanced project, and on 26 June 1939, Wallis complained to Walter Runciman that RAF officers who argued against putting 'too many eggs in one basket' did not consider 'the mathematical chances [of accuracy and effect] operating against five bombers in place of one with superior speed and armament'.

An interview with Lord Beaverbrook, Minister of Aircraft Production, on 19 July 1940, had particular significance for Wallis, however. Believing that they were to discuss another of his projects – to prevent enemy aircraft landing on open spaces in Britain – Wallis was nonplussed when Beaverbrook asked him to go to the USA to investigate pressurised cabins for high-altitude flight. Wallis pointed out that he had already done that work on a Wellington and, in any case, he preferred to remain in Britain to build 'a monster bomber to smash the Germans.' Impressed by a brief outline of Wallis's ideas, Beaverbrook told him to come back with fuller details. Later that day, after consulting Pierson at Weybridge, Wallis summarised the specifications of a 'High Altitude Stratosphere Bomber,' which would soon acquire the name 'Victory'. Designed to carry a bombload of 20,000lb and to operate at 40,000ft, it would have a maximum speed at 35,000ft of 330 mph and a range of 4,000 miles. Powered by six Hercules VIII engines and with a wing span of 160ft, it would need 1,200 yards to take off at an all-up weight of 107,000lb. Wallis argued, correctly, that no bomber then flying could meet this standard of performance even in theory, and that, although the amount of material and number of engines involved would be treble the figures needed for the Wellington, the number of crew and volume of equipment would remain the same. No defensive armament was planned, it being believed that speed and height capability could give adequate protection. He used this paper at a second interview with Beaverbrook on the following day, 20 July, and it is possible that he also over-enthusiastically claimed then that the earthquake bomb, which the Victory bomber would carry, could end the war. Beaverbrook was unable to commit the Government, the Air Ministry or even his own Ministry to positive action, but he did instruct Air Vice-Marshal A. W. Tedder, responsible for research and development, to give Wallis full co-operation; thereafter Wallis corresponded with, met and telephoned Tedder frequently. By the close of 1940 responsibility for implementing the operational requirements of the Air Staff and ensuing levels of production had centred at the MAP on the Controller of Research and Development (CRD) and his immediate staff through specialist directorates of Armament Development (D Arm D), Engine Development (DED), Scientific Research (DSR) and Technical Development (DTR).

Sir Charles Craven, Vickers-Armstrongs' chairman but seconded to the MAP during July–November 1940, arranged for Wallis to visit the English

Steel Corporation, a part-subsidiary of Vickers-Armstrongs, at Sheffield on 9 August with drawings of the ten-ton bomb to consult experts on a bomb casing capable of withstanding high-velocity impact, yet light enough to allow a high explosive content. Craven was almost certainly instrumental in gaining the support of the Vickers-Armstrongs board for this project. On 1 November 1940, at the MAP Gp Capt A. Dunbar submitted a lengthy paper on the Victory bomber to Beaverbrook. Recalling that the Minister had requested this appreciation from him on 23 October, Dunbar noted the need for suitable bombers to launch an attack on the Axis 'which might result in a complete stoppage of all sources of power in both Germany and Italy, and, if necessary, their conquered territories for a sufficient period to bring their war activities to a close.' He reminded Beaverbrook that 'large industrial areas' in Germany and the whole of northern Italy 'derive their power from large hydro-electric installations', and pointed out that 'the most important of all dams in this connection [the Möhne]' measured 'upwards of 110ft' at its base and held back several million gallons of water. His line of argument then came very close indeed to that of the erstwhile WA5 plan: 'By striking at sources of power rather than widely distributed targets such as power stations and factories, the number of targets becomes so limited that a few squadrons of bombers carrying the requisite size of bomb might be sufficient to bring the war to a conclusion within the course of two or three weeks.' But he continued with pure Wallis; and Wallis is thought actually to have drafted the letter for Dunbar. With the help of the Admiralty (the Mine Design Department at Leigh Park), Ordnance Board and National Physical Laboratory, experiments were in progress on development of a ten-ton (22,000lb) bomb, and Dunbar attached a summary of Wallis's specifications for a Victory bomber with an all-up weight of 109,000lb – a mistake for 107,000lb – to carry it. Assuming that 25 per cent of the days in a year were suitable for bombing from 40,000ft, 'it is considered that in the undisturbed conditions of high-altitude flight the accuracy would be as great as is at present possible from 15,000–20,000ft under gunfire'.

At the end of the month Wallis himself claimed that enemy dams could undoubtedly be destroyed by this method of attack. 'Greatly distressed' to learn that Tedder had been posted from the MAP at Millbank to the Middle East, he thanked him for his help: 'I am sorry to lose the encouragement and support which you have so consistently given to me,' stressing that Tedder's help had not been in vain. The 'Road Research Labs' had reported favourably on the effect of shock waves on underwater structures, confirming 'my forecast that we can, without much difficulty, destroy all the Italian Dams . . . A second report to hand to-day [28 November] shows that a ten-ton bomb will probably destroy the Möhne Dam.' His impatience at official reticence warranted a rueful postscript, which underlined his lack of appreciation of the issues concerning allocation and application of resources facing those involved in formulating policy: '. . . if only all concerned had been as ready to accept our original suggestions as you were this scheme could have been very much further ahead than it actually is. As a result of the continued opposition that we have met it has been necessary to resort to these laborious and long winded experiments in order to prove that what I suggested last July can in reality be done.' During these months the Battle of Britain had been fought, as German invasion forces lurked ominously across the Channel and U-boats drove uncomfortable inroads into vital supply convoys.

In a 'strictly private and confidential' communication to Wallis, Dunbar revealed that Air Cdre Huskinson, now D Arm D at the MAP, was 'very sceptical' of upscaling data from small experiments, although Air Chief Marshal Sir Wilfrid Freeman, newly appointed Vice-Chief of the Air Staff, appeared 'very keen' on the ten-ton bomb. 'The only difficulty is that it requires a big machine to carry it and they [the Air Staff] do not know where the machine could be built without serious interference with existing production,' even though Dunbar's letter to Beaverbrook had stated that Vickers-Armstrongs would undertake the large bomber's development and construction. And on 9 January 1941, in a letter to the firm, Beaverbrook gave the first real hope of official backing for Wallis. Laying down that 'high-altitude bombers are to be developed intensively,' he emphasised that this referred to the Wellington V with a pressurised cabin, but added: 'Subject to the above work taking precedence, you should continue your research on your 50-ton bomber.'

This encouragement came at an opportune moment, as Wallis finalised a comprehensive summary of his work from the past year. With appendices, footnotes and diagrams prepared by his design team and reproduced photographs, 'A Note on a Method of Attacking the Axis Powers' totalled 117 pages. Two full-page diagrams at the beginning illustrated the foundation for Wallis's thinking about his project. The first set out strategic bombing doctrine in visual form. At base were shown 'natural sources of power . . . concentrated and immovable targets,' from which power stations, oil wells, gasworks and hydroelectric facilities distributed power to 'industrial proceases . . . dispersed and movable targets' involved directly in the war effort and constituting the enemy's 'ability to wage war'. The second showed the distribution of 11 hydroelectric power stations in a semi-circle from San Remo on the Mediterranean to Sesto Calende in the foothills of the Alps superimposed on a map of north-west Italy. At the outset of the main text

Wallis summarised his arguments: all the belligerent air forces (Allied and enemy) possessed only 'relatively small bombs designed to attack surface targets such as factories and houses,' a form of attack 'effectively countered by Dispersal' and making it impossible simultaneously to destroy '*all* the [enemy] factories and *all* the generating stations'. However, factories relied upon 'highly localised Stores of Energy in the form of Coal, Oil and Water Power', which were 'so concentrated and so massive that they cannot be dispersed'; unfortunately, they were also invulnerable to contemporary bombs. Wallis proposed to demonstrate that 'these stores of energy are vulnerable to very large bombs; by sterilising their Stores of Energy the Industries of Germany and Italy can be quickly paralysed; the very large bomb and appropriate bomb carrying aircraft are practicable and can be produced in this country.' Eight chapters followed, backed by five appendices, eight tables of relevant data, 32 pages of diagrams, countless formulae and a photograph of Hamm marshalling yards.

Prefacing his work with a quotation from Thomas Hardy, 'experience is as to intensity and not as to duration,' Wallis began by discussing three axioms: 'Modern Warfare is entirely dependent upon industry,' 'Industry is dependent upon adequate supplies of power' and 'Power is dependent upon the availability of natural stores of energy such as coal, oil and water (white coal)'. Emphasising that 'coalfields, oil fields and districts suitable for development as hydro-electric catchment areas and underground storage tanks for oil . . . are impossible to disperse,' he articulated the central tenet of pre-war strategic thinkers: 'If their destruction or paralysis can be accomplished THEY OFFER A MEANS OF RENDERING THE ENEMY UTTERLY INCAPABLE OF CONTINUING TO PROSECUTE THE WAR.' Thus far the RAF's 'puny efforts,' recognised by experts as 'quite powerless to inflict any but minor and therefore reparable damage,' had made German and Italian 'great sources of energy . . . for all practical purposes invulnerable'. It was clear that to achieve success 'a new technique of air attack must be required.' Wallis did not confine this solely to dams, nor even to supplies of electricity, but his sharp dismissal of current bombing effort with its implied criticism of official policy would scarcely warm the hearts of civil servants, Government ministers or Service officers. Nor would their blood pressure be lowered by the ensuing analysis of the ineffectiveness of small bombs (up to 1,000kg or 2,200lb) and 'stick bombing . . . by which range errors are covered by a wide distribution in the direction of flight while line errors are covered as far as may be by flying over the target in two or more different directions.' Air bombardment had therefore become trapped in a mesh of small bombs, requiring direct hits for effect, which in turn could only be sought through dropping a large number of bombs and the stick technique. This might be justified if the means of industrial production (factories) were seen as the primary target, but enemy attacks on England had shown that even direct hits with small bombs created only temporary inconvenience. And accuracy of 'the so-called land mine' could not be predicted 'within several hundred yards'; when these weapons were dropped from 15,000ft, a modest crosswind of 10 mph would create 200 yards' inaccuracy.

Wallis then introduced the basis of his new technique by analysing the 'destructive characteristics of a bomb,' concluding that most damage occurred not through the expansion of gases or 'bubble' produced by detonation of the charge but by the wave created in the surrounding medium, which continued to travel outwards after the velocity of the gases had decreased. This, occurring in air, earth or water, would better be termed the 'pressure wave or shock wave' rather than 'blast' (normally associated with air). Deliberate use of this 'agent of destruction' formed the basis of Wallis's new technique. Noting that 'the pressure pulse,' the basic term he now adopted, involved 'a wave motion' whose characteristics were definable, Wallis proceeded to a minute examination of 'wave characteristics' and their relevance to the use of explosive charges of different types and sizes. In concluding this section, he argued that small bombs had hitherto been preferred because explosion in the air was unavoidable. Wallis held that, in reality, a choice between air and water or air and earth always existed.

He went on to look at the impact of the wave motion on structures built from materials such as glass, steel plates or concrete, each of which was specifically affected by different characteristics of the wave. Experiments on concrete and masonry structures had shown that they could be destroyed by detonation of charges either within a certain distance to cause shattering or beyond this to effect 'severe cracking,' which could never be entirely prevented by reinforcement. Intensity was closely concerned with the destruction of concrete, because if 'the applied energy is highly concentrated' fracture would occur before the strain could be absorbed throughout the structure. Wallis was convinced 'that concrete structures which are *quite unharmed* by a charge bursting *in air* are destroyed by an equal charge at the same distance, when the explosion occurs *in deep water or in earth*.' He further reasoned that experiments carried out on models representing masonry dams, tanks or conduits actually underestimated the impact on full-size counterparts. As illustration of this was the more severe effect of the derailment of a fast-moving train rather than a slow-moving or stationary one.

Reiterating that the Axis powers' 'ability to make war is entirely dependent upon natural or adapted sources of energy, coalfields, oilfields, hydro-electric reservoirs and underground storage tanks for oil and petrol,' which were massively constructed and 'practically invulnerable' to attack by existing weapons, Wallis once more maintained that 'a new technique in bomb attack' could be developed to deal with these truly vital targets. This entailed construction of a larger bomb than any hitherto employed and 'utilisation of the *pressure wave set up* by the detonation in the surrounding medium to destroy the target instead of relying upon a direct hit.' The 'operative characteristics' required to break the massive targets under consideration were best developed not in air but in water or earth, with one of which elements all important Axis targets were fortunately in contact. Wallis then stated the crux of his theory: *'To attack these targets successfully it is necessary to inject the largest possible charge to the greatest possible depth in the medium (earth or water) that surrounds or is in contact with the target.'* So far as hydroelectric dams were concerned, the depth of water at the face would always be great and liable to penetration by 'a relatively light case bomb'. But for earth penetration a special bomb would be needed to obtain a suitable depth for maximum camouflet (an explosion at such a depth that the surface of the ground is not disturbed). Interestingly, diagrams of the proposed bomb, which were appended, depicted a pointed nose rather than an 'R100' rounded shape, suggesting that Lockspeiser's original criticism of limited penetration had been accepted or sustained by experiment.

During the early months of the war Wallis had considered the size of bomb, concluding that one of ten tons and carrying six to seven tons of explosive would be necessary for the larger targets. By restricting the bomb size, Wallis felt, design and construction of the necessary aircraft could be achieved 'within a reasonable period.' Later, in mid-1940, 'in order to utilise existing aircraft and to obtain valuable information regarding the behaviour of large bombs,' he planned 'intermediate sizes' of two and four tons for conveyance in a Wellington or Warwick respectively. Three sizes – two (4,480lb), four (8,960lb) and ten (22,400lb) tons – were therefore under review, but experiments showed that only the latter would be effective against the largest targets. He had virtually discounted an alternative method by 'the sympathetic detonation of several large bombs,' which he considered very difficult to accomplish and of doubtful value.

Detailed technical explanation of the characteristics and requirements of the large deep-penetration bomb were then expounded. Having discussed the specifications of his Victory bomber based on the paper of 19 July 1940, he moved on to consider bombing from high altitude. In this section he cited evidence from firing trials on a Wellesley at Shoeburyness, experiments on gun turrets remotely controlled from the Wellington's pressurised cabin, and the improbability of fighter interception at such an altitude to argue that 'high-altitude bombers of the type described will be relatively immune from attack, but will be capable of putting up a sound defence if and when they are attacked.'

With the method of attack theoretically settled, Wallis discussed targets. He dealt fully first of all with petrol and oil storage tanks, concluding that 'no practical number of standard bombs can ever damage these tanks,' which were sunken and reinforced with concrete or steel. Destruction could only be achieved 'by high-altitude aircraft carrying *very large* earth penetration type bombs.' Shafts and galleries of coal mines offered a similar target: 'It should be a relatively easy matter to get even the 4,000lb bomb within lethal distance of a winding shaft.' Wallis continued: 'A few squadrons of high-altitude aircraft such as Wellington V [could] bring the German and French [sic] coal industry to a standstill in the course of two or three weeks . . . with little risk to our aircraft and the expenditure of an almost negligible amount of HE.' Against oilfields he held out little hope of success, except that a ten-ton bomb placed certainly within 25 yards and possibly 80 yards of vital machinery might well render it useless. He considered this accuracy from 40,000ft feasible and further indicated that the Romanian oil fields were 'within easy reach of a high-altitude pressurised cabin bomber with 4,000 mile range' operating from England. But hydroelectric dams were much more promising. Noting that 'the railways and industrial plants' derived their power supplies from installations of this nature and that the Tirso Dam in Sardinia created power 'for the electrolytic reduction of bauxite for the production of metallic aluminium,' he argued that 'if the principal hydro-electric dams in North Italy could be put out of action, that country would be utterly unable further to carry on the war.' In Germany hydroelectric schemes were not so numerous, 'but the destruction of certain important dams such as the Möhne would probably do immense damage if only from the extensive flooding of industrial districts.' The two types of dam involved – multiple-arch and gravity – could be rendered vulnerable to 'the destructive agent . . . [of] the pressure pulse' by dropping 'one or more large bombs in the water, as close as possible to the water face.'

Experiments suggested that the multiple-arch dam was susceptible to the 4,000lb or ten-ton bomb 'when dropped within the lethal radius appropriate to the bomb'. But 'gravity type dams offer a more serious problem'. Constructed of strong masonry or concrete walls roughly triangular in cross-section, they resisted the thrust of the water pushing against them by 'sheer weight' and firm foundation in the rocky bed of each valley. To demonstrate this type, he produced a diagram of the Möhne Dam, emphasising that the base of the dam was 112ft thick and when the lake was full the depth of water at the face of the dam was 128ft. He believed that the water face of this and similar dams would be protected by nets against torpedo attack and, although the air face might be vulnerable to dive bombing, heavy defences would effectively prevent this. Moreover 'recent experience' had shown that the accuracy of dive bombing had been 'over estimated'. Nor could destruction be assured if a large charge were detonated on the water side of the dam, for the pressure pulse would not necessarily be lethal against this type of construction. Undermining of the foundations by a large bomb penetrating deep into the earth from the air side of the dam, however, would benefit fully from the pressure pulse. The hydrostatic uplift so created, combined with the lateral thrust of the water, would overwhelm the limited drainage system devised to cope with inevitable seepage and 'overturn the dam'. An alternative way of critically damaging multiple-arch and gravity dams might be to shatter the valves which regulated the flow of water to the turbines, though Wallis did not place much faith in the success of this tactic.

He concluded the main part of his paper by looking at docks, dock gates and surface transport (including canal locks, aqueducts and canals). Small bombs were virtually useless against docks and dock gates, but dock gates could be severely damaged by exploding a ten-ton bomb dropped from a high altitude within '121ft' of them. The cratering formed by this type of bomb could also cut railways and canals 'not for a few hours as is at present the case, but for weeks at a time, thus bringing internal transport to a virtual standstill.' Wallis was unable to decide whether a surface or penetration type of attack would be preferable against canals and aqueducts, though 'it is possible that the seismic disturbance caused by the penetration type will do more damage by causing cracking and leakage than the rather more local effect of surface detonation.'

Copious notes and diagrams supported all of Wallis's points and the appendices dealt in depth with such subjects as 'Visibility of Objects from Great Heights,' 'Variation of Wind Speed with Height,' 'Earth Waves and Coalmine Shafts' and 'Bomb Craters,' the latter, for instance, analysing possible repair times. Each specific point appeared scientifically and persuasively argued, and by any standard this paper was a tribute to Wallis's engineering ability, professional integrity and sheer determination. But, despite a later claim to Professor Andrade that he had produced it for Service officers, it was militarily insensitive, and the practical difficulties of its implementation were largely outside Wallis's comprehension. The method of destroying the Möhne Dam may have been theoretically sound, but execution posed a multitude of complex operational problems. As a civilian Wallis had in reality condemned Air Staff strategy and specifically criticised the bombing effort. Far from suggesting a means of attacking one target, he was proposing a method capable of employment against a number; hydroelectric dams, and the Möhne in particular, formed only a small portion of his paper. So fertile was Wallis's imagination that he saw the big bomb dropped from a high altitude as actually capable of altering 'the course of a river such as the Rhine'. To the sceptical this must have verged on science fiction.

Completed during March 1941, the Note thus represented over a year's research, experiment and thought. Anxious to secure support for it, Wallis circulated about a hundred copies to scientific, political, military and other interested figures. Wg Cdr S. O. Bufton, later Director of Bomber Operations at the Air Ministry at the time of Operation Chastise, had heard Wallis expound his views on the ten-ton bomb and explain his 4,000lb version over lunch at the RAF Club and subsequently on visiting Wallis at Burhill was given a copy; one also went to Oliver Stewart of the *Evening Standard*. Four copies were sent to the USA, which was then still neutral and where sensitive details might have fallen into enemy hands. Much later Wallis defended this proliferation of copies on the grounds that wide distribution was in itself a form of security: nobody would think the contents very important.

Not surprisingly, the Note provoked official reaction. Sir Henry Tizard, scientific adviser to the MAP, received a copy via Wg Cdr F. W. Winter-botham, Head of the Air Section of M16. But he was not the prime mover in establishing a committee 'to advise the Director of Scientific Research, Ministry of Aircraft Production, on the experimental work necessary to establish the technical possibilities of aerial attack on dams,' which became known as the Aerial Attack on Dams (AAD) Advisory Committee. Dr D. R. Pye, the DSR, had already convened an *ad hoc* body of four civilian scientists (Professor E. N. da C. Andrade, Professor J. D. Bernal, Professor G. I. Taylor and Dr W. H. Glanville) and Air Cdre P. Huskinson to observe the experiments at Harmondsworth and Garston, and he was clearly well aware of Wallis's ideas before formal production of the Note. Almost certainly, the experiments that the *ad hoc* body saw, rather than the Note itself, led to formation of the committee. On 18 February Pye wrote to Stradling referring to 'our discussion' of a week previously about Wallis's proposals to destroy dams, which, focusing as they did on an area of particular pre-war concern, now seemed especially attractive. Pye advanced the idea of a formal investigatory committee with himself in the chair and comprising Stradling (or his representative), Glanville, Wallis, Taylor and Mr R. S. Capon (concerned with armament development at the MAP), with Mr W. H. Stephens of Pye's staff as secretary. Pye subsequently agreed to Dr A. H. Davis being added at Glanville's request, and on 6 March he informed Dr E. Appleton (Secretary to the Department of Scientific and Industrial Research, the body in overall control of establishments like the Road Research Laboratory and Building Research Station) that, as with the model experiments, Glanville would exercise responsibility in scientific matters for the full-scale work in Wales, the cost of which was to be borne by the MAP. It is not clear when precisely MAP had assumed financial responsibility for the model tests, although February 1941 seems likely.

Taylor's full diary meant that the AAD Committee did not meet for the first time until 10 March. Then, and at future meetings, Professor W. N. Thomas represented the Ministry of Home Security instead of Stradling. Pye claimed 'that the work on the possibilities of aerial attack on dams had been started at the instigation of Mr Wallis.' Capon reminded the committee, however, that attacks on gravity dams had been under discussion 'for a number of years,' and three methods had previously been proposed: torpedo attack, with a number dropped to achieve a cumulative effect (abandoned because nets could foil it); attack on the air face with rocket bombs (the need to develop delayed explosion for protection of the aircraft effectively disqualified this); detonation of bombs in the water, which was eschewed by the Air Staff 'just before the war' because no suitable site could be found for trials. Wallis then explained his idea. At length, agreeing to further experiments, the committee decided to omit all reference to the Möhne Dam from circulated papers.

On 11 April 'a special meeting' of experts chaired by Pye, possibly the *ad hoc* body but not the AAD Committee, though later called 'Tizard's committee' by Wallis, met 'to consider the soundness of the suggestions made by Mr Wallis as to the destructive effect produced by detonating a very large bomb under the ground'. 'Tentative conclusions' were that on the available evidence Wallis's calculations of the depth to which a bomb of this nature might penetrate 'when dropped from a great height' and its 'likely' extent of damage to an underground tank were 'not unreasonable'. This meeting was therefore convened to examine the method for destruction of underground oil storage tanks explained in the Note. Writing five days later to Tizard, Pye argued that its findings were 'an essential preliminary to any further consideration of the project [against oil storage tanks] as a whole,' emphasising that neither the construction of the ten-ton bomb nor the 'special aeroplane' to carry it was discussed.

In fact, Wallis's proposals encountered varying degrees of scepticism before and after the Note. Winterbotham had however come to believe by mid-1940 that he 'must summon the Air Staff to adopt his [Wallis's] plan for a larger penetrating [sic] bomb without delay,' while nevertheless being 'well aware that half-baked, untried schemes had little chance of a hearing at this critical stage of hostilities, especially where new types of construction were involved.' Winterbotham decided to put out unofficial feelers to the Prime Minister's office, and on 5 July Maj Desmond Morton replied that he had 'consulted certain goodwill experts without disclosing your identity.' The view was that the project could not reach fruition until at least 1942, and Morton suggested that 'if the plan is to be put into effect in a reasonable period,' the Boeing Company or another suitable American firm should be approached. 'Thus modified there is no need why your plan should not be a perfectly practicable one.' This lukewarm response annoyed Wallis for, as Winterbotham wrote, 'in those very early days Barnes could not envisage the possibility of anybody not falling in with his ideas at once.' But Winterbotham encouraged him to produce the Note, a copy of which he sent to 10 Downing Street in 1941, and he 'indirectly' learned that Prof F. A. Lindemann considered that no such bomb nor aircraft to carry it could be completed before the end of the war. The situation was thus infinitely less encouraging than after Morton's letter the previous year, and Wallis became 'completely dejected'. In fairness to Lindemann, at different times Tizard, Pye and Huskinson (none of them unsympathetic towards Wallis) counselled caution against acceptance of his working figures. Winterbotham continued to canvass support, and, three days after Wallis appeared before Pye's committee of experts on 14 April 1941, he responded to a phone call from the DSR. Noting that he had supported 'the potentialities of the very large bomb' in 1940 partly due to 'the trend of development in Germany and the USA,' Winterbotham told Pye that the Germans appeared to be constructing a 'new large aircraft' in Czechoslovakia and reminded him that Beaverbrook had instructed Tedder, when at the MAP, 'to give all assistance' to Wallis. Winterbotham realised the need to ensure that the conclusions of Wallis's Note were not based upon 'moonshine,' but 'at the same time exhaustive enquiries made during the past eight months, together with the interesting discussion at your meeting, appear to me to make it evident that neither the actual effect of a ten-ton bomb can at present be accurately predicted, nor the suggested effect disproved.' However, Winterbotham appreciated the scientific objection that one major difficulty, given the current state of explosive development, would be to detonate the entire 19ft length of bomb instantaneously to produce a shock wave of the requisite intensity.

After the first AAD Committee meeting Andrade wrote a memorandum attacking the scientific basis for many contentions in the Note and, although Wallis defended himself in a detailed reply on 10 April 1941, this open disagreement about the value of such a revolutionary technique inevitably discouraged Service support for it. Winterbotham was still enthusiastic and Tizard, promising to secure more information on underground shock waves, did favour continuing work on the big bomb. Nor was the War Office implacably opposed: in a letter to Lt Col Charles Wallis, Barnes' brother, one official welcomed the idea of dropping a ten-ton bomb from the stratosphere as 'an attractive way of shortening the war'. And clearly, because it continued to co-operate with him, the Admiralty had not lost faith in Wallis. But as Charles told his brother early in April, his real task would be to convert the CAS. Later that month, 23 April, noting that some time previously he had discussed the destruction of dams with Wallis, Professor R. V. Southwell at the Ministry of Home Security put up another idea. It involved dropping into the water close to a dam a mine which immediately sank to a predetermined depth attached to a float and which was dragged into position by the force of water flowing over the spillway of the dam while its progress was slowed by a drogue or small parachute linked to the float. Stradling promised to put this before the AAD Committee.

Within weeks the Air Staff rejected the twin concepts of big bomb and Victory bomber. Writing to Wallis on 21 May and conveying on paper the substance of that decision, which he had clearly already discussed with him verbally some days before, Tizard underlined that 'the Air Staff has no interest in a specialised big bomber solely designed to carry one big bomb, and your view that the single-purpose bomber offers a high probability of winning the war is not accepted.' This was an 'operational decision,' not one of the MAP, but under the prevailing circumstances Tizard agreed with it. He had understood from Wallis, however, that he had greater 'elasticity' of use in view for the big bomber: it could carry a large bomb, a heavy total weight of smaller bombs, or a large number of troops over long distances. He asked Wallis to confirm this and Tizard's added impression 'that you would design in units so that you could attach different body units to the wing and tail units,' because this flexibility would make 'a great deal of difference to my interest in your proposals.' Tizard revealed that the Air Staff wanted the Wellington V in operation as soon as possible and 'the utmost energy' directed towards production of the high-altitude Warwick. Wallis should understand that attention to the big bomber must not interfere with these priorities, which could be interpreted as oblique encouragement to continue with this work. Tizard ended with renewed support for 'the ten-ton penetrating bomb' and a note that he was still making every effort to collect evidence for Wallis on the effect of underground shock waves.

As Tizard intimated, the Air Staff's reasons for eschewing the ten-ton bomb and the large bomber at the time were sound. Both weapon and aircraft – neither of which had left the drawing board in any realistic sense – would need time to develop. Wallis held that this might be achieved in a 'reasonable period . . . quickly and economically,' but made no attempt to predict a timescale. The discouraging estimate of a two-year development period seemed reasonable, considering that introduction of a new bomber type had hitherto taken up to six years. Furthermore, concentration on Wallis's project would entail transfer of personnel and facilities away from production of four-engined bombers, which was only just getting under way. In the context of the current war situation, this was plainly unacceptable, and Vickers-Armstrongs finally abandoned the Victory bomber in September 1941. The Air Staff could not be expected to sanction primary effort on a bomber to carry one bomb, especially when expert opinion voiced by scientists like Lindemann and Andrade did not fully support it.

3

Tenacity

EVOLUTION OF THE BOUNCING MINE FOR SEPARATE ADMIRALTY AND AIR STAFF TARGETS, 1941–1943; WALLIS'S SECOND SCHEME

Determined to prove the Air Staff's decision wrong, Wallis almost immediately received encouraging news. In May 1941 in another report from Harmondsworth Collins revealed that, once the right-hand tower had been removed and adjacent masonry blocks dismantled, a more thorough examination of the model of the Möhne Dam used for tests in February showed it to be 'more extensively damaged than appeared visible on the surface'. In a separate paper the civil engineer W. T. Halcrow agreed and argued that the chances of destruction would seem 'not unreasonable' if charges could be detonated 'near the downstream toe' of the dam 'more or less simultaneously' with those dropped upstream, especially as an 'attack by aircraft flying in formation has been contemplated.'

Then, on 6 June, Wallis learned that the AAD Committee would hold its second meeting 13 days later to discuss the 'Tirso model experiment, model gravity dam experiment, gravity dams; Elan Valley experiment.' Acutely aware that he had little positive evidence to present, on 19 June Wallis arrived early at ICI House, Millbank, which housed the MAP. He privately convinced the chairman that his project should not be abandoned and, with Pye's support, induced the members to allow further experiments. In addition to those at the first, Halcrow, H. D. Morgan of Halcrow's firm and Wg Cdr J. Baker-Carr were in attendance for this second meeting, and without calling him before it the committee rejected Southwell's scheme of 23 April.

Precisely how Wallis secured Pye's special support is not certain, but it is unlikely that he was as yet considering a contact explosion against the dam wall. For during the summer and autumn of 1941 the effects of explosions at a distance from reinforced concrete were further examined with a variety of different explosives, first on slabs and then on two 1/50-scale Möhne models at Harmondsworth (one with clay foundations, one with concrete). Collins reported that 'most damage' was achieved by RDX/TNT, 'slightly less damage' by Compound Explosive (CE) and Plastic Explosive and 'least damage' by Polar Ammon gelignite. He noted that 'a charge of 15,000lb detonated 100ft away from the face of the dam would cause severe damage but not complete failure,' although 'it is possible that failure might occur from the static forces, due to gravity, imposed by the water after the explosion.' However, 'the overall situation was still both complex and unhopeful.' On 21 November Stephens, the AAD Committee's secretary, acknowledged that progress concerning gravity dams had been 'slow' and revealed why nothing had yet been done at Nant-y-Gro: two 1/10-scale models for preliminary tests had only just been completed at Harmondsworth, following a detailed examination of the original in Wales by Collins and his team. These models, and two others built afterwards, had construction joints similar to those of the Nant-y-Gro dam and, if not severely damaged, could be repaired for further use. Two models of the Nant-y-Gro reservoir were also made at Harmondsworth and the four models of the dam used in conjunction with them.

The AAD Committee, chaired by R. S. Capon in Pye's absence and attended by Collins, met for the third time on 10 December 1941. Discussion covered much old ground, including bombing techniques dismissed in the Note: Capon suggested employing the stick method with a number of small bombs, because this provided 'greater statistical probability of a direct hit.' Despite Wallis's lack of enthusiasm, the possibility of damaging valve systems and sluice gates with a large bomb was to be further investigated and experiments carried out with multiple charges (a return to sympathetic detonation of mines). The next series of tests at the Road Research Laboratory was fixed for the morning of 22 December.

Wallis sensed that the AAD Committee was once more close to withdrawing its support and by now he too felt 'the growing conviction that my original suggestion was impracticable [which] led me to seek for other methods of destruction . . . Early in 1942 I had the idea of a missile, which if dropped on the water at a considerable distance upstream of the dam would reach the dam in a series of ricochets, and after impact against the crest of the dam would sink in close contact with the upstream face of the masonry.' Wallis could not explain how this concept occurred to him. It certainly had no direct link with children bouncing pebbles across a pond, for they revolve around a vertical axis, whereas Wallis's weapon spun around the horizontal. He knew that American airmen had dropped bombs from low-level and skipped them over the waves towards enemy ships, and he was intrigued to hear a BBC broadcast ascribe this type of attack to an RAF Coastal Command bomber in the Channel. Only after he had settled on his method did Wallis discover that naval gunners in the past had deliberately made their round shot ricochet to increase range. This reinforced his theoretical conclusion, but he insisted that knowledge of these techniques did not initiate his train of thought. And it is clear that Wallis now foresaw explosion of a charge in contact with a dam as his only hope of success.

By the beginning of April Wallis believed his idea 'sufficiently mature' to commence experiments 'in a Surrey garden,' the patio of his house over-looking Effingham golf course. Commandeering a supply of his daughter Elisabeth's marbles, he fired them out of a catapult device to ricochet from the surface of the water in a tub and then, clearing a taut string, land second bounce on a table, where the fall of each missile was marked in chalk by the Wallis children. As Elisabeth's dwindling supply of marbles was supplemented by 'half-inch diameter spheres of fibre and wood,' Wallis patiently collected valuable data, though he was far from establishing the reliable Law of Ricochet which he sought. The shape of the ultimate projectile ('sphere or oblong') also concerned him. He explained to Winterbotham (now Group Captain) that in a spherical bomb, if detonated from the centre, the explosion would reach all points of the surface at the same moment, thus disarming one major criticism directed at his deep-penetration weapon. Without giving him a reason, Wallis asked about the behaviour of a spherical bomb on impact with a surface. Winterbotham rang an Air Ministry contact, who told him that far from achieving deep penetration 'it would bounce like a football'. Wallis's reaction surprised Winterbotham: 'But my dear boy, splendid! Splendid!,' and picking up his briefcase he left. A few days later he telephoned Winterbotham to explain that he now intended to bounce the bomb across the surface of water against suitable targets. He was confident that his new scheme would work, although Winterbotham begged him to produce 'a properly baked pie – no under-cooked blackberries' this time.

By the middle of April 1942 Wallis was ready to commit his idea to paper and approach a friend, Professor P. M. S. Blackett, scientific adviser to the Admiralty, because he regarded his invention 'as essentially a weapon for the Fleet Air Arm.' At the same time, Winterbotham may well have encouraged him to seek Blackett's assistance, knowing that he would inevitably consult Tizard, who would in turn involve the Air Ministry. Winterbotham was present on 22 April, when Wallis explained his thoughts to Blackett and gave him a preliminary copy of the paper 'Spherical Bomb – Surface Torpedo,' which was circulated more widely in its final version on 14 May. In this Wallis held that the bomb bay of any aircraft could be converted to carry a large spherical bomb, and that the sphere would not be susceptible 'to initial disturbance by the under-body turbulence of the carrying aircraft at the moment of release, and thus its flight path should in fact be more accurate than that of the ordinary bomb.' Acknowledging its unsuitability for penetration bombing, he nevertheless maintained that a sphere would be ideal . . . for under water bombing, where rapid deceleration and good water stabilising are required.' Quoting past naval experience with round shot and in particular the experimental work of the German Ramsauer, who fired 11mm brass balls with a muzzle velocity of 2,000ft/sec onto the surface of water, Wallis explained that if the angle of incidence exceeded 7° the sphere would not regain the surface after discharge, but if it were less the angle of reflection from the surface of the water would always be less than the angle of incidence. To ensure success the attacking aircraft must 'attain a high velocity close to the surface . . . By approaching the target in a fast glide and flattening out the bomb should be dropped from a height not greater than 26ft when travelling at a speed of 470ft/sec.' Available data, which would be important in deciding the date of Chastise due to the height of the water in the Möhne reservoir, proved that a distance of 3,500ft (approximately two-thirds of a mile) could be covered in five bounces, the first of which would be half the height of the aircraft on release, the last about four feet. Noting that the density of the sphere was important, Wallis recommended 'a double skin,' bridged by 'a series of light timber beams or roughly welded steel girders,' which would allow this to be varied.

Narrowing the scope of targets discussed in the Note, as the bouncing technique only concerned water, Wallis saw this type of attack as 'particularly suitable' to 'the hydro-electric dam or reservoir and floating vessels moored in calm waters, such as the Norwegian fjords.' 'The charge should sink in close proximity [to the target] and may be detonated by a hydro-static valve at any pre-determined depth, the rate of sinking being comparatively slow.' Experiments showed that to destroy hydroelectric dams, the charge must be exploded close to, if not in contact with, the water face: 'This method of attack, permitting the aircraft to turn away at a distance upstream where short-range defences are unlikely to be situated, offers a promising means of obtaining the necessary proximity without undue risk to the aircraft and crew.'

Blackett was impressed, especially as the Admiralty had for two years been seeking an effective method of dealing with enemy capital ships. He did not share Wallis's view that this was exclusively 'a naval weapon,' saw operational relevance for the RAF and, perhaps as Winterbotham had hoped, informed Tizard. Sir Henry, whose influence spanned the Air Council, MAP and Chiefs of Staff Committee and with whom Wallis had already dealt concerning the Note, went to see him at Burhill next day, 23 April. Wallis found him 'very pleasant and easy to get on with . . . kindly and very knowledgeable'. More practically, Tizard's strong support was once more secured. And 'within two days' through Benjamin Lockspeiser permission had been obtained from Dr G. S. Baker, Superintendent of the William Froude Laboratory, to use facilities at Teddington again. Independently, employing spherical and oblong metal shapes produced by Vickers-Armstrongs, towards the end of April Wallis carried out another series of tests on Silvermere Lake near the Weybridge works, conveniently screened from prying eyes by a belt of trees and close to Foxwarren. Once more using a special catapult to bounce the projectiles across the water, he deployed Amy Gentry, his secretary and a stalwart of the Weybridge Ladies' Rowing Club, in a rowing boat to chart their progress. On the basis of these tests he settled for the sphere. Writing to Blackett on 29 April, he gave details of his findings: the 'golf balls' (spheres) were less satisfactory for ricochetting, but more suitable for aerial bombing and had better 'ballistic properties'.

The William Froude Laboratory at Teddington included two tanks: No 1, also known as the 'Alfred Yarrow,' and No 2. The former, 550ft in length, was the smaller and was utilised by Wallis only once when the other tank was not available. Thus for virtually the whole of his time at Teddington in 1942 Wallis used the No 2 tank, which was 640ft long, 23ft wide and 9ft deep, decreasing to two feet over the final 200ft. Because many other projects were simultaneously under way, Wallis had only limited time set aside for him. He worked with his own staff and equipment, which arrived from Burhill in a special van, and so secret were the experiments that even Baker did not understand their significance. To Fred Rayment, working on another task in No 1 tank, Wallis represented 'the perfect scientist' – one who 'rolled up his sleeves and joined in' – as from a specially rigged catapult mounted on a platform over the water his staff fired balls down the tank. Work at Teddington began on 9 June and occurred on 22 other days up to 22 September. Essentially this second series of tests there centred on refinement of the delivery technique. When he completed his paper on the Spherical Torpedo early in 1942, Wallis had decided to impart backspin to the weapon, without revealing it in writing. Why he decided on backspin is not certain. Another employee at Weybridge, George Edwards, is reputed to have discussed spin bowling in this context with Wallis at the time of the Silvermere Lake experiments, and Herbert Jeffree, one of Wallis's design team, knew about a proposal advanced over a decade earlier at Boulton & Paul for a surface vessel supported by forward-spinning wheels. German scientists later thought that the weapon had been spun to achieve greater stability in flight, and the need to attain this with a sphere may have started Wallis thinking about spin – an explanation favoured by the Road Research Laboratory scientist A. R. Collins.

A document produced by Vickers-Armstrongs in August 1942 explained: 'The enhancing life force due to the reverse spinning motion applied to the missile has three advantageous effects. (a) It increases the distance which the missile will travel after release from the carrier, before striking the water (b) It diminishes the tendency of the missile to plunge downwardly on impact with the water surface (c) It increases the distance which the missile will travel whilst ricocheting. As will be understood, all of these effects contribute to the improvement of the effective range.' The paper referred to two previously-registered patents (10889/1915 and 7198/1912). Both these 'earlier devices' for forward movement over ground or through the air derived 'translational movement' from rotation before discharge. Wallis's new method relied on 'the positive impulsion towards the target either by a carrier aircraft or a catapult or other projection means'.

Meanwhile the immediate aim of the new set of tests was to examine the practical difficulties of imparting backspin to the weapon. So 2in-diameter spheres made of materials ranging from lead to balsawood, either dimpled or smooth, were used, with the additional objective of deciding the ideal weight of bomb. To help to discover the elusive Law of Ricochet, A. D. Grant of Wallis's staff timed the bounces, as Wallis heard the spinning spheres 'kiss, kiss, kiss the water.' One part of the experiments concerned the determination of the distance below the surface at which a projectile might run. This was achieved by lowering a sheet of steel into the water: 'by varying the depths of immersion of this sheet . . . we were able to determine closely the depth at which a store (bomb or mine) immerses itself as an audible click was given out when the sheet was close enough to the surface for contact to be made.'

An apparently precarious method was employed to film the underwater trajectory of a spinning sphere after it struck the target. Two rectangular galvanised cisterns, open at the top and each fitted with small windows in one side, were loaded with cast iron ballast until they rested on underwater scaffolding with an inch or so of freeboard. A photographer with camera occupied one, taking pictures through the submerged window; the other contained the necessary lights. The experiments themselves were by no means quickly successful: one of the early spheres cleared the side of the tank first bounce and another shattered a window. Surface tension and the nature of the wetting of the surface of missiles ('wettability') affected results, and the water was skimmed at regular intervals by drawing a stick stretched across the tank from the far end towards the gantry.

Writing to Tizard on 16 June 1942, Wallis expressed renewed doubts about the spherical form for his weapon. Referring to results from the first four tests at Teddington, he argued 'that a cylindrical form might be more effective than the spherical and it certainly looks much more practical from the manufacturing point of view.' Proposing to carry out tests with spherical and cylindrical shapes, he had in mind that 'the torpedo' would be released from an aircraft at 50ft and slide down 'a rope' to the water, for which purpose a cylindrical form would be more appropriate. The idea was that ultimately the weapon would be suspended below an aircraft by two ropes wound round the ends of an axle and travel down yo-yo fashion to achieve spin. If preliminary tests with cylindrical shapes were successful on 19 June, Wallis intended to proceed to dropping 'a full size wooden dummy suspended by ropes in the proposed manner from a gantry in the roof of the shed.' This second stage was never reached, and it must be presumed that the tests on 19 June were unsatisfactory. A pity, for a cylindrical weapon, though not this method of spinning, would be used for Operation Chastise but only after much nail-biting delay.

From the start a succession of visitors descended upon the National Physical Laboratory to witness tests. On 12 June Tizard informed Pye that he had been to Teddington that afternoon: 'It looked very promising . . . I certainly think now that a full-scale test is desirable with a Wellington'; Pye (DSR), Air Vice-Marshal F. J. Linnell (CRD) and Norbert Rowe (DTD) at the MAP made the pilgrimage on 21 June to watch 'metal balls bouncing across the water.' Rear-Admiral E. de F. Renouf was another important visitor. When Lt Cdr L. H. M. Lane from an Admiralty experimental organisation, the Directorate of Miscellaneous Weapon Development (DMWD), went to see Wallis about a scheme involving the launching of a radio-controlled plane from a cruiser, he learnt of Wallis's new idea. On the advice of his director, Dr C. E. Goodeve, he told Renouf, who was also engaged in experimental work and had the ear of members of the Board of Admiralty. At Teddington Renouf immediately saw the potential of the proposed weapon and the very next day returned with other senior naval officers. Wallis recorded: 'For their benefit I moored a wax model of a battleship several hundred feet up the tank, broadside on. We then fired 2in. dia [sic] balls at it, when of course after hitting the freeboard of the ship, the sinking velocity of the ball combined with the back-spin to move it towards the ship, and by adjusting the mean density of the ball we were able to get it to pass right underneath "the soft underbelly" of the hull, to quote Winston Churchill.' Wallis recorded that the Admirals were '*tremendously* impressed,' appointed Lane to attend future tests and looked to the production of a version of the weapon capable of fitting into a Mosquito's bomb bay. Wallis would always remain grateful for Renouf's valuable support at this point and later stages of the project, but by mid-1942 he saw air force as well as naval uses for the new weapon and was concerned at the RAF dragging its feet. On 25 June, however, following his visit four days earlier, Linnell gave permission for a Wellington to be used for another series of tests. Wallis envisaged the ultimate weapon measuring about 7ft 6in diameter, but considered extrapolation from the Teddington experiments with 2in balls 'beyond the bounds of reason'. Conversion of a Wellington to carry a 4ft 6in sphere would provide an intermediate point, and subsequent installation, ground and air testing from Weybridge took place entirely under Vickers-Armstrongs' control.

Air Cdre G. A. H. Pidcock, Huskinson's successor as D Arm D, and his deputy, Gp Capt W. Wynter-Morgan, now took an active interest in Wallis's work. So did Wg Cdr Bufton, by then Deputy Director of Bomber Operations (D/DB Ops) at the Air Ministry, and Flt Lt Green was assigned to observe Wallis's work in a similar role to that of Lt Cdr Lane. The RAE at Farnborough provided a photographer, Mr J. Woolls, and Vickers-Armstrongs made two test pilots, Capts Summers and Handasyde, available. But for all this, an attack on enemy surface vessels still seemed the only possibility: on 9 July Pye wrote: 'I think we can safely say that the gravity dam is a hopeless proposition'. His view appeared to be shared by the Air Staff, and Wallis wrote to Maj P. L. Teed, a personal friend at the MAP, somewhat bitterly on 21 July: '. . . the profound effect of water impact waves has not yet been realised by the Air Force, but is now appreciated by the Admiralty.' He was trying to 'educate' airmen in this respect, but 'there is no doubt that the Air Staff have been singularly stupid over this point.' The following day Wallis learned that the Admiralty wanted 12 experimental weapons dropped from a Wellington and that the MAP had authorised the Oxley Engineering Company Ltd in London and Leeds to construct them.

During spring 1942 more tests were conducted at the Road Research Laboratory, where the 1/10-scale models of the Nant-y-Gro dam in layered mortar were constructed and subjected to scaled explosions at various distances from them. Then, on 1 May, Wallis and his wife were among a small group to witness the first test at Rhayader. Despite a great deal of disturbance in the water, the dam held and Collins therefore concluded it 'unlikely' that a single charge of less than 30,000lb would destroy a gravity dam 150–200ft high, if exploded at a distance from it. Back at Harmondsworth, meanwhile, there had been an interesting development. The possibility of using contact charges had been informally discussed at an early stage of the experiments and discarded on account of the accuracy of bombing required. Collins therefore had this possibility in mind as an ideal solution, but he was not tasked to carry out the relevant tests and at length did so virtually by accident. Towards the end of February or in early March 1942 (this unofficial and unscientific test was not formally written up) he decided to see if a contact explosion would breach one of the damaged models and was astonished to see pieces of mortar flung thirty feet away. Even while work went ahead to prepare for the first full Nant-y-Gro test in May, Glanville agreed that Collins should now prepare for a second with a contact charge.

The unscheduled contact explosion carried out at Harmondsworth by Collins almost certainly had an important effect on Wallis's thinking and thus represented a special contribution towards the success of Operation Chastise. Thirty years later Wallis told Collins: 'The bouncing bomb was originated [? invented] solely to meet the requirement so convincingly demonstrated by your experiments that actual contact with the masonry of the dam was essential.' And in another post-war summary, he wrote: 'Just before this [April 1942], in view of the discouraging results obtained from the experiments authorised by the AAD Committee, I had approached Dr Pye in confidence, telling him that I had an idea which would probably enable a charge to be placed *in contact with the dam face* and *exploded at any required depth*, asking him if he would guide the Committee before issuing their report to recommend a final series of experiments with the object of determining the smallest possible charge that would breach the dam when detonated in actual contact with the masonry together with the depth below the surface at which it should explode.' In view of the chronology, this too suggests that Collins' contact experiment had an important influence upon development of the weapon which would ultimately breach the Möhne and Eder dams. For evidently Wallis broadly settled on its nature and mode of operation in March 1942. This particular Harmondsworth test, therefore, may well constitute one of those happy, unexpected occurrences which can change the direction of scientific enquiry.

Collins believed, too, that a suggestion made by Glanville at this time represented 'a crucial turning point in the experimental work because it gave us the confidence to undertake the second test on Nant-y-Gro with a real hope of success. If this test had failed, and the dam had been severely damaged but not breached, the case for an attack would have been seriously weakened.' All those involved in the test programme realised that to crack or crater the surface of a gravity dam would not cause a breach: a substantial part of the wall had to be pushed back far enough to make it tumble over the air side. In Collins' words: 'We had, in effect, to use a battering ram rather than a hammer or pick-axe.' The amount of energy needed to achieve the required result related to the weight of the parts being moved, but it was known that effectively the distance moved by fragments of the model under current conditions was ten times that for the prototype Nant-y-Gro. Glanville therefore proposed that appropriate pieces of the model should be moved back nine-tenths of the scaled distance and this was done for all future model tests.

Glanville now set about procuring a 500lb anti-submarine mine with approximately the correct scaled-up weight of explosive (279lb, as opposed to the 20z charges used on the models). This mine was suspended by means of a scaffolding structure at the mid-point of the dam and 7½ft from its crest, and at 1700 on Friday 24 July the second test on the Nant-y-Gro dam was carried out with a contact charge (contained in the 500lb mine) before a much larger audience. It resulted in a spectacular success: a flash of water whitened the surface of the reservoir before water at the point of the explosion was drawn upwards into a huge spout so high that Collins, who was filming with a ciné camera, momentarily took his finger off the button as he followed its course. Then the centre of the dam was punched out. So in August Collins reported that a breach about 50ft deep could be caused by a contact charge of approximately 7,500lb exploded 30ft below the water level. Even allowing for casing, that made a much more acceptable weapon in terms of weight and was within the carrying capacity of a Lancaster. It would cause an estimated 70 per cent of the water in the Möhne reservoir to escape, although Collins later admitted that this figure and others of up to 85 per cent were only rough calculations 'derived from the assumption that the reservoir was a trapezoid – a solid with four faces like half a pyramid cut across the angles and laid flat.' The precise contours of the bed of the reservoir were unknown and the steepness of the banks would affect the potential outflow of water. In retrospect, Collins felt that his paper of August 1942 was 'the crucial report of the Road Research Laboratory tests . . . It not only showed that (with Glanville's adjustment to allow for gravity) a model would give a reasonable estimate of the size of the breach but also introduced, for the first time, the concept that the "scale" of an attack with a contact charge was determined by the depth of the charge and not the size of the dam.'

On 20 October Wallis used one of the 4ft 6in practice spheres produced by the Oxley Engineering Company for the Admiralty for spinning tests on the ground with a special rig installed in the fuselage of a Wellington to check aircraft stability. Following further tests of this nature, on 2 December Summers took the Wellington into the air over the Queen Mary reservoir north of Weybridge and Wallis spun four of the spheres simultaneously at maximum revolutions using the hydraulic system installed to operate the bomb doors. Summers was unaware that the spheres were spinning, and this convinced Wallis that fears of gyroscopic effect on an aircraft were unfounded, although some Chastise crews would disagree on the night. Meanwhile Lindemann (now Lord Cherwell) remained unimpressed. In later years Wallis claimed that he was 'always against me' and, in contrast to Tizard, 'not pleasant,' and as Wallis never met Churchill Cherwell's attitude was important. On the morning of 29 September, Wallis noted: 'I see Lord Cherwell and find him very unresponsive . . . [he] doubted if the Dams were of any consequence.'

Perhaps anticipating this response, on 14 September Winterbotham had initiated a different approach through G. M. Garro Jones, Parliamentary Private Secretary to the Minister of Production. Sketching Wallis's pre-war achievements and work in 1941–2 towards destruction of 'enemy water dams,' he outlined his invention of a 'surface torpedo' or 'Rota-mine,' about which the Admiralty was very enthusiastic and considering equipping 'every destroyer . . . with catapult apparatus capable of projecting Rota-mines along the surface of the water to distances of about three miles at an average speed of some 200 mph.' Yet, in spite of 'conclusive proof' obtained in Wales in July that a 'Rota-mine' with an '8,000lb charge' carried in a modified Stirling or Lancaster could destroy 'the largest dam in Europe,' no further action had been taken and the AAD Committee had not been re-convened. 'If this new weapon is intelligently used e.g. for simultaneous attacks on all German capital ships and main hydro-electric power dams, there is little doubt but that Italy could be brought to a complete standstill, and that industry in Germany would be so crippled as to have decisive effect on the duration of the war.' Far-reaching claims indeed. Tizard, too, gave support. Having re-examined the official file and especially noted conclusions drawn from the experiments at Harmondsworth and Rhayader, on 30 September he wrote: 'I should myself be inclined to advise that Wallis be instructed straight away to submit an opinion as to whether a bouncing bomb of this size could be fitted to a Stirling or a Lancaster.'

The AAD Committee eventually did assemble for its fourth meeting on 12 October 1942, but, apart from finally rejecting the idea of using multiple charges on the basis of tests carried out by Charlesworth at the Road Research

Laboratory, it gave Wallis no specific encouragement. So the following month Garro Jones arranged for him to address the new Tribunal of Scientific Advisers to the Ministry of Production at Gwydyr House, Whitehall, chaired by Dr T. R. Merton. Possibly because this was its first case, the tribunal showed interest and sympathy during 'a long interesting examination,' but its influence was limited and it could not override Cherwell. However, a meeting at the Institution of Mechanical Engineers on 16 November 1942, attended by Pidcock, Huskinson, Wallis, representatives of the experimental staff at Shrewsbury, MAP and Woolwich Arsenal, noted that detonation trials with Torpex explosive had been carried out in connection with Wallis's proposed weapon and would continue with a view to progressing to static detonation trials with 'a full-size store'.

In the meantime, a meeting at Vickers House in London on 25 August, attended by representatives of the MAP, Air Ministry, Admiralty and Vickers-Armstrongs, had decided that trials of 'the Spherical Bomb' should take place off the Dorset coast between Chesil Beach and 'the mainland known as East and West Fleet.' Wallis later claimed: 'We did our first actual full-size dropping experiments at Chesil Beach some time in September [1942], the Wellington having done considerable flying trials with the sphere spinning at full speed for some weeks before.' But no other written evidence supports this.

There is no doubt, however, that at 1340 on 4 December, with Wallis acting as bomb-aimer and Handasyde in the second pilot's seat as flight test observer, Summers did take off in Wellington BJ895/G from Weybridge. The aircraft, with its bomb-bay doors removed and a special apparatus for spinning and releasing two practice bombs, flew direct to the test range behind Chesil Beach near Portland for what official records term the 'First Trial'. Wallis considered the experience 'rather exciting', although the belief that naval gunners en route, puzzled by its strange outline, opened fire on the Wellington has been firmly discounted by Handasyde. Whatever the truth of this alleged incident, the bomb tests were certainly unsuccessful: the welded spheres burst on impact with the water. Undismayed, Wallis ordered that the outer casings be reinforced with a mixture of granulated cork and cement.

Wallis briefed Woolls, the RAE photographer, on 9 December for the next series of tests. No camera had been carried on the Wellington during the First Trial, although one had been positioned on the ground. The scheme in future was to supplement the ground camera, whose operator acted on a flash from the aircraft when the bomb was released, with one in the aircraft mounted in the bomb-bay to record the first bounce. In accordance with normal experimental procedure, the RAE had overall responsibility for the Chesil

Beach tests, and scientists at Farnborough analysing the First Trial declared that the store speeded up during flight, which Herbert Jeffree of Wallis's staff dismissed as 'rubbish'. On seeing the film for himself, he agreed that this did appear so, but concluded that the theodolite sighting rods were sticking. After proving his point, by hand-copying enlarged projected images of frames from the film, he was given the task of analysing the results of all future airborne trials.

On 12 December Wallis travelled to Weymouth once more for the 'Second Trial,' planned for 1230 next day. Stormy weather prevented flying throughout that day, though Wallis contrived a working dinner with Renouf. Even that had its problems. As a waiter lifted a tankard of beer from his tray, the bottom of the receptacle cracked, depositing a generous quantity of local brew over the Admiral. Eventually test conditions were favourable on 15 December. At 1100, with Handasyde again as observer and Woolls aboard with his camera, Summers took off from the grass runway of RAF Warmwell, north of Weymouth. He was instructed to dive BJ895/G at top speed and to release two spheres (one smooth, one dimpled) from a height of 60ft. Both spheres apparently shattered on impact, but after rowing around for two hours Wallis managed to recover one from five feet of icy water. It was badly damaged, but not broken. Two days later, at Vickers House, Renouf chaired a meeting, including representatives of the Oxley Engineering Company, which had manufactured the bomb casings, Admiralty, Air Ministry, MAP and Vickers-Armstrongs personnel (including Craven), to evaluate these tests. The ciné film showed that the height of release varied between 45 and 220ft, the speed between 230 and 255 mph, and the rotation of the bomb before release between 250 and 750 revolutions per minute (rpm). Renouf made clear that these trials were 'primarily to ensure the safety of the aircraft when releasing the rotating bombs.' The meeting noted however that the casings had 'failed badly' and agreed to further strengthening of them. Vickers undertook to produce two wooden spheres as standby weapons in case the modifications could not be completed before the next series of trials.

Experiments on the weapon now gathered pace. The Admiralty was especially keen to press ahead with a smaller version of the weapon, which seemed appropriate for anti-ship operations, and another trial was arranged at Chesil Beach below Langton Herring for Monday 28 December and subsequent days if the weather were suitable. Three variations of the weapon were to be tested: smooth and dimpled stores strengthened only by extra welding; this type plus additional ribs; and wooden ones fitted with equipment to record impact forces. It was hoped to recover all practice stores for further use.

In the event, this trial did not proceed until the New Year, and on 9 January Summers again flew from Warmwell for the 'Third Trial'. One steel ball was dropped on the water just after mid-day and it broke up on impact; a malfunction of the release mechanism meant that the second fell on land. After additional welding had been carried out at Warmwell, another smooth sphere was dropped next day from 100ft, revolving at 980 rpm and at an indicated airspeed of 289 mph: it broke on striking the water, though Wallis noted with delight that it 'did one enormous bounce to a ht. [sic] of 55 feet.' Saturday 23 January saw the 'Fourth Trial,' for which one wooden sphere was used. Released just east of the Coastguard Station at an indicated airspeed of 283 mph, height of 42ft and revolving at 485 rpm, it bounced 13 times. Technical difficulties prevented another test that day and a frustrated Wallis complained of 'blisters on bottom!' Next morning a second wooden sphere bounced '20–22' times and at dusk Summers easily propelled another over a special boom on the range. This was the first use of wooden spheres at Chesil Beach. Further tests at Chesil Beach on 5 February with 3ft 10in-diameter smooth wooden balls, dropped individually from heights of 80–145ft at an estimated airspeed of 300 mph and revolving at 425–450 rpm, achieved a range of approximately 1,315 yards, almost twice the distance predicted in the model experiments. A delightful postscript to these trials was the complaint of an irate local that the breeding of swans at nearby Abbotsbury had been seriously disturbed.

Two versions of Wallis's weapon were now being considered for aerial use: a smaller one (Highball) to be delivered by a Mosquito against surface vessels, and a larger (Upkeep) destined for a Lancaster operating against enemy dams. A third variation (Baseball) also received Admiralty attention in a number of meetings chaired by Capt F. W. H. Jeans, Director of DMWD, at Dorland House early in 1943. This involved mounting a large mortar in the bows of a motor torpedo boat or motor gun boat to launch a bouncing bomb against enemy ships. Though this never became a practical proposition, it remained a possibility for another two years. A fourth variation, designated the 'heavy type' Highball for a Wellington or Warwick (as distinct from the 'light type' for a Mosquito) operating against Italian multiple arch dams, merchant ships and canal locks, did not proceed beyond preliminary discussion. One Upkeep would be carried by a Lancaster, two 'light type' Highball bombs by the Mosquito. Highball, Upkeep and Baseball were all grouped together under the codename Golf Mine.

At 1230 on 28 January, Wallis showed the film of the Chesil Beach trials at Vickers House in London to Pidcock, Wynter-Morgan, Winterbotham, Air Cdre R. Faville and Sydney Barratt of the MAP, and in the afternoon to

Craven, Sir Wilfrid Freeman, Admiral Wake-Walker, Summers, Handasyde, Lockspeiser, Kilner and Linnell. Next day Vickers-Armstrongs undertook to manufacture 250 Highball bombs at their Crayford works, and that afternoon Wallis showed his film in the Admiralty cinema to 'the Deputy First Sea Lord, Admiral Boyd etc. etc.'

Meanwhile, towards the end of 1942 Wallis had finished his second major paper on the bombing of enemy industrial targets, which synthesised his work, thoughts and experimental results connected with the bouncing bomb. Entitled 'Air Attack on Dams,' it was sent to Renouf on 9 January 1943 (as it also included material on attacking ships), and then to a total of 19 other people during the next three months. A copy was despatched to Jeans on 20 January, and Wallis believed that this was in turn copied and extensively distributed within the Admiralty. Air Marshal R. S. Sorley, Assistant Chief of the Air Staff Technical Requirements (ACAS[TR]), was the first RAF officer to receive a copy, on 5 February, although others at the Air Ministry, like Gp Capt Bufton and Air Cdre G. H. Vasse, followed soon afterwards. In turn Bomber Command officers and other responsible civilian and Service figures were gradually added to the distribution list. On 30 January Wallis sent a copy by hand to Cherwell at the Cabinet Offices with a detailed covering letter. He described his paper as a report on 'the effect of destroying the large barrage dams in the Ruhr Valley, together with some account of the means of doing it.' Trials on 3ft 10in-diameter spheres – the dropping tests from Wellingtons – had 'more than justified' hopes raised by the Teddington experiments with 2in spheres. So the Admiralty and MAP had agreed to 'full priority' in the development of 3ft spheres (Highball) for use by Mosquitoes against 'naval targets'. Wallis claimed that the first of these aircraft would be 'available for operations' in six to eight weeks. Indirectly Wallis showed that he was relying on Cherwell to stimulate RAF interest for 'unfortunately the possibilities of this new weapon against naval targets appear to have overshadowed the question of the destruction of the major German dams.' Yet this had been his own initial view in April 1942. Now he emphasised that his paper, based upon information supplied by Winterbotham, '. . . clearly shows that the destruction of the five major dams in the Ruhr district would have a powerful effect on the Ruhr industry.' Wallis continued: 'Large scale experiments carried out against similar dams [sic] in Wales have shown that it is possible to destroy the German dams if the attack is made at a time when these are full of water (May or June).' 'It is felt that unless the operations against the dams are carried out almost simultaneously with naval opera-tions, preventative measures will make the dam project unworkable and that therefore the development of the large sphere of five tons weight should be given priorities equal to those for the smaller weapon.' He proceeded to a rash promise: if 'a high level decision' were taken to give equality of priority to smaller (Highball) and larger (Upkeep) weapons, 'we could develop the large sphere to be dropped from a Lancaster bomber within a period of two months.' And another assertion would be proved much too optimistic in time. Modifications to Lancasters destined to carry. Upkeep bombs would be 'small . . . and the aircraft can be restored to their original use after having achieved this particular object in a few days.'

Although it was much shorter, the format of the 'Air Attack on Dams' paper resembled that of the Note: 19 pages of text, interspersed with tables and backed by footnotes, followed by eight pages of diagrams and illustrations. Opening with a 'General Discussion of the Problem,' Wallis recalled that the AAD Committee had been formed early in 1941 'to investigate proposals for the destruction of German and Italian dams'. Subsequently experiments on small-scale models of gravity and multiple-arch dams culminated in an exercise carried out on the Nant-y-Gro dam, which effectively proved that 6,500lb (7,500lb in Collins' paper of August 1942) of Mineol or RDX (Research Department Explosive) in contact with the masonry wall 30ft below the water level would breach 'the largest gravity dams in Germany.' The Welsh dam was one fifth the size of 'the Möhne or the Eder dams,' so he was confident that destruction of them could be achieved by a similar extrapolation of data; the overall weight of the bomb was well within the carrying capacity of a Lancaster II.

Wallis explained that he had developed a novel method of placing the charge against a dam face. One important German dam, the Sorpe, comprised a concrete core with earth supports sloping away each side of it, and 'at first sight' it appeared invulnerable to the bouncing bomb. However, earth dams with concrete cores became 'practically self-destroying if a substantial leak can be established within the water-tight core.' This had happened with the Bradfield Dam, near Sheffield, whose collapse in 1864 was initiated by a small crack on the crest, resulting in $3\frac{1}{4}$ millions tons of water escaping from the reservoir in three-quarters of an hour and 'a very large loss of life' (but, in fact, with a clay core the Bradfield Dam was not comparable). The Sorpe could be destroyed if detonation occurred on the upstream side of the dam 'at a suitable distance below the surface'. Wallis argued that, if an attacking aircraft released its sphere 'at extreme range' to reach the sloping face as it was virtually spent, 'it would drop back into the water rather than leap over the crest.' Alternatively, the range of release might be such that the sphere would sink within lethal range of the sloping bank 'without actually having made contact while above the surface.' Wallis pointed out that experiments with 'tamped explosions' showed that an earth wave would crack 'a substantial thickness of masonry' at distances far in excess of that envisaged in this instance. Once the concrete core had been cracked water would seep through to erode the earth bank on the downstream side, and ultimately the concrete core would collapse through lack of support.

Examining the catchment area of the River Ruhr, he listed five dams (Möhne, Sorpe, Lister, Ennepe, Henne) which held back a total of 254 million cubic metres of water; seven smaller dams together controlled a mere 12 million. The primary function of these dams was to provide '*domestic and industrial water supply* of the Ruhr district.' He concluded that any breach in its retaining dam would empty the Möhne reservoir in ten hours and that 'the capacity of this reservoir alone was therefore evidently great enough to cause a disaster of the first magnitude even in the lower reaches of the Ruhr.'

Wallis argued that interference with the flow of the Ruhr would interrupt traffic on the river and 'presumably' as a result disrupt heavy industry. Floods would also damage the railway system, which crossed the river in numerous places and ran beside it for considerable distances. As the Dortmund-Ems Canal reached its summit at Dortmund, although alternative pumping facilities might well exist on the Rhine to compensate for deficiency, loss of the Ruhr reservoirs' contribution to its supply must lower its water level. Water supplies for the population of approximately five million and industry in an area of 6,500km^2, which stretched as far as Hamm and Ahlen in the north-east, comprised a most important provision from the Ruhr river. Published statistics suggested that the electricity produced by stations associated with the Ruhr reservoirs was not large. But the maximum output of 13 stations between the Möhne Dam and the mouth of the river at Mülheim did total some 250,000hp; several of these would be damaged or destroyed by floodwater and all affected by loss of water supplies.

Wallis then turned to the Weser area, in particular the Eder and Diemel dams, which held back 222 million cubic metres of water. As with the Ruhr the maximum flow occurred in March, with June–October the dry period. Before its dam was constructed, the Eder river suffered frequent floods which affected the Werra, Fulda and Weser rivers, towns like Kassel, Hameln and Minden, and agricultural land. And by examining the original governmental authority for establishment of the two dams, Wallis concluded that their 'principal function' was to 'provide a regular supply of water for pumping *from the Weser into the Mittelland Canal.*' Two power stations at Hemfurth, below the Eder, had combined output of 44,000hp, and others such as that at Bringhausen were dependent upon the Eder reservoir. These and other installations 'lying along the rivers concerned' would be damaged or destroyed by breaching the dams.

In summary, interpreting available evidence in the light of the increase in demand which must have taken place in three years of war, Wallis concluded: 'IN THE RUHR DISTRICT THE DESTRUCTION OF THE MÖHNE DAM ALONE WOULD BRING ABOUT A SERIOUS SHORTAGE OF WATER FOR DRINKING PURPOSES AND INDUSTRIAL SUPPLIES;' 'IN THE WESER DISTRICT THE DESTRUCTION OF THE EDER AND DIEMEL DAMS WOULD SERIOUSLY HAMPER TRANSPORT IN THE MITTELLAND CANAL AND IN THE WESER, and would probably lead to an almost immediate cessation of traffic.' To those well versed in the subject, this section of Wallis's paper covered old ground spiced with some new, illustrated material.

The third section was a description of 'the Spherical Torpedo'. Calculations suggested that, if dropped from an aircraft at high altitude, it might double the horizontal distance achieved by a bomb released in the ordinary way and 'falling under the normal acceleration due to gravity'; it might be launched against any waterborne target or one in contact with water; and it could be projected from the deck of a naval craft, 'giving a longer range at a much higher velocity than is obtainable by an ordinary under-water torpedo' (in fact, Baseball). Once the bomb had struck its target, it would rebound and sink at 10–20ft/sec, being held in contact with the target surface by lateral force. Detonation could be achieved by means of a pistol activated by water pressure. Previous attempts to use this method had not always succeeded, because a bomb entering the water at high velocity would carry a large bubble of air with it and thus effectively prevent the water from activating the pistol as required. With the new technique, no air bubble would be formed and the depth of the explosion could therefore be 'controlled within satisfactory limits'.

Wallis concluded his argument by noting that, in the first section of the paper, he had discussed specific targets. Experiments had shown that 'massive masonry dams' were 'invulnerable' to any charge within the carrying capacity of existing aircraft unless exploded at a lethal depth below the surface of the water and in contact with the face of the dam. Given the known problems of attaining such accuracy with current methods and the 'erratic flight path' of bombs under water, only the spinning bomb could achieve this.

Cherwell reacted swiftly: at 1500 on 2 February he saw Wallis again, watched his Teddington film and displayed altogether less antagonism. Immediately afterwards, at 1615, Wallis met Lockspeiser (now DSR in succession to Pye) to secure permission in principle to press ahead with preliminary design work on the Lancaster bomb, and he gave him a copy of 'Air Attack on Dams'. Next day Lockspeiser telephoned to say that Linnell 'approved preliminary design work on Big Highball.' Unhappy at this limited approval, on 4 February Wallis rang Lockspeiser to ask for a decision on developing, as opposed to simply planning, 'Big Highball'; and that afternoon the DSR phoned back to state that Linnell was reluctant to sanction this for fear that development of the B.3/42 (Windsor) four-engined bomber would suffer; Linnell was therefore preparing a file and circulating it for comment.

Meanwhile, on 29 January, faced with an estimated delay of one week if he were denied immediate access to National Physical Laboratory facilities for further experiments to test impact resistance, Wallis had impressed Renouf with the need for priority over the requirements of Sir Amos Ayres. The views of admirals tend to prevail: next day Wallis and his team returned to Teddington.

Wallis's diary for the beginning of February showed a succession of meetings, working lunches, visits, telephone calls and design conferences concerning development of Highball, Upkeep and the B.3/42. Few working days finished before 2000 and on occasions stretched to 2300. On 10 February, however, Wallis met a serious administrative setback. Although Highball work must continue, Linnell ruled that nothing more should be done about the Lancaster project. Erroneously, perhaps mischievously, Green told Wallis that, having ensured Linnell's veto, Lockspeiser 'now pretends to back the scheme'. The following day the third of three practice spheres ordered from Crayford on 1 February was delivered to Woolwich for inert filling, preparatory to aerial drops on concrete at Porton on Salisbury Plain to test resistance; and Wallis made arrangements to record on film more experimental data at Teddington, fearing that, with Highball clearly advancing, facilities there would soon be denied to him. Yet again the galvanised cisterns were called into service and a female photographer from the Physics Department of the National Physical Laboratory recorded the underwater progress of spheres as they struck the hull of a model ship and crawled down its side.

On 12 February ACAS (TR), Sorley, received an appreciation of Upkeep from Linnell: 'Model experiments, mathematical analysis and full-scale drops of a smaller weapon, all indicate that the Upkeep project is technically feasible.' But Vickers-Armstrongs admitted to being four to six weeks behind on the B.3/42 project due to Mosquito work and, if Upkeep went to this firm, further delay of some months must be expected: Avro's (A. V. Roe & Co Ltd) programme of Lancaster production would inevitably suffer too. Linnell concluded that an Upkeep attack should be carried out in sufficient force, otherwise surprise would be lost. He did not dismiss the project out of hand, but advised caution, and this explained his decision two days earlier. Upkeep should wait until completion of Highball tests.

The fortnight of 13–26 February proved decisive. On the morning of 13 February at the Air Ministry Sorley chaired a critical meeting of 13 representatives from the Air Ministry, MAP, Bomber Command and Admiralty; neither Wallis, nor anybody else, represented Vickers-Armstrongs. Explaining that they were 'to discuss the development and possible operational use of the spherical bomb,' Sorley outlined the project put forward by Wallis, whom he named, for use against ships and dams. Lockspeiser gave details of experiments at Teddington and Chesil Beach, pointing out that two bombs were envisaged: Upkeep (11,000lb in weight, including a charge of 7,500lb – after Collins' paper – and 84in in diameter) and Highball (950lb, the same charge/ weight ratio and 35in in diameter). Air Cdre Pidcock, D Arm D at the MAP, acknowledged the Chesil Beach success, but observed that there was no proof that the bomb would be in a fit state to function once it had hit the target; and other MAP authorities held that no full-size Upkeep bombs could be produced before April. Admiralty representatives only stayed to discuss the feasibility of dropping a number of mines close to the base of the dam. When all present agreed that for all practical purposes sufficient accuracy was impossible, they withdrew. In their absence Sorley said that now the spherical bomb 'had been brought to the attention of the Air Staff,' its development should be watched; in particular, Bomber Command must keep in touch with Highball trials. Lockspeiser pointed out that 'considerable modification' to a Lancaster would be necessary for Upkeep, and he favoured development of Highball stores first. Sorley, however, argued that to use Highball against a ship would 'give away the idea and that it was a small step to imagine the use of such a weapon against a dam.' He then summarised. It appeared that the earliest possible date for attacking with Upkeep would be six months hence. In the meantime Highball work should continue with a view to two of these bombs being carried by a Mosquito. RAF Bomber Command would now be brought fully into the picture, and Gp Capt S. C. Elworthy was detailed to brief the AOC-in-C, Air Chief Marshal Sir Arthur Harris. And further advice was to be sought from experts, including Wallis. If this proved satisfactory, notwithstanding Highball, MAP should be urged to go ahead with development of Upkeep. That day Sorley wrote to Wallis: 'I have started the operational people off on the subject.'

On 14 February SASO Bomber Command, Air Vice-Marshal R. H. M. S. Saundby, produced a lengthy minute about Sorley's meeting, probably based on a briefing from Elworthy, to which he attached a copy of Wallis's 'Air Attack on Dams' paper. Explaining the characteristics, purpose and behaviour of Highball, which had been 'specially designed for the attack of capital ships,' he then considered the possibility of producing 'a similar weapon' of '10,000lb' containing a '6,500lb' charge and about seven feet in diameter 'for the special purpose of destroying dams, the Möhne Dam in particular.' If dropped from a 'specially modified Lancaster' at 80–120ft and 220 mph, it would travel 1,200 yards over the water, and calculations from the results of scale-model tests suggested that the Möhne Dam would be breached if the weapon were detonated 'within 10 feet of the up-stream side of the dam at a depth of 30 feet.' The attack would need to be made when the dam was full, 'or nearly full,' a depth of 30ft being necessary to achieve 'the necessary tamping effect.' Saundby noted that Sorley had addressed urgent questions to the MAP, DB Ops and Bomber Command so that he might make a final decision on the project on 15 February, and he appended draft replies to the tactical queries. One squadron would have to be nominated, depriving Bomber Command of its strength for the 'two or three weeks' of training which he envisaged, for 'the tactics are not difficult'. He considered the operation feasible in clear moonlight with radio altimeters.

Apparently Harris did not immediately grasp the difference between using Highball in Mosquitoes against ships and Upkeep in Lancasters against dams. His hand-written condemnation appended to Saundby's minute was scathing: 'This is tripe of the wildest description. There are so many ifs & buts that there is not the smallest chance of its working.' Unless the bomb were 'perfectly' balanced round its axis the vibration at 500 rpm would either 'wreck' the aircraft or 'tear the bomb loose'. 'I don't believe a word of its supposed ballistics on the surface.' Harris argued that it would be 'much easier' to produce 'a "scow" bomb to run on the surface, bust its nose in on contact, sink & explode,' maybe a reference to Finch-Noyes' scheme. As for Upkeep, 'at all costs stop them putting aside Lancasters & reducing our bombing effort on this wild goose chase.' It was, he opined, 'another Toraplane – only madder. The war will be over before it works – & it never will.' In retrospect Harris's assessment proved wildly inaccurate: but, in the circumstances and on first sight, his reaction was not unreasonable.

The meeting at the Air Ministry on 15 February was chaired by DB Ops Gp Capt J. W. Baker, not Sorley. Bomber Command and MAP representatives were joined this time by Wallis and Summers. Development of the larger sphere for an attack upon the Möhne alone was discussed. It was decided to produce a single Upkeep bomb and one modified Lancaster for experimental purposes. Special cradles would only be fitted to other Lancasters if and when the weapon had been proved and the attack decided upon; a MAP representative said that cradles could be fitted to an ordinary Lancaster in 48 hours and removed in a further 24. The following day Vasse, Bufton, Rowe, Wg Cdr Collier and Lockspeiser went to Teddington again. But there was still opposition to Upkeep, and on 17 February Wallis forwarded 'a simplified version' of 'Air Attack on Dams' to Barratt at the MAP. Pointing out that all his references could be checked in the library of the Institution of Civil Engineers, he enclosed translations of relevant articles from *Gas und Wasserfach* and *Der Bauingenieur* and emphasised that before 'I hit upon my own solution . . . many other possibilities' had been considered. Accurate bombing by ordinary methods was 'impracticable' and an aerial torpedo would carry too small a charge for effect. Defenders could foil a charge dropped and carried forward on the surface by a combination of self-propulsion and current or, more imaginatively, one dropped from an aircraft and towed into position by men using a dinghy ejected from another. The only feasible method was Wallis's own: by dropping a charge arranged to develop 'dynamic support whenever it touches the water thus leaping through or over obstacles until it strikes the freeboard of the target.' He had carefully weighed the first four methods '. . . and cast about in my mind until I stumbled upon the method of dynamic flight . . . which I am advocating.' That Wallis was evidently conversant in detail with all of these previous schemes suggests that he had access to a large number of official papers.

Now apparently 'a rival' – an interesting choice of noun – had suggested floating a charge down the reservoir. In fact this emerged from a plan early in 1943 by Combined Operations to attack the Möhne Dam, which its chief, Lord Louis Mountbatten, described as 'one of the great strategic targets'. Special Operations Executive also put up Operation Cornet for 'the demolition of the Möhne Dam' quite independently, using paratroopers to place destructive charges. Neither plan survived the third week of February, and Mountbatten's assertion that his was 'held in abeyance when Wallis came along with his rolling bomb' suggests that an informal agreement to defer action was made at the RAF's request.

Indeed, RAF interest had by no means slackened. On 18 February Saundby summarised the results of the Air Ministry meeting three days earlier for Harris in another minute. The AOC-in-C immediately despatched a personal letter to the CAS (Portal), which reinforced the impression given in his scribbled appendix to Saundby's minute of 14 February that he had confused Highball and Upkeep, though this error scarcely detracted from his general dislike of the entire concept. 'Linnell rang me up this morning about the

Highball proposition. He is as worried as I am about it . . . all sorts of enthusiasts and panacea mongers [are] now careering round MAP suggesting the taking of about 30 Lancasters off the line to rig them up for this weapon, when the weapon itself exists so far only within the imagination of those who conceived it.' Harris 'strongly' deprecated the diversion of Lancasters 'at this critical moment in our affairs' on the assumption that 'some entirely new weapon, totally untried, is going to be a success . . . I am now prepared to bet that the Highball is just about the maddest proposition as a weapon that we have yet come across – and that is saying something.' He moved on to detailed criticism: 'The job of rotating some 1,200lbs. [sic] of material at 500 rpm on an aircraft is in itself fraught with difficulty. The slightest lack of balance will just tear the aircraft to pieces, and in the packing of the explosive, let alone in retaining it packed in balance during rotation, are obvious technical difficulties.' These objections were understandable from somebody unfamiliar with Wallis's work, and Harris continued with some warmth: 'I am prepared to bet my shirt (a) that the weapon itself cannot be passed as a prototype for trial inside six months; (b) that its ballistics will in no way resemble those claimed for it; (c) that it will be impossible to keep such a weapon in adequate balance either when rotating it prior to release or at all in storage; and (d) that it will not work, when we have got it.' 'Finally we have made attempt after attempt to pull successful low attacks with heavy bombers. They have been, almost without exception, costly failures.' '. . . while nobody would object to the Highball enthusiasts being given one aeroplane and told to go away and play while we get on with the war, I hope you will do your utmost to keep these mistaken enthusiasts within the bounds of reason and certainly to prevent them setting aside any number of our precious Lancasters for immediate modification.' An unsigned, hand-written note to Portal on the Air Ministry copy of this letter indicated that Harris had also voiced his misgivings more widely: 'I understand that ACAS (Ops) had discussed the Highball with the C-in-C [Harris]. He is sending you a note on it through ACAS (TR).'

Support for Wallis did come from another quarter, however. On 20 February Lockspeiser informed him that he had 'in the past day or two' held discussions with Admiralty officers, including Renouf, on 'the question of trials which will be necessary with this smaller version of your toy to bring it into operational use as quickly as possible.' It had been agreed by Linnell, that 'a small body . . . of all interested parties' be brought together under Lockspeiser to investigate the project fully, and he proposed to hold the inaugural meeting of this body, to which Wallis was invited, six days later. Wallis learned, too, that the First Sea Lord, Admiral Sir Dudley Pound, had described Highball as 'the most promising secret weapon yet produced by any belligerent.'

Wallis himself was making good use of the test films. He showed one of the Chesil Beach trials after the Air Ministry meeting of 15 February and four days later at Vickers House ran this and another of the Teddington tests for a larger audience which included Pound, Portal and Craven. Although Wallis spoke at length about his ideas and answered questions, he received no overt encouragement. This may have prompted him to write next day to Cherwell, noting that since last seeing him 'no opportunity' had occurred to carry out 'full-scale tests with rotating spheres,' so he had concentrated on 'getting some underwater photographs showing the behaviour of spheres striking the target.' The Physics Department of the National Physical Laboratory had 'some remarkable pictures' capable of being shown in slow motion. 'They confirm the theory that the sphere will develop a horizontal force directing it towards the target.' He offered to show this film at the Cabinet Offices the following week or send it up, if preferred. On receipt of this letter, Cherwell sent for Lockspeiser.

Two days later Wallis made an optimistic journey with his two existing films to Headquarters Bomber Command at High Wycombe. Cochrane, following the visit to Teddington, convinced Harris (his commanding officer in Mesopotamia twenty years previously) that he should see Wallis, who took Summers with him to answer questions about flying aspects. They found Harris distinctly hostile. Before Wallis even crossed the threshold of his office, Harris roared: 'What the hell do you damned inventors want? My boys' lives are too precious to be thrown away by you.' He still believed that a squadron of Lancasters would be sacrificed to the heavy armament of a German capital ship. Harris later summarised his feelings at this time: 'I was damned if I would have my pilots out-Kamikazing the Kamikazes!! Quite apart from the fact that obviously a battleship under way would be a mile away by the time a bomb had hit it, bounced back, sunk 20 feet or more, crawled underneath and finally exploded!!!!!' Despite such an unnerving overture, Wallis explained the outline of his scheme, the two types of bomb, targets and aircraft involved. Although less abrasive, Harris remarked pointedly that he had heard about destroying the Möhne before. But he agreed to see the Chesil Beach film, sending unnecessary personnel away from the area for security reasons. Only Wallis, Summers, Harris and Saundby were therefore present when the film was shown, with Saundby acting as projectionist. In the face of Wallis's pleas, Harris remained obdurate – with good reason, as Cochrane later held, for Wallis was proposing to project 'a five ton lump of iron across a lake.' And overall Harris's problems were acute. Bomber Command possessed 59½ operational squadrons, many of these with light or medium aircraft; there were but 33½ squadrons of heavy bombers, only 15½ of them equipped with Lancasters. Although increased by half during the first three months of 1943, forecast Lancaster production for April was 123. Wallis wanted a quarter of that figure committed to the preparation and execution of one operation. Understandably, like the two Chiefs of Staff two days earlier, Harris would not commit himself. However, for the first time Wallis had been shown an aerial photograph of the Möhne Dam with its anti-torpedo boom in position.

Unknown to Wallis, official support was in fact massing in favour of a dams raid with Upkeep. During their meeting Harris inadvertently revealed to Wallis that Portal had authorised conversion of three Lancasters for Upkeep trials; Wallis had therefore secured the backing of the CAS, which in April 1941 his brother had warned was so necessary. As Cochrane's faith in Wallis had persuaded Harris to see him, personal contact may have favourably influenced Portal, who met Wallis when sitting for his portrait to be painted by Wallis's long-standing friend Egerton Cooper. So the engineer was no anonymous pedlar of wares. On the day that he saw the films at Vickers House, 19 February, Portal wrote to tell Harris that he could not dismiss Wallis's idea out of hand. He was anxious that its feasibility for use against the German dams be investigated, but promised Harris that he would not permit 'more than three of your precious Lancasters to be diverted' until the bomb had been thoroughly tested. The clear inference was, however, that satisfactory trials would result in the allocation of more aircraft. In the same letter, unlike Harris, Portal did not confuse the two versions of the bomb or their different targets, although he considered them part of the same project. The conclusions of conferences, such as those chaired by Sorley and Baker on 13 and 15 February, and possibly Wallis's film show on 19 February, probably had a cumulative effect on Portal's thinking, so that he now had fulfilment of his 1940 aim in view. It is just possible, too, that he held out more hope of a dramatic achievement by Upkeep than any other responsible authority associated with it then or later. He told Harris: 'If you want to win the war bust the dams.' In 1940 he had told Air Vice-Marshal Gibbs: 'The Germans won't win the war by dribbling bombs on London.' It was a sentiment close to Wallis's contempt for a sprinkling of small bombs.

Following his unhappy reception at High Wycombe that day, Wallis was cheered by MAP final, formal approval at long last on 22 February for modifications to two Mosquitoes for Highball trials. The intricate contractual details, whereby Vickers-Armstrongs at Weybridge took charge of the machines, covered a multitude of columns and several pages of typescript, with a stern warning that the RAF Special Accounts Section at Abingdon would only authorise a total expenditure of £6,000 on alterations. But any elation Wallis felt was dashed the very next morning. Early on 23 February, he was summoned to Kilner's office at Weybridge and informed that both of them were to go straight away to Vickers House, London, to see Craven. There Wallis was told officially by the chairman of Vickers-Armstrongs that he must drop further work on the larger bomb. Craven said that Wallis was making a thorough nuisance of himself at the MAP, by involving Vickers-Armstrongs directly or indirectly was damaging the firm's interests and, moreover, had offended the Air Staff. Linnell had told him 'to stop his [Wallis's] silly nonsense about the destruction of the Dams.' The CRD had not attended any of the previous week's meetings about Upkeep and evidently was not aware of Portal's decision to allow modification of three Lancasters, communicated to Harris four days previously. In fact, Linnell's decision – probably taken unilaterally – was not altogether unreasonable, and the ban did not affect Highball. Upkeep was only on the drawing board and, like Harris, Linnell would have been acutely sensitive about the need for heavy bombers to carry out Main Force bombing of German targets. He was worried, too, that development of the Windsor aircraft would suffer.

A shocked Wallis offered to resign. Sir Charles, to whom Wallis's project represented but a very minor part of Vickers-Armstrongs' work, reacted with vigour, accusing Wallis of 'mutiny'. As he left the room, Wallis told Kilner that he really wanted to go and, of Craven's news, wrote enigmatically in his diary: 'What happened on the Golf Links at Ulverston?'

After lunching with Winterbotham, Wallis went to Richmond Terrace to see Merton and Barratt. He expressed bitter disappointment at the morning's turn of events and yet once more talked enthusiastically about his ideas. Both seemed impressed by his arguments, but it is unlikely that either exerted decisive influence in the matter at this late stage. And Wallis did not stop his work, possibly on reflection treating Craven's words as an aberration or simply displaying yet once more stubborn resolution not to be thwarted. There was also a prompt indication that Craven's discouragement need not, after all, be regarded as final. On 25 February Wallis received a letter from Lockspeiser inviting him to attend a conference chaired by Linnell, as CRD, at the MAP the following morning. Wallis had received notification of this meeting, to discuss Golf Mine, five days earlier, and Lockspeiser's letter could have been in response to a request for confirmation of Wallis's invitation to it after the interview with Craven. Wallis learnt therefore that Linnell, and not Lockspeiser as planned on 20 February, would be in the chair and Roy Chadwick, Avro's designer of the Lancaster, had also been invited. In telephoning Kilner at Vickers-Armstrongs' Blackpool works, Wallis spoke of the conference 'to arrange development of the Lancaster Highball' – in other words, Upkeep.

Discussion at this conference – originally planned for 1000 on Friday 26 February but postponed until 1500, and attended by representatives of the Air Ministry, MAP, Vickers-Armstrongs (including Craven) and Chadwick – could not therefore have been a complete surprise to Wallis, and he evidently went armed with necessary data. Linnell, in stressing the need for utmost security, announced that the CAS wanted 'every endeavour' to prepare aircraft and weapons for use in spring 1943. Thus Upkeep had priority over the B.3/42 (Windsor) at Vickers-Armstrongs and other Lancaster projects at Avro. Three Lancasters should be prepared for trials as soon as possible with full Upkeep apparatus; eventually another 27 would be similarly modified and 150 mines produced. DB Ops (Baker) noted that 26 May would be the latest date for carrying out an operation against the dams that year, so all aircraft and mines should be delivered by 1 May 'to allow a reasonable period for training and experiments.' Wallis pointed out that 'no detailed scheme' for preparing the modified Lancasters had been agreed, and following discussion, 'the line of demarcation between the two firms' was settled: Avro would deal with strongpoint attachments to the airframe, bombcell fairings, bomb-release electrical wiring and the hydraulic powerpoint for the rotating motor; Vickers-Armstrongs would handle the attachment arms carrying the mine (including the driving mechanism) and the mine itself. To finalise these details, Avro undertook to send draughtsmen to Weybridge 'at once'. DTD (Rowe) would 'take immediate steps' to allocate a Lancaster, which could be located either at Farnborough or, if feasible, Brooklands airfield at Weybridge. Wallis revealed that no 'detailed drawings' of Upkeep were in existence yet, but hoped to give these to the works manager at Newcastle 'in 10 days to a fortnight'. D/D Arm D (Wynter-Morgan) reported that Torpex explosive was available, although three weeks would be required to fill 100 mines; the self-destructive mechanism could not be designed until final Upkeep drawings were ready. Air Staff representatives agreed to radio altimeters being provided for the three experimental aircraft, but held that they were 'not essential' for the rest. In summary, Linnell emphasised 'the extremely tight programme' ahead: of the eight weeks available 'at least four' had been identified for completing drawings and filling of the mines. Time was not now on Wallis's side, especially as the meeting also made clear that Highball work should not slacken: the first modified Mosquito had to be ready by 8 April. After the meeting, at 1745, Wallis showed his films to a captive audience in the Admiralty cinema.

On more than one occasion Wallis had claimed that only eight weeks would be required for developing Upkeep, and this was almost precisely the timescale now envisaged. As he left Linnell's room that Friday afternoon he felt 'physically sick' because 'somebody had actually called my bluff' and realised 'the terrible responsibility of making good all my claims.' Sensing Wallis's despair and aware that he needed 'enormous help' during a period of intense activity and worry, Rowe offered to send him the prayer to St Joseph which he used in times of personal stress: 'I knew Wallis had spiritual depths and I felt he needed spiritual help then, more than anything else, to strengthen and reinforce his own powers to enable him to do what he alone could do, and to carry an enormous load.' Wallis was deeply touched by this spontaneous gesture of friendship, and he subsequently made frequent use of this prayer in the weeks ahead. For now the advance to Chastise had begun in earnest. Tenacity was about to bear fruit.

4

Development

Garro Jones warned Winterbotham that Wallis's troubles had only just begun, and to Air Cdre R. Mansell at Boscombe Down Wallis himself wrote on 27 February: 'It appears that we are to go ahead at full speed, and my only fear now is that this important decision may have been arrived at too late.' The unavoidable pressure of constant meetings in a wide variety of far-flung locations, endless correspondence, delays, difficulties and changes of emphasis, which form an integral and inescapable part of design and production in any major project, were now exacerbated by a fast approaching deadline. Nevertheless, Upkeep matured to the point of delivery in 11 weeks, for on 26 February it was scarcely more than an inventor's dream.

In his final design Wallis projected a near-spherical steel weapon 7ft 6in in diameter and with its poles cut back to flats; like the smaller Highball, it would be back-spun before release. But, contending with so many other demands on its resources, the Ministry of Supply estimated a two-year wait for steel to make the dies, so Wallis settled on a smaller steel cylinder which could be cold-rolled and welded. The full diameter of the sphere would be achieved by putting packing round it and binding 'great staves of wood' outside with six 1½in-diameter steel bands sunk in grooves.

Shortly before noon on Saturday 27 February Wallis began the first full-scale drawings of Upkeep, completing them in time for a meeting at Burhill the following evening chaired by Wynter-Morgan, and attended by three other RAF officers and civilian representatives from the Royal Ordnance Factory, Woolwich, and Vickers-Armstrongs' works at Crayford and Weybridge. Wallis explained that the steel casing of the cylindrical core to hold the charge would be $\frac{3}{8}$ in rather than $\frac{1}{4}$ in thick. For detonation three hydrostatic pistol pots, standard Admiralty types with steel tubes of $3\frac{1}{4}$ in inside diameter but each carrying twice the normal number of CE pellets, would be required. These were to be armed by hand immediately before the aircraft left the ground, so normal Admiralty horseshoe washers would be safe enough. A fourth self-destructive fuse, to be armed 'when the store leaves the aircraft,' would be positioned centrally at the same end of the store as the hydrostatic pistols. All fittings coming into contact with the HE charge were to have every crack securely welded, and tie-bars were to be cased in paper tubes to prevent friction.

The following day, 1 March, Wallis revealed that Lt Cdr Broadhead of DMWD had undertaken to secure the necessary $\frac{3}{8}$ in plate by short-circuiting the naval supply system, and he wrote to C. H. Smith, chief engineer of the Hoffman Manufacturing Co Ltd at Chelmsford, about provision of special bearings for the 'Type 464 (Lancaster) Aircraft'. Wallis despatched six copies of 'preliminary Upkeep sketches' to Wynter-Morgan at the MAP on Tuesday 2 March. And that morning Wynter-Morgan, in company with civilian and Service representatives of the MAP and Ministry of Supply, and Vickers-Armstrongs at Crayford and Weybridge (including Wallis), gathered at Burhill for a meeting chaired by Chadwick, the Avro designer, at which detailed arrangements for 'filling and handling Upkeep stores' were laid down. Vickers-Armstrongs Crayford would be responsible for producing complete stores, although manufacture might be redeployed to other works; in practice, Upkeep steel cylinders and wooden casings were produced at Elswick, Newcastle-upon-Tyne, and Barrow, while Crayford dealt with Highball. The cylinders would go to the Royal Ordnance factories at Chorley and Woolwich for live and inert filling respectively before ultimately being assembled with the exterior wooden casings at a nominated operational station by Vickers-Armstrongs personnel. One inert-filled store, however, would be sent to the Vickers-Armstrongs detachment at RAE Farnborough so that balancing, hoisting, spinning and dropping gear might be tested on the ground, and Avro hoped to have the first modified Lancaster flown there for this purpose by the end of the first week in April. The decision of the meeting on 28 February concerning fusing was confirmed. Finally, Chadwick suggested that to reduce drag the Lancaster's top turret should be removed, and Wynter-Morgan undertook to refer this to the Air Staff for a decision. That same afternoon Chadwick and Service and civilian representatives of the

MAP travelled the short distance from Burhill to Weybridge for a meeting with other Vickers-Armstrongs personnel, plus Wallis and Summers. Conclusions of the morning's meeting were broadly supported, though 'in order to maintain secrecy' fitting of the calliper arms to modified Lancasters by Vickers-Armstrongs would now be delayed until the aircraft arrived at the operational station.

Next day, 3 March, Chadwick wrote to 'Wallace' from Avro at Middleton, Manchester, about a 'Type 464 Provisioning' aircraft, for which plans had been drawn up two days before. With a maximum annual output of 18,000, Rolls-Royce had found itself unable to meet the demands of the wide variety of fighters and bombers requiring Merlin engines. Bristol Hercules air-cooled radial engines were therefore used to power the Lancaster II, which Wallis at one time considered suitable for carrying Upkeep. This type was not a success, however, and soon Merlins built under licence by the Packard Motor Company of Detroit became available. Based upon the British Merlin 22 but complying with American 'standards and measures' with magneto and carburettor modifications, they were named Merlin 28. Aircraft fitted with them in Britain were designated Lancaster III, and some of these were modified as 'Type 464 Provisioning' for Chastise.

Even as Chadwick began this work in Manchester, Wallis discovered that Vickers-Armstrongs at Barrow and Newcastle had informed Craven of their inability to produce more than 20–25 of the steel cylinders and additional wooden casings in the available time. To both works Wallis wrote on 4 March that 'a good mechanical engineering job' was not necessary: 'the workmanship required is of the mine class, produced by rolling and welding' without machinery. The wooden segments needed only to be smoothed off with plane or spokeshave after being clamped into position with the steel bands, and he urged them to re-examine their pessimistic estimates. Next day Wallis sent further technical details about the lifting and spinning of 'the Lancaster golf mine' to Wynter-Morgan, and to Avro he confirmed 'yesterday's conversation' with Messrs Taylor and Walsh that the belt drive on the 'Type 464 Aircraft' would be on the starboard side and that the belt would have a standard 195in inside measurement. A speed indicator would be fitted to the countershaft and led to a suitable position near the hydraulic control valve, so that the operator could keep the unit at the correct speed. Wallis suggested that the standard rpm indicator, either electrical or mechanical, fitted to aero engines be used for this purpose. From Barrow Wallis received acknowledgement that his modified drawings for the charge casings had been forwarded through Kilner. Wallis himself wrote to Sqn Ldr Freeman, who had attended the Burhill meeting on 28 February, at the Ministry of Supply,

Fort Halstead, Sevenoaks, Kent. Enclosing drawings of the Type 464 hub, he explained that the inner hub was fixed and that the wheel would rotate on two large ball bearings driven on one side by 'a large V belt,' with the store running on the wheel driven by friction. In his drawing he showed the pot for the self-destructive fuse; Vickers-Armstrongs was to supply 'the screwed fitting' to be welded to the end plate, but the actual part would be a 'free issue' and depend upon Freeman's design. As the Vickers-Armstrongs fittings were already in hand, Wallis hoped that Freeman would make his design suitable for them. He reminded Freeman that any projections were to be kept within the recess at the end of the store to prevent damage on release.

Writing to Craven at Vickers House on 6 March, Wallis noted that drawings of 'the big bomb' had been finished 'on Thursday 4 March' and despatched through Kilner to Barrow and Newcastle. Wallis revealed that Barrow had 'almost completed' the first five casings, a surprising achievement considering the doubts of a few days previously. He noted that these had been constructed from 'the very rough undimensional full-scale sketches' and, unfortunately, were too long to fit into a Lancaster's bomb bay. Wallis was 'in touch with Avros' over this problem and hoped to finish all drawing-office work on Upkeep 'by the end of the week,' presumably Saturday, 13 March. 'My impression is that we shall come through all right as things are going far better than I thought would be possible.' The same day he wrote to Mr W. Mitchell at Barrow about a number of detailed technical points and, in particular, instructed him to avoid the problem with the Lancaster bomb bay by making the charge cylinder $59\frac{7}{8}$in, not 61in, overall. Had Wallis been able to study design details this hiccough could have been avoided, and he now secured sight of a set of Lancaster plans through Winterbotham. Then from Mr R. C. S. Hunt at Newcastle came an important objection. He opposed any separation of steel cylinder and wooden casing for transportation and filling. The diameter of the cylinder would be liable to vary plus or minus $\frac{1}{4}$in, he held, and perfect re-assembly at the operational station could not be guaranteed.

On 7 March Wynter-Morgan informed Wallis that he had chosen the location for Upkeep trials (Reculver Bay on the north coast of Kent), and the following day Freeman wrote to Wallis from Fort Halstead to report progress. A separate unit for electrical ignition of the self-destructive device, which would not affect Wallis's design, had been almost completed. He opposed Wallis's plan, however, to pull out the arming forks of the hydrostatic valves after 'the machine' (for spinning the weapon) was in position in case entanglement with the operating wire of the self-destructive device produced 'awkward results'. To remove the forks before the machine was installed would not be dangerous. And that day, too, Kilner replied to Hunt, reversing the previous decision to separate cylinder and casing. Such details of production were thus clearly outside Wallis's sphere of influence. But he did receive an encouraging letter from Craven. Expressing his satisfaction with progress, the Vickers-Armstrongs chairman added: 'I have seen the Chief of the Air Staff twice in the last week, and also Sir Wilfrid Freeman. They are taking intense interest in the whole scheme.'

On 8 March, as well, Chadwick signed the first conversion order for a Type 464 Provisioning Lancaster, and dropping trials purely in connection with Upkeep were carried out at Chesil Beach for the first time, four days after completion of the first full-scale drawings. Two high-density spheres in welded steel and 3ft 10in in diameter – one smooth, one dimpled – were filled with a cork and cement mixture to give the 'anticipated density of Upkeep,' 75lb/ft^3. Wallis explained that they were to be 'regarded as models of Upkeep' and would provide 'a useful comparison between smooth and dimple in high density.' They were to be dropped in not less than five feet of water from a height of 40–50ft at 300 mph and rotating at 500 rpm. Should the depth of water on the inland side of Chesil Beach be insufficient, the trial would be transferred to the open sea, provided this were calm. The second trial with low-density spheres, however, had to be conducted in open sea, provided that a trawler were available for recovery. All bombs would be dropped from the aircraft under the same conditions, so that, once the sea conditions had been taken into account, the performance of low and high-density spheres could be obtained. Before he and his team moved to Reculver Bay Wallis collected valuable data from the high-density results of these last two trials with Wellington BJ895/G flying from Warmwell to the Chesil Beach range on 8 and 9 March 1943, although no trial actually occurred over open sea.

Before the Reculver trials a number of technical and administrative problems had to be resolved. On 13 March Wallis confirmed a telephone message to Mitchell at Barrow that the Air Ministry required the exterior of all inert-filled stores to be painted grey and that of live ones dark green. Two days later he told Craven that the Barrow and Newcastle works were 'performing miracles' and that five of 'the new large stores' would be ready for despatch from each on that day. Despite the previous arrangement, three were to be filled with 'aerated concrete' and sent to Weybridge for balancing and spinning tests; the rest would go to a filling factory. On 17 March Sqn Ldr Freeman informed Wallis that he had arranged for the fusing equipment to work on the starboard side of the Type 464 aircraft, as requested, and that fusing in the air would be quite safe. The same day Wallis wrote to Dawnays of Battersea about provision of testbed and balancing equipment; the net of sub-contractors for important equipment was rapidly expanding. Two days afterwards he wrote again to Mitchell at Barrow: the three inert-filled stores had reached Weybridge and were 'a magnificent job'. But he warned that securing tackle had cut into the wooden casing in what was perhaps an indirect criticism of the decision to transport assembled cylinders and casings.

That same day, 19 March, Air Cdre B. McEntegart chaired a meeting at the MAP, attended by Chadwick and Air Ministry, MAP and Vickers-Armstrongs representatives (Kilner and Mr T. Gammon, works and general managers at Weybridge, but not Wallis). It was now clear that 23, not 30, Lancasters would be modified: three were destined for Farnborough so that Vickers-Armstrongs could fit the necessary equipment, while the other 20 were to be modified 'in every way' by Avro. The modified Lancasters would be test flown by Avro and delivered to Farnborough for clearance by a Vickers pilot before delivery by him to a destination nominated by the MAP. McEntegart ruled that at no time were aircraft to be flown with stores aboard unless under trial conditions. The engine which would rotate the store in the Lancaster had also been settled. Initially Wallis approached staff at Vickers-Armstrongs to construct one to his specifications. To his astonishment, the works at Newcastle replied that it already mass-produced a similar four-cylinder machine for use in submarines. So Sir Arthur Harris could later claim, with some glee, that to make Upkeep function the RAF had 'pinched a small engine from the Navy.' Once Wallis was satisfied that a spinning mine would not unduly affect the stability of the aircraft, his only problem was to determine the most effective number of revolutions per minute. Should the mine be spun too fast, the charge would expand and possibly split the steel cylinder. Later Wallis strenuously denied that use of electrics was ever considered for this purpose: employment of the hydraulic system installed for working the bomb-bay doors had been envisaged from the start, although Saundby's minute of 14 February did mention an electric motor revolving Highball in a Mosquito.

Upkeep development now pressed on at a furious pace. On 27 March Wallis sent Chadwick full details and weight estimates of the fittings which would be applied to Type 464 Lancasters in addition to the modifications to bomb doors, fairings and other work undertaken by Avro. The Vickers-Armstrongs fittings, such as ball races, side drums and changes to the hydraulic system, would mean an extra 1,178lb on each Lancaster. In thanking Wallis for this information, which would affect calculations concerning maximum fuel and oil capacity and therefore range, Chadwick regretted that the first machine would be a week later than the planned 1

April. He wrote, too, that a telephone message had just been received cancelling the order for fitting radio altimeters. This he found 'rather amusing,' because a letter requesting them had arrived only that morning.

The previous day, 30 March, an Admiralty scientist, Dr E. C. Bullard, had answered Wallis's queries about wave disturbance after an explosion. In 'open water' he predicted that the spreading circle of disturbed water would reach a radius of three miles in little over five minutes. A 6,600lb charge of Torpex (rather than Collins' original '7,500' or Wallis's '6,500' and a figure determined by the maximum possible in the chosen cylinder) would give waves one foot high over 7½ square miles, and even allowing for reflection from the dam wall or sides of an inlet, Bullard believed 'there is nothing to fear from the direct wave . . . I feel confident that after five minutes the height of the waves will be measured in inches rather than feet.' Four days later he re-emphasised that five minutes after the explosion the problems associated with reflection of the waves from the side of a lake would have been minimised: 'The area is too big for the energy in the explosive to cover it with waves of any height that matters.' That Saturday, too, McEntegart chaired a meeting on the progress of Upkeep and Highball at the MAP. To the nine officers present he stressed the need for the utmost secrecy. They learned that ten inert-filled stores were already at RAF Manston; balancing and spinning tests had begun on 2 April and five should be ready 'in a day or two'. Filling of cylinders with HE had begun at Chorley. Sixty Upkeeps with inert filling and 60 with HE were now on order; 20 of the inert-filled were to go to Manston, the remaining 40 plus all those filled with HE to RAF Scampton. Not until 7 April, following tests at Foxwarren, was Wallis free from his fear that, if rotated at 400 rpm or more, Upkeep would leap clear of its retaining arms. That day also Bufton sent Wallis 'two photographs and two interpretation reports of a certain objective' (the Möhne Dam). And three days later the Barrow works informed Wallis that its complement of fifty Upkeep cylinders and wooden casings had been completed, the last two being despatched to Chorley for filling on 9 April.

The first Type 464 Provisioning Lancaster (ED765/G) arrived at RAE Farnborough on 8 April; the second (ED817/G) went to RAF Manston 12 days later and the third (ED825/G) to the A&AEE, Boscombe Down. The first destined for 617 Squadron (ED864/G) arrived at RAF Scampton also on 8 April, while the last and twentieth (ED937/G) arrived just three days before Operation Chastise. Meanwhile, on the same day that ED765/G flew into Farnborough, Handasyde took the Wellington used at Chesil Beach from Weybridge to Manston. As Wynter-Morgan had indicated, Upkeep trials were now to be carried out on a bombing range in the Thames Estuary off the

North Kent coast at Reculver. This bay, dominated by the twin towers of an old Norman abbey church on a promontory, was secluded, as agricultural land to the south sloped up towards the promenade and no private houses overlooked the sea. When each bomb was released a bulb flashed in the aircraft, and A. D. Grant of Wallis's staff was equipped with four stopwatches to time the first three bounces, to help determine their height and record the duration of the whole run. RAF Manston served as the base for this latest series of trials, and there the test aircraft were bombed up by Service personnel under the supervision of Vickers-Armstrongs staff. On one occasion Jeffree had to prepare a weapon before loading by putting a detonator into guncotton. A curious but nervous throng retreated a full four feet from this activity. As Jeffree observed, that flimsy *cordon sanitaire* would have been 'a fat lot of good' had an explosion occurred.

Upkeep trials with the Lancaster aimed to determine 'the range and the trajectory of the large store with particular reference to the heights and speeds considered suitable by the Air Staff'. Initially a height of 100ft and indicated airspeed (IAS) of 200 mph was suggested, with rpm about 300. As no Type 464 Provisioning Lancaster was yet available, on 9 April Handasyde flew from Manston in Wellington BJ895/G to survey the proposed dropping area from the air. That same day, with his report to hand, Service officers and representatives of Vickers-Armstrongs met at Manston to discuss the first series of trials. Wallis did not attend this meeting, which concentrated on Highball, but arrived at Manston on the evening of 10 April in the modified Lancaster (ED765/G), which had been used to test 'the carrying and launching gear' with a sphere in the Vickers-Armstrongs shed at Farnborough and was now piloted by Summers. The following morning, exactly six weeks before Operation Chastise, Wallis briefed Vickers-Armstrongs staff and arranged a programme for the initial Upkeep trials at Reculver.

During Sunday 11 April and Monday 12 April balancing, spinning and the necessary test flights were carried out. As the Lancaster spun its store, problems were experienced with the rev counters, which had to be altered. By early Monday evening all aircraft were ready to begin the trials, but 'generally overcast and hazy' weather frustrated plans. Next morning, 13 April, weather and tide were suitable. Among those gathered on the promenade east of the Norman towers to watch were Guy Gibson and his bombing leader, Flt Lt R. C. Hay. At 0920, flying parallel to the beach towards two white buoys bobbing in the water as markers, Handasyde dropped an inert-filled Upkeep spinning at 520 rpm from the Wellington at a height of 80ft and 289 mph IAS. The woodwork shattered on impact, but the steel cylinder ran on, 'remaining stable until the extreme end of run,' which Wallis pronounced 'excellent'. At 1108 and 1907 Sqn Ldr M. V. Longbottom (attached to Vickers-Armstrongs for test flying) dropped similar bombs spinning at 300 rpm from the Lancaster. A variation in recording technique from that used at Chesil Beach occurred for this and all subsequent Lancaster trials. No camera was carried in the dropping aircraft. A high-speed ciné-theodolite camera was mounted on the shore, broadside to the dropping aircraft, to deal with range, while a second camera on the headland below the towers about a mile ahead of the point of release was used to cope with line. In addition, another device, consisting of a tripod with peephole which rotated on a vertical axis surrounded by a piece of cylindrical perspex sheet, was used for some of the drops. The operator looked through the peephole as the store cleared the aircraft, rotated the apparatus through 180° as he followed the weapon, and drew its track and the number of bounces in chinagraph on the perspex. The trace of each run was copied onto tracing paper and the perspex then wiped clean for the next.

The first sphere released by Longbottom at 250ft entered the water and shattered. Wallis waded out at low tide to recover the fragments for analysis, but he had already issued instructions for another bomb to be strengthened at Manston for a further test that afternoon. He reasoned that Longbottom had flown too high in the morning and thus on the second run the drop was to be made from a mere 50ft. Once more, therefore, as dusk fell an aircraft appeared offshore, flying east to west. The bomb dropped and a massive fountain of spray and splinters climbed skywards. Although the wooden casing clearly shattered – damaging an elevator on the Lancaster, which had difficulty in landing at Manston – the cylinder continued to run on for some distance. That, together with Handasyde's similar experience earlier in the day, was encouraging. But Wallis had no plans as yet to abandon the spherical shape, believing that further tightening of the metal bars would prevent fragmentation of the wooden casing. And this work was put in hand at Manston on 14 April.

The second series of Upkeep trials were due at Reculver on Saturday 17 April, watched by Linnell, McEntegart, Rowe, Professor G. I. Taylor and Wg Cdr H. Arnold. But at the scheduled time, 1245, visibility was unsuitable for flying. Despite the overcast conditions, the sea was 'so inviting' that Wallis, Taylor and Rowe stripped off and plunged in for a nude bathe, afterwards drying themselves 'with a pocket handkerchief' to 'the delighted hoots' of the assembled onlookers. After a late lunch at Manston, when all hope of a test flight had been abandoned for that day, Wallis returned to Reculver at 1715. This time, more conventionally, he rolled up his trousers and at low tide with Taylor and members of his own staff tried to recover more fragments of the bombs shattered on 13 April. They soon gave up the attempt: 'water too deep and cold,' Wallis wrote. That evening he and Taylor had a 'deep and long discussion' about the problems so far encountered.

At 1100 on Sunday 18 April, however, Summers was able to drop the first of three spheres. While two sank completely, the third, at 1330, 'held up'. But the cylinder broke out of the wooden casing and continued to bounce for some 700 yards, the third time that this had happened at Reculver. Over a sandwich lunch Wallis discussed the implications with Taylor. They decided that a steel cylinder, without wooden casing, would meet all requirements, and overnight the outer wooden casings of the remaining stores at Manston were removed.

Three days later, 21 April, in Wallis's absence and with Handasyde as observer, Avro chief test pilot Capt Sam Brown unsuccessfully dropped the first bare cylinder from low level and the following day he had no better luck when dropping another from 185ft at 260 mph. Wallis recorded that, because it too shattered and sank, the trial was 'a complete failure'. Chastise lay little more than three weeks away. But Wallis was certain that he had all difficulties solved: such was his confidence that he lost 'not a wink of sleep' over the project and has vehemently denied that at this time, or any other, it became an obsession with him. Nevertheless, on 24 April Longbottom flew Gibson to Brooklands, Weybridge, in a Mosquito for an urgent conference. A tired Wallis explained that unless the height of release and speed of the attacking aircraft were modified, the operation would fail. Using diagrams of the Möhne to emphasise his points, he stressed the need for release from 60ft at precisely 232 mph groundspeed. Gibson agreed; had he demurred, Operation Chastise could have collapsed. There is some doubt, too, as to whether a full-size Upkeep had yet been used in the trials. On 15 April Portal informed Air Vice-Marshal W. F. MacNeece-Foster in Washington that trials had commenced 'this week . . . with the actual weapon,' but other surviving papers suggest that the scaled-down 4ft 6in version was used until the end of the month.

An entry in Wallis's diary about this meeting with Gibson, Summers, Longbottom and Renouf 'to discuss height and speed of drops with bare cylinders or spheres on Lancasters' suggests that, despite recent events, he had not yet finally determined the shape of Upkeep. And this uncertainty appears to be confirmed by Flt Lt M. W. Hartford, the A & AEE test pilot who took ED825/G, which would unexpectedly be flown on Chastise, to Manston from Boscombe Down on 24 April. Next day he saw 'a 12,000lb steel ball' fitted in retaining arms for a test programme on 26 and 27 April, after which the store, which Hartford insists was spherical and not cylindrical, was removed and he took his Lancaster back to Boscombe Down on the evening of 27 April. However, no such large steel spheres were manufactured and Hartford may have been confused by the circular ends of the full-size cylindrical weapon.

The fourth series of dropping trials, which began at Reculver on 28 April, confirmed the choice of a cylinder. The first day was occupied with Highball flights, but with Gibson among the watchers on shore at 0915 the next morning, Longbottom dropped a bare Upkeep cylinder (possibly the first full-size one) rotating at 500 rpm from 50ft at a speed of 258 mph (less 5 mph headwind). It bounced six times in covering a distance of 670 yards over the water, but was seen to deviate 30ft left off course towards the end of its run. In the afternoon Wallis travelled to London for a progress meeting on Highball and Upkeep with civilian and Service personnel, including Gibson and chaired by McEntegart. He returned to Reculver in the evening and at 1030 on Friday 30 April Longbottom dropped another bare Upkeep rotating at 520 rpm from a height of 65ft and at a speed of 218 mph in flat calm. The bomb bounced four times and ran for 435 yards despite deviation of 50ft to the left. Wallis declared this 'a very good performance'. In pouring rain in the afternoon an attempt was made to recover the pistols from the cylinder dropped by Longbottom on 29 April, but it proved impossible to overturn the weapon, which had stuck in the mud on the seabed. Two days later, at 1130, Longbottom dropped a cylinder revolving at 680 rpm from 80ft, with the aircraft flying at 190 mph over rough seas with 2–3ft waves. The result was less successful – three bounces, a distance of 360 yards, and 40ft left of track – but Wallis was now fully satisfied that the operation could go ahead as planned. However, at Manston on 2 May McEntegart and Wynter-Morgan secured his agreement for the dropping of five more Upkeep cylinders at Reculver at groundspeeds between 210 and 220 mph from a height of 60ft and spinning at 500 rpm. Precisely 14 days remained before Chastise.

At the same time as the Reculver trials, either complementary to or in conjunction with them, experimental work connected with Upkeep was being carried out at other locations. At Boscombe Down the aircraft flown to Manston on 24 April, ED825/G, was used for range and manoeuvrability tests. On 30 April, with two guns mounted in nose and tail and 'one free ball-mounted in the ventral position,' it performed 'brief handling and performance trials.' The A & AEE report noted that 'the bomb doors have been removed and the fuselage underside modified, and two external carrier arms fitted, one on each side of the fuselage . . . [and] the normal saucer-shaped transparent moulding carrying the bomb-aimer's window had been replaced by a more nearly hemispherical type'; de-icing equipment had not been fitted and the boxes for barrage balloon wire-cutters were sealed. During the next week there came a series of tests which would directly affect Chastise. With a store in position and at weights of 63,000lb and 44,670lb the aircraft responded normally during climbing, diving and stalling tests. An indicated airspeed of 160 mph and a weight of 61,000lb was considered 'practical . . . for the operation,' with an increase of 15 mph causing a three per cent effective loss of range. An outward journey at 2,000ft, return without the store at 15,000ft and an initial weight of 63,000lb, including 1,774gal of fuel, would give a maximum still-air range of 1,720 miles. At Foxwarren Vickers-Armstrongs personnel refined the important spinning and balancing tests without which Upkeep could never have been perfected. Early spinning tests were conducted on the modified Wellington in the former Hawker shed at Brooklands, Weybridge, but by 1943 two rigs had been constructed at the Foxwarren annex on the Redhill Road, Weybridge, which comprised three sheds close to Silvermere Lake. One rig, with a Wellington unit, checked vibration and the effectiveness of the release gear by dropping a store onto plates to roll between sand-bags, while the other concentrated on spinning and balancing data; both used inert-filled stores. It was at Foxwarren that Jeffree solved the balancing problems by devising a special pendulum system with a sensitive galvanometer. With this he and Grant balanced all inert-filled Upkeeps by fitting plates behind the screws in the recesses at the ends of each store, later despatching the pendulum apparatus to Scampton so that live stores could be similarly balanced. No live Upkeep was thus spun at Foxwarren, although one was in Richmond Park.

Two important meetings were held in London on Wednesday 5 May. McEntegart, as D/CRD, chaired one at the MAP during which the fitting of air position indicator (API) and spotlight altimeter equipment by RAE staff to the Lancaster at Scampton was agreed. AOC 5 Group, Cochrane, under-took to have two of the six modified aircraft required by ACAS (Ops) for the testing of Upkeep at Manston by the following evening. Then Wallis, Cochrane, McEntegart, Saundby, Glanville and Bufton attended another meeting at the Air Ministry chaired by ACAS (Ops), Air Vice-Marshal N. H. Bottomley. Wallis and Glanville explained the plan to detonate Upkeep stores 30ft beneath the surface but insisted that the water level be no more than five feet below the crest of the dam for maximum effect. Wallis estimated that withdrawal of water from the reservoir would cause the level to fall about ten feet per month and that withdrawal had started in April. The attack, therefore, must be launched quickly. He told Bottomley that tests had confirmed detonation of the hydrostatic fusing to be accurate within one or two feet. In reply to Saundby's question about the cumulative effect of explosions in contact with the dam face, Wallis agreed that this would be 'likely'. Noting that it had been decided to attack during the moon period 14–26 May, Bottomley queried whether postponement until the June moon period were possible, but Glanville and Wallis pointed out that an accurate assessment of the level of the water required further photographic reconnaissance. This was agreed, with the proviso that in an emergency the reconnaissance pilot should bale out over enemy territory rather than force-land, so that the photographs would be fogged in the resulting crash. Wallis said that with airspeeds of 210–220 mph a range of 450–500 yards – of which 250 would be on the surface of the water – would be obtained with Upkeep. He had in fact specifically calculated that, if the weapon were dropped from 60ft at 210 mph, the range from point of release would be 476 yards.

Eight days before Chastise, Wallis wrote to the MAP about its request for a list of the people to whom he had sent a copy of his 'Air Attack on Dams' paper. Explaining that it was impossible to remember precisely to whom he had distributed a copy during a crowded meeting, he attached a list of 21 names with approximate dates of despatch: it ran from Admiral Renouf on 9 January to Flt Lt Green at the MAP on 30 March, but he cautioned that it might be incomplete. Four days later – and just another four before 617 Squadron Lancasters carried out their attack – Wg Cdr H. Arnold replied: 'The opinion here is that to withdraw or to impound the copies which you have issued would at this juncture only focus attention on the project and as far as I can ascertain Air Min'y [sic] share this view.'

In the meantime a change in the trial procedure had taken place. During the first week in May for some test flights the aircraft changed their angle of approach 90° so that they were flying towards the promenade, where between 6 and 10 May two screens were erected east of the Norman church to simulate dam towers. Released at sea and propelled towards the shore, the inert-filled stores (some of them fitted with self-destructive pistols) were to come to rest on the inclining beach, but frequently cleared the promenade to land in pasture beyond. Handasyde knew that these meadows were mined as an invasion precaution, and hoped that one of his long hops would cause a spectacular detonation. In reality, only grazing cows suffered.

On 6 May Longbottom flew four times (twice each in modified Lancasters ED765/G and ED817/G) with Handasyde as observer, but Wallis thought only one 'shot' satisfactory. The following day at Manston he supervised adjustment to the calliper arms of the Lancasters, which were 'badly out,' and at 1530 returned to Reculver, where, he wrote in his diary, 'Shorty did two good drops – direct hits.' Then for the ensuing three days bad weather interrupted trials. However, on 11 May, flying parallel to the shore, Longbottom dropped an Upkeep store on two separate runs. Both were spun at

500 rpm, the first dropped from 75ft at 230 mph, the second from 500 feet at 245 mph. Neither deviated from track, the former bounced five times over 430 yards, and the latter six times over 450 yards. The following day Handasyde did a similar drop from ED817/G. Then on 13 May Longbottom carried out perhaps the most significant test to date. Abandoning Reculver for security reasons, he flew south-west to north-east and dropped a Torpex-filled and fully armed Upkeep from 75ft five miles off Broadstairs. Spinning at 500 rpm, it bounced seven times over 'almost 800 yards' without deviation. For this trial the theodolite camera was positioned ashore on the North Foreland almost broadside to the aircraft's track, and Handasyde flew the other Lancaster at 1,000ft and 1,000 yards away from Longbottom, with two cameramen aboard to operate the normal-speed camera. Handasyde had Gibson as observer, and Wynter-Morgan flew in Longbottom's rear turret to watch the behaviour of the mine after release, as it slowed to 55 mph behind the aircraft.

The film of this test showed that the water-spout when the mine exploded rose to about 500ft above Handasyde's aircraft, and the estimated depth of detonation was 33ft. For all concerned the day was eminently successful. Jeffree witnessed the drop from the North Foreland lighthouse. Conscious that the keeper must not be allowed to see what happened, he contrived to borrow his binoculars just in time. Without benefit of their magnifying effect, the keeper remarked how 'terrific' it was to get 'eight bombs' together and explode them simultaneously underwater. Wallis independently recorded the event: 'We obtained a "dome" or rise of solid water about 20 feet in height and 200 to 300 yards in diameter at the instant of detonation. This was followed by the "plume" which arose to a height of about 750 feet and was probably between 100 and 200 feet in diameter.' At the time of writing he had not seen the film, which proved that the plume went considerably higher. Officially, Upkeep was now 'sufficiently robust to withstand repeated impact with the water and soft targets and has satisfactory balance.'

Two days later, 15 May, with Jeffree among those aboard, Handasyde flew off Broadstairs again to jettison the remaining live Upkeep held at Manston in a straight drop. Officially the height of release was 500ft for safety reasons, though Handasyde maintained that he dropped the store from 4,000ft. The mine did not explode, either in contact with the water or below the surface, for no hydrostatic nor self-destructive pistols were fitted and the stated aim of the test was to see whether the mine (filled with Torpex, whose stability when used in this way was uncertain) would explode on such violent impact with the water. There had been doubts, too, as to whether the mine fell immediately the release button was pressed or whether an appreciable delay occurred. Such fears were dispelled as the aircraft lifted suddenly and dramatically. In a sense that applied to events during the last week after two and a half months of intense, often frustrating, activity since 26 February.

As the Lancasters flew from Manston on this final, successful series of tests, on 9–10 May Mosquitoes from RAF Turnberry carried out Highball trials on Loch Striven. All three aircraft experienced trouble with the release gear and none of the weapons worked properly. Despite the encouraging signs at Reculver, Highball had proved an abysmal failure. This led to serious inter-Service friction virtually on the eve of Operation Chastise which threatened to render it still-born. The deadlock would be broken at the proverbial eleventh hour, neither at Manston, Loch Striven, Weybridge nor London, but over 3,000 miles away – in Washington.

5

Training

Control of the detailed planning, preparation and execution of the operation which would use Upkeep lay with Bomber Command, and the AOC-in-C (Harris) chose Air Vice-Marshal the Hon R. A. Cochrane, AOC 5 Group, to exercise direct responsibility for it. On 15 March Harris told Cochrane that he must form a special squadron without reducing Main Force effort and that the dams would be its first, not only, task. Harris nominated as the commanding officer Wg Cdr G. P. Gibson, who had served under him previously in 5 Group but was unknown to Cochrane; the same day Gibson was posted to HQ 5 Group for 'operational duties'.

On the evening of 11 March, Gibson flew as commanding officer of 106 Squadron for the last time. In his logbook he wrote that he went to Stuttgart and back on '3¼ engines . . . My last trip. 71st bomber'. He prepared to leave Syerston on 15 March after a total of 42 sorties on Hampdens, 99 on Beaufighters and 29 in Manchesters or Lancasters during one night-fighter and two bomber tours; although his rear gunner on 106 Squadron believed Gibson did not record every operation on which he flew, and this was certainly true later when he quite unofficially flew from East Kirkby following the Dams Raid. Promoted Acting Wing Commander in April 1942 and holder of the DSO and DFC and Bar, he was still only 24 years of age and clearly deserved the leave in Cornwall to which he now looked forward. News of his posting to Grantham thus came as a shock, which was not lessened when he learned over the phone from Cochrane's SASO, Gp Capt H. V. Satterly, that 5 Group wanted him to write a book. At his new posting he

Air Chief Marshal Sir Charles Portal. *(IWM)*

Air Vice-Marshal N. H. Bottomley. *(IWM)*

Air Vice-Marshal R. H. M. S. Saundby. *(IWM)*

Air Vice-Marshal A. W. Tedder. *(IWM)*

Sir Charles Craven. *(Vickers)*

Maj Hew Kilner. *(Vickers)*

Capt J. "Mutt" Summers. *(Vickers)*

Capt R. C. Handasyde. *(Vickers)*

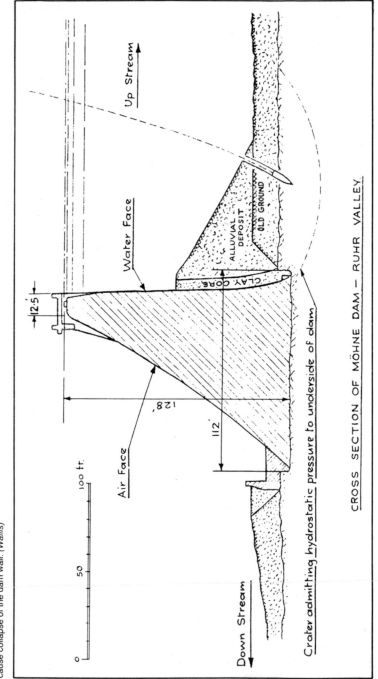

Illustration from "A Note on a Method of Attacking the Axis Powers," showing the path of Wallis's deep-penetration bomb, which would theoretically create an earthquake effect and cause collapse of the dam wall. (*Wallis*)

Up Stream

Water Face

Air Face

Down Stream

100 ft.

50

0

12.5'

128'

112'

CLAY CORE

ALLUVIAL DEPOSIT

OLD GROUND

Crater admitting hydrostatic pressure to underside of dam

CROSS SECTION OF MÖHNE DAM — RUHR VALLEY.

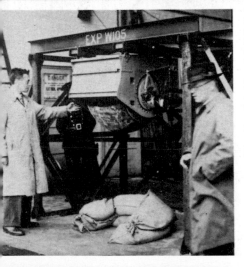

Top: The patio of White Hill House, Effingham. Here Wallis conducted early experiments connected with the bouncing technique. He sits far right under the balcony of his upstairs study overlooking the golf course. A table used in the experiments is visible extreme left. *(Vickers)*

Above: Wallis post-war with A. D. Grant of his Weybridge staff. Grant assisted with Upkeep experiments and trials at Teddington, Chesil Beach and Reculver. *(Vickers)*

Left: Foxwarren, near Weybridge. Herbert Jeffree (left), responsible for analysing results of dropping trials from aircraft and for balancing Upkeep, indicates a rig used for static tests. *(Vickers)*

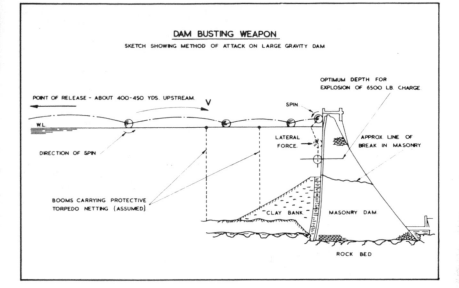

Above: The bouncing technique. Wallis's later diagram, using the Möhne as an example, demonstrates how backspin allowed Upkeep to crawl down the face of a dam. *(Wallis)*

Below: Extract from Wallis's diary, covering two busy days during the development of Highball and Upkeep. Note the variety of firms, ministries, test facilities and individuals mentioned. *(Wallis)*

Top: Early, experimental form of Upkeep. Note the flattened poles and metal bands securing an outer wooden casing around the charge cylinder. *(BAC)*

Above: Close shave. This simulated Highball, released from a Mosquito at Reculver, veered sharply off track and almost felled the cameraman. *(John Cura)*

Left: Reculver trial. Modified Lancaster, minus dorsal turret and bomb-bay doors, drops an experimental sphere with wooden casing on April 13 or 18, 1943. *(BAC)*

First of several sketches by Barnes Wallis in 1977, when he was aged 89. This shows "golfball" and "oblong" shapes used during experiments on Silvermere Lake in April 1942, after which Wallis opted for a spherical weapon with flattened poles. *(Author)*

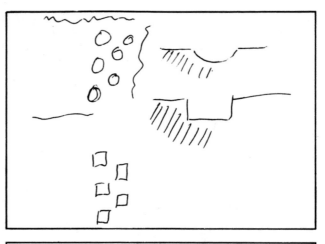

Illustrations showing how a pebble projected across the surface of water revolves around a vertical axis (left), whereas Upkeep revolved around a horizontal one (right). *(Author)*

Beams from angled spotlights fitted to aircraft penetrate water, intersect and are liable to give a false impression of height. Chastise navigators needed to ensure that the circles were touching on the surface, not under the water. *(Author)*

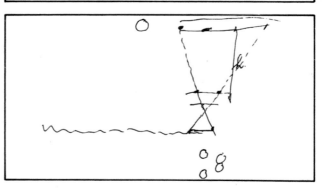

Wallis's free-hand sketch illustrating the technique of destruction at the Möhne, completed without notes or other aids and demonstrating his clear, retentive memory a generation after the event. *(Author)*

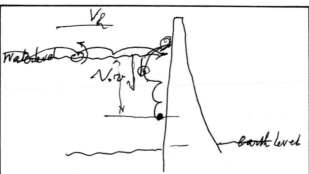

A. R. Collins. *(Collins)*

Dr W. H. Glanville. *(G. Argent)*

The Road Research Laboratory, Harmondsworth, where tests with models of the Möhne and Nant-y-Gro dams took place in connection with Wallis's two schemes for destroying gravity dams. *(Road Research Laboratory)*

1/50-scale model of the Möhne Dam at the Building Research Station, Garston, with apparatus for measuring the effect of charges exploded at various distances from it. *(Building Research Station)*

Two 1/10-scale models of the Nant-y-Gro Dam (itself one fifth the size of the Möhne) at the Road Research Laboratory. Note straight, not curved, wall. *(Collins)*

Nant-y-Gro model after destruction by a scaled contact charge. Damaged models could, after a lengthy process, be repaired for further tests. *(Collins)*

First test at Nant-y-Gro proved that, if detonated away from it, 30,000lb of explosive would be required to breach the Möhne Dam. *(Collins)*

Scaled charge showers, but does not destroy, the Nant-y-Gro Dam, May 1942. *(Collins)*

Impressive aftermath of the second Nant-y-Gro test with a contact charge. *(Collins)*

Air Chief Marshal Sir Arthur Harris. *(IWM)*

Air Vice-Marshal The Hon R. A. Cochrane. *(IWM)*

Gp Capt H. V. Satterly. *(Crown Copyright)*

Gp Capt J. N. H. Whitworth. *(IWM)*

Barnes Neville Wallis.
(Wallis)

Wg Cdr G. P. Gibson.
(IWM)

Möhne Dam, showing the two towers and extension of crest (far side of valley), on each of which a single 20mm flak gun would be mounted, and the larger power station demolished during Operation Chastise. *(Ruhrtalsperrenverein)*

Eder Dam, showing the two power stations at its extremities, compensating basin, twin towers, Edersee village (foreground) and road beneath Waldeck in the distance. 617 Squadron attacked from left to right. *(Ruhrtalsperrenverein)*

Henne Dam, included in the draft operation order but omitted from the final version. Attack would have been from left to right. After the war the dam wall was completely and differently rebuilt. *(Ruhrtalsperrenverein)*

Lister Dam, showing a single tower, not two as Wallis believed. An attack would have been from left to right. *(Ruhrtalsperrenverein)*

Right: Model of Sorpe Dam used for briefing. Pilots would dive over Langscheid village (centre), attack along the crest of the dam and turn to port beyond the compensating basin. *(IWM)*

Ennepe Dam. Note that the "island" on maps is a tree-covered spit and that any approach run towards the dam is very restricted. *(Ennepe-Wasserverband)*

Diemel Dam with the reservoir at near-maximum capacity. Note absence of towers on the dam wall. *(Author)*

Right: Briefing model of Möhne Dam. Aircraft would fly left to right along the lower arm of reservoir, clear the central spit and attack dam at bottom right. *(IWM)*

Chastise Lancaster, with ventral gun position which was soon removed. Flown to Scampton on the mid-afternoon of May 16, 1943, it went to the Sorpe Dam that night. *(IWM)*

Modified (Type 464 Provisioning) Lancasters flying in formation, unusual for British heavy bombers. This photograph is post-Chastise. *(Crown Copyright)*

Gibson's aircraft at dispersal, with mine in position and belt linked to the hydraulic motor mounted in the fuselage for rotating Upkeep. *(Crown Copyright)* encountered all the paraphernalia of bureaucracy which were anathema to an active pilot. But on 18 March Cochrane asked him, without giving details, to do one more operation, and Gibson agreed. The following day Cochrane sent for him again. This time Gp Capt J. N. H. Whitworth, station commander at RAF Scampton, was present. Cochrane still told Gibson little, except that this would be 'no ordinary sortie' and that he would command a new squadron with personnel drawn from other squadrons in the group. The operation would not be carried out for about two months, but meanwhile low-level flying must be practised at night.

Squadron X, as Gibson's new charge was immediately known, officially came into existence on 17 March 1943, when Air Vice-Marshal R. D. Oxland, SASO Bomber Command, described 'Up-keep' to Cochrane as a spherical bomb, which if spun and dropped from a height of 100ft at about 200 mph would travel 1,200 yards. 'It is proposed to use this weapon in the first instance against a large dam in Germany, which, if breached, will have serious consequences in the neighbouring industrial area . . . The operation against this dam [the Möhne] will not, it is thought, prove particularly dangerous, but it will undoubtedly require skilled crews. Volunteer crews will, therefore, have to be carefully selected from the squadrons in your Group . . . Some training will no doubt be necessary and this will probably consist of demonstrations in the first place for the air crews at the Chesil Beach, and later practice at or near Penrhos in North Wales.' Saundby, Harris's Deputy AOC-in-C, confirmed that 'volunteer tour-expired crews' were to be used for the new squadron, and subsequently Bomber Command laid down that it should be recruited from those who had completed or nearly completed two tours.

Emerging from the second interview with Cochrane on 19 March, Gibson knew that his squadron would be based at Scampton, where he had served with 83 Squadron as a Hampden pilot during the first 12 months of the war. Choice of this station explained Whitworth's presence at the briefing and came about because 49 Squadron had been moved out in preparation for the laying down of hard runways, so currently 57 Squadron occupied accommodation designed for two squadrons.

Squadron X began to gather at RAF Scampton on 21 March, and that evening Gibson arrived to take charge. Later the impression formed that all the aircrew were young veterans and hand-picked by Gibson, all highly decorated and present on the station then. In reality they assembled over a period of days (up to a month in extreme cases): seven crews were ordered to report by 24 March, seven by 25 March and seven more by 31 March. Not all the pilots were personally known to Gibson; aircrew ages ranged from 20 to

32; the majority were not decorated (including six of the pilots); and far from having finished two operational tours some had not done one. Many who would fly to the German dams in May 1943 had completed fewer than ten operations against enemy targets.

Of the 21 pilots who initially joined Gibson for the operation, twelve were RAF (including one Australian), three RAAF, five RCAF (including one American) and one RNZAF. Flt Lt J. V. Hopgood DFC, F/Sgt (soon promoted Plt Off) L. J. Burpee DFM RCAF and Flt Lt D. J. Shannon DFC RAAF came from 106 Squadron, although Shannon did so indirectly. Posted with his crew to 8 (Pathfinder) Group, on 25 March he seized the opportunity to rejoin Gibson, though only his navigator agreed to go with him. At Scampton he acquired a bomb-aimer and flight engineer from 57 Squadron who approached him because their own pilot had been grounded, and he did not permanently get a wireless operator until 20 April. Sqn Ldr H. M. Young DFC, Plt Off G. Rice, Flt Lt W. Astell DFC and Sgt Lovell and their crews comprised C Flight of 57 Squadron, which was posted across the station *in toto* on 26 March despite Rice's protests. A former Oxford rowing blue and married to a Californian, Young, who had completed two bomber tours and had a large amount of staff experience, was a natural choice as one flight commander and Gibson's deputy; Leonard Cheshire, later to command 617 Squadron and win a VC, freely acknowledged Young's intellectual ability and cogency in argument. The second flight commander, old Etonian Sqn Ldr H. E. Maudslay DFC, arrived on 25 March from 50 Squadron together with Plt Off L. G. Knight RAAF, whose wireless operator, Sgt Kellow, observed: 'The offer presented to us sounded interesting and with our faith in each member's ability, we made up our minds there and then that we would accept the offer and move over as a crew to this new squadron.'

44 Squadron supplied F/Sgt K. W. Brown RCAF and his all-NCO crew, who were posted to Scampton on 30 March when partly through their tour. As the bomb-aimer, Sgt Oancia, later drily remarked: 'I do not recall volunteering for this transfer.' From 97 Squadron on 25 March came the only RNZAF pilot, Flt Lt J. L. Munro, Flt Lt J. C. McCarthy DFC RCAF (an American citizen who had joined before Pearl Harbor and wore dual shoulder flashes, 'USA' and 'Canada'), and Flt Lt D. H. Maltby DFC, and their crews. 61 Squadron supplied Fg Off R. N. G. Barlow DFC RAAF, and 49 Squadron Sgt C. T. Anderson and Sgt W. C. Townsend DFM and their crews; Barlow was promoted Flt Lt, and Anderson and Townsend F/Sgt before the operation. Townsend's wireless operator declined to join the new squadron, as he was about to get married, but the rest of the crew agreed and went to Scampton on 25 March. There they were joined by F/Sgt G.

Chalmers, who chose this crew by accident. He deliberately joined an all-NCO crew, though neither he nor any of the others knew that the navigator, Howard, had been commissioned in January.

From 207 Squadron Plt Off W. H. T. Ottley DFC brought his own crew, though they did not reach 617 Squadron until 6 April. Unlike Townsend, who had refused a transfer, Ottley volunteered his crew for the Pathfinders, but no vacancy existed. Then he heard that Gibson (whom he knew and respected) was forming a new squadron and arranged a posting to 617. Flt Lt H. B. Martin DFC – a very experienced Australian serving in the RAF who had gained a reputation for brilliant flying, especially at low level, and until recently with 50 Squadron – gathered his own crew at 1654 Heavy Conversion Unit and joined 617 Squadron on 31 March.

Gibson assembled his experienced crew at Scampton. The wireless operator, Flt Lt R. E. G. Hutchison DFC, joined him via RAF Wigsley on 25 March after finishing an operational tour with 106 Squadron; the rear gunner, Flt Lt R. D. Trevor-Roper DFM, had completed two and a half tours in Bomber Command; the bomb-aimer, Plt Off F. M. Spafford DFM RAAF, had served on 83, 455 and 50 Squadrons. The two RCAF men, Plt Off H. T. Taerum and F/Sgt G. A. Deering, navigator and gunner respectively, would fly to the dams unaware that they had been promoted, one to Fg Off, the other commissioned as Plt Off. The passage in Gibson's later book suggesting that Deering was inexperienced and only brought into the crew for the operation at the last minute is inaccurate. Other pilots posted in from the beginning were Sgt (promoted Plt Off) V. W. Byers RCAF, Flt Lt H. S. Wilson and F/Sgt G. Lanchester (or Lancaster) RCAF. In all, 22 pilots converged on 617 Squadron, although until the arrival of Type 464 Provisioning Lancasters only ten aircraft on loan from other squadrons were available to them.

By the morning of 27 March non-flying personnel had all reported to Scampton, where they came under F/Sgt G. E. Powell. Flight Sergeant (Discip), in charge of 57 Squadron's administration, Powell was transferred in this capacity to 617 Squadron. Drawing the newcomers up in a hollow square and knowing most 5 Group squadrons, he was alert for those who had offloaded 'scruffy buggers'. His suspicions were well founded, and several unwelcome guests swiftly returned whence they had come.

Other more worthy men received a different shock. Arriving at the guardroom on 23 March, an RCAF radar specialist, LAC H. K. Munro, could at first find nobody to admit knowledge of the mysterious new squadron. Eventually he was directed to a group of dilapidated wooden billets of First World War vintage, which he discovered later had been condemned as unfit for human habitation. Each hut was to house 24 men of all ground crew trades (riggers, fitters, signallers, radar specialists, etc.) and different nationalities; washing facilities – with cold water – were close by. Munro decided that the best way to bring this motley collection of 'Rhodesians, Canadians, Scots, Welsh, "Geordies" and English personnel' together would be 'to convince them all to do callisthenics for fitness before retiring each night.' This therapy soon produced results, but an additional signals man who arrived unexpectedly in the middle of one evening performance retreated in utter confusion. He explained afterwards that the limb-jerking convinced him he had stumbled on an annex of the local mental institution. With justifiable pride Munro noted that, once persuaded to the contrary, the newcomer 'soon joined our lunatic actions'.

Initially the new squadron had no chairs, so raiding parties were despatched to lift unguarded furniture from 57 Squadron. Powell mused that 'nobody knew where chairs for the crew room came from, but I know.' With nearly 700 men to house and dubious accommodation at his disposal – as Munro found to his dismay – Powell faced an administrative cul-de-sac until 'an erk' mentioned that three-tier bunks had just been thrown out of billets at another station. A quick phone call followed by an excursion in a 'Queen Mary' waggon, and 617 Squadron could sleep 66 men in a space designed for 22. At first, less success seemed likely at Scampton itself. Powell submitted a list of requirements – uniforms, paper, blankets, etc. – to the station stores officer, who replied with a brusque: 'You won't get 'em'. Sharp intervention from Gibson followed, and soon orders came from the Air Ministry that top priority must be given to the new squadron. The fact that 5 Group's pool of ground handling equipment was at Scampton considerably eased transportation problems once official pressure had been applied: spare spark plugs, tools, starter motors, bomb trolleys and winches suddenly appeared, and the squadron workshops, signals, armoury and other facilities began to take recognisable shape.

Squadron records show 24 March as the day on which the squadron 'formed on ordinary Lancasters'. That afternoon, Flt Lt H. R. Humphries arrived from Syerston to act as adjutant, replacing 'the officer selected by Bomber Command for that duty but who was found to be unsuitable.' The following day, 25 March, Gibson was awarded a bar to his DSO and Humphries, whose administrative efficiency would make an invaluable contribution to the smooth running of the squadron, reported it ready to fly.

Two days later, with the more serious equipment deficiencies made good, Squadron X acquired specific orders and an identity. Gp Capt Satterly issued Gibson with 'most secret' written orders, which outlined the general plan of attack to be carried out against the dams without naming them. It proved a remarkably accurate forecast. 'No 617 Squadron will be required to attack a number of lightly defended special targets . . . These attacks will necessitate low level navigation over enemy territory in moonlight with a final approach to the target at 100ft at a precise speed, which will be about 240 mph.' Noting that the exact speed would be determined later and visibility might well 'not exceed one mile' at the target, Satterly expected aircraft to be despatched at ten-minute intervals to attack Target A. Once this had been destroyed, subsequent aircraft would be diverted in the air to 'Target B, Target C and so on'. Gibson must therefore ensure accurate navigation in moonlight or simulated moonlight 'at a height which will best afford security against fighter attack'. Although air position indicators would be made available, training should not be delayed for their arrival. Giving no specific clue to the targets, Satterly nevertheless advised that in preparation for the low-level final attack 'it will be convenient to practise this over water,' and all crews should be able to release their 'mine' within forty yards of a specified release point. Satterly warned that the route to the target must be planned to avoid light flak, aerodromes and other defended localities. He laid down that during daylight training pilot and bomb-aimer should wear dark goggles to simulate moonlight, and a second pilot must also be carried to mark in the actual tracks followed and to be available in an emergency. Satterly noted that nine suitable lakes were available for practice, particularly in Wales and the North Midlands.

That afternoon, 27 March, Astell was despatched to photograph these lakes on the pretext that they might be needed for training crews at conversion units, and it was significant that Satterly no longer referred to 'Squadron X'. So, with its orders clear and most of its personnel now on the station, 617 Squadron could commence full training. Two pilots took advantage of the lack of aircraft, however. Townsend and McCarthy persuaded Gibson that their crews required leave, McCarthy's request being backed by the wedding on 3 April of his bomb-aimer, Sgt G. L. Johnson. HQ 5 Group showed 27 March as the first day that 617 Squadron actually flew, though not until four days later did any crew fly one of the long cross-country routes – none under three hours' duration – which Gibson had approved for use in training.

Meanwhile Gibson had found out something more – though not much – about the proposed operation. On 20 March Wallis learned that the Lancaster squadron destined to deliver Upkeep would be based at Scampton. Three days later the name of its commander was certainly revealed to him, although the single word 'Gibson' in a small diary suggests that he may have heard of him on 20 March. With charming indiscretion, Wallis wrote in his diary for

23 March: 'a.m. phone from Group Capt. H. V. Satterly SASO No 5 Group Grantham 200 to introduce Wing C. Gibson who is doing the big job.' The next day Gibson received orders to travel south and meet a 'scientist' in connection with the work of the new squadron. After a journey by road and rail Gibson was met at Weybridge station by Summers and driven to Wallis's temporary office overlooking the golf course at Burhill. To his astonishment and the Wing Commander's chagrin, Wallis found that as yet Gibson had not been cleared for a full briefing. So 617 Squadron's commander received a general summary of the ideas put forward in Wallis's original Note. Wallis then ran the trial films, explaining that the weapon being tested was about a half the size of the final version, which must eventually be delivered within accuracy of a few yards from an aircraft travelling at 240 mph and 150ft above smooth water after pulling out of a dive from 2,000ft. With these daunting words ringing in his ears, Gibson returned to Scampton by following the same combination of rail and road travel, so that even his driver should not know where he had been. In his diary Wallis briefly noted: '4.20 W/Cr Gibson & Summers.'

Then, on 28 March, Gibson took a Lancaster with Hopgood and Young aboard over the Derwent reservoir near Sheffield to test his ability to fly at the required height. During daylight, despite the problems of surrounding hills and some industrial haze, this proved comparatively easy, but when tried at dusk it very nearly committed senior 617 Squadron officers to a watery grave. The day after this flight Gibson discovered the nature of the squadron's targets. At Grantham Cochrane showed him models of two dams (Möhne and Sorpe) and instructed him to make another journey south to see Wallis. The relieved Wing Commander mused that at least it was not to be an attack on *Tirpitz*. This time Wallis could expand on his previous information, explaining the targets, their construction and their importance to German industry. Summers, who was present again, said that if the bomb were dropped accurately, the blast of the explosion would be some 300ft behind the delivering aircraft, which would in any case be protected by the dam's parapet. This optimistic forecast could not be challenged, but Gibson firmly and decisively rejected Wallis's suggestion of a daylight attack.

By 13 April some crews were still incomplete, although four of the 157 aircrew on strength were surplus to requirement. And of those originally posted in to the squadron, that of Lovell had by now returned to 57 Squadron and been replaced by Sgt (soon Plt Off) Divall's. The manner of Lovell's departure, three weeks after the formation of Squadron X, underlined the rigorous requirements laid down by Gibson: the crew 'did not come up to the standard necessary for this squadron.' Shortly afterwards another crew went for similar reasons. Gibson proposed to replace Lanchester's navigator, to which the pilot objected. He and the entire crew opted to leave 617 Squadron, which was thus reduced to 21 crews at 16 April. Other changes also took place: Gibson agreed with the medical officer that one officer who was unable to endure the unusual strain should be posted out, and by 24 April the extra manpower had been shed. With few exceptions, the 19 crews which would fly on Operation Chastise were now settled.

During April the squadron's operations record book recorded: 'Daily intensive flying training carried out, when weather permitted.' At the end of the month Gibson reported to Whitworth that all crews were competent to navigate from pinpoint to pinpoint at night at low level by map reading; they could bomb accurately using a special rangefinder sight; and fly safely over water at 150ft. Training would now be consolidated into one tactical operation at the Eyebrook reservoir two miles south of Uppingham, and from 5 May ten aircraft at a time would operate there at 60, not 150, feet. Because of the advanced state of their training the crews were to be given three days' leave in rotation spread over the next ten days. In the meantime, cross-country exercises, bombing and further training with the Gee navigational aid would be undertaken. Initially crews had used the normal ground targets at the Wainfleet bombing range on the Wash, but 'two white cricket boards' (30ft × 20ft) had since been erected 700ft apart to simulate sluice towers on a dam. A gale on 26 April blew the screens down, but they had been put up again. Since 26 April the crews had been briefed to bomb from 60ft at a true airspeed of 210 mph. During the succeeding week 31 exercises had been carried out and 284 bombs dropped with an average error of 39 yards. Air-to-air gunnery practice with a towed target and air-to-sea practice with floats had also taken place. The squadron did not yet know the precise nature of the Upkeep weapon, but Plt Off Watson, the armament officer detached to RAF Manston for nearly a month, was due back at Scampton on 1 May with full details.

The Eyebrook reservoir, with a straight dam wall at its southern end and usually full in May, supplied water for the Stewart & Lloyd steel works at Corby. Appearing in all Chastise documents as 'Uppingham Lake,' it was ideal for 617 Squadron as aircraft frequently practised in that area, and its activity need not attract undue attention. Curiously, Wallis's brother had once fired field guns loaded with rifle ammunition across the reservoir in the course of War Office experiments, and Charles Wallis told the manager of the Corby (Northants) & District Water Company responsible for the reservoir, Mr G. C. S. Oliver, that his brother was working on a bomb to destroy German dams. Oliver remarked: 'Such was the security instilled in us that I mentioned this to no-one and thought no more about it.' Only after the attack 'did the penny drop'. Years later Cochrane recalled taking the manager of 'the local steel works out for a slap up lunch' and persuading him to allow Lancasters to practise over the reservoir. Oliver regretted in retrospect that this example of 'bribery and corruption' did not benefit him.

On 3 May Mr G. Le Mare, director of the Corby (Northants) & District Water Company, met RAF representatives, who 'explained that they want a sheet of water for special and urgent tests of some new device during the next three weeks. On their assurance that they will drop nothing, and fire nothing, and damage nothing, I said we would do anything they wanted.' So the following day a Service party under Flt Lt Lake erected 'four special canvas targets, approximately 20ft × 12ft . . . on top of the dam on poles fixed in barrels of concrete' standing behind the parapet wall and fastened to it. The four 'targets' were grouped in twos linked together with camouflage 'scrim' and spaced to simulate the towers on the Möhne. Thus at 1600 on 4 May, to the initial consternation of local inhabitants, practice commenced, though the squadron had already made use of the reservoir for training purposes before erection of the dummy towers. On 5 May Oliver recorded: 'Lancaster Bombers have been flying low over the reservoir last night and to-day. They fly between two targets which are put up on the dam. The targets are light structures and are in no way doing any harm.' People nearby were not so equable. Residents leapt from their beds fearing an enemy attack, but gradually they got used to the repeated low flights over the water, with aircraft pulling up sharply over the dam wall as they fired 'purple flares,' and often gathered in the road to watch the nightly performance. One villager explained that at times 'the roar of the planes became a little frightening.' Once his wife dived under the table thinking that the roof would be hit: 'The house shook as the plane, making a deafening noise, passed overhead and after this incident we realised that there was in fact no danger of planes striking the house.' When one of the targets, which had blown down, had to be re-erected on 11 May, the work was done by water company employees under the supervision of Plt Off MacIntosh from RAF Wittering. A postscript to this episode was that, after the war when the mysterious targets had long been removed from the dam, the RAF Angling Association held an inter-unit trout-fishing competition in the Eyebrook reservoir and many of the locals recalled the practices in May 1943.

The Abberton reservoir, also used for practice and shown in Chastise documents as 'Colchester Lake' or 'Colchester reservoir,' was three miles south of Colchester. A dam, carrying the Abberton to Maldon road just south of the Layer-de-la-Haye pumping station, crossed it and although without towers this provided an acceptable practice target for the Eder Dam. Mr A. A. Lowes, a local resident, was barred by Service police from using the road across the dam when practice flights took place, exclusively at night. But by the change in engine noise and trail of exhaust flames, which he observed from his house on a hill overlooking the reservoir just over a mile from the road dam, he realised that (as at the Eyebrook) the aircraft climbed steeply after firing a flare on crossing the dam.

In fact, over 1,000 hours had been flown in training by 617 Squadron up to the end of April, when it had a total of 58 officers and 481 other ranks. Individual crews perfected their own method of quick and accurate map-reading for, as Munro's bomb-aimer Clay observed, fixing a feature 'immediately below . . . [was] well-nigh impossible.' So 'the trick was 1) to keep your map(s) orientated 2) pick out salient features ahead or to either side 3) pass the pinpoint to the pilot and navigator 4) mark your map and check back.' Although map-reading responsibility fell mainly on the bomb-aimer, in this crew it was 'more of a team effort' with the gunners taking drifts from time to time also. Low level tactics were not however entirely to the liking of the civilian population: stories of panic-stricken clergymen forsaking bicycle saddles for sodden ditches, labourers diving headlong from the apex of hayricks and cattle imitating a Wild West stampede as Lancasters approached in formation were by no means all the result of too much Mess alcohol. On one occasion Maudslay returned with foliage sprouting from the underside of his aircraft after a low foray, and on another residents near Lake Bala in Wales were terrified as the Lancasters swept over low at night. An intelligence officer at Scampton, Sec Off Fay Gillan, was required to alert military and civilian authorities of the time and direction of all low-level exercises, but her task proved as daunting and about as successful as that of King Canute. Crews took off individually at irregular intervals when aircraft became available, and harassed navigators did not always feed her the necessary information in time for effective action. The result was a stream of complaints, even involving farmers who blamed fluctuations in milk yield from their cows on 617 Squadron, which occupied an undue proportion of Gibson's time. One unsympathetic squadron member, however, applauded the shaking-up of 'some of the cocky farmers'. There was an unpleasant side-effect of continuous low-flying for the crews, too, to which the squadron medical officer could personally testify after a trip with Maudslay on 25 April: airsickness. Fg Off M. W. Arthurton was therefore sympathetic to requests for 'appropriate medication' from other sufferers.

The high standard of training could not have been achieved without four important provisions. The first involved equipment developed by the

USAAF, comprising blue celluloid fitted to the windscreen, side windows in the cockpit and the front and rear gunners' positions, and amber-tinted goggles with three grades of interchangeable lenses to give varying degrees of intensity, all with the aim of simulating night flying during the day. On 11 April the first Lancaster fitted with 'Synthetic Night Flying Equipment' in the Scampton workshops became available for squadron use. A week later Gibson reported: 'There is no doubt that this equipment is the answer to all night map reading problems.' His early hopes of six aircraft so equipped were not fulfilled, however; the squadron never had more than two, although these were 'very efficient' and were used 'extensively'. When the goggles were taken off outside the aircraft, everything appeared red. Aircrew soon learnt to put on dark glasses until their eyes readjusted, but Shannon's bomb-aimer felt that a permanent deterioration in his sight may have resulted from these long hours spent in conditions of simulated darkness.

Examination of published technical details and reconnaissance photographs showed that the two sluice towers on the Möhne Dam were about 700ft apart, hence the position of the sight screens at Wainfleet. Following preliminary tests at the RAE, Wg Cdr C. L. Dann (supervisor of aeronautics at Boscombe Down) employed this information to achieve accurate release of Upkeep. Using calculations based upon the width of the sluice towers, he devised a simple triangular wooden sight, with a peephole at the apex and two nails at the extremities of the base. The bomb-aimer held this by a piece of wood attached to the underside of the apex and looked through the peephole. When the two nails and the towers or the sight screens coincided, as the aircraft approached the target, he pressed the release mechanism for the weapon. A trial flight, using the two towers of the Derwent Dam, convinced Dann and Gibson that the device would work and Wallis later worked out appropriate sight data based upon the towers of the gravity dams due to be attacked.

The difficulty of maintaining a specific height at low level over water, which had proved near-fatal for Gibson on 28 March, posed another severe test of ingenuity. After his fearsome experience Gibson told Satterly that he could see no effective method of judging the required height, although 617 Squadron made several unsuccessful attempts to solve this problem, one involving trailing a wire of specified length from the aircraft as Finch-Noyes had suggested. The civilian Director of Scientific Research at the MAP, Lockspeiser, solved this problem, and the answer had nothing to do with Gibson watching spotlights in a theatre converge on a line of chorus girls; for attempted use of spotlights shining down from an aircraft was not new. When told of this latest idea to determine height by Cochrane, Harris replied:

'I tried that with flying boats and it didn't work because the spotlight went through the water.' In 1942 Coastal Command had briefly and unsuccessfully attempted to use spotlights in Hudsons to assist depth-charging of submarines at night in shallow water. Lockspeiser remembered this, read up the papers and concluded that the double beams had failed due to choppy water. At Grantham he convinced Cochrane that this might not be so over a calm lake and went back to Farnborough to mount a spotlight on the underside of each wing. But the structure of the Lancaster made it difficult for the pilot to see converging spotlights set under the wingtips. A series of tests were therefore carried out at the RAE, and it was eventually decided to fit an Aldis lamp in the front camera slot, by the bomb-aimer's position on the port side aft of the clear-vision panel in the nose; cameras would be ineffective at such low altitude and would not therefore be carried on the operation. The second Aldis would be fitted in the rear of the bomb bay, where its beam would not be obstructed by bomb-bay doors in the Type 464 Provisioning Lancaster. The beams of the two lamps were arranged to form a figure of eight – that is, two touching circles – just forward of the leading edge of the starboard wing. This allowed the navigator to observe them and advise the pilot on altitude by looking through the perspex blister on the starboard side of the cockpit, while standing in the gangway leading to the nose. Three positions for the spotlights were considered during experiments, the third being that towards the rear of the fuselage designed for the downward-firing ventral gun, which was removed for Operation Chastise. The positions eventually chosen were 20ft apart: the forward one to port of centre, the rear precisely in the centre of the fuselage, and respectively angled 30° and 40° to starboard, with the rear lamp additionally slanted forwards.

Maudslay took one aircraft to Farnborough for the two lamps to be fitted to converge at a height of 150ft, and flew back to demonstrate their effectiveness before a sceptical audience at Scampton. Gibson, however, was satisfied and arrangements were made for all 617 Squadron aircraft to be similarly equipped. But, unwittingly, Gibson contributed to later confusion about the position of the Aldis lamps by informing Whitworth on 4 April that 'spotlight altimeters' were to be fitted 'to nose and tail'; it is however possible that these positions were used at this time and the rear one altered a month later. Before setting off over water, crews practised above Scampton's runways, and Plt Off Whittaker spent many hours of darkness cross-checking their height with a theodolite. Very soon crews graduated to flying over the Wash and canals, and the Spotlight Altimeter Calibrator – its official name – quickly proved its worth. Nevertheless, Gibson was worried that even if the lights were switched on only for the attack run they would act as a magnet to enemy gunners, and that 'a glass calm' had not yet occurred during trials. At the end of the month he revealed that the spotlights were still causing concern. Due to the need for attacking at 60 rather than 150ft, adjustments had to be made; in training oil was also found to be smearing the rear light, and still no means of shielding either from the ground had been found. Answers to these problems were not discovered until the first week in May, though the necessary modifications were completed by 10 May. A maximum of nine days then remained for the operation: 19 May, not 26 May, had been agreed as the last possible date.

The fourth critical provision was the modified Lancaster. The first did not reach 617 Squadron until 8 April, but by the end of the month 13 had arrived, allowing the last of the borrowed aircraft to be returned to its original squadron. Surveying the disembowelled bombers, squadron humorists dubbed them 'abortions' and the two 'cymbal-like contraptions' dangling from the exposed bomb-bay as 'clappers'. All the modified Lancasters were in the ED series, with the suffix 'G' (for Guard) to their individual numbers denoting that special equipment had been installed. Unfortunately the original plan for Avro to complete modifications at its factories and for the firm's test pilots to fly the Lancasters to Farnborough, where they would be given acceptance trials by Vickers-Armstrongs before going on to Scampton, foundered for lack of time. Aircraft went straight to Scampton, where the workshops, in conjunction with Avro, RAE and MAP supervisors, agreed to carry out some modifications originally allotted to Avro, including removal of the mid-upper turrets. And, under the direction of the squadron engineering officer, Flt Lt C. C. Caple, 617 added some modifications of its own. Gibson therefore reported that although twelve Type 464 Provisioning Lancasters had reached 617 by 29 April, only nine were actually serviceable pending the necessary local work.

Throughout the training period, much readjustment was called for among ground-crew as well as aircrew. On other squadrons, if an early morning phone call warned that the station was not on operations that night, the maintenance personnel tended to carry out daily inspection routines with a reduced sense of urgency. But night and day flying at Scampton meant that ground maintenance – on the exposed dispersal points – took place virtually throughout the hours of daylight (with Double British Summer Time operating, sunset being about 2130), under constant pressure to meet deadlines as a steady stream of military and civilian visitors demanded yet further modifications before the next exercise. The ten borrowed aircraft were flown so often that structural fatigue was feared. After one aircraft returned from an exercise, maintenance personnel discovered that the sturdy IFF

(Identification Friend or Foe) equipment had been torn from its mounting by a practice bomb bouncing upwards and hitting the underside of the fuselage. Airframe mechanics thus had a repair job to do and an IFF apparatus in pieces. On another occasion Rice and Gibson were shown an aircraft on which four of the bolts which held the outer panels to the centre section had sheared. Gibson was worried, and Rice hardly decreased his anxiety by suggesting that the continuous buffeting at low level must produce serious additional stress. The squadron was irrevocably committed, however, to further training and an attack at low level. This was a further mental burden of which the squadron commander must have preferred to be rid, as was the discovery that the rigid security exercised at Scampton had not been repeated elsewhere.

On 2 May he sent a personal handwritten note to Satterly at Grantham. Watson, the squadron armament officer, had just returned from a three-week course at RAF Manston, where within three days of his arrival he had been shown: 'Sectional drawings of certain objectives, a map of the Ruhr showing these objectives [and] various secret sketches in connection with Upkeep.' Gibson pointed out that Watson therefore knew more about the operation than either flight commander or, at the time, himself. With some warmth he emphasised that he had constantly enforced strict security, the breach of which could lead to the 'most disturbing results'. Satterly referred the matter to Cochrane, who reacted swiftly. The following day, 3 May, the AOC wrote to Saundby at Bomber Command enclosing Gibson's letter. Cochrane reminded the Deputy AOC-in-C that in 5 Group details of the operation were confined to himself, Satterly, Whitworth and Gibson: 'No other member of the Squadron has been told, nor will they know until they are briefed for the operation.' He was therefore extremely disturbed to find that somebody at Manston possessed 'a most secret file, which he has been showing to Junior Officers.' This action was 'criminal,' and Cochrane suggested that the file be withdrawn from that individual forthwith. A memorandum from Saundby to Bottomley at the Air Ministry on 4 May confirmed his scrambled telephone message of the previous day, supporting Cochrane's recommendation and adding: 'Incidents such as this let down those of us who are trying to "play the game" by drastically restricting the number of people in the know and make our precautions look absurd.' Two days later in a personal note Bottomley assured Saundby that appropriate action had been taken.

Despite the official explanation that the smaller of the two gunners was deployed in the front turret, most crews put the more experienced man in the rear, whatever his size. As Fg Off Rodger pointed out, every operation involved 'seven men against the Reich,' and this one demanded even greater expertise and higher standards of crew co-operation. Introduction of the Dann sight provided a good example of professional initiative, for in practice the triangular contraption proves less than satisfactory. At low level thermals caused severe buffeting and, as the bomb-aimer needed one hand for the bomb-release mechanism, he could not use two hands to steady the new sight. Problems associated with enemy fire at the target would compound these difficulties. So in Shannon's crew Walker and Sumpter dispensed with the wooden sight. Sumpter used instead two blue chinagraph marks on the clear-vision panel, with string attached to the screws each side of the panel and drawn back taut to the bridge of his nose. Lying full-length on the floor and supported by his forearms, Sumpter could then achieve a much more stable position during the bombing run. In Knight's crew Hobday and Johnson quite independently devised a similar system based upon the largest possible triangle and involving the practice sight screens, marks on the clear vision panel and the bomb-aimer's eye. Like Sumpter, Johnson used taut cords attached to the retaining screws as a guide to the release point, but with an additional refinement: two double marks were used on the panel to take into account the width of the practice sight screens. Clay, Munro's bomb-aimer, developed yet another variation: instead of marks on the clear-vision panel, he effectively used the retaining screws at the side of the clear-vision panel in place of Dann's nails. To these he attached string of a predetermined length in consultation with the navigator. Holding this string to meet in front of his right eye, he pressed the release mechanism when eye, screws and towers were in line. However, some crews did retain the Dann sight for use. Dr Merton heard of the difficulties in attaining the required accuracy of release, and after studying the reconnaissance photographs of the Möhne in April he told Lockspeiser that 'tape inside the windscreen would do the trick'. But the Dann contraption was developed and bomb-aimers and navigators left to experiment with chinagraph and string. Sgt Oancia, F/Sgt Brown's bomb-aimer, noted that two sets of double lines on the panel 'could allow for differences between the Möhne and Eder dams and be accurate for either'. Flt Lt Shannon's bomb-aimer, F/Sgt Sumpter, has explained that a variation of 50 yards in the point of release coupled with the distance between the water level and crest of the dam at the point of impact allowed crews to use Dann's nails or two single (as distinct from double) marks to achieve the same effect.

The tight schedule required the crews to be kept busy, even though lack of aircraft severely restricted flying time; and there were administrative burdens too. In the interests of security, though officially 'for passport purposes,' all aircrew were photographed. Simpson, Martin's rear gunner, recorded in his diary on 22 April: 'Bags of security gen and various threats to those who are found from now on speaking or writing about our job . . . I think it is something to do with combating U-boats.' This impression was reinforced by a suggestion that he should carry all armour-piercing ammunition, although this was reputedly 'pretty savage on gunbarrelling'. Inevitably, too, came inspections from senior officers. Cochrane's visit on 30 April was preceded by 24 hours of 'spit and polish'. There was more of the same when AOC 5 Group was succeeded by the revered old warrior Lord Trenchard and C-in-C Bomber Command on 5 and 6 May respectively.

During April the respect for authority without which no squadron could function efficiently was firmly established. Gibson fully justified his reputation as a strict disciplinarian, and frequently emphasised the need for total security. At one pre-operation aircrew meeting he publicly reprimanded an officer, who in the event did not fly on Chastise, for indiscreet use of the telephone. But Plt Off I. Whittaker held that this insistence upon discipline and security was fully justified: with so much at stake Gibson could neither tolerate inefficiency nor brook any hint of slackness. So when Sec Off Ann Fowler, later to marry Shannon, arrived without the requisite documentation, she was confined to the station until clearance had been obtained. Later, during training, a more senior intelligence officer returned from a visit to the Air Ministry in London, stating that he knew the squadron's target. After a visit to Gibson's office that officer became strangely reticent. Plt Off Howard later summarised his feeling that Gibson was the 'outstanding' influence on 617 Squadron: 'Though we did not see a lot of him he seemed to set a standard of perfection in all our training and the final preparation. It's called leadership – how do you define it?'

On 1 May Gibson rang Wallis to say that, in the light of training performances at the lower altitude, he was absolutely confident that the squadron could carry out the operation. And three days later, in submitting his weekly report to Whitworth, he underlined this. All crews were now 'ready to operate'. In all, 31 exercises were flown between 30 April and 6 May, involving 168 bombing attacks at Wainfleet. Only 52 per cent success had been achieved in these attacks, which Gibson ascribed to the use of flags to simulate the towers. As a result the sight screens had been re-erected there instead of going to Uppingham. He reported officially that Dann's hand-held sight had not proved a success, but incorrectly conveyed the impression that all bomb-aimers had dispensed with it. Modifications to the spotlights now ensured that they were shielded from the ground and the rear one no longer smeared by oil. It had been decided to use 100 per cent tracer for the guns to achieve the maximum 'scare effect'. Eighteen modified Lancasters had been received and all would be grounded in the next 48 hours for VHF radio to be fitted. A mere nine days before the operation Gibson noted that the form of Upkeep had finally been decided; 20 were stripped and ready for balancing, which should be completed in three days. The weapon would thus be available less than a week before Chastise. Practice Upkeeps had also been stripped and balanced for crews to use off Reculver in moonlight 'on or about 10, 12 or 13 May'. Gibson added that all squadron leave would be stopped with effect from 1200 on Friday 7 May.

On 6 May he had held a conference for all pilots and the squadron's armament and engineering officers (Watson and Caple). Agreeing that to achieve the required accuracy in navigation had been 'absolute hell,' he explained the night exercise mentioned in his report to Whitworth two days before: three formations each of three aircraft would fly a special route to the Eyebrook and Abberton reservoirs in turn, attacking singly at precisely 60ft and exactly 232 mph groundspeed, as directed by Gibson by R/T on the spot. He could not reveal that this would be the form of attack intended for use against the Möhne and Eder. Six other crews would carry out a practice attack on the Derwent Dam, flying south over the Howden and Derwent reservoirs to simulate the type of attack envisaged for the Sorpe. The remainder – intended to form the mobile reserve – were to practise bombing with spotlights over the Wash. While stressing the need for absolute security, in answer to a question from Young, Gibson admitted that the operation would take place within a fortnight. From Caple he required 'maximum service-ability' and round-the-clock availability of ground crews, and he informed Watson that all Upkeep mines must be ready by 12 May. Young was to calculate the all-up weight of the aircraft on the night, which could not exceed 63,000lb, and have his figures checked by a flight engineer. Stirrups for each front gunner to keep his feet away from the bomb-aimer below him must be fitted in all aircraft, and a second altimeter fixed to the windscreen in front of the pilot's face to prevent him having to look down at a vital moment.

Other technical problems had also become apparent. At the low altitudes at which training sorties had been flown, great difficulty had been experienced with the TR 1196 R/T set. Air-to-ground reception during day and night was satisfactory, but air-to-air was not, and became even worse at night. Ajustments were made, but on 4 May a final trial was declared 'completely unsatisfactory'. As a result, Flt Lt Bone from the Radio Department of the RAE advised installation of the VHF Type TR 1143 sets used in fighters. The necessary equipment was swiftly installed by an RAE team under his guidance, and with justification Cochrane reported: 'The fact that all available eighteen aircraft were fitted with VHF by 1730 hrs on Sunday 9 May indicates the drive and enthusiasm with which this apparently impossible task was handled.' On the evening of 9 May Maudslay and Young tested the TR 1143 sets satisfactorily, although some further modifications were later necessary. Effectively installation of the sets took two days, for on the night of 6–7 May 617 Squadron flew the exercise pattern over the Eyebrook and Abberton reservoirs, Derwent Dam, Wainfleet and the Wash. The Lancasters were not therefore available until 7 May, when the RAE representatives, one officer and 35 men from 26 (Signals) Group, arrived at Scampton. However, with the aid of a carpenter the squadron signals leader, Hutchison, had already organised booths in the crew rooms for practice of R/T procedure, so that maximum use could be made of the sets once the squadron became airborne.

During the second week of May, in accordance with Gibson's instructions, Watson and the armourers worked hard to get the mines ready, performing the important modifications that had to be done at Scampton. Although each mine (as Upkeep was now officially called) arrived complete from the filling factory, a certain amount of machine work had to be carried out for the weapon to be balanced. As a preliminary to this work LAC A. Drury was given a requisition order and sent to the Ruston Hornsby boiler works at Lincoln in a van to collect slabs of steel plate measuring approximately $8 \times 6 \times 1\frac{1}{4}$ in. Back at Scampton he drilled two holes in each slab of metal. When the mines arrived from the filling factory, they were hung in turn under one of the modified Lancasters for centrifugal balancing between the two retaining arms. One piece of plate with the drilled holes was bolted to the lighter side of the mine: if it proved too heavy to allow correct balancing, it was removed and returned to the machine shop. There Drury machined metal off the plate to reduce its weight, and the process of bolting to the mine, removal and further machining was carried out as many times as necessary. No matter the time of day that a mine arrived nor the job currently in the lathe, Drury had to machine the plate. In addition he needed to machine 'a few one thousandth parts of an inch' off the brass cup which formed part of the fuse gear to the mines. Ignorance of the urgency and importance of this work almost proved his undoing. One day he was about to go to lunch when the sergeant armourer brought in one of the brass cups for machining. Drury indicated that it could wait until after his meal. The NCO observed that he could start machining immediately or proceed to the guard room under escort. Drury chose a late lunch.

On 10 May Sqn Ldr F. Fawssett, an intelligence officer at Bomber Command, sent Satterly 20 copies of a prepared information sheet on the Eder, for which no model had been built, and promised that illustrations of it would be forwarded as soon as possible. He confirmed that a plan of the dam showed the towers 750ft apart. That day, too, Fawssett forwarded a detailed analysis of the Möhne defences, promising notes in due course about the other two targets, and confirming that models had been produced of the Möhne and Sorpe reservoirs only, which 5 Group already held. Photographs showed that the top of the 'tent-shaped' roofs on the Möhne towers had been removed to leave a gun platform of approximately 20ft × 15ft, and a single light anti-aircraft gun was on an extremity beyond the right-hand (northern) tower. Three light anti-aircraft guns were positioned north of the compensating basin, with each gun occupying a 'slightly raised square' about 18ft × 18ft and surrounded by a wall of sandbags. The possibility of a searchlight position in the vicinity could not be ruled out. The double-line boom, with timber spreaders floating on the main reservoir 100–300ft from the barrage, was possibly anchored to the northern, but not 'visibly' to the southern, shore; the distance between the two lines of the boom varied between 10 and 20ft. A third, perhaps the most important, document involved Satterly on 10 May. He wrote to Whitworth at Scampton, enclosing the only draft operation order in existence, 'written as you will see all by my own fair hand'. Satterly requested: 'Will you please get down to it right away with Gibson and either re-write it completely to suit yourselves or pin on it slips of paper giving any amendments you want to suggest.' He did not want his original altered, because it would be more convenient to compare that with suggested amendments. So that there would be enough time for typing and distribution, Whitworth should get the draft order and comments to Satterly 'personally' no later than 1600 on Wednesday 12 May.

Gibson did produce detailed comments. He wanted to designate the targets ABC, instead of XYZ, because training had been carried out in this way (Eyebrook A, Abberton B, Derwent C). At this stage an attack by 20 Lancasters was planned, which Gibson suggested should be by three sections of three aircraft at ten-minute intervals, followed by single aircraft taking off at three-minute intervals, making a total take-off time of 39 minutes. Once A had been destroyed, aircraft would be diverted to B and C in that order; at the same time C would be attacked by five Lancasters at five-minute intervals to 'create a diversion and avoid undue congestion.' The use of 'diversion,' which was clear in this context when linked with avoiding 'congestion,' would lead later commentators wrongly to state that the Sorpe was considered as a minor, secondary target. Gibson agreed that aircraft should cross the North Sea at 60ft, but erased an instruction to climb 'rapidly' to '3,000 feet' to make a pinpoint at the enemy coast. Low altitude would be maintained throughout over the Continent, although the formation leader should climb to 500ft in order to check landmarks, and ten miles from the target area to 1,000–1,500ft.

On seeing this No 2 and No 3 would listen out on VHF. Gibson then envisaged the leader making an immediate attack, firing 'a red star' over the dam to signal his attack to the others, 'fox flak men' and help the rear gunner by illuminating dam defences. Once his attack was finished, the leader would wait 90 seconds (timed by stopwatch) before detailing No 2 to attack, and repeat the procedure for No 3. 'By this time' the second formation, led by No 4, would have arrived, and the leader would also control the attacks of aircraft in this and the third formation; each aircraft would fire 'a red star' over the dam after dropping its store. Should the leader 'fall out,' No 2 and No 3 would act as leader and deputy leader respectively.

When A was destroyed, aircraft would divert to B. The same procedure was to be followed there, with Nos 4 and 7 acting as substitute leader and deputy leader in case of emergency, Nos 2 and 3 having returned to base. After destruction of B, the leader would send all remaining aircraft to C, where individual attacks were to be carried out on the initiative of pilots not under the leader's control; Nos 1, 4 and 7 would however fly to C to make a reconnaissance. Gibson explained that firing of a flare over the dam was imperative to ensure that the safety limit was observed before another attack, and that no aircraft was blown up by another's store, the spinning of which would commence approximately five minutes before each attack. The different method of attack at the Sorpe (C) showed that by 12 May the original plan of bouncing the mine towards it had already been abandoned. After their attacks all aircraft should return to base 'by the most widely diverged routes, at a very low level and a very high airspeed'. Gibson scored out a suggestion of a Mosquito raid on Soest at Z-60 to check visibility in the area of the Möhne. He then listed his attacking force, which would be adjusted on the night, and reinforced the impression that the final round of practices did lead to redeployment of certain aircraft.

Even as Gibson briefed his pilots and 26 (Signals) Group installed the VHF radio sets to ensure squadron efficiency, Upkeep had still not been satisfactorily dropped from the air. On 3 May Saundby voiced his general pessimism. Allowing that the trial of 1 May appeared more promising, he noted nevertheless that no live Upkeep had yet been properly tested. And the strain, particularly on those with crucial responsibility for the operation, mounted. During the first ten days of May Longbottom and Handasyde carried out more trials at Reculver and on 11 May 617 Squadron aircraft dropped inert-filled Upkeep cyclinders there for the first time. Due to the necessary R/T modifications and night exercise of 6/7 May, Cochrane had been unable to fulfil his promise, given at the MAP meeting of 5 May, to have two 617 Squadron Lancasters at Manston by the evening of the following day.

It was not until 11 May therefore that three attacked the simulated towers on the promenade and rolled practice Upkeeps up the beach: Gibson wrote in his logbook: 'Low level Upkeep dropped at 60ft. Good run of 600yds.'

The following day more 617 Squadron aircraft, including those of Shannon, Knight and Munro (who had Townsend as his second pilot), went to Reculver. The sight of Upkeep bouncing across the water and rolling up the beach remained vividly scored in Fg Off Hobday's memory thereafter, but F/Sgt Sumpter recalled that day for another reason. He dropped his Upkeep 20 yards short, and the following morning had to face Gibson to do penance. It was the only time before the operation that Gibson and Sumpter spoke to one another. And 12 May was significant for a further reason: Munro damaged the tailplane of ED921/G by dropping his practice Upkeep from below a height of 60ft. This aircraft could be repaired.

That unfortunately was not true of ED933/G. When more 617 Squadron crews flew to Reculver on 13 May, Maudslay damaged his aircraft far more extensively. It was officially 'badly damaged,' and the necessary repairs would normally have been beyond local workshops. Nevertheless, in view of the urgency of the task and despite a gloomy prognosis of five days for completion, work went ahead at Scampton round the clock. Hours before the operation, defeat would be finally admitted, leaving the squadron with just 19 aircraft for 21 crews. For the fourth day running, on 14 May, 617 Squadron aircraft practised at Reculver, and Martin's crew dropped their second Upkeep store. Wallis recorded that these practices showed individual crews' ability 'to put stores on the beach with remarkable accuracy,' and so prove that the tight release constraints of the operation would indeed be met. Forty-eight hours remained before the live show. And that night the 19 available Type 464 Provisioning Lancasters flew for the last time as a squadron before Operation Chastise. Armed with a supply of his own airsickness pills, Arthurton, the medical officer, flew once more with Maudslay on that final exercise without knowing its significance: 'We took off at 2150 hours and flew for four hours. I have not the foggiest notion where we were nor exactly what we were doing except that we were doing low flying . . . people said very little and I did not embarrass them with very difficult questions as I realised that there was something in the wind.' Whitworth went with Gibson, who noted in his logbook: 'Full dress rehearsal on Uppingham Lake and Colchester Reservoir. Completely successful.'

6

Planning

DECISION-MAKING PROCESS, FEBRUARY TO MAY
1943

The relevance of 617 Squadron's training, however, depended on high-level policy decisions. And on 28 February, two days after the critical meeting in Linnell's office, the Air Staff injected an important constraint into the strategic reckoning. Even if it matured before Upkeep, Highball must not be employed independently; the naval operation against *Tirpitz* by Mosquitoes in daylight was considered 'problematical,' possibly 'costly,' and therefore liable to compromise the bouncing technique. On the other hand, no such betrayal of method would occur with Lancasters at night. So notwithstanding progress with Highball, Upkeep should be dropped as soon as possible.

The very day that Chadwick signed the first conversion order for the Type 464 Provisioning Lancaster – 8 March – the Chiefs of Staff established an *ad hoc* committee 'to co-ordinate the plans and preparations for Operation Highball and to report progress fortnightly to the Chiefs of Staff.' It was perhaps an indication of the confusion which prevailed that Highball was referred to as an 'operation,' when it was clear that the committee was to monitor the development of the Highball and Upkeep weapons and plans to attack *Tirpitz*, and the German dams. Mindful perhaps of the Air Staff's conclusions on 28 February, the Admiralty moved swiftly to protect its interests by securing Rear-Admiral Renouf's appointment to the chair. Within three days an RAF counterattack ousted Renouf in favour of Air Vice-Marshal N. H. Bottomley, Assistant Chief of the Air Staff (Ops).

With representatives from the Air Ministry, Admiralty and MAP present, this committee held its first meeting on 18 March. Examining its terms of reference, it assumed that Upkeep as well as Highball should be discussed 'since the use of the one vitally affects the successful use of the other'. Noting that 'the two most important dams vulnerable to attack in Germany are the Möhne and the Eder,' the committee 'ruled out' the Sorpe 'as being unsuitable for attack, for tactical and technical reasons'. Of the other two, the Möhne 'constituted the more important and tactically more suitable for attack.' 'We consider that an adequate effort should be devoted to this objective as the one of highest priority . . . initially the planning of operations for Upkeep should be confined to attacks on the Möhne and possibly the Eder Dam in that order of priority.' Admiralty fears were reflected, however, in the contention that use of Upkeep against the Möhne would prejudice Highball, and the MAP was urged to make every effort to synchronise development of the two weapons and their associated equipment.

The committee recommended that preparations be made for attacks using Highball against *Tirpitz* or another capital ship in Norwegian waters, and Upkeep against the Möhne and 'possibly' Eder dams, but concluded: 'It may be necessary for the Chiefs of Staff to decide whether or not to release the weapon for the Möhne Dam and the Eder Dam to the prejudice of possible later attacks on capital ships.' Should delay be necessary, due to summer lowering of the water level in the reservoirs, any attack would be postponed until early 1944. This would leave a residue of aircraft modified to no purpose and a long winter in which unwelcome security leaks might occur. A cautious postscript underlined the precarious state of the weapons' development: the committee's proposals were based upon the assumption that Upkeep and Highball would achieve the results predicted by their advocates. In forwarding to Harris next day a copy of a memorandum to the Chiefs of Staff, based upon this meeting, Bottomley noted that a conference would shortly be held to brief Bomber Command Ops staff on all aspects of the proposed plans. And on 21 March Oxland informed Bottomley that the modified Wellington (BJ895/G) would be flown from RAF Warmwell to Scampton, and Plt Off H. Watson, a 5 Group armament officer, had been posted to the 'special squadron'. Oxland suggested that a 'misleading idea' of the function of the new squadron be circulated, perhaps 'something on the lines of the American "skip" bombing, which has already been used against ships at sea.'

At 1500 on 25 March in the Air Ministry, King Charles St, London, Bottomley chaired another important meeting in connection with Highball and Upkeep. Present were seven other Air Ministry representatives, Renouf on behalf of the Admiralty, Lockspeiser with three others from the MAP, Saundby, Cochrane and Oxland from Bomber Command, AOC-in-C

Coastal Command, and Wallis and Summers from Vickers-Armstrongs. Bottomley explained that their purpose was to determine technical requirements and details of trials and training, and that Coastal Command was represented as it had assumed responsibility for Highball. Trials of this weapon with Mosquitoes should begin on 11 April, and those with Upkeep on Lancasters on 17 or 18 April. Dropping trials at sea were foreseen for both Highball and Upkeep, but for the latter additional 'stringent tests against a cliff' and more for the hydrostatic fuse were planned. An appendix to the summary of this meeting noted that special operations against enemy shipping involving Highball would be codenamed Servant, those with Upkeep against enemy dams Chastise. It was the first time that the operations' code name had been acknowledged.

That same day, referring to an Air Ministry 'most secret' letter of 19 March, the Director of Intelligence (Security) at the Air Ministry circulated a cover story: 'The weapon is a special type of mine and the wooden casing surrounding it is provided for protection in handling. This is particularly necessary as the mine is designed for use in localities where it will be man-handled by native labour. The spinning device is in connection with the fusing which is effected by centrifugal action. The uses of the weapon are in the main anti-submarine, but it will also function against shipping. Units armed with the weapon are to be known as Special Mining Squadrons.' This romance, with its broad hint of translation to another hemisphere, was altogether more ingenious than allusions to skip-bombing.

While these administrative and operational arrangements were under way, the economic worth of destroying the dams had come under scrutiny, quite apart from the operational reservations expressed by Bottomley's committee. Bombing policy and target selection evolved from a complicated series of authorities. The Defence Committee of the Cabinet, on advice from the Chiefs of Staff and in accordance with Anglo-American aerial policy, laid down the general aims of bombing, which were contained in a directive to Bomber Command by the Air Staff with recommendations about objectives to be attacked. Bomber Command, however, decided upon how and when a particular target should be attacked. One important element in the development of bombing policy was the Ministry of Economic Warfare (MEW) – sometimes backed by information from the US Committee of Operations Analysts – which liaised with the DB Ops at the Air Ministry. The MEW had no direct contact with Bomber Command, although it was represented with the Admiralty and War Office on the Bomb Targets Information Committee. It did however have an avenue to the Air Staff for comment upon economic matters connected with bombing.

During February and March 1943 the MEW sought to establish an effective means of carrying out the aims of the Anglo-American Casablanca Directive, with its accent upon destruction of German submarine and aircraft construction capability. It settled for attacking specific sections of those industries – such as ball-bearings – at almost precisely the moment that the American Committee of Operations Analysts reported: 'It is better to cause a high degree of destruction in a few really essential industries or services than to cause a small degree of destruction in many industries.' The prize proffered by destruction of specific targets vital to the enemy war industry was therefore once more very much in the forefront of Allied thinking. And on 15 March the MEW produced a memorandum on the 'Economic Significance of the Mohnetalsperre and Edertalsperre,' which Renouf forwarded under 'most secret' cover to Wallis a week later. In essence, it had no new information but it did heavily emphasise the importance of the Möhne and point out that the economic functions of the two dams were 'quite different'.

During March, too, the Air Ministry revised its 'Operational Numbers of Bomb Targets in Germany,' originally produced in October 1940. The 1,600 targets in the GO (power) section included pumping stations, electricity generating stations, reservoirs and dams. An electricity generating station at Waldeck near the Eder Dam (GO 1129) and the Baldeney reservoir below the Möhne (GO 1129) were listed together with the seven dams from Wallis's 'Air Attack on Dams' paper GO 933, Helminghausen near Brilon (Diemel); GO 934, Hemfurth near Bad Wildungen (Eder) together with its two hydroelectric power stations; GO 935, Holthausen near Hagen (Ennepe); GO 936, Meschede near Arnsberg (Henne); GO 938, Attendorn near Olpe (Lister); GO 939, Günne near Soest (Möhne); and GO 960, Langscheid near Arnsberg (Sorpe). The power stations at Hemfurth (Eder) had previously been targets in their own right (GO 1233) – so an attack on that dam would effectively deal with three desirable objectives – and the Günne (Möhne) and Langscheid (Sorpe) dams were also shown as special targets. In fact all of these dams were more generally known by the name of the river on which they stood, and nearby villages and towns were given by the Air Ministry merely to facilitate navigation.

Towards the end of the month Portal 'demi-officially' circulated to members of the Chiefs of Staff Committee a 'note . . . extracted from the dossier prepared for the Chief of Combined Operations by the Scientific Advisers to the Minister of Production,' entitled 'The Economic and Moral Effects of the Destruction of the Möhne Dam and the Added Effects which will result from Destruction at the same time of the Sorpe and Eder Dams.' In forwarding a copy to General Sir Alan Brooke, the CIGS, on 27 March Portal erroneously ascribed it to the 'Office of Scientific Advisers to the War Cabinet,' while stressing that its contents and the identity of 'a certain objective in Germany' be confined to the smallest number of people. The following day, in asking for his 'authoritative opinion' on it as soon as possible, Bottomley correctly identified its authors for Col C. G. Vickers VC of the MEW. The Chief of Combined Operations also distributed a paper which appears to have been prepared in his office from information supplied by the Scientific Advisers and the MEW, for phrases in it virtually correspond with passages in the MEW memorandum of 15 March. A table on the construction of the five Ruhr dams and the capacity of their reservoirs and, indeed, much of the more general data were identical to those contained in Wallis's 'Air Attack on Dams' paper, which suggests that either Wallis supplied this information to one of the official sources or, alternatively, he received it from them.

The paper circulated by Portal argued that direct destruction by escaping water from the Möhne would be 'appreciable': low-lying districts of the Ruhr, including Herdecke, Wetter, Witten, Hattingen, Linden, Kettwig, Mülheim and Duisburg, would suffer. An averate rate of flow of 3,720m^3/sec would empty the Möhne reservoir in ten hours: 'The capacity of this reservoir alone is, therefore, great enough to cause a disaster of the first magnitude,' which would spread to 'densely populated areas' between the Ruhr and Dortmund-Ems canal. 'Substantial' loss of electricity would occur due to the destruction of 13 hydroelectric plants between the Möhne Dam and Mülheim on the Ruhr river, of which the Herdecke station was the most important. Even if complete destruction were not achieved, variation of flow in the Ruhr river due to loss of reservoir control should adversely effect electricity production, and the thermo-electricity generating stations would also be affected during the summer months. In addition, a 'most serious effect' would occur for foundries, coal mines, coke ovens, blast furnaces and chemical plants if water supplies were restricted. Navigation on the Ruhr would inevitably be interfered with and, in the narrow valley, damage to railways and bridges could not be avoided. So far as domestic water supplies were concerned, the entire Ruhr area eastwards to Hamm and Ahlen depended upon the Möhne reservoir. Priority had inevitably to be given to the domestic user and firefighting needs, which in turn would have an additional adverse effect upon industry. Furthermore, morale in the Ruhr area had been weakened by the recent months of 'devastating' bombing, culminating in two heavy raids on Essen; breaching of the Möhne Dam 'would undoubtedly have further and serious repercussions on morale'. Increased danger to the population, due to lack of water for firefighting, 'could be exploited by Political Warfare methods as an excellent opportunity for spreading panic among the population.' Destruction of the Sorpe Dam, which with the Möhne supplied 75 per cent of the Ruhr's water, would 'produce a paralysing effect upon the industrial activity in the Ruhr and would result in a still further lowering of morale.' With reference to the Eder, 'destruction of this dam would be speculative, [and] economic effects would be problematical.' No important industrial complex would be denied water and the effect on the Weser river and Mittelland Canal would probably not be of long duration: 'From the economic standpoint, therefore, this dam cannot be considered as a first-class objective.'

Evidently answering Bottomley's request to Vickers, Mr O. L. Lawrence of the MEW advised caution on 2 April. He agreed that if the Möhne were breached there was 'every prospect that both the physical and moral effects of the flood' would in themselves justify the operation even if other effects were not significant. Nevertheless there would 'not necessarily' be a 'large or immediate effect' on industrial or household water supplies. These depended upon 'underground water-bearing strata, supplemented by colliery water, water pumped back from the Rhine and water drawn from the Emscher river and canal systems.' The main purpose of the Möhne reservoir was to maintain the level of underground supplies through conserving rainfall. If there were heavy demand on the underground supplies, the effect might be felt in 'some months', but the amount of subsequent rainfall, rate of repair and possible additional supplies from the Rhine would be important considerations. If all of these factors were 'unfavourable' to the Germans, 'a difficult situation' might develop by the end of the summer, but Lawrence pessimistically concluded: 'It is not possible to state that a critical shortage of water supplies in the Ruhr would be a certain and inevitable result of the destruction of the Möhne Dam.' However, if the Sorpe were simultaneously attacked and destroyed, it 'would be worth much more than twice the destruction of one.'

Lawrence repeated once more that the Eder had no connection with the Ruhr. Probably agricultural land and possibly the low-lying districts of Kassel would be flooded, but he thought that the Weserand Mittelland Canal would not be 'critically' affected. The four power stations below the dam would 'probably' be destroyed; although this could cause 'a useful measure of interference with the Prüssenelektra supply system,' it would have no 'major economic importance'. On the other hand, the effects of the destruction of the Möhne and Sorpe would be witnessed by thousands and 'whatever the facts . . . alarmist rumours' about lack of drinking water, spread of disease and loss of firefighting capability would develop, giving 'exceptional opportunities . . . for successful measures of political warfare.' Because the area below the Eder, with the exception of Kassel, was not densely populated, 'the total moral effect, though by no means negligible, would inevitably be much smaller than in the case of the Ruhr.' Lawrence pointed out that the immediate impact on industry had been overstated, but it is significant that he and the other writers mentioned a basic element of strategic bombing theory: the undermining of enemy morale.

Three days after Lawrence produced his paper, Bottomley reminded Portal that a summary of the Chief of Combined Ops' memoradum had been circulated to the Chiefs of Staff, but, as Lawrence underlined, the Scientific Advisers to the Ministry of Production now claimed that they had been misrepresented in it. In fact they agreed with Lawrence, and his paper had been prepared 'in consultation' with them. Bottomley meanwhile had already drawn tactical conclusions from these various comments. On April 1 he produced a memorandum for the Chiefs of Staff based upon the second meeting of his *ad hoc* committee. Twenty modified Lancasters would suffice for attacks on the dams, which the committee envisaged being spread over two to three days (not the single night eventually used). The committee counselled against ordering more of the modified aircraft on the grounds that the Germans were bound to take defensive measures so that further attacks would become 'completely ineffective,' a conclusion that may well have affected the later decision not to follow up Operation Chastise. Four days after this memorandum, Bottomley suggested a change of emphasis to the CAS: simultaneous attacks should be launched on the Möhne and Sorpe, with an attack on the Eder to follow only if the circumstances were favourable.

Independently, the Joint Planning Staff, responding to a Chiefs of Staff Committee instruction to investigate uses of Highball and Upkeep and noting establishment of the *ad hoc* committee to look at development of the big and small weapons as well as 'another' in view, had listed possible groups of targets on 17 March. These comprised anti-U-boat targets (shelters, lock gates etc); in connection with Husky, the invasion of Sicily (naval units in harbour, hydroelectric dams); Germany (for example, dams in the Ruhr); heavy units of the German fleet (apart from assisting supplies to Russia, this would free destroyers for the anti-U-boat campaign and British heavy units for action against Japan); German transportation (shipping, locks and dams in waterways, especially those connected with oil centres); Japanese Navy (in harbour or at sea); and cross-Channel operations (such as dams or inland waterways affecting enemy reinforcements). It seemed therefore that planners were concentrating on acquiring the weapon from Wallis with little regard for his appreciation of targets.

The Chiefs of Staff considered the first report of Bottomley's *ad hoc* committee on 23 March, but due to 'the highly secret nature of the operation' recorded only 'a token minute'. Bottomley was to make Highball and Upkeep 'available for operational use at the earliest possible moment and on the largest possible scale. The decision as to how and when to employ this weapon is one for the Chiefs of Staff,' a significant codicil in view of later inter-Service disagreement. Four days later Portal reported that the three American service chiefs (King, Marshall and Arnold) had shown 'great enthusiasm' about 'Operation HIGHBALL [*sic*],' requesting that drawings and full information be released to them as soon as possible. On April 7 the First Sea Lord, Sir Dudley Pound, raised the matter in more detail at a meeting of the committee. He believed that Highball (and by implication Upkeep) must be developed with all speed 'since it was always possible that the enemy might be developing a similar weapon.' But 'a really good dividend' should be ensured before the enemy could institute counter-measures, so he wanted a simultaneous attack against 'Objective X' (Möhne), German capital ships, the *Graf Zeppelin* aircraft carrier and Italian capital ships. Perhaps with Lawrence's memorandum of 2 April (which had been copied to the Admiralty) in mind, he emphasised that 'the effects of an attack on Objective X were now considered to be less far-reaching than had previously been estimated.' Whilst agreeing, Portal argued that it would still be 'an operation well worthwhile'. 'Recent intelligence' suggested that X might be attacked later in the year than hitherto anticipated, 'but if the attack on naval targets was deferred too long an attack against "Objective X" would have to wait until next year.' He alleged that 'so many' knew about Highball, 'that a leakage regarding it was an unfortunate probability'; it must be used quickly. In reply to Pound's contention that more Mosquitoes were required for a simultaneous attack against German and Italian naval units, Portal said that a 'slight delay' after the German attacks would not give the Italians adequate opportunity to produce effective countermeasures. The Chiefs of Staff then decided to postpone discussion of Highball and Upkeep until the results of further trials were known.

At their meeting on 12 April the Chiefs of Staff agreed that Admiral Stark, General Andrews and not more than one other American officer be invited to witness Highball trials and they approved the codenames suggested in the second report of Bottomley's committee, together with its cover plan. The same day, Portal despatched a 'most secret private personal' cypher telegram to MacNeece-Foster in Washington. 'A spherical bomb which will be dropped from low-flying aircraft and act in the nature of a surface torpedo' was under trial. It would be suspended under the bomb bay of an attacking aircraft and back-spun at about 500 revolutions per minute: 'This spin lengthens initial flight before impact on water, increases the angle of incidence of ricochet and serves to counter the action of water drag and the tendency of the sphere to roll under water.' Two versions of the weapon were planned: the first for use against capital ships, the second for use against 'important dams' and measuring 84in in diameter, weighing 11,000lb and including a charge of approximately 7,000lb. 'Experiments up to date indicate that the weapons are technically feasible but we cannot guarantee success until we have seen results of the trials. The potentialities, however, are so great that we have taken a gamble and pressed on with development of the weapon as quickly as possible.' The CAS concluded: 'Intended to launch major initial operations simultaneously so as to exploit surprise and avoid possible counter measures.' Next day, 13 April, he sent MacNeece-Foster the agreed codenames and cover story concerning native labour and special mining squadrons. A rapid exchange of telegrams then occurred between Washington and the Air Ministry, and on 15 April the RAF Delegation in Washington emphasised that Arnold wanted to put the weapon into production in the United States. That day also the CAS learned that Arnold and King were sending officers to the United Kingdom to get the necessary details. Eight days later, General McClelland was reported to be on his way.

On Wednesday 14 April another meeting took place at the MAP, chaired by McEntegart and attended by ten representatives of interested organisations, including Mr Whitfield from RAE Farnborough and Gp Capt Marwood Elton from Bomber Command. The meeting learned that certain equipment, such as the Air Position Indicator, would now be fitted to the Lancasters at Scampton, and heard officially about development of the converging spotlights to aid height-finding. And 15 days later 14 people, including Wallis, Summers and Gibson, attended a further progress meeting chaired by McEntegart at which details of the recent Reculver trials, equipment modifications and despatch of an impressive array of special apparatus to Scampton, including one ten-ton crane, six modified bomb trolleys and two mobile gantries, were discussed.

Close attention was also paid to tactical matters. On 15 April a Bomber Command minute from Marwood Elton noted that 5 Group wanted the speed of attacking aircraft reduced to 205–210 mph and considered that the height of the splash created by Upkeep might well limit its tactical use. Saundby appended his dissent from this view for Harris: 'I think that the remarks about speed limitation are nonsense, and I feel sure that experienced crews can drop at 250 mph under good moonlight conditions.' The AOC-in-C's retort was not encouraging: 'As I always thought, the weapon is balmy.' And he continued: 'Beams of spotlight will not work on water at glassy calm. Any fool knows that . . . I will not have aircraft flying about with spotlights on in defended areas . . . Get some of these lunatics controlled & if possible locked up!' Two days later, however, Marwood Elton indicated to 5 Group that 617 Squadron would enjoy some permanence. Recalling that it had been formed 'to perform a special operation which entailed using new equipment of a most secret nature,' he explained that on completion of the initial task it would not revert to 'normal bombing operations' but remain 'a Special Duty Squadron under the operational control of AOC 5 Group.' It would not be required 'to take part in sustained operations' but would be used for tasks 'that entail special training and/or the use of specialist equipment.' As far as possible aircrew for the squadron would be recruited from within the group, and he then virtually repeated Oxland's misleading comment of a month previously: 'As the work is not expected to be arduous full use should be made of crews who have completed two operational tours and who apply to take part in further operations.'

Bottomley presided over another *ad hoc* committee meeting at the Air Ministry on 5 May, attended by Saundby, Cochrane, McEntegart, Wallis, Glanville and Bufton, and this proved a valuable forum for briefing and decision. Reconnaissance photographs of 19 February had shown water in the Möhne reservoir six feet below the top of the dam, while those of 4–5 April revealed two feet. As Wallis calculated that water would be withdrawn probably at a rate of ten feet per month from mid-April, the level must now be even lower, and another reconnaissance was requested.

Discussion then centred on timing of the operation: Cochrane wanted it as soon as possible after 14–15 May, although Saundby stressed the danger to the security of Highball if the dams operation proceeded independently. He conceded, however, that enemy observers might confuse the method of attack with skip-bombing as a result of the comparatively short range at which the weapon would now be released. Cochrane sketched the plan of attack for Chastise, which Satterly sent to Whitworth on 10 May without going into detail. The bulk of the squadron was to proceed to Target X (the Möhne), where local VHF R/T control would be used to direct the attack, and then to Y (the Eder). 'At the same time, he proposed detailing about four of the crews who [sic] did not reach the highest standard of accuracy in practice to attack Z (Sorpe),' explaining that 'the method of attack against this dam was simpler and should prove effective.' Wallis agreed that the (unspecified) different method of attacking the Sorpe had 'very good prospects' of damaging Z to an extent which would bring about its destruction, although seepage through the cracked concrete core would not be immediately obvious to attacking crews. During the afternoon of 5 May Wallis had a further meeting with McEntegart and Cochrane on details of the operation, and then went to see Col Langley of Combined Ops at Richmond Terrace, possibly because his organisation had not yet abandoned all interest in the Möhne Dam.

Just five days before the operation, on 11 May, Wallis wrote to DB Ops (Bufton) about the Sorpe. Perhaps after reconsidering the discussion about attacking the dam with Gibson, Summers, Longbottom and Renouf on 24 April, or because he had now discovered that the Bradfield Dam data were unsound as the core of the structure was clay and not concrete, he moved away from the tactic advanced in his 'Air Attack on Dams' paper and possibly considered at the Air Ministry meeting of 5 May. However, he still believed that a chance of 'real success' did exist. After studying aerial photographs he concluded that the sloping face on the air side of the dam 'appears to be made of pretty heavy material,' which he felt might not disintegrate even if the central core of the dam were cracked. Wallis therefore suggested that craters be made on the air side before any attack took place from the water side: this would be 'most helpful'. In his workings Wallis included the calculations that if Upkeep were dropped 41ft from the core of the Sorpe Dam, it would roll 113ft down the slope before exploding 30ft below the surface of the water. The Torpex charge of '6,600lb,' exploded at this point, would cause a lateral movement of 16–20in. Rather mysteriously in his diary that day, 11 May, beneath notes about meetings in London, watching three 617 Squadron aircraft drop Upkeep at Reculver range at 1800 with '100% success,' and a working dinner with Bufton, he wrote: 'Invented new Range Finder!' with a small sketch vaguely resembling a variation of the Dann sight.

Another meeting on the progress of Upkeep and Highball at ICI House on the afternoon of Thursday 13 May decided that, as the squadron was satisfied with range tests at Boscombe Down, one of the three prototype Lancasters there (ED825/G) should be flown to Scampton and adapted for use by 617 Squadron. Unknown to the meeting, that decision would allow 19, not 18, Lancasters to set off on Chastise. Successful Upkeep drops had been achieved since the last meeting, although release below 50ft would cause damage to the aircraft. In contrast Highball had not been conclusively tested against a target ship. And it is noteworthy that HQ 5 Group considered that there had been two 'avoidable accidents' during 617 Squadron's training.

But all was now set for the operation, and Gibson regarded his squadron as 'rather like a team of racehorses still standing in the paddock'. Then on the very day (13 May) that national exultation greeted the news of the Axis surrender in North Africa, and a mere three days before it was launched, Chastise teetered on the brink of obscurity. A Highball and Upkeep progress meeting, attended by Gibson, learned that armament deliveries, including 56 HE-filled Upkeeps to Scampton, had been satisfactorily completed, since the last meeting 617 Squadron pilots had carried out 'several successful drops' with inert-filled Upkeep stores at Reculver, and that 'no difficulty' was anticipated in maintaining 'the correct height of 60 feet' for release. But Highball trials conducted in Scotland had proved totally unsatisfactory: 'The bombs have failed to stand up to the force of impact and have broken up.'

That day, too, the Vice-Chiefs of Staff met in London in the absence of their superiors. Air Chief Marshal Sir Douglas Evill reported that Upkeep trials had been successful, but not those for Highball. He argued that if an aircraft with Upkeep aboard were captured 'the particular characteristics of this type of weapon' would be disclosed, but Highball would not be compromised. Pointing out that Upkeep targets were only vulnerable to attack during the next few weeks, Evill pressed for separation of the different efforts and authority for Upkeep to proceed independently from 14 May. The Vice-Chief of the Naval Staff could not agree, having received specific instructions from the First Sea Lord before his departure, so it was decided that the gist of a paper on the subject submitted by Evill should be signalled to the Chiefs of Staff in Washington for a decision as soon as possible. Bufton drafted the signal, which was despatched by Brig C. L. Hollis at 1855 Double BST on 13 May. Bufton argued that Upkeep was less likely to affect Highball because it was cylindrical and the release point from the target was now only 450 yards: 'Method of attack might well engender belief that special form of depth charge had been dropped between the boom and dam. This would be confirmed by attack on target Z (Sorpe) in which aircraft will fly close and parallel to dam face.' Bufton went on to suggest that bounces at such short range, for the figure of 450 yards included the air path before Upkeep hit the water, would resemble the normal skip effect of a bomb dropped short. The best time for the operation was now, with 23 Lancasters 'frozen' for it and the crews 'keyed up'. He went on, spuriously considering that 617 Squadron and its aircraft would not attack Main Force targets, that to delay until June would deny this force to the main Bomber Command effort for a further month. However, more realistically, he thought it 'improbable' that the enemy would associate Upkeep with a 'spherical weapon against ships,' and that a 'devastating effect' could be expected. Bufton concluded that Bottomley's *ad hoc* committee and AOC-in-Coastal Command, whose Mosquitoes were detailed for Highball and Servant, agreed that the dams operation should go ahead.

The Vice-Chief of the Air Staff followed this with a second message. At 1040 BST on 14 May, Evill sent a 'most immediate and personal' cypher to Portal. Re-emphasising support from the *ad hoc* committee, which comprised representatives from Navy and RAF, Evill stated: 'We are fully convinced that balance of factors is strongly in favour of disassociating the two operations and getting on with the heavy.' The combination of favourable weather with the full-moon period now confidently forecast might not recur and he assumed that the CAS did 'not envisage prior reference to Defence Committee necessary before Action.' The final test on 13 May (Longbottom's live drop) had proved 'entirely satisfactory technically and tactically'; 'immediate action' would be undertaken if the separate operation were approved. Evill's message probably had no effect, having arrived during the night in Washington; as at 1440 BST on 14 May (breakfast time locally) a signal from Washington to the Air Ministry read: 'For reasons stated by you, Chiefs of Staff agree to immediate use of Upkeep without waiting for Highball.' Thus at 1555 BST on 14 May, the time at which this signal was decoded, Operation Chastise was finally set to go. There is no evidence that the messages from either Hollis or Evill came before the Chiefs of Staff formally, but they were in the habit of holding daily 'domestic meetings' of their own before each session of the Trident talks with their American counterparts, and this they did at 1730 local time on 13 and 14 May. It appears likely that Hollis's message, which would have arrived at about mid-day local time, was discussed at the informal British meeting of 13 May and a reply despatched early the following morning (14 May). Common sense, and Bufton's persuasive arguments, had prevailed. A decision made 3,000 miles away from Scampton thus ensured, just 48 hours before take-off, that Operation Chastise would proceed. Later Wallis believed that Winston Churchill personally gave the go-ahead for the operation, but there is no corroborative evidence for this.

On 14 May also a letter from Bufton to Wallis suggested an element of late confusion among the planners in England. Enclosing a set of reconnaissance photographs taken 'yesterday,' Bufton observed that 'Y' (Eder) was overflowing. Enigmatically, he added: 'I have arranged for our own interpretation experts to give you the distance between the two prominent points on objectives "X" and "Y" '. Possibly Wallis needed only to double-check information on the Eder Dam, for which comparatively less had been forthcoming than for the Möhne. Even so, it was uncomfortably close to the eleventh hour.

Another decision made in Washington on 14 May was relevant. The Combined Chiefs of Staff approved the Pointblank plan for a combined bomber offensive against Germany from the United Kingdom. Although the associated document stated: 'All our attacks imply precision bombing of related targets by day and night,' it made clear that RAF Bomber Command would carry out 'area bombing' at night, with the US 8th AAF attacking 'precision targets . . . in daylight.' The implication that the RAF could not hit 'precision targets' was reinforced by 8th AAF claims, based upon the period 3 January–6 April 1943, that in the face of enemy fighters it had proved able 'to conduct precision-pattern bombing operations against selected targets from altitudes of 20,000 to 30,000ft.' For a number of reasons, and more especially from Bomber Command's standpoint, it was important that Gibson's stable should win.

7

Take-off

Urgent, at times frantic, activity centred on RAF Scampton and HQ 5 Group during the 48 hours between the Chiefs of Staff decision to go ahead and take-off. At 0900 on 15 May ACAS (Ops) sent a 'most immediate most secret' message to High Wycombe: 'Op. CHASTISE. Immediate attack of targets "X" "Y" "Z" approved. Execute at first suitable opportunity.' Shortly afterwards at Grantham Satterly took from his office wall safe the hand-written operation order, which he had gradually compiled in solitude after each day's work and then locked away. The version which he now held incorporated some, but not all, of Gibson's suggestions forwarded through Whitworth on or about 12 May: for example, the targets remained 'X, Y, Z' not 'A, B, C'. During the morning Satterly studied the revised draft, then at midday instructed the 5 Group chief signals officer, Wg Cdr W. E. Dunn, to read it and devise appropriate procedures for the operation. As he did so, Cochrane travelled the short distance to Scampton to tell Whitworth and Gibson that the operation would take place next day, Sunday 16 May.

Few 617 Squadron aircraft took to the air on 15 May, most being grounded for thorough maintenance checks or fitting of the mines. Not all the Lancasters were bombed up that day, however, for the special process required approximately half an hour for each aircraft and entailed the use of loading equipment in rotation. So Barlow took Byers as his second pilot on a bombing exercise to Wainfleet and Astell carried out an air test on AJ-B. Byers, together with Sgts Gillespie, A. N. Whittaker and Whillis, learned on 15 May that they had been commissioned, as Divall and Fuller had done two days previously. MacLean and Deering would not receive the news until 18 May, the day that Maltby similarly learned of his promotion to Sqn Ldr.

During the afternoon of 14 May Sgt Goulden had flown a photo-reconnaissance Spitfire XI of 542 Squadron from RAF Benson at 30,000ft over targets 'in the Soest area,' and on the morning of 15 May Fg Off F. G. Fray similarly photographed the Dortmund, Duisburg and Soest regions so as not to draw particular attention to the dams, landing back at base at 1310. By mid-afternoon of 15 May the results of these reconnaissance flights and interpretations of them, together with information from RAF Medmenham on the Sorpe and Eder dams which showed no unusual defensive activity, were available at Grantham. At 1540 5 Group received a cypher message from High Wycombe repeating the earlier order of ACAS (Ops) to execute Chastise.

Just before 1600 Cochrane left Scampton once more for his headquarters, as Wallis and Kilner touched down from Weybridge in a new Vickers-built Wellington piloted by Summers. On his return journey Cochrane took Gibson with him and together they discussed the draft operation order with Satterly and Dunn at Grantham, concentrating on Dunn's proposed signals procedures. It is probable that an important alteration to the draft operation order was also agreed at this conference. A copy dated 15 May shows seven target dams, with the Diemel as Target G (Reference GO 933) and the Henne as Target F (GO 936). However, the version dated 16 May, which appears as Appendix C to AOC 5 Group's post-operational report, lists only six dams with GO 936 omitted and the Diemel promoted to Target F.

After Gibson returned to Scampton, at 1800 in the station commander's house Gibson and Wallis briefed the two flight commanders (Young and Maudslay), Hopgood and Hay. Initially, for security reasons, Cochrane had insisted that only Young and Maudslay be briefed before the day of the operation. The decision to extend the information to the other two was almost certainly taken verbally that afternoon, because Hopgood would act as Gibson's deputy leader for the attack on the Möhne and Hay was squadron bombing leader. Their inclusion in discussions on 15 May proved significant. Hopgood pointed out that the proposed route would take the aircraft near Hüls, where a heavily defended rubber factory had not been marked on the flak map; this would be avoided on the night.

Late in the evening, as the informal briefing broke up, Whitworth gave Gibson the distressing news that his beloved dog, Nigger, with him since a puppy, a companion on several flights and adept at consuming alcohol, had been killed. Earlier in the evening the labrador had dashed out of the camp gate and been struck by a passing car, whose driver and passenger were injured in a vain attempt to avoid him. Nigger's body was carried into the guard room and placed in a detention cell. Summoned by a telephone call from the Service police, F/Sgt Powell confirmed the identity of the body and informed the adjutant of the tragedy. In turn Humphries told the station commander, who decided to break the news personally. It proved a depressing epilogue to the meeting; Wallis feared it was a dreadful omen and a loss which might unduly affect Gibson. His anxiety proved totally unfounded. And, contrary to a later assertion, neither Gibson nor any other member of the squadron was specially dosed with sleeping pills that night.

The following morning Wallis slept late while intensive activity went on around him in the hangars, workshops and offices of RAF Scampton. It was difficult to conceal that an operation was imminent, as tracer was loaded into machine guns and armourers laboured with the assistance of the crane and modified trolleys to complete the bombing-up of the Lancasters. Compasses needed to be swung with and without the mine in position, because Upkeep was found to affect the compass needle extraordinarily. Humphries drew up the order of battle – thinly disguised at Gibson's insistence as a 'Night Flying Programme' – and Powell quietly set in motion preparations for an evening meal for aircrew. Not all went smoothly. Once the mine had been painstakingly and slowly hoisted into position and pronounced secure, Martin and some of his crew entered Lancaster AJ-P to carry out routine checks. Suddenly the mine fell out of its retaining arms onto the tarmac, a premature release ascribed in squadron mythology to one WAAF officer's attraction for a lever in the cockpit. Fearing that the mine had been armed, bodies poured from the fuselage as Martin dashed off to fetch the armament officer. On arrival, with obvious disdain, Watson pronounced the monster safe. Sheepish figures shuffled from behind cover and the mine was once more laboriously heaved into position and painted black, rather than green, by the crew to merge with the fuselage. Meanwhile, Ottley had taken up AJ-C for an air test. That afternoon an armoury flight lieutenant went into the machine shop to collect a grease gun which LAC Drury had modified for use with Upkeep mines. Acknowledging that Drury 'had been put to a great deal of trouble and had shown a great deal of patience' on the squadron's behalf, he asked if he would like to see what he had been working on, adding that if he did not see it that day he would never see it at all. With that the officer led Drury into the aircraft hangar, where a Lancaster stood 'with what appeared to be a large steel drum hanging underneath the fuselage and a chain drive [sic] to revolve it in its bearing.' Looking at such 'a massive object,' Drury still had no inkling of its true nature or its purpose.

During the morning Satterly's instructions, finalised in consultation with

Gibson and approved by Cochrane, were typed in 'No. 5 Group Operation Order No. B.976' with three appendices: A 'Routes and Timings'; B 'Signals Procedure for Target Diversions etc.'; C 'Light and Moon Tables'. Twelve numbered copies were made under 'most secret' cover: two went to Whitworth at Scampton, three to HQ Bomber Command for personal delivery to the Deputy AOC-in-C or, in his absence, Marwood Elton. The remaining seven copies – destined for addresses or files within HQ 5 Group – were not to be distributed until after despatch of the executive signal for the operation, which would not be until late that afternoon.

Operation Order B.976 opened with general data about the targets, based upon information supplied by Bomber Command which had itself leaned heavily upon Wallis's paper 'Air Attack on Dams,' reconnaissance data and the many different economic, strategic and tactical appreciations on the subject. Noting that the 'inhabitants and industry' of the Ruhr relied 'to a very large extent on enormously costly water barrage dams in the Ruhr District,' it stated: 'Destruction of TARGET X (Möhne) alone would bring about a serious shortage of water for drinking purposes and industrial supplies.' The effect of this deficiency might not be 'immediately apparent but would certainly take effect in the course of a few months.' Satterly went on to note that 'additional destruction of one or more of the five major dams in the Ruhr Area would greatly increase the effect and hasten the resulting damage,' adding: 'TARGET Z (Sorpe) is next in importance'. But he re-emphasised that breaching of Target X would produce 'substantial' damage, 'considerable local flooding,' and 'a large loss of electrical capacity in the Ruhr' through destruction of hydroelectric plants and denial of cooling water for the thermal plants. His conclusion, however, fell short of a definitive claim: 'In fact it might well cause havoc in the Ruhr valley.' To the east of the Ruhr 'in the Weser District the destruction of TARGET Y (Eder) would seriously hamper transport in the Mittelland Canal and in the Weser (river), and would probably lead to an almost complete cessation of the great volume of traffic now using these waterways.'

At Target X 'three objects' on the crest of the dam were thought to be light AA guns, a three-gun light AA position was certainly situated 'below and to the north of the dam,' that is close to the village of Günne, and there was a possible searchlight position close by. Floating on the reservoir, some 100–300ft from the dam, was 'a double line boom with timber spreaders'. No other defences had been identified in the vicinity of the target. Relevant information about Targets Y and Z would be circulated separately once the results of reconnaissance photographs were known, and it was considered 'unlikely' that any target other than X would be defended. Satterly laid down that the dams should be breached in order of priority: X (Möhne), Y (Eder), Z (Sorpe). Three 'last resort' targets – D (Lister), E (Ennepe), and F (Diemel) – were then listed. This was an unfortunate use of a standard description, tending to underrate the value of their destruction, which Satterly had earlier explained. Their demolition was of less importance only with reference to the initial three: added to success at X and Z, breaching of D and E would have a potentially catastrophic effect on the Ruhr, while a successful attack on F would be a bonus to the emptying of the Eder reservoir.

The operation, by 'twenty Special Lancasters from 617 Squadron,' would take place on 'the first suitable date after 15th May, 1943'. The aircraft would fly from base to target area 'in moonlight at low level' by the detailed routes laid down in Appendix A and be divided into three waves. Air Vice-Marshal Cochrane later explained that he envisaged roughly the same number of Lancasters attacking X, Y and Z, with a reserve to cover emergencies at any of these or to attack remaining targets, because he was uncertain how many bombs would be needed to breach the Möhne. The first wave was to comprise three sections (each of three aircraft) to take off at ten-minute intervals and fly 'the Southern route [across the Scheldt estuary] to the target area and attack TARGET X.' It would do so 'until the Dam has been clearly breached . . . [and] it is estimated that this might require three effective attacks,' though who produced this estimate is unclear. Wallis always believed that one mine would do the job, so the figure of three almost certainly came from RAF staff officers more aware of the operational problems connected with such a precise method of delivery against a defended target. Once X had been breached, the remaining aircraft of this wave were to divert to Y, 'where similar tactics are to be followed'. When X and Y had been destroyed, those aircraft still carrying mines would proceed to Z. Meanwhile the second wave of five aircraft, 'manned by the specially trained crews,' would fly 'the Northern route' across the North Sea to the island of Vlieland, then roughly south-east over the Ijsselmeer (Zuider Zee) to join the route flown by the first wave in the area of the German border. Timings were to be arranged so that this wave, which would take off singly and fly thereafter separately to attack Z, would cross the enemy coast at the same time as the leading section of the first wave further south. The third wave would consist of the remaining six aircraft acting as 'an airborne reserve' under direct control of HQ 5 Group using a special W/T frequency. In the event this wave would comprise only five Lancasters due to lack of crews and aircraft. The third wave would fly the same southern route as the first and take off so that it could be recalled before crossing the enemy coast if the first two waves had breached all the targets. If possible 5 Group would signify which target each third-wave aircraft must attack before it crossed the enemy coast. Should no W/T message be received, aircraft were to proceed to X, Y (not Z) and last-resort targets 'in that order, attacking any which are not breached.' No recall for any reason would be possible unless the first section of the first wave and the third wave reached a point over the North Sea some 70 miles due east of Harwich and 35 miles north-west of the island of Walcheren (51°51′N – later in the order twice shown as 51°52′ and therefore probably a typing error here – 03°00′E). Allocation of individual aircraft to 'specific last resort targets' was left to Whitworth.

A most comprehensive and detailed plan for executing the operation followed. Each section of the first wave was to fly in open formation and not exceed 1,500ft over England. Crossing the North Sea coast the aircraft were to descend to low level and set altimeters at 60ft, using the two converging spotlights 'for calibration'. Aircraft should remain at low level to and from the target, at least until reaching 03°00′E on the return flight. Satterly emphasised the importance of crossing the enemy coast precisely as ordered, but added that aircraft should not turn back 'if their landfall is not quite accurate'. 'Good map reading and crew co-operation is essential' to make sure that each aircraft kept to the planned track, which 'should be free of all major opposition from flak.' The enemy coast must be crossed 'as low as possible' on the outward and return journeys, even if more height were later necessary for map-reading purposes. On reaching a point ten miles from the target, the leader of each section (Gibson, Young and Maudslay) was to climb to 1,000ft, whereupon all other aircraft should listen out on VHF and report by it to the wave leader on arrival at the target. Spinning of 'the special store' was to commence ten (not five) minutes before each aircraft attacked. The leader (Gibson) would attack first, then control other attacks by first-wave aircraft on X and Y via VHF R/T and in accordance with the signals procedure laid down at Appendix B. No 2 of the leading section (Hopgood) would act as deputy leader for the entire first wave at X and take over the leader's role if for any reason Gibson should be prevented from doing so; in that event No 3 (Martin) would become deputy leader. For the attack on Y No 4 (Young) would become deputy leader or leader in Gibson's absence, in which case No 7 (Maudslay) would assume responsibility as deputy leader. All other aircraft should return to base on completion of their attack via routes designated at Appendix A.

Target X should be attacked at right angles to the length of the target, that is by flying approximately south-east to north-west. No aircraft should be sent to Y until Target X had been breached, but Gibson was given licence to use up to two more aircraft to widen the breach at X, provided at least three aircraft remained for Y. Care should be taken to distinguish between water spilling over the dam as a result of turbulence following the explosion of the mine, and a breach. Once X had been breached 'beyond all possible doubt,' remaining aircraft would divert to Y and carry out a similar attack, in this instance from north-west to south-east. Once Y had been breached 'beyond all possible doubt,' remaining aircraft would be sent by Gibson to attack Z independently 'using the same tactics as the 2nd wave'. For the attacks on X and Y the special rangefinder (the Dann sight or 617 chinagraph variation) would be used, and aircraft would fly at 60ft and at a groundspeed of 220 (not 232) mph.

Proceeding by the northern route over the island of Vlieland and the Ijsselmeer, aircraft of the second wave were to cross the enemy coast 'in close concentration but not in formation at the same time, although at a different point, as the leading section of the 1st wave.' The leader (McCarthy) would control aircraft of this wave on the alternative VHF channel. Most crucially, the form of attack against Z would differ from that on all other targets. Stores would not be spun and attacks would take place north-west to south-east along the length of the dam (not at right angles to it), with the object of dropping each mine in the water just short of the centre point of the dam and 15–20ft from the edge of the water. Each attack would be made 'from the lowest practicable height' at an IAS of 180 mph, and after completion aircraft were to return to base independently by the briefed routes. The third wave, under direct control of HQ 5 Group, would fly to X 'in close concentration but not in formation' along the same northern route as the first wave and at low level. Aircraft of this wave were separately to attack X and Y in a similar manner to that laid down for the first-wave and last-resort targets.

The method of attack would be that already practised, with the pilot responsible for line, the navigator for height, 'Air Bomber' (bomb-aimer) for range and flight engineer for speed. To allow turbulence from the preceding explosion to subside, the interval between attacking aircraft at each target should not be less than three minutes. At all targets except Z, aircraft would fire a red Very cartridge as they passed over the dam during its attack; at Z the cartridge would be fired on release of the 'special store'. All aircraft would fly left-hand circuits in the area of targets, keeping as low as possible while awaiting their turn to attack. Satterly stated that the precise time of attack at each target was 'not important to within a few minutes', but that of crossing the enemy coast was, on the contrary, 'all important'. Bomber Command would be asked for 'the maximum possible diversionary attacks' without crossing the enemy coast in the hour preceding the third wave's arrival there, but reaching 'maximum strength' fifteen minutes after it did so and continuing until third-wave aircraft cleared enemy territory on the return journey. Satterly went on to give meticulous information about navigational aids, stress the continued need for security, and cover the timings, turning points and distances involved in all outward and return routes in minute detail. The routes were based closely, though not slavishly, on recommendations contained in a long memorandum from RAF Tempsford on 7 April.

Appendix A laid down three return routes, which ultimately crossed the Helder peninsula at different points, and allocated individual aircraft to them. Until the English coast was reached a true airspeed of 220 mph and maximum height of 500ft were to be maintained, with an additional warning that the enemy coast should be crossed 'at the lowest possible height'. Appendix B concerned signals procedures and a number of important codewords: Pranger (attack X), Nigger (X breached, divert to Y), Dinghy (Y breached, divert to Z), Mason (all aircraft return to base), Tulip (No 2 take over at X), Cracking (No 4 take over at Y), Gilbert (attack last-resort targets as detailed). The code-word on R/T for the aircraft was Cooler. Once individual aircraft had released their weapon they were to change to Group Frequency (3,680kc/s) to transmit Goner (signifying release), the agreed code letter indicating the target attacked and a figure to denote the effect of the mine as follows: 1, failed to explode; 2, overshot the dam; 3, exploded over 100 yards from the dam; 4, exploded 100 yards from the dam; 5, exploded 50 yards from the dam; 6, exploded 5 yards from the dam; 7, exploded in contact with the dam; 8, no apparent breach; 9, small breach; 10, large breach. So '710A' would indicate a mine exploding in contact with the Möhne and causing a large breach in it; in contrast to the operation order, which required the letters X, Y and Z for the Möhne, Eder and Sorpe respectively, signals procedure called for A, B and C. Appendix C gave such details as the times of twilight and rising and setting of the moon: the moon would rise in the target area, for example, at 1700 on 16 May and set at 0431 on 17 May, all times being Double British Summer Time, which coincided with that in Germany and the Low Countries as they were one hour in advance of Central European Time.

617 Squadron Lancasters were therefore ordered to attack six of the seven dams (four of them in the Ruhr) detailed in Wallis's 'Air Attack on Dams' paper, which had been finalised five months earlier. The Möhne Dam (Target X, Reference GO 939) lay seven miles south of Soest and 26 miles east of Dortmund, where the Möhne and Heve rivers merged before flowing northwards into the Ruhr. The dam, which held back 134 million cubic metres of water, was of the curved gravity type, tapered from the base upwards and measuring 40.3m (132ft) high, 650m (2,133ft) long, 34.02m (112ft) thick at

the bottom and 6.25m (21ft) at the top, wide enough for a roadway. Built mainly of limestone, but with some sandstone and diorite, it had a volume totalling 267,000m^3 of masonry and it effectively controlled an annual flow of 240 million cubic metres of water through its sluices. Astride the structure, crowning access to the machinery and inspection galleries below, were two towers 196m (639ft) apart.

On the upstream side of the Möhne Dam alluvial deposits had built up to a third of the dam's height, sloping away into the reservoir. Any bomb not exploded before it reached this shelf would therefore roll along it and away from the dam face. From the centre of the dam, looking up the reservoir, a heavily wooded spit of land topped by the Hevers Berg (262m) divided the Möhne and Heve valleys, whose sides were also tree-covered. The rising land on both sides enclosed the dam, and rolling hills, angled valleys and tall trees would effectively shield aircraft from anybody on the dam until the last few hundred yards of an attack. Then, however, the aircraft would be cruelly open to flak guns, which covered the widest expanse of the reservoir, where the two rivers merged; the removal of 18 balloons in August 1942 and heavy guns shortly afterwards did not significantly reduce this potential menace to low-flying aircraft. Approaching from the Hevers Berg spit, they would be totally exposed, with their spotlights giving added help to enemy gunners. Behind the dam, and in the centre of it on the downstream side, stood a large power station set among ornamental gardens on the edge of the overflow or compensating basin. A smaller power station lay on the western side of the basin, on three sides of which were rising hills and to the north-east the village of Günne. So aircraft flying a left-hand circuit after crossing the dam would need to negotiate hills rising to 291m.

The Sorpe Dam (Target Z, Reference GO 960) had a different structure, hence Wallis's late fear expressed to Bufton on 11 May that his proposed method of attack might not succeed and Cochrane's decision to adopt another tactic, an attack along the 600m (1,965ft) length of the dam with the bomb not spun and dropped near the crest. The 58m (190ft) high dam was situated at the northern end of a reservoir, which contained 72 million cubic metres of water and stood six miles (not ten as in the route details) south-west of the Möhne Dam on the Sorpe, leading to the Ruhr river. A watertight core of concrete ten metres wide was buttressed by high stabilising banks of earth covered with stone slabs which sloped away at an angle on both the air and water sides. Lined by rolling tree-covered hills with numerous peaks exceeding 400m, the Sorpe Lake had a steep rise at each end of its dam. That to the west, immediately above the dam, rose to 340m and was covered by the village of Langscheid, whose church spire stood virtually in the path of each attacking aircraft. To the east the ground rose more sharply to 324m, so the aircraft commanders were briefed to approach from the west over the village and line up the nacelle of the port outer engine with the top of the dam to give the correct lateral position for release of the mine. As Harris remarked, this tactic had 'a poor chance of success,' and the decision to go ahead with it was taken by the Air Staff over his head and against his advice. Curiously, years later both Cochrane and Wallis believed that crews were told to drop their mines on top of the dam so that it would crumble, a tactic recommended pre-war and later tried unsuccessfully by No 9 Squadron. The War Cabinet was informed: 'The intention was to cause leakage on a sufficient scale to force the Germans to empty the reservoir in order to effect repairs'; and Harris considered that the aim was to create the sort of gradual erosion which the legendary Dutch boy's finger had prevented at Leyden four centuries before. The aim of this particular attack did not therefore seem clear. And after the operation Collins, leader of the Road Research Laboratory team, professed to being surprised and 'a little irritated' to learn that the Sorpe had been bombed 'because we could easily have made some model tests which I am sure could have made the attack more successful.'

The third Ruhr dam detailed for attack was the Lister (Target D, Reference GO 938, in some papers shown as 'Attendorn'). Measuring 264m (866ft) long and 40m (131ft) high, it was of similar curved masonry construction to the Möhne. It held back 22 million cubic metres of water, contained in a narrow reservoir about three miles long and fed by the Herpel and Lister rivers. Situated in hilly country 55 miles south-east of Duisburg and close to the small town of Attendorn, it fed the Lenne tributary of the Ruhr. The approach for an attacking aircraft to the dam over the village of Eichen from due west was relatively simple, with 500m of open water and a direct line between the spit of land on which Eichen stood and the dam. But a significant error in information misled Wallis here. Only one tower existed on the Lister Dam, whereas his calculations showed two, 271m (886ft) apart. The source of this false information is unknown.

The Ennepe constituted Target E (Reference GO 935). Like the Möhne and Lister, it was a masonry dam with a convex curve into the reservoir and a capacity of 12.6 million cubic metres. Measuring 51m (165ft) high, 330m (1,083ft) long and wide enough for a road to pass over, it had semi-circular sluice towers 183m (600ft) apart. The figures Wallis set out in his 'Air Attack on Dams' paper – height 45m and capacity 15 million cubic metres, clearly taken from Kelen – differ slightly from those quoted authoritatively elsewhere, but the difference had no practical significance. Situated 20 miles due south of Dortmund and 30 miles south-west of the Möhne Dam, it nestled in very hilly terrain with a most difficult approach run for any attacking aircraft. The dam lay at the northern end of an irregular L-shaped reservoir edged with steeply wooded slopes, meandering just over two miles (3,500m) south-east and fed by the Ennepe river. Beyond the dam, this river ran into the Ruhr near Herdecke and was principally used to supply drinking water. A peculiar feature of this target, almost exactly in front of the mid-point of the two sluice towers, 300m upstream and preventing a perfect approach run, was a tree-covered spit of land. However, with maximum water level in the reservoir envisaged, this appeared on all maps as an island.

Logically, following Wallis's paper and the opening paragraph of Satterly's order, the fifth target should have been the Henne Dam at Meschede, 15 miles south-east of the Möhne and a mere 1,500m from the Ruhr river. Wallis identified this as the fifth most important Ruhr dam, holding back 11 million cubic metres of water. Although he claimed that it had a 'masonry wall' he did not supply details of the height of 38m and 364m length, as given in Kelen. It may have been this lack of information which caused the dam to be excluded from the list of targets at a very late stage in planning, probably during the afternoon conference at the HQ 5 Group on 15 May. But photographic reconnaissance would have revealed its inaccessible nature. The outskirts of the small industrial town of Meschede, which was situated on the banks of the Ruhr river and likely to have some anti-aircraft defence, virtually abutted the dam. Even if an aircraft were not directly exposed to flak guns during its attack run, it would most certainly be vulnerable as it cleared high ground beyond the target.

So the Henne was excluded and only four targets were connected with the Ruhr. The other two concerned the Weser area. The Eder Dam (Target Y, Reference GO 934) was the more important. Very similar in construction to the Möhne, it was 42.4m (139ft) high, 399m (1,309ft) long and 5.8m (19ft) wide at the top and 35m (115ft) at the bottom (though published figures on the height, in particular, vary). Surmounted by two towers 238m (781ft) apart, it presented a much more difficult approach for attacking aircraft, even if it were undefended. Situated close to Hemfurth, two miles south of Waldeck – perched with its castle high over the Eder Lake – 20 miles south-west of Kassel and 50 miles south-east of the Möhne, it held back 202 million cubic metres of water contained in a reservoir which wriggled like a giant caterpillar some 12km west to east between sharp, wooded hills. Unlike the Möhne Dam, the Eder had two small power stations below the wall, virtually at its extremities and not vulnerable to a central breach.

Two metres below the road along the top of the Eder Dam were 39 outlets capable of coping with a flood of 610m^3/sec and, together with six drainage

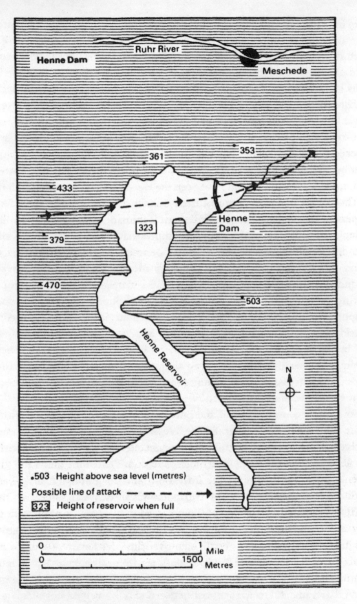

Henne Dam

Ruhr River

Meschede

361   353

433

323

Henne Dam

379

470

503

Henne Reservoir

N

.503 Height above sea level (metres)

Possible line of attack

323 Height of reservoir when full

0   1 Mile
0   1500 Metres

outlets controlled by Hemfurth II, of 900m³/sec. Twelve emergency sluices were situated 12m below these and were capable of dealing with the same amount of floodwater. This system had been installed to prevent undue damage to the dam wall when the reservoir was full. Further to regulate the flow of water for the lower Fulda and Eder rivers, an equalising basin had been constructed below the dam with a capacity of 3.8 million cubic metres. And the 0.65 million cubic metres from a storage lake 300m above the equalising basin could be released when required. The Eder reservoir itself fulfilled another, less obvious purpose. Worried by the potential effects of a naval blockade similar to that experienced during the First World War and loss of North Sea fishing grounds, the German government had deliberately stocked numerous inland lakes to guard against food shortages. In the last year before the breaching of the dam the Eder reservoir contained 23,000kg of fish, mainly pike and perch.

The Germans no doubt considered that its natural position afforded an impenetrable defence, for flak defences initially positioned there were redeployed to the more pressing protection of urban centres elsewhere. The dam itself arched west-north-west into the reservoir; immediately west of it stood a large tree-covered spit rising to 241m. To the north undulating ground soared in places to some 400m, and a mere 350m east of the dam the land rose steeply to 343m. Considering that the mine had to be bounced as at the Möhne, the only possible approach for aircraft – described by Cochrane as 'very confined, very tricky' – was from the north, using Waldeck Castle in its eyrie as an aiming point to dive towards a point west of the spit before executing a sharp port turn to hop over the spit and line up with the sluice towers. Small wonder that attacking crews would require several practice runs on the night before they released their mines.

With the Möhne and Sorpe, the Eder constituted a major target. The sixth dam, the Diemel (Target F, Reference GO 933, and in some documents 'Helminghausen'), in concept closely connected with the Eder, was the third so-called 'last resort' target and the second connected with the Weser river. Twenty miles north-west of the Eder Dam and 30 miles west of Kassel, it stood at the northern head of two narrow valleys, each some two miles (3,000m) in length. From one of them flowed the Diemel river, providing an easy approach run directly in front of the dam wall, which nestled between two hills respectively 557m and 596m high. Below the dam the Diemel wound itself through Helminghausen and past its tiny church before at length joining the Weser near Hoxter. The dam itself was 194m (637ft) long and 40m (131ft) high, of masonry construction and holding back 20 million cubic metres of water. For the attacking aircraft it had one serious disadvantage: there were no superimposed towers for guidance. Yet, as with the Lister, Wallis unaccountably believed that there were, in this instance 220m (721ft) apart.

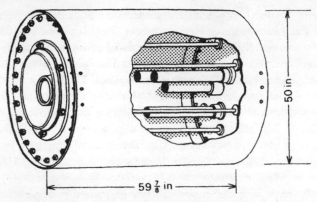

50 in

59 ⅞ in

The Upkeep mine weighed a total of 9,250lb, including 6,600lb of Torpex underwater explosive. The three outer pistols shown were hydrostatic and set to activate at 30ft, with the central, self-destructive, pistol set to act 90sec after release from the aircraft. Originally 61in, the length had to be reduced for Upkeep to fit into the Lancaster bomb bay.

The final version of Upkeep, with which it was hoped to breach the dams, comprised a cylinder approximately 60in (actually 59⅞ in) long and 50in in diameter, made of metal ⅜in thick and weighing 2,650lb. Containing 6,600lb of Torpex underwater explosive compound, three hydrostatic pistols set to explode at 30ft and a fourth self-destructive pistol timed to go off 90 seconds after release (all with the powerful initiating explosive Tetryl), the weapon had a total weight of 9,250lb. The two V-shaped calliper arms protruding from the bomb bay held the mine between their points, and a 20in-diameter disc mounted on the inside of these extremities engaged a track at each end of the cylinder. A belt running at an angle of 45° and linked to the Vickers Jassey Variable Speed Gear hydraulic motor, used for steering by the hydroplane operative in submarines, was mounted on the floor of the fuselage in the facing of the bomb-bay and caused the mine to rotate at the required 500 rpm. Since it was not needed to operate the mid-upper turret or bomb-bay doors in Type 464 Provisioning Lancasters, the hydraulic system had a cut-out arrangement which allowed power to be diverted to the Vickers motor after the undercarriage had been retracted. This imparted back-spin when the wireless operator manipulated the valve of a compressor to regulate the speed, which he estimated with the aid of an attached gauge. The bomb-aimer was responsible for releasing the weapon by operating powerful springs which made the calliper arms spring outwards, allowing the mine to drop. As the flight engineer controlled the speed of the aircraft on the approach run, the navigator would switch on the spotlights. Watching them through the perspex blister on the right of the cockpit, he advised the pilot of height corrections until the necessary figure-of-eight was achieved.

To deliver Upkeep, the 617 Squadron Lancaster IIIs had to combat strong enemy defences to and from their targets. Light anti-aircraft guns posed formidable problems for low-flying aircraft. The basis for nearly all early German 20mm models was the Flak 30, capable of 120 rounds per minute and a ceiling of 6,630ft. The 20mm Flak 38, firing the same range of 3.6–5.2oz shells at 480 rounds per minute, and a four-barrelled version (20cm Flakvierling 38) were developments of the Flak 30. Gibson observed that the distinctive 'bok! bok!' of the 20mm could have an unnerving effect on bomber crews, and it was single-barrelled 20mm guns, each with a crew of six and capable of reaching the Hevers Berg spit when depressed, which were stationed on the Möhne Dam. A wide range of heavier flak guns, including those mounted on concrete towers or formed into mobile railway batteries, would also prove dangerous if Chastise crews flew high or strayed too close to military or industrial centres.

As anti-aircraft guns were manned by Luftwaffe personnel and searchlights were under Luftwaffe control too, a system of integrated defence with fighters had been developed. The night-fighter arm was organised into XII Air Corps commanded by Major-General Josef Kammhuber, and in his headquarters at Zeist near Utrecht Kammhuber was ideally placed to direct operations against bombers from England. The German night-fighter force at that time comprised five *Nachtjagdgeschwadern* (night-fighter groups), sub-divided into *Gruppen* (wings) and *Staffeln* (squadrons). Each unit was numbered according to its *Gruppe*: thus I/NJG 3 represented the first *Gruppe* of *Nachtjagdgeschwader* 3. The *Staffeln* were numbered consecutively within each *Geschwader*: *Gruppe* I always had 1, 2 and 3 *Staffeln*, *Gruppe* II 4, 5 and 6. To avoid long numerical descriptions 3/NJG 3 was often used instead of 3/I/ NJG 3. The vast majority of night fighters were Messerschmitt Bfl 10 and Junkers Ju88 twin-engined aircraft, which had forsaken their early bombing role and since also proved inadequate in a fighter capacity by day. Faster than the Lancaster, even one unencumbered with Upkeep, their main difficulty early in 1943 was in detecting bombers.

In this respect radar provided great assistance. *Freya* stations on the coast gave the direction and range of attackers up to 100 miles, but they could not determine altitude. Mobile *Würzburg* sets with a range of 45 miles were used by ground controllers inland and many fighters had airborne *Lichtenstein* sets accurate up to two miles. A system of interception, known as *Himmelbett*, was devised whereby the ground controller with two *Würzburg* sets, one trained on the fighter and one on the bomber, guided the fighter into a position for its wireless operator to stalk the quarry with his *Lichtenstein*. This system was in turn linked to a series of geographical zones which a sub-committee of the British Operational Research Committee had identified fairly accurately in February 1943.

So 617 Squadron Lancasters involved in Operation Chastise had to contend with this defensive organisation: interlocking *Himmelbett* zones (the Scheldt estuary, which aircraft of the first and third waves would cross, was covered by four), fighters with airborne radars, and a strong array of flak weapons assisted by searchlights and radar and often grouped around vulnerable targets. Night-fighter units were stationed within easy range of the planned routes at Venlo, Gilze Rijen, St Trond/Brusthem, Twente/Enschede and Leeuwarden. Their means of interception were dictated by a rigid zonal system which required aircraft on patrol to orbit a radio beacon and await instructions from the ground controller. Furthermore, each *Himmelbett* zone could cope with only one enemy aircraft at a time. Although a 50 per cent overlap in zones theoretically helped to reduce this problem, in reality the system lacked flexibility. NJG 1 and NJG 2 covered the Ijsselmeer and Scheldt estuary areas, but could not call upon other units for short-term reinforcement. This gave the RAF scope for intruder operations and other diversionary raids to confuse the defences. Moreover, as the German fighters did not carry IFF equipment, each had to return to its zone's radio beacon after every interception or attempted interception to re-establish contact and identity. *Konaja* zones, linking searchlights, flak and night fighters, were in existence over specific areas, such as Cologne (codename *Kolibri*), and Düsseldorf-Duisburg-Essen (*Drossel*), and the entire defensive system came under Luftwaffe Command Centre at Berlin, commanded by Colonel-General Hubert Weise.

A carefully planned route to avoid known flak concentrations and airfields, such as the base of 1/NJG 1 and 10/NJG 3 at Gilze Rijen between Tilburg and Breda in Holland, was therefore imperative, and a low-level approach justified. Ground radar would find it difficult to track aircraft below 1,000ft, especially in the relative haven of valleys near the targets, airborne *Lichtenstein* sets were not effective in scanning downwards, and a bomber's exhaust flames were virtually impossible to detect from a night fighter. But the immense difficulty involved in keeping to the briefed track at low altitude underlined the inherent dangers in this tactic, and the vulnerability of low-flying aircraft to light flak was an added peril.

As maintenance and bombing-up preparations went ahead and the final version of Operation Order B.976 was being typed, at 1000 on Sunday 16 May Wg Cdr Dunn learned that the operation would take place that night.

Pausing only to gather papers and equipment, he set off from Grantham for Scampton, arriving an hour later at about the time Wallis rose for a late breakfast. Gibson recorded that 617 Squadron did not formally break for lunch that day, for from noon onwards many of the aircrew were grouped in various conference rooms. In F/Sgt Powell's words, the hangars and offices were 'very quiet, like a morgue,' and Martin's rear gunner, Simpson, wrote: 'It was the longest briefing I ever attended.' There was, however, one discordant note late in the morning. Gibson asked F/Sgt F. O. Brown in the station workshop to build a coffin for Nigger, which Brown refused to do. As an observer recorded: 'With that the Wing Commander lost his temper, there were high words with very little wisdom, and the Wing Commander went on his way without getting a coffin made for his dog.'

Shortly after noon Wallis and Gibson briefed all pilots and navigators, as Dunn dealt with the wireless operators, giving them specific messages to practise on a buzzer circuit under his supervision. Both groups broke for refreshment after two hours, with all committed to reveal absolutely nothing. Sgt Tees was unperturbed by this reticence, musing: 'Well, it can't be any worse than others.' At different times during the afternoon, bomb-aimers and gunners joined pilots and navigators to study models of the Möhne and Sorpe, and photographs and maps of the other targets, and to talk over aspects of the routes with which they would be involved as special map-readers that night. Thereafter discussion and briefing became virtually continuous for over five hours. During this period a major variation of route from the operation order was introduced. As a result of Hopgood's observation about Hüls the previous evening, the intermediate navigation point between Rees and Ahlen on the northern edge of the Ruhr at Ahsen was changed to lakes near Dülmen, north of Haltern. This would give a wider berth to the Ruhr, but bring aircraft over an unexpected, well defended position east of Rees and expose them to another between Dülmen and Ahlen.

As the operational problems were under examination by 617 Squadron aircrew, DB Ops (Bufton) considered press releases. To Harris he emphasised the need for security even after the operation, and stressed that newsmen should receive information only from the Air Ministry, and communiqués would be issued in accordance with the cover plan agreed on 25 March. 'A mine of great size' had been dropped by a number of selected crews 'specially and rigorously trained' for an operation 'which demanded an extra-ordinarily high standard of flying and the highest degree of accuracy in dropping the mines sufficiently close to the target to be effective.'

With meteorological forecasts favourable, the operation was definitely on.

At 1315 HQ Bomber Command signalled Fighter Command, requesting provision of 'intruder operations . . . between 2330 and 0030 and again between 0145 and 0300 hrs.' in a defined area. Three-quarters of an hour later a more general signal was sent to the USAAF, Fighter Command, Coastal Command, Army Co-operation and all bomber groups, warning them of 'special operations tonight 16/17 May.' At 1615 5 Group sent a 'secret and immediate' telex message to the officer commanding at Scampton: 'Code name for 5 Group Operation Order B.976 is Chastise'. Until that time, outside an intimate circle, the operation had been a number. A half-hour later a cypher despatch followed: 'Executive Operation Chastise 16/5/43 zero hour 2248'. The way was now clear for general briefing of all 617 Squadron aircrew destined to fly that night. And at 1817 indication occurred that pressure of time can cause clerical errors which also elude proof-readers. Saundby pointed out to 5 Group a mistake in Bomber Command's copies of B.976, where the dams were listed 'X,Y,X', and at this late hour an amendment to read 'X,Y,Z' was quickly circulated from Grantham.

One special problem was the number of serviceable aircraft. Early in the afternoon the workshops finally admitted defeat: ED933/G, damaged by Maudslay on 13 May, would not be in the air that night. This left only 19 modified Lancasters. Sickness meant that the crews of Flt Lt Wilson and Plt Off Divall could not fly, which conveniently left 19 crews too. But there was no reserve Lancaster in case of last-minute emergency. Only three other Type 464 Provisioning Lancasters had been produced: two were still in use by Longbottom and Handasyde at Reculver, and the third (ED825/G) was at Boscombe Down. Fortunately, as it turned out, Commander H. C. Bergel of No 9 Ferry Pilots Pool was called upon to collect this aircraft from Boscombe Down and fly it to Scampton as a matter of extreme urgency. The strange contraption, with the bomb bay faired over and its doors removed, seemed to Bergel like a 'gutted fish'. The hefty metal arms with small wheels at their extremities, the driving belt from the starboard side to a pulley attached to a hydraulic motor bolted to the cabin floor, and the instructions connected with it in the cockpit, all were utterly beyond his comprehension. Testing the engines before take-off, however, he did identify an unpleasant feature: No 3 engine would not run at full throttle with the fuel booster pump off. Due to the pressing nature of his orders, Bergel decided to 'ignore' this condition, which should have rendered the machine unserviceable. On arrival at Scampton at approximately 1530 he discovered 'a large number' of other 'gutted' Lancasters parked round the perimeter, some of them carrying objects 'about the size and shape of the front wheel of a steam roller' in their vast claws. He noticed that on one aircraft this object was slowly rotating, so on leaving his charge he set off for a closer look. Swiftly intercepted, he was informed (with a pinch of exaggeration) that those connected with this top secret project had been confined to camp 'for the past eleven weeks'. So Bergel beat the proverbial hasty retreat to a waiting Anson and spent the homeward flight pondering the nature of his discovery. His deliberations were not illuminating, as he later admitted: 'I had no idea what this peculiarly modified aeroplane was required to do, and it was made clear that curiosity was most unwelcome!' He was never told that his flight allowed McCarthy to bomb the Sorpe Dam and 617 Squadron to put 19, not 18, aircraft into the air that night.

Even as Bergel took off again, maintenance crew were converging on ED825/G. Munro, the erstwhile gymnast, discovered that a 16-strand coaxial cable had a bakelite insert missing from the end that fitted into the Gee box. This in itself presented a major problem. No spares were available, so Munro had either to declare the aircraft unserviceable or gamble that he could solve the problem. Slowly and carefully he spaced out the 16 small wire-end sockets, lined them up with the male plugs and pressed them together. When the engines were tested, he held his breath, but no shorting occurred. After the raid, Munro wrote: 'Joe McCarthy flew close to Hamm with more than just a poor compass swing.'

During the afternoon Wallis and Summers moved among the maintenance crews examining weapons and aircraft. At one point a flustered Wallis rushed up to Gibson. The wrong oil had been used with sensitive equipment connected with Upkeep and he feared that the weapon would not work in anger. Local stores did not have the correct fluid. Disaster could occur. Preoccupied with administrative tasks, Gibson gave Wallis *carte blanche* to sort the matter out, which presumably he did. Gibson heard no more of the affair – and the mines worked. Ammunition may also have created a special problem. For, according to one gunner, 'we could not get from RAF sources the tracer that we wanted (one that would burn from the gun barrel to impact) and it was made up for us by the Ordnance Corps, and only delivered on the morning of 16 May.'

At 1800 came the final briefing, for which all aircrew 'noisily assembled' in the large upstairs briefing room. Service policemen were stationed outside the closed door but did not deter one intruder. Late that afternoon Longbottom flew ED817/G from Manston to Scampton, taking Handasyde with him. Having nothing to do and not having been there before, Jeffree hitched a lift with them. On arrival Handasyde saw that 'a flap was on and tight security about to close the station,' so he and Longbottom agreed to depart without delay. Jeffree, with neither authority nor instructions, decided to stay.

Hearing that a briefing was in progress, he approached one of the sentries, saying that he was one of Wallis's team and producing a numbered pass which was authority for places like Reculver and Manston but certainly not for the final briefing at Scampton. Temerity brought its reward. Opening the door, he joined the briefing, which had already begun. Sitting down at the back, Jeffree noted the senior officers and Wallis on a raised area immediately opposite the door with their backs to the window. The temperature of that hot day had only marginally fallen in the early evening, he realised, as he became aware of the models of the dams, enlarged reconnaissance photographs, map of Europe with red tape pinned on it to indicate routes, and all the other trappings of an operational briefing. This was the first time he had attended any pre-raid briefing.

Gibson had opened the proceedings by briefly telling the aircrew that they were 'to attack the great dams of Germany' and then introducing Wallis. Repeating details which he had already explained at the mini-conference on 15 May and earlier that day, with occasional use of a blackboard and a cross-sectional drawing of the Möhne Dam, Wallis described the weapon, how it had been developed, some of the many problems encountered in the experimental stage and arguments for attacking the German dams. By destroying them the squadron would strike a blow at the enemy from which he would not recover 'for a very long time'. Concentrating on the importance of damage to enemy industrial capacity, he emphasised that German methods of production required eight tons of water to make a single ton of steel, although on other occasions he used the ratio 100:1. He could not have known that on 11 April, faced by mounting losses at sea and on land, Hitler had ordered Albert Speer to increase steel production. Thus a major blow against the steel industry would indeed have a most serious effect upon the enemy war effort. He went on to discuss the characteristics of the dams and principles of his method of destruction. There were few moments of light relief, though he did observe that as the Kaiser had personally opened the Möhne in 1913 it must be a good target. F/Sgt Chalmers found Wallis's sketch of the effects of destruction on the Germans 'lasting and impressive'. Recalling that most of those present had previously heard of Wallis through his work on the Wellington, in which many had flown, Sgt Clay reflected how 'detailed and clear' was his explanation of the development of the bomb and construction of the dams. But he could not avoid feeling that 'it seemed incongruous that this kindly and quietly spoken white-haired man should be involved with devastation.' McCarthy similarly thought him 'a genial man'.

When Wallis had finished, Cochrane rose to speak. He believed that the crews would do 'a tremendous amount of damage' and that the operation would become 'historic' – prophetic words. Following the line laid down by the Air Ministry, he stressed that details of the weapon and its peculiar characteristics must remain secret after the operation, for other targets were destined to feel its impact. He concluded simply but strongly: 'I know this attack will succeed'. As he spoke Wallis and Gibson had a quick exchange of words, and two remarks by Wallis were significant: 'I hope they all come back . . . I look upon this raid as my last great experiment to see if it can be done on the actual thing'; Garston, Harmondsworth and Nant-y-Gro, now the Möhne. Essentially an engineer, despite his concern for the crews, professionally he continued to focus on the scientific principles of Upkeep.

After Cochrane, Gibson went over operational details once more and repeated the three waves of aircraft, which he had announced earlier to pilots and navigators. Wave 1 (nine aircraft), whose Lancasters would take off in groups of three at ten-minute intervals and were destined for the Möhne, Eder and Sorpe; Wave 2 (five) would go to the Sorpe independently; and Wave 3 (five) would act as airborne reserve, taking off some two and a half hours after the other waves. The interloper Jeffree intervened, arguing that to return with an unused store could be dangerous. There might be peril for an aircraft returning with a mine whose self-destructive fuse had been armed when crossing the enemy coast. It was ruled, to Jeffree's recollection, that no Upkeep mines would be brought back, and this may explain why Sgt Webb remembers that crews were told that to drop the mine on land would not endanger the aircraft. It may also go some way to explaining Gibson's later anger with one crew which did bring one back. Then Dunn ran over signals procedures, and before the crews finally dispersed for a meal at 1930, he talked with wireless operators in the three separate waves about their different responsibilities. Other groups gathered round the models, photographs and route maps to re-check details. Yet once more details of callsigns, weather, ammunition and routes were mulled over as crews huddled haphazardly in the briefing room (although the three waves tended to group separately) to discuss salient features and likely defences. Rice, detailed for the Sorpe attack, realised that to drop the mine at a relatively low speed without spinning after diving over the steep hill meant that he would have to put the Lancaster's flaps down, and he was concerned about having to 'wriggle round' the church steeple at Langscheid to get the correct approach run. Despite the obvious dangers and difficulties, in excess even of a normal operation in the Ruhr, Clay noted: 'Everyone was in high spirits and ready to go.'

After the briefing, reversing the normal order of events, crews went for a meal. As F/Sgt Powell noted, preparations for that meal of eggs and bacon and gathering of coffee, sandwiches and fruit to go into the aircraft for in-flight consumption were impossible to conceal. Waitresses in the officers' mess felt that something was afoot, and Section Officers Fowler and Gillan noticed two eggs on each crew member's plate (traditional pre-operational fare) but made no comment. With the meal over crew members went back to their quarters, some to undertake the grim task of composing letters to next of kin in case they failed to return. Predictably Young tidied up his office. So conscious were crews of security that an NCO who made a remark in the mess after supper about the operation was brusquely rebuked by his fellows. The squadron medical officer, who shared a room with Shannon's rear gunner, only sensed that an operation was imminent that evening when he asked Buckley if he could fly with him on the practice flight and received an evasive reply. And, attempting shortly afterwards to telephone a member of his family who was ill, he discovered that rigid security prevented any outside calls.

With time now for reflection, the confidence exuded at the briefings began to ebb: Townsend confessed to feeling sick, convinced that they were 'all for the chop,' and Hopwood told Shannon that he would certainly not return. Sgt O'Brien noted that some crew members talked quietly together, while others, in nervous outbursts, joked in unnaturally loud voices. Elsewhere on the station tension also mounted. Cochrane later reported that nobody outside squadron aircrew knew that the operation would be mounted that night. Strictly that may be true. But while they could not be sure, many groundcrew realised that this was no ordinary practice; loading of the mines alone indicated an operation. LAC Munro recorded: 'The interaction between ground crew and aircrew was such that your sixth sense told you that this was "it", by the way the crews acted. If it's just another exercise, aircrews are quite relaxed and talkative. If it's the real thing, there is tension in the air, as well as a general quietness in communication.' One intelligence officer, looking at the full list of 19 aircraft scheduled to take off that evening, similarly remarked: 'They're off!' Meanwhile, in the bar Jeffree stood drinks for those whom Wallis had inadvertently omitted to reward for their help. Such is administrative parsimony, later he had great difficulty in recovering his outlay from Vickers-Armstrongs' accountants. More adventurous spirits made unscheduled and premature trips to the aircraft after supper. Sgt Feneron tried to lift the mine slung under Brown's Lancaster, and Sgt Garshowitz chalked on AJ-B's mine: 'Never has so much been expected of so few'. It was a poignant note of defiance: Garshowitz would not return. Earnshaw, Hopgood's navigator, prophesied, precisely and correctly, that eight aircraft would not come back. His Lancaster would be one of them.

Gradually, towards 2000, crews converged in little clusters on the squadron hangar to collect parachutes and other equipment. The 90 minutes before take-off was always a trying time on any station, but the long prelude to this operation made this occasion even more testing. As the adjutant recorded: 'This was Der Tag for 617 Squadron . . . [and] from eight o'clock onwards the scenes outside the crew rooms were something to be remembered.' Gibson arrived with his entire crew packed into his car, radiating complete confidence. To Humphries he appeared 'fit and well and quite unperturbed,' which later caused Gibson to comment: 'This was a complete lie.' The squadron commander, in keeping with his command responsibility, managed to conceal his true feelings well. Outside the hangar some squadron members lounged on the grass in the evening sun, while others sat in deckchairs. Then the time came to move. Equipment was piled into buses and trucks, men clambered aboard and off they moved to dispersal points. Here many, like O'Brien, saw Upkeep for the first time. Their surprise at the massive object suspended beneath the bomb bay vindicated the obsession with security.

At the aircraft superstition prevailed before crews of the first and second waves climbed aboard for final pre-flight tests and pilots formally signed the acceptance Form 700 proffered by the maintenance NCO. As was his wont, Whittaker watered the tail wheel of Martin's Lancaster, and Martin himself tucked a toy koala bear into his jacket as a good luck charm. Once the checks had been satisfactorily completed, the captains shut down the engines and waited for the time to depart. For some that period of waiting was 'the worst half-hour of the day'. At take-off, each aircraft carried 'I UPKEEP; 6 loose 4lb. INC.; Pyros'.

Shortly after 2100 Hutchison fired the red Very light as a signal for all first and second-wave aircraft to start engines, and pilots prepared to move from dispersals onto the perimeter track preparatory to take-off. At 2128 a green light flashed from the Aldis lamp at the control caravan and Barlow's aircraft – the first in the second wave – began to move northwards up the grass runway of RAF Scampton to set Operation Chastise in motion. Carrying maximum weight and such a cumbersome cargo, AJ-E was gradually hauled over the perimeter track and boundary fence before turning eastwards towards the North Sea.

F/Sgt Powell and his staff, who were still working at that late hour on a Sunday evening, briefly emerged from their offices. Herbert Jeffree and other civilian workers also looked on. Jeffree noted the long run necessary to get the laden aircraft off the ground against the background of a beautiful sunset and reflected that, although his job was done, theirs was about to begin. Another interested spectator noted the unusual shape of the Lancasters, with their bulging bellies, as they laboured skywards and, unusually, climbed away from the station without circling to gain height. LAC Drury was cycling home to his family in Lincoln on that beautiful, cloudless evening. He realised that these strange silhouettes had some connection with his recent work and, more especially, directly related to the aircraft which he had seen with its bulbous freight that afternoon. But Cochrane was right: Drury had no idea of the purpose or target to which the aircraft were directed. And a Royal Observer Corps post, reporting their progress to its control centre in Lincoln, commented prophetically: 'Looks like the Lancs. are going to do a bit more low-flying to-night.'

When the last aircraft of the first two waves had faded into the distance, the five reserve-wave crews drifted away. Over two hours of uncertainty remained for them: perhaps they would not be needed. Several passed the time with the aid of dice and playing cards, others behaved less predictably. Sgt Webb, convinced that he would not be coming back and determined to 'die clean,' took a bath. As he did so a 617 Squadron Lancaster was falling in flames off the Dutch island of Texel – the first, but not the last, to be lost that night.

8

Attack, Wave 1

MÖHNE AND EDER DAMS

That tragedy lay in the future as Gibson held AJ-G (ED932/G) ready for take-off, with Hopgood in AJ-M (ED925/G) to his right and Martin in AJ-P (ED909/G) on his left – though neither these nor any other Lancaster flew with the 'G' suffix on its fuselage. At 2139 the Aldis lamp from the control caravan signalled them on their way. Even without the sagging cargoes (which caused Gibson to dub his plane 'pregnant duck') and the enveloping framework of a setting sun, the spectacle of heavy bombers in a vic-three fighter formation would have been unusual. Gradually, almost painfully for onlookers and crews, in 'perfectly clear' weather and with a ghostly full moon already in the sky, each captain laboriously hauled his charge over the northern perimeter fence and then turned south-eastwards across the Wash and the familiar Wainfleet bombing range towards South-wold. Martin's navigator, Leggo, discovered that his compass read 5° low and thereafter made the necessary allowance.

Crossing the English coast on schedule, just under 40 minutes after take-off, Gibson's flight descended well below the maximum, although crews knew that their approach must be detected at some stage over the North Sea by enemy flak ships, other hostile vessels, reconnaissance aircraft or *Freya* radar. Behind, the Aurora Borealis neatly presented them in silhouette for the benefit of attacking fighters, which mercifully did not appear. The sea was so calm that the Lancasters could virtually skim the surface while the crews methodically performed more checks and drills. Navigators in all three aircraft threw out flame floats for rear gunners to estimate drift, which on this occasion proved virtually nil (1° starboard). In Martin's aircraft Simpson squinted down his gunsight at a second float to verify the first reading, but he did not test the guns, arguing that this wasted ammunition and that careful pre-flight checks on the ground should detect any malfunction. Each aircraft did try out its spotlights, however. Otherwise little happened to disturb a quiet passage, punctuated by frivolous messages passed between the aircraft by Aldis lamp. Gibson experienced trouble with his automatic pilot, which he eventually declared useless, and once a friendly convoy flashed a recognition challenge.

Stronger winds than anticipated were encountered over the North Sea and, moreover, the aircraft found themselves to starboard of the scheduled track. So not only did they reach the enemy coast late, but in the wrong place. Instead of turning in the mouth of the Scheldt river between Schouwen and Walcheren islands, they made landfall on Walcheren. Crossing that heavily defended island and South Beveland, the Lancasters hastily adjusted course for Roosendaal. Fortunately the enemy gunners did not react and the attackers were not punished for their error. Bomb-aimers now carried out initial fusing of the self-destructive pistol, which would be fully armed once Upkeep left the aircraft. Swiftly realising that they were indeed off course, Gibson climbed to 300ft to identify the expected windmill and wireless masts, and Taerum worked out an amended course. With Spafford in the bomb-aimer's position using a special roller, rather like 'a roll of lavatory paper' in his skipper's words, to assist the navigator in pinpointing salient features and avoiding dangerous high-tension cables, Gibson took the three aircraft towards Roosendaal and the intersection of three main railway lines 25km west of Breda. There, setting course almost due east, they soon picked up the Wilhelmina canal some 10km east of Goirle and followed its line, which conveniently ran between the fighter airfields at Gilze-Rijen to port and Eindhoven to starboard. At Beek, near the town of Helmond, the canal met another at right angles, and from this 'T' junction, so clear in the moonlight, the Lancasters turned towards the Rhine. So far they had experienced no opposition. Crossing the German frontier, in theory less than 45 minutes' flying time from the Möhne, they flew on completely unmolested; on the ground and in the air nothing stirred. Ahead the Rhine glistened attractively, but suddenly the crews realised that they were off track again, some six miles too far south. Banking sharply to port, Gibson flew up the Rhine towards the briefed turning point, a bend in the river near Rees. During this short flight, as the other two aircraft strove to regain formation, they experienced the first uncomfortable hostile reaction when barges on the Rhine and flak positions on its banks threw up a phalanx of shells, to which the air gunners responded with some warmth. The Lancasters reached the required bend without

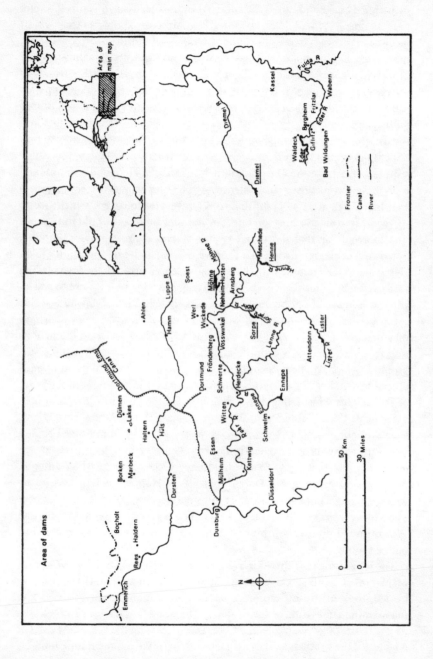

Area of dams

incurring damage and turned east along the amended track towards the lakes near Dülmen. When flying at such low altitude complete accuracy of navigation proved impossible. The aircraft again drifted off track and, moreover, surprise pockets of flak caused trouble. In the Buchholt-Borken area heavy concentrations of light flak backed up by an estimated 50 searchlights were identified, with a large number situated in emplacements south of Buchholt. North-west of Dorsten a defended position caused particular trouble: all three Lancasters were caught in its searchlights and the flak proved distinctly uncomfortable. A further dangerous concentration of light flak guns and approximately 12 searchlights east of Dülmen (possibly around a seasonal airfield) damaged the port wing of Hopgood's aircraft and caused Gibson to break radio silence. At 0007 his wireless operator sent a warning of flak at 51°48′N 07°12′E to 5 Group Headquarters, which Group rebroadcast to all attacking aircraft four minutes later. So low did the aircraft sink to avoid flak that shortly afterwards Hopgood's rear gunner, Burcher, noted with some trepidation that they were flying under high-tension cables. Flying north of Hamm, with its strong defences around the marshalling yards, Gibson led his flight on to the last major turning point, close to Ahlen, where a number of railway lines conspicuously met. Then flying almost due south between Werl and Soest, with its clutch of church spires, at length they breasted a tree-covered range of hills and looked down on the Möhne reservoir. The laconic words of an official report scarcely conveyed the problems which had been encountered: 'Various small [sic] flak posts opened up and as the aircraft flew over a defended area they were caught in the beam of searchlights while flying at a very low level, but their low level and high speed helped them escape from the searchlights and flak. Several searchlights were shot out of action.' Later maps show no deviation from briefed routes, and many accounts of the operation portray Gibson triumphantly leading his force to the target area. Simpson's diary recalled a somewhat different picture. After crossing the Dutch coast: 'Lost Hoppy! later picked up by some searchlights near Rhine – shot some out somewhere – bit off track over some town – bags of shooting – lost Winco – arrived Möhne Hoppy and Winco turned up'. Gibson himself admitted to being off course more than once en route.

The second flight of three aircraft, led by Young in AJ-A (ED877/G), with Maltby in AJ-J (ED906/G) to his right and Shannon in AJ-L (ED929/G) on his left, took off from Scampton at 2147, eight minutes after Gibson and followed the same route to the Möhne. In his log AJ-J's navigator noted that its last-resort target would be the Lister Dam. Crossing the Wash, the crew of AJ-J tested the spotlights. They switched off the IFF equipment nine minutes after leaving the coast and reached the turning point in the Scheldt estuary accurately, if late, at 2312 despite being well starboard of the planned track for some distance over the North Sea. The mine was then fused and almost

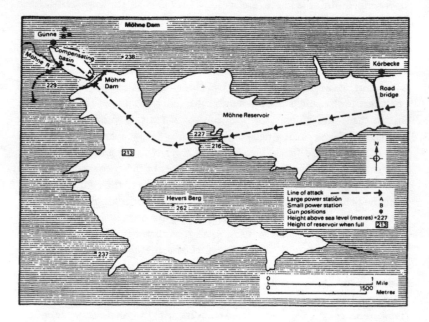

immediately 'evasive action' became necessary to avoid flak short of Roosendaal. Maltby's navigator noted that Young 'turned too soon' at the canal intersection near Beck, but did not record 'Gee jammed something chronic' until 15 miles short of the Rhine. Just after turning at Dülmen the pilot took more evasive action to avoid flak north of Ludinghausen and again near Ahlen, finally reaching the Möhne at 0026. Unlike Spafford, Shannon's bomb-aimer (Sumpter) did not use a roller to assist his map reading, but had folded 1:250,000 maps with high-tension wires brilliantly etched in red. Turning points, starkly illuminated in the bright moonlight, were easily seen and he had no difficulty in spotting danger in sufficient time for the Lancaster to hop over in safety. Perversely, Sumpter did not wear a parachute, seeing no point in trying to bale out at treetop height. Young persisted in flying too high (still only some 500ft), to the alarm of Shannon and Maltby, both of whom made their feelings known over the R/T. This tendency not to hug contours closely would cost the crew their lives later that night, but as formation leader Young did need to climb before the turning points to assist identification. Nor was navigation perfect with this flight. Shannon arrived at the Möhne after the other two. Flying over the right-hand tower, the Lancaster was 'hosepiped' by the gunners, to the verbal consternation of Sumpter. In this encounter AJ-L suffered its only structural damage of the operation, a tiny hole in the fuselage.

The final flight of the nine aircraft directly under Gibson's control experienced rather more discomfort and lost one of its number before the Möhne. Led by Maudslay in AJ-Z (ED937/G), with Astell in AJ-B (ED864/G) and Knight with AJ-N (ED912/G) to right and left respectively, it left Scampton at 2159. As with the two previous vic threes, although the approach to the Dutch coast was unchallenged, crossing the North Sea took longer than anticipated. This was due to two major variations from the planned track over East Anglia and the North Sea, the stronger winds and drift of 2° starboard. The mine was fused in AJ-N as the aircraft crossed the English coast over Southwold at 2248, and short of the enemy coast Hobday noted that the API was 'not working'. Nevertheless, the three Lancasters flew over the Scheldt estuary accurately though slightly behind schedule at 2321. Like Simpson, O'Brien in Knight's rear turret did not test his guns in anger over the sea, nor did Hobday, the navigator, use flame floats to estimate drift. And although the aircraft did fly in formation, Hobday insisted on strict individual navigation, which paid off in following 'the excellent route . . . with its recognisable turning points and short distance between them.' Once over land O'Brien was conscious of the illuminating effect of the full moon: 'Farm houses, canals, some people, rivers, canals, roads, haystacks, gun positions were easily seen.' Somewhat wistfully he later observed: 'I would like to do it again, now that I could enjoy the thrill.' Shortly after crossing the Dutch coast, O'Brien noted in the distance what he thought was an aircraft on fire to starboard; it is just possible, though unlikely due to the distance and the low altitude of AJ-N, that this was Barlow's crash on the east bank of the Rhine. In the bomb-aimer's position Johnson carried out, in his own words, 'super map reading' with a roller map, while Hobday checked pinpoints and Gee readings, calculating the new heading and time to the next turning point. Fortunately he had 'extraordinarily good Gee' well over the Continent and, in contrast to some other navigators, beyond normal range. Johnson and O'Brien agreed that for AJ-N there was 'no real trouble – some flak, some searchlights'. But that did not apply to one aircraft of their three.

Between the turning points near Rees on the Rhine and Dülmen, Astell crashed. The defended position north-west of Dorsten, over which Gibson, Hopwood and Martin had flown some 20 minutes earlier, caused his destruction. Up to this point Maudslay's three aircraft had kept formation with little difficulty. Just short of the position, Astell seemed uncertain of an intermediate pinpoint, hesitated to turn with the other two and thus trailed some way behind them when he did eventually do so. Looking back through the astrodome, Knight's wireless operator, Kellow, saw two lines of tracer intersecting in a brilliant criss-cross. Through this Astell flew at 0015, and although his gunners vigorously returned fire he did not survive the ordeal. When eight miles north-west of Dorsten Kellow watched the aircraft become swiftly engulfed in flames about two miles astern, and shortly afterwards he and Hobday reported an explosion on the ground. Strangely, 617 Squadron's operation record book would suggest that Astell was leading the formation, 'appeared uncertain of his whereabouts, and on reaching a canal crossing actually crossed at the correct place, turned south down the canal as though searching for a pinpoint. He fell about ½ mile behind his accompanying aircraft doing this and got slightly off track.' Another curious feature is that some records suggest that Astell was shot down over an airfield. But no airfield, 'temporary or otherwise,' could later be traced within 30km of Dorsten to the north-west; and it seems likely that after the event the defended position west of Dülmen and the seasonal airfield east of it were confused.

Virtually at the precise moment that Astell crashed, Martin crested the ridge immediately north of the Möhne. When Hopgood and Gibson joined him, the Wing Commander remarked how 'grey and solid . . . squat and heavy and unconquerable' the dam looked. As they orbited, however, the crews of AJ-G, AJ-M and AJ-P admired the moonlit scene in a detached way, even though the defences were already proving spiteful. Briefing had been accurate: no balloons and no searchlights, but active light flak – the battery seemed intent on belying its caustic nickname of the 'Möhne Flak Sanatorium'. 20mm or 37mm weapons were identified on each sluice tower. Another position on an extension of the wall beyond the right-hand tower and others in meadowland north of the dam and east of the equalising basin in the area of the village of Günne led Gibson erroneously to report 'two positions on the north bank of the Lake on each side of the dam'. Up to 12 guns were estimated, three of which would be able to fire practically horizontally at aircraft over the final exposed approach run. The drama which was now unfolding contrasted with the peaceful Sunday scene on the lake a few hours earlier as people flocked there to celebrate Mother's Day, the officer in charge of the flak battery enjoyed his birthday (curiously, 16 May was also the birthday of Gibson's father), and other military personnel took advantage of the fine weather to sunbathe. The Lancaster crews heard Gibson say 'stand by, chaps, I'm going to look the place over' and saw him make a dummy run over the dam, a manoeuvre which confused German records into claiming that six

Lancasters attacked the Möhne. AJ-G passed through the brilliant lattice of flak unharmed and without revealing the proposed method, direction or altitude of attack. As the aircraft turned to port and flew back over the high ground west of the Heve valley towards Körbecke, the others heard Gibson say that he 'liked the look of it'.

At this point the second flight – AJ-A, AJ-J and AJ-L – arrived. Sumpter, Shannon's bomb-aimer, immediately noticed the steepness of the hills and Walker, the navigator, had time to reflect that light flak would be 'beautiful in all its different colours' if it were not so dangerous. But the time for reconnaissance was over, as the darkness imperceptibly ebbed. Every moment's delay increased the danger of night fighters and, furthermore, the enemy coast had to be cleared before dawn.

The agreed tactic was for aircraft to attack individually on instructions from the leader. After diving over the Körbecke bridge, each would fly along the Möhne sleeve of the reservoir and hop over the convenient spit which jutted out from the northern extremity of the tree-covered Hevers Berg, dividing the two lakes. The aircraft would then line up to attack the dam from a distance of 1,500m. This manoeuvre would provide cover from defending guns until that last open stretch over the water, but would require aircraft to adjust their line of approach and achieve the correct height and speed while under heavy fire. For the convenient spit was to the right of an ideal approach, a difficulty which possibly caused two mines to fall short or veer harmlessly left.

Over the R/T Gibson warned the other five aircraft to be prepared to attack when ordered, and he reminded Hopgood to assume control if anything happened to him. As the aircraft crossed the spit for the last stretch, Taerum switched on the spotlights and gave Gibson instructions until he was satisfied that the Lancaster was flying at precisely 60ft. Pulford ensured the correct speed and Hutchison checked that Upkeep was back-spinning in its retaining arms at 500 rpm. In the nose Spafford concentrated on releasing the mine at exactly the required position, while Deering sprayed the defences. Threatened by the angry flak, Gibson suddenly felt his aircraft 'very small' and vulnerable. He experienced spasms of extreme fear, but resolutely flew on. Brave men are those who overcome fear, and Gibson was a very brave man. Despite the hot fire, possibly because the low-level approach confused the gunners, AJ-G once more crossed the dam unscathed, having this time dropped its Upkeep at 0028 at a ground speed of 230 mph on a bearing of 330°M (variation – 5°8') in 'bright moon, no cloud, very good visibility'. Looking back, Trevor-Roper in the rear turret saw the bomb bounce three times and, after some ten seconds delay as it sank, a tremendous sheet of water surge high over the wall.

In Shannon's crew Walker noted from afar how the flak tracer increased in intensity as Gibson neared the dam. When 'a great spout of water' went up after 'a terrific explosion' he felt sure that the dam wall must have been broken. Wishful thinking. The water subsided, and the dam still held. Hutchison signalled to 5 Group that the mine had exploded 5–50 yards from the dam without breaching it. 'Goner 68A' signified bitter disappointment.

Five minutes passed before the water settled and the spray obscuring the dam cleared. Gibson then called Hopgood to attack, and as he prepared to do so Maudslay and Knight arrived. This time the flak gunners were not surprised. As Hopgood crossed the water, crews of the other aircraft saw the Lancaster hit several times. Gibson noted a hit in the port outer, but the inner engine was also damaged for Burcher found that his power-operated turret, which relied on this source for its power, would not work. Clearly, too, the starboard wing had been hit, and amid all this confusion AJ-M dropped its Upkeep late. Instead of striking the face of the dam, the mine bounced over the wall and landed in the vicinity of the power station beyond. As the stricken aircraft crossed the dam, in accordance with the operation order and as Hutchison had done during Gibson's attack, Hopgood's wireless operator fired a red Very cartridge. From the rear of Martin's aircraft, Simpson noticed that AJ-M was enveloped in flames at this point and concluded that a petrol tank must have been hit. From Shannon's aircraft the navigator, Walker, noted 'a sheet of orange flame out from the side of the aircraft – he'd been hit'. Gibson, Maltby and Shannon's bomb-aimer, Sumpter, saw the aircraft struggle to about 500ft before exploding. One wing fell off and it finally plunged to the ground near the village of Ostönnen 6km north-west of the dam, where it burned furiously throughout the ensuing action. In his report Gibson suggested that some of Hopgood's crew might have baled out, thanks to their skipper's valiant efforts to gain height. Three did escape, though only two survived to become prisoners of war.

When the loss of hydraulic power occurred, Burcher had to crank his turret round by hand until he could get back into the fuselage, where his parachute was stacked. As Hopgood fought to get the Lancaster up, Burcher had no choice but to escape via the crew door at the starboard rear of the fuselage, an exit officially discouraged for fear that the escaper would injure himself against the tail section. Burcher realised that the aircraft was on fire at about the time that the mine dropped, heard the flight engineer confirm the seriousness of the situation over the intercom and prepared to bale out. The last words he recalled were from Hopgood: 'For Christ's sake get out of here.' As he left his turret to collect the parachute, he saw Minchin, the wireless operator, crawling down the steeply inclined fuselage towards him. Wounded as he was, Minchin must have made a supreme effort to get over the main spar. Knowing that he had a parachute buckled on, Burcher pushed his colleague out of the aircraft, pulling the ripcord as he did so. To no avail, for Minchin did not survive; AJ-M was too low for a conventional parachute drop. In a less orthodox manner, Burcher pulled his parachute open as he crouched in the doorway and held the billowing silk in his arms. Suddenly there was a tremendous explosion and he came to on the ground. Recovering full consciousness after a while, he appreciated the wisdom of not using the crew entrance door as an escape hatch. His back was severely damaged, and thus immobile he was captured without resistance. Some time later, back in England, survivors heard that he had been thrown out of the aircraft as it hit the ground; but this was a garbled version of a report referring to another rear gunner who survived that night.

Hopgood's bomb-aimer, the Canadian F/Sgt Fraser, was the other member of the crew to escape from the doomed aircraft and live. He did not use the chinagraph variation of the special bomb sight, but the original Dann version, which he described as 'a wooden box with two points on it'. Approaching the dam, he waited for the two sluice towers to appear to move outwards until they coincided with the 'two points,' when he would press the button to release Upkeep. As AJ-M steadied over the water, he had time to reflect that for the flak gunners it would be 'pretty simple duck shooting,' with the victim conveniently illuminated by its own lights. He mused, too, over Gibson's R/T call to attack: 'Cooler 2, it's your turn to attack. It's a piece of cake.' Far from true. The defences knew what to expect and weapons on the towers 'crossed up on us,' reinforced by the light flak gun in the third position on the dam wall. The fire was 'intense,' though there was 'no alternative but to fly through the middle of it'. Orders were that if the mine could not be dropped accurately, the aircraft must overshoot and go round for another attack. Just as Fraser considered doing this, the aircraft was hit. He released the mine, knowing that he had done so late. From terse intercom exchanges – the same ones to alert Burcher – he gathered that fire had broken out in the starboard wing, with one engine immediately alight. Attempts by the flight engineer, Brennan, to quell the blaze failed and about 25 seconds after crossing the dam the pilot ordered his crew to bale out. In the nose Fraser had no idea how serious the situation was behind him or who had been hit. Lying over the escape hatch, he reached behind for his parachute, pulled the hatch open and, as the manuals prescribed, knelt facing forward. Peering through the gaping hole he was not impressed by the view: 'trees looked awful damned close'. Realising that he had no chance of survival if he jumped out before pulling the ripcord, he decided to do so inside the aircraft, let the parachute billow out in front and pull him after it. This unorthodox exit, not dissimilar from Burcher's, worked. Later he recorded: 'The tail wheel whizzed passed my ear,' before he swung to a vertical position and two or three seconds later touched the ground. He had escaped uninjured, but while in the air had seen the Lancaster crash. Meanwhile the mine had fallen between the dam and the main power station, exploding at about the time that AJ-M hit the ground. The self-destructive fuse, fully armed on release from the aircraft, worked. Although little damage occurred to the dam wall, the power house suffered severely and its seven transformers, containing 2,700gal of oil, exploded with 'a gigantic flash'.

At 0038 Martin carried out the third attack, precisely ten minutes after Gibson. At this point, with evidence of Hopgood's failure burning fiercely, Gibson's leadership and Martin's courage ensured that the operation would not disintegrate. As Martin attacked, Gibson flew slightly ahead of him to starboard to distract the gunners and perhaps silence some of the guns on the dam and beyond before Martin came within range. He crossed the dam close to the right-hand tower and the third flak position, turning to port over the equalising basin near the small power station for Trevor-Roper to engage positions below Günne. In the meantime Martin was attacking. The right-hand sluice tower was clearly visible but smoke from Hopgood's mine partly obscured the left-hand one, as AJ-P approached at a ground speed of 217 mph on a bearing of 335°M. The aircraft was hit by flak though Whittaker, the flight engineer, knew that none of the full tanks had been holed; the extent of the damage remained obscure until the aircraft landed at Scampton again. Martin experienced no difficulty in handling the Lancaster over the water and at 0038 Hay dropped the mine, which had been spun at 480 rpm. Chambers fired the Very pistol over the dam and the aircraft pulled up safely, turning to port away from the Günne flak. Martin reported a huge explosion and a waterspout rising high above the smoke, which prevented the rear gunner from seeing how many times the mine bounced. In fact once more the dam had not been breached, for this mine sheered off to the left of the dam, finishing close to the western banks of the reservoir. It thoroughly drenched gunners on the left-hand tower and officially burst 'almost twenty yards short'. Of his experience at the Möhne, Simpson baldly wrote: 'Hoppy shot down. We were next – shot up badly, got through however.' Once more a disappointing message went back to Grantham: 'Goner 58A'.

Three aircraft had thus attacked the Möhne without success. Gibson now called in AJ-A, the fourth. This time Gibson patrolled the air (northern) side of the dam beyond the line of attack, in an attempt to draw the fire of guns

on the dam away from Young and occupy the attention of those near
Günne. As a further distraction Martin flew in with Young on his left. Five
minutes after Martin completed his attack, Young came over the spit to the
exposed stretch of water and his navigator switched on the spotlights.
Gibson's gunners engaged the enemy fire from the far side of the wall, and
AJ-G also flicked its identification lights on and off further to distract them
from the approaching Lancaster. Gibson noted that Young's mine made
'three good bounces,' apparently hit the dam and exploded in contact with it
exactly as Wallis planned. A vast column of water rose up and splashed over
the dam wall down into the basin beyond. Young – and momentarily Gibson
– was convinced that the wall had been broken, but yet again the turmoil
subsided and no breach became apparent. Although 'Goner 78A' – indicating another failure – was sent, Gibson felt sure that the structure had been
damaged.

He called in his fifth Lancaster, piloted by Maltby. For this attack Gibson
joined Martin in engaging enemy positions from the water side of the dam as
the two aircraft orbited to starboard and port respectively. Visibility for
Maltby was good, though later he argued that it would have been better to
attack with the moon behind the dam rather than behind the aircraft, which
were so conveniently silhouetted for the enemy gunners. Both towers were
clearly visible and, after establishing the correct height, AJ-J attacked at a
groundspeed of 223 mph on a course of 330°M. Suddenly Maltby realised
that 'the crown of the wall was already crumbling . . . [with] a tremendous
amount of debris on the top' and that there was a 'breach in the centre of
the dam': Young, the fourth attacker, had been successful after all, and
Wallis's theory had been vindicated. Neither Gibson, Hopgood nor Martin
had dropped their mines as predicted, and the first mine to strike the dam
correctly had breached it. Maltby veered to port and at 0049 dropped his
mine. It bounced four times, struck the dam and exploded: but in the
confusion of fire from ground and air and the inevitable swirl of water, its
effect could not be gauged. Maltby recorded: 'Our load sent up water and
mud to a height of a thousand feet. The spout of water was silhouetted
against the moon. It rose with tremendous speed and then gently fell back.
You could see the shock wave at the base of the jet.' Unaccountably, at 0050
Stone, the wireless operator, sent another disappointing 'Goner 78A' to
Grantham. Gibson warned Shannon to prepare for his attack, when as the
water subsided he suddenly realised that the dam had been shattered, though
why Maltby had not reported Young's breach by R/T is a mystery. Flying
closer, Gibson noticed water pouring through the shattered dam: even as he
looked it surged down the valley, 'looking like stirred porridge in the

moonlight'. Nicholson, Maltby's navigator, dubbed the result 'wizard' in his log but remarked as well 'flak none too light'.

Warning Shannon not to attack, at 0056 Gibson told Hutchison to signal 'Nigger' – the code word for success – to 5 Group, which repeated the message for confirmation to avoid misunderstanding. The seven surviving 617 Squadron Lancasters at the Möhne congregated to see evidence of their success as the embers of Hopgood's aircraft still glowed in the distance. A single gun position on the dam sought to engage them, but was swiftly silenced. The watchers above, feeling strangely remote, observed without comprehending the full significance of the scene unfolding below them. Shannon described it as 'a most fabulous sight' to see the water pouring through the dam and down the valley, gaining visible momentum. He found it 'almost impossible to describe the elation in success'. Gibson later wrote: 'This was a tremendous sight, a sight which probably no man will ever see again,' and Simpson recorded: 'I have vivid memories of seeing a huge sheet of water as the dam gave way.'

Aware that they must yet attack other dams, Gibson curbed the excited R/T chatter. In accordance with the operational plan, Martin and Maltby turned for home. The three Lancasters still carrying Upkeep – those piloted by Shannon, Maudslay and Knight – and Young, who would act as deputy leader in an emergency, were ordered by Gibson to follow him to 'B target,' the Eder. Under instructions from him, but without flying in formation, the five aircraft set out on a south-easterly course from the southern tip of the Möhne Lake for an estimated 14-minute flight.

Back in England, those anxiously awaiting news of the operation relied entirely upon W/T transmissions from the aircraft. Harris admitted that those who knew that the operation was under way were 'in a considerable state of excitement'. Cochrane and Wallis saw the nine aircraft of Gibson's wave and the five detailed for the Sorpe Dam off from Scampton, and at 2300 left by car for HQ 5 Group at Grantham. Almost at that exact moment, Munro's aircraft sustained damage which would lead it to abort the operation, and AJ-K crashed into the Waddenzee. At Grantham, Cochrane and Wallis joined Harris, Satterly and duty staff in the underground operations room. A long, narrow construction, it had a raised platform down one side where the chief signals officer, Dunn, sat. On the opposite wall was the operational board chalked with details of Chastise, which would soon show returning and missing aircraft, and at one end a vast map of Europe. To the usual cluster of WAAF and RAF personnel it was another operation, another night on duty, even though the presence of Harris and Wallis suggested something extraordinary afoot. To Satterly it was all 'very exciting,' especially as this was the first time that 5 Group could contact attacking crews direct by W/T. At Scampton Jeffree, and others aware of the unique nature of the operation, waited for news to filter through via the well worn grapevine. Summers lounged in a mess chair and somebody was prevailed upon to reopen the bar.

In the 5 Group ops room nobody relaxed. While senior officers talked quietly, Wallis designer Chadwick (who had wanted to fly on the operation himself) talked quietly, Wallis paced up and down in a state of acute anxiety. To Cochrane he seemed to be 'having kittens'. As each W/T morse message came through, it was so clear that Dunn read it over the telephone, which he had plugged into the radio receiver, quickly decoded it and passed the gist to the waiting throng. Transmission proved so simple that Cochrane could question Gibson 'and obtain the reply within the minute'. When the first signal of 'Goner' came in, Wallis muttered in despair: 'No, it's no good'. Then came a long delay of 13 minutes between Gibson's 'Goner,' not sent until 0037, and Young's, for some reason received three minutes before that of Martin. Young's 'Goner' made Wallis bury his head in his hands. It also created considerable alarm among the Service officers, who knew that Hopgood and Martin were due to attack before him, and Satterly had a mental vision of utter disaster. Within two minutes of the fourth 'Goner' message, however, 'Nigger' had been received and confirmed by Hutchison. Satterly saw Wallis leap in the air and pump both arms vigorously upwards. Officers vied to shake his hand, and in that brief moment elation replaced despair. As Harris congratulated the engineer, he said: 'Wallis, I didn't believe a word you said, when you came to see me. But now you could sell me a pink elephant.' The reaction and exact words remained indelibly stained in the minds of both men thereafter. Equally, the image of that scene stayed vividly with Satterly and Cochrane. It was one of those emotional moments which persist in memory for a lifetime. The Möhne Dam had been breached.

The five aircraft flying to the Eder encountered no hostile activity on the cross-country flight, but they had great difficulty in finding the dam. Below, the steep valleys and tree-covered hillsides were laced with rivers and dotted with small lakes and isolated villages. Unwary pilots could breast one hill to discover a dangerous Spion Kop immediately behind, and electricity pylons signalled an ever-present additional peril. Gibson reached the Eder Lake too far west. Flying east, he spent a hazardous five minutes discovering the dam, tucked beneath its steep hill beyond a sharp bend in the reservoir. Navigation was much hampered by early-morning mist gathering over the water, and the narrow, winding nature of the reservoir, with its sharp, tree-lined banks, also contributed to the general murkiness. The neighbourhood of the dam was relatively clear, but only Young and Gibson found it quickly. The other three aircraft were nowhere to be seen. Like Gibson, Shannon reached the Eder too far west, then compounded his error by initially flying in the wrong direction. Corrected onto an easterly course by his navigator, he reached what he thought was the target at Rehbach, 2.5km west of the Eder Dam. Extraordinarily, it too was situated on the eastern side of a sharp bend and its attacking approach lay roughly along the expected bearing. Although puzzled by the non-appearance of the others, Shannon was about to begin a run over the dam when Gibson's voice came up on R/T. He announced that he would fire

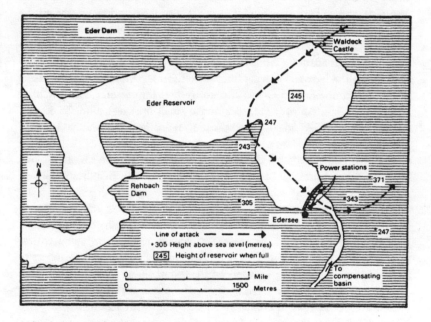

red Very lights from his position over the dam, which enabled Shannon to join him and the other three Lancasters. The firing of these lights created a myth that during subsequent attacks Gibson sent up Very cartridges behind the target to illuminate it. As they circled to port, the five aircraft took stock of the situation. The formidable task of diving from some 1,000ft over Waldeck Castle and down to the lake, executing a tight port turn, hopping over a spit of land and then settling at 60ft for the final approach seemed even more daunting than at the briefings. There was one bonus – no flak. The dam was defended by two sentries armed with rifles.

With the time now approaching 0130, Gibson was anxious to press on with the attack and start for home. He ordered Shannon in first. Three or four times he flew over the dam without releasing his mine because it proved impossible to achieve the correct height after the steep dive and sharp turn. Maudslay then tried twice, but experienced similar problems, until at length Shannon executed his attack after two more dummy runs. Approaching on a course of 150°M (variation −05°04′) at a ground speed of 220 mph in 'bright moonlight, no cloud and visibility of ten miles' – the latter figure was altered to 'three miles' on one post-raid report – he dropped his mine at 0139. It bounced twice before making contact with the dam and its explosion was followed by the now familiar upsurge of water, estimated at 1,000ft high. With his landing lights on to aid illumination of the dreaded hill beyond the dam, Shannon rose to safety. Gibson and Knight's crew, which attacked later, could not identify specific damage from the mine and officially 'no result was seen,' although Shannon felt certain that he had made a breach in the Eder wall. Inexplicably, even allowing for problems of terrain and organisation of the attacks at the Eder, 5 Group did not receive the message 'Goner 79B' – explosion in contact with the Eder and a small breach – until 0206, after messages from AJ-Z and AJ-N and the crucial one from Gibson that the dam had been breached.

Maudslay then made his third run on the target. Gibson saw something hanging down from the Lancaster, which he believed to indicate damage suffered between the Scheldt and Rhine. He and other watchers saw Maudslay's mine drop too late, hit the parapet hard and detonate 'with a cordite flash,' as Wallis had predicted it would if the store struck with great velocity. But, significantly, before the explosion, a red Very light went up from the aircraft, indicating that it was then crossing the dam. Members of Knight's crew – especially Johnson and Hobday – were adamant that AJ-Z was beyond the explosion when it occurred. Gibson recorded that the mine had struck the parapet of the dam and exploded 'with a slow, yellow, vivid flame which lit up the whole valley like daylight for just a few seconds,' and that he saw the aircraft 'banking steeply a few feet above it'. As Knight's crew reported, AJ-Z was actually beyond the explosion, not above it. Shannon's crew did not see the sequence of events, only the lurid flash; though they and Knight's crew reinforced Gibson's contention that he made faint contact with Maudslay after the explosion. To his urgent second enquiry by R/T if he were 'OK,' Maudslay replied: 'I think so, stand by'. Sgt O'Brien thought the sound 'very faint,' unnatural and almost dehumanised. But it was most definitely heard. Gibson reported: 'The mine overshot and struck the parapet, detonating instantaneously. The pilot was spoken to afterwards by R/T and was heard to reply once, when he sounded very weak.' Nevertheless, effectively

Maudslay had vanished, and the official verdict was that he had 'probably' been killed at 0156 by the force of the explosion of his own mine as it hit the crest of the dam. Yet, even if the R/T contact were imagined, 5 Group noted 'Goner 28B' – mine released and 'overshot' with no damage to the dam – from AJ-Z. However, '0156' – 17 minutes after Shannon's attack and four minutes after Knight's – is clearly an inaccurate record of Maudslay's time of attack. More probably this occurred at about 0145, which suggests that the 5 Group report may include a typing error for '0146' (although yet another official record states '0150') or rationalised that AJ-Z must have attacked at 0156 because its wireless operator sent a W/T message a minute later. Later evidence supports the conclusion that Maudslay did in fact survive at the Eder.

This was not certain at the time, however, and with darkness fast paling Gibson had still not broken the dam. Strangely, for the first time on W/T, he called up Astell in AJ-B at 0147 and 0150. There was no reply, so he knew for certain that only AJ-N could finish the job. Like Shannon, Knight had great difficulty in securing the required speed and alignment after the steep drop from the castle. He made one dummy run, during which O'Brien 'never thought we would get over the mountain' beyond the dam. Throughout this period the R/T hummed continuously with advice from the other aircraft, but for the actual attack Knight told Kellow to switch it off. O'Brien recalled how meticulous Knight was in ensuring the correct conditions, as he approached at a ground speed of 222 mph on a course of 135°M, 15° left of Shannon's approach run, in 'perfect visibility' with a bright moon on the starboard beam. The mine was released at 0152, bounced three times and hit the wall slightly right of centre. In the rear turret O'Brien confessed to considerable qualms about the outcome, 'waiting for it to explode [under the aircraft] like Maudslay'. Nothing happened until they had climbed to a safe height. Knight then reported: 'Large breach in wall of dam almost 30ft below top of dam, leaving top of dam intact. Torrent of water pouring through breach caused tidal wave almost 30ft high half a mile down valley from the dam.' Flying above Knight's aircraft, some 500m to starboard, Gibson had a clear view of the earthquake effect of the explosion on the base of the dam and of the structure collapsing 'as if a gigantic hand had pushed a hole through cardboard'. From his grandstand perch in the rear turret of AJ-N as it rose steeply over the far hill, O'Brien saw the destruction from a different angle: 'I was the only one of our crew to have a front centre seat at the breaching of the Eder as our aircraft was standing on its tail for the climb out. Simultaneously, the dam broke and a column of water rose vertically behind us. It is the column of water that I remember most vividly . . . it was like a plume. I exaggerate when I say it rose a 1,000ft, it only seemed like it.' He had never dreamed that the water would rush up to meet him in quite such an alarming manner. In fact, O'Brien was not alone in witnessing the scene from Knight's Lancaster. Kellow, the wireless operator, was standing with his head in the blister of the astrodome, also looking behind: 'When we passed over the dam wall at the Eder we had to clear a large hill directly ahead of us. After the mine had been dropped Les [Knight] pulled the nose up quite steeply in order to clear this hill and in doing so I could look back and down at the dam wall. It was still intact for a short while, then as if some huge fist had been jabbed at the wall a large almost round black hole appeared and water gushed as from a large hose.'

Neither Knight, Grayston the flight engineer, Sutherland the front gunner nor Johnson the bomb-aimer was in a position to savour these delights, as Johnson recorded: 'The recovery from low level as the bomb was released to clear the large hill immediately facing the dam wall was quite hair raising and required the full attention of the pilot and engineer to lay on emergency power from the engines and a climbing attitude not approved in any flying manuals and a period of nail biting from the rest of us not least me who was getting a too close view of the approaching terra firma from my position in the bomb-aimer's compartment.' In Shannon's aircraft Sumpter heard 'one hell of a bang' and almost immediately the rear gunner, Buckley, yelled over the intercom: 'It's gone!' Flying over the crumbling masonry, the crew saw water rushing down the valley and Sumpter watched in fascination as car lights disappeared beneath the flood, changing colour perceptibly as they slipped into permanent darkness. By the time that Knight had lifted over the hill, recovered flying equilibrium and circled for a closer look at the results of his efforts, the bridge which had remained over the hole in the dam had been swept away and in his excitement Knight began to follow the wave down the valley until recalled by Gibson. O'Brien thought the murky flood resembled treacle and, like Sumpter, saw a car sink beneath the torrent, its lights turning green. Meanwhile, the ether crackled with excited comments, many of them unprintable. O'Brien experienced a feeling of 'great joy. We felt the exquisite pleasure one feels when he had completed a difficult task perfectly.'

Undeterred by the prevailing enthusiasm and the sight below, at 0154 Hutchison sent 'Dinghy' – the signal for success at the Eder – to 5 Group, which asked for and received confirmation a minute later. Not until over six minutes had passed did AJ-N transmit 'Goner 710B,' indicating a large breach in the dam. And now came the sobering reality that, although they had completed the operation most successfully by breaching the Möhne and Eder dams, the crews had to face a long journey home. Undoubtedly the defences would be thoroughly alert and night fighters no longer conspicuous by their ineffective absence. Over the R/T Gibson said: 'Good show, boys, let's all go home and get pie.' O'Brien agreed that 'we didn't stick around too long'. Nevertheless, as the crews set off they were still chattering excitedly to one another. Indeed, so elated were they that at 0257 Shannon's crew repeated their message to 5 Group: 'Goner 79B'. Meanwhile, receipt of 'Dinghy' at Grantham had provoked an encore of mutual congratulation. Harris immediately phoned Washington, and a delightful story thereafter circulated that instead of calling the White House in the United States a confused operator connected him with a local hostelry of the same name. As with all such fictions, the truth dims by comparison. Harris was put through to Washington very quickly and spoke to the CAS, Portal, without difficulty. Portal congratulated him and all civilian and Service personnel responsible for the night's successes, and he undertook to inform Churchill without delay. But the operation was not yet over. At 0210 5 Group asked Gibson how many aircraft of the first wave were available to attack the Sorpe. His reply, 'none,' meant that the work of the first wave had officially ended. All that was left for the survivors was to make their way back to Scampton. One would not succeed, and others were to experience many problems before at length they touched down.

When Gibson led Young, Shannon, Maudslay and Knight off to the Eder, Maltby flew back from the Möhne to Scampton via the designated exit route 1, skirting the Ruhr to the east, then flying north-west to the Ijsselmeer and out over the North Sea across the neck of the Helder peninsula north of Alkmaar at 0153. Except for brief 'evasive action' near Ahlen, his return flight was largely uneventful, although he reported 'flak north of coast and searchlight' (possibly on the southern tip of Texel) and the navigator had great difficulty with Gee, which was 'still no dice' over the Netherlands and 'faint but workable' 15 minutes later. Over the North Sea AJ-J for some reason again tested the spotlights and finally landed unscathed at Scampton at 0311, the first of the attacking aircraft to reach base. Martin also flew back to Scampton direct from the Möhne as laid down in the operation order and along the same exit route. His rear gunner recorded: 'On the way back we saw nothing, thank goodness, but by then I think we were flying at less than 50ft.' Martin's celebrated habit of brushing treetops on the return from an operation had given him ample practice for this. In his diary Simpson also noted a reaction to the loss of Hopgood: 'Felt madder than Hell – returned to base OK.' To Whittaker, the flight engineer, the homeward flight was 'no problem'. On landing at 0319, he discovered that the starboard 3 (outer) fuel tank had been ruptured at the Möhne. Fortunately it had already been emptied in accordance with the normal practice of draining the outer wing tanks first. Damage to the starboard aileron had been incurred too. In all it was relatively minor, but Martin reacted violently in the atmosphere of operational tension. When the test pilot, Summers, arrived at the aircraft to greet him, he complained bitterly about the impertinence of flak gunners in holing 'Popsie,' his pet name for AJ-P.

Shannon was the next to land. Although he followed the same route as Maltby and Martin in its later stages over the Ijsselmeer and Helder, he did not fly via the Möhne, as the operation order required. Like the two preceding aircraft, he had an uninterrupted flight, which added to the crew's high spirits. Shannon admitted to being 'terribly elated' and aching to get back for the inevitable party. Three miles short of the North Sea, over the Helder peninsula, he took AJ-L up to an unprecedented 800ft and crossed the shore in a fast dive at almost 300 mph, reaching base at 0406, after six hours and 29 minutes in the air. One tiny hole, suffered when flying too close to the right-hand sluice tower on arrival at the Möhne, represented the sum total of the damage to ED929/G.

Nine minutes later Gibson landed. He flew from the Eder via the Möhne, where for three miles below the dam the river had swollen to 'several times its normal size'. The level of the reservoir had dropped appreciably, with pleasure boats already stranded on exposed mud and sand. Fearful lest he be caught over enemy territory in daylight, Gibson did not linger to admire the squadron's handiwork, but set course for the Ijsselmeer. He followed the third exit route, which crossed the Helder peninsula north of Haarlem and south of the track flown by Maltby, Martin and Shannon, but deviated through a known gap in the coastal defences near Egmond. At one point, warned by the rear-gunner of a possible night fighter in pursuit, he dropped low enough to tickle hedges at a speed of some 240 mph. If it were a fighter it did not come within range. Away to port the crew saw an aircraft shot down over Hamm and hoped perversely that a fighter had fallen victim to flak guns. In reality they had witnessed the end of a reserve wave aircraft on the way to its target. Fifteen minutes from the coast Gibson called up Young by R/T: there was no reply. Like Shannon, Gibson climbed shortly before the coast and crossed it in a fast dive. To the pilot the North Sea looked 'beautiful . . . perhaps the most wonderful thing in the world' at that time. Already the sky was appreciably lighter in the east. After a completely peaceful crossing of the North Sea, ED932/G landed safely at 0415 at Scampton; the only damage it had sustained comprised three small holes in the tail.

In Knight's aircraft the exuberant chatter gradually petered out as the prospect of fighting the way home loomed nearer. Following orders, Knight flew first to the Möhne, where, like Gibson, the crew saw a torrent raging down the narrow valley below the dam and a much reduced water level in the reservoir. Kellow admitted to being 'fascinated by the amount that the water had dropped'. They did get one shock, however: a flak gun resented their intrusion, and Knight wisely took evasive action. Thereafter it was a trouble-free run and no hostile aircraft were seen. Flying as low as possible at maximum speed, they followed the second exit route. Knight's aircraft trekked home absolutely alone and relatively undisturbed, although it did find itself to port of the planned track in the area of Zutphen and Harderwijk. There were a few unpleasant flak bursts near Borken, and Sutherland raked a train which was stationary in a small town. O'Brien was the only horrified witness of a near-miss which would have spelt disaster for them all: 'We were flying very low during the return journey, at the Dutch coast the terrain rose under us, Les pulled up, over and down. On the sea side of this rise in the terrain and invisible to Les was a large cement block many feet high. This block passed under our tail not three feet lower. As the rear gunner, I was the only one to see it.' Fortunately for his peace of mind, that was the final alarm. Crossing the Dutch coast at 0259 and switching on his navigational lights when nearing England, Knight alighted on the runway at Scampton at 0420.

Including two early returns from the second wave, seven Lancasters had now returned safely. Two others from the first wave which set off after attacking did not reach England. Despite the observations and conclusions at the time, Maudslay almost certainly survived to be shot down close to the Dutch border some 45 minutes later. Reported sightings of his aircraft above or beyond the explosion, from several observers in Gibson's and Knight's crews, were consistent with a Lancaster rising after release of its mine, which – since the aircraft was moving faster than the mine – would have struck the dam behind it, however late the weapon had been released. The weak R/T transmission may be explained by damage caused by the explosion of the mine on top of the dam rather than 30ft below the water, and the loss of contact thereafter by the aircraft's being out of range beyond the hills. Damaged as his aircraft was, and aware that the operation order required him to proceed to base immediately after dropping his mine, Maudslay must have decided to head back to England at once. His single W/T message to 5 Group, giving details of his attack and sent at 0157, would again have been in keeping with orders that use of W/T should be kept to a minimum. The relevant Luftwaffe records of that night have not survived, but later German sources, based upon the statements of eyewitnesses, claim that the aircraft was shot down by light flak as it approached from the east near Emmerich, an oil-refinery centre on the Rhine which had been an Allied target since 1940 and therefore well defended. A flak gunner was reputedly decorated for bringing the aircraft down. This is corroborated to some extent by a post-war official British report that AJ-Z was shot down 3.5km east of Emmerich, just 2km inside the German border, at 0236. But the casualty records upon which this much later summary is based are not open to public inspection, and it is therefore impossible to conclude with certainty that Maudslay did survive at the Eder. There are however fairly strong indications that he did so and that he and his crew then struggled valiantly to fly their damaged aircraft to safety. If he did indeed attack at about 0145, it would have taken him some 50 minutes to reach the position at which he apparently crashed, a distance of 140 miles if he followed the briefed return route. This low speed might be explained by serious damage to the aircraft and a decision to make an even wider diversion round the defended area of the Ruhr, thus increasing the theoretical distance to Emmerich, east of which lay the third return route.

Young's fate is more certain. In accordance with orders, he apparently flew back via the Möhne and followed return route 3, which took him close to Ijmuiden. Here the tendency to fly relatively high, noted by Shannon and Maltby on the outward flight, possibly cost Young his life. At 0258 gunners near Castricum-aan-Zee, north of Ijmuiden, reported shooting down a Halifax over the North Sea just after it crossed the coast. The Lancaster could be confused with the Halifax even by experienced gunners, for from the rear only the different configuration of the tail section distinguished the two types. Ijmuiden, with its E-boat pens, ironworks and important harbour, was a frequent target for Allied bombers and heavily defended by 3 and 4/Marine Flak 246, 2, 4 and 6/Marine Artillery 808, and 8/Flak Abteilung 45. Several of these units reported firing at the aircraft, which crashed off the coast north of the town, and the official German report thus credited its destruction to flak in the Ijmuiden area. Between 25 and 27 May bodies washed up along 15 miles of the shore from Wijk-aan-Zee to Bergen-aan-Zee confirmed that the 'Halifax' was indeed AJ-A.

At 0400 on Monday 17 May, Harris, Cochrane and Wallis left Grantham by car for Scampton. By the time that they arrived, all the surviving first-wave aircraft had landed and the crews were being debriefed. The new arrivals then mingled with them, as official photographers recorded the scene for posterity. Apart from the usual crew debrief, each pilot had to complete a special questionnaire about visibility at the target, number and height of bounces of Upkeep, rpm at which the mine was spun, particulars of the explosion and damage caused to the target, effectiveness of the system of control, and value of the 100 per cent tracer. It concluded with an invitation to add general comments or criticisms. Commenting on the Möhne, Gibson wrote: 'There are two holes in the dam,' indirectly confirming that Young had caused the initial breach. Of the Eder he recorded: '1st. and 3rd. hit 2nd. overshot,' thus undermining his later contention that Maudslay had attacked first, followed by Shannon and Knight. He considered that VHF had provided a 'perfect' method of control and approved of 100 per cent tracer: 'Very satisfactory against gun positions. No dazzle. Perfect for this job.'

Martin agreed with Gibson's conclusions on VHF and tracer, adding a lengthy comment: 'Very good trip. Numerous searchlights and light flak positions north of the Ruhr against which gunners did wizard work. Rear gunner extinguished two searchlights. Front gunner shot up other flak posts and searchlights. Navigation and map reading wizard. Formation commander did a great job by diverting the gun fire from target towards himself. Whole crew did their job well.' Martin made no mention of his own diversionary tactics to help Young and Maltby at the Möhne. About use of tracer, Maltby merely commented: 'No trouble and slightly easier to aim.' But he found the VHF control 'excellent,' adding: 'In two cases a second aircraft flew alongside the one bombing and machine gunned ground defences on north side of objective,' a reference to Gibson flying to Martin's starboard and Martin on Young's port side. Maltby also noted: 'Good route, flak free and easy to map read.'

Shannon was equally enthusiastic about the route, effect of tracer, VHF control and perfect execution of the plan. He claimed: 'Made gap 9 feet wide towards east side' (or right-hand looking down the valley), and that the third aircraft (Knight's) had 'widened gap'. A significant comment was then appended, supporting Gibson's observation: 'Saw second aircraft overshoot.' Shannon and Gibson had thus confirmed that the order of attack at the Eder had been Shannon, Maudslay, Knight. While agreeing with the others about VHF, Knight proved less enthusiastic about the ammunition: '100% tracer dazzled gunner but appeared to frighten searchlights and gun crews. Opinion of gunner – ordinary night tracer would have caused greater accuracy because of reduced dazzle.' Knight concluded: 'Routeing excellent. Reports from aircraft ahead re flak found to be very useful. Attack straightforward and as predicted. It was found possible to gain 1,000 feet easily after dropping the mine. Satisfied that the raid was successful.' In his logbook F/Sgt Sumpter would insert a rather more bald epitaph on Operation Chastise: 'Op No 14 via Holland to the Hun. Satisfactory attack on Eder Dam 18 miles west of Kassel. Average ht. 100 feet.' And Gibson wrote in his: 'Led attack on Möhne and Eder Dams. Successful.'

In the early hours of Monday 17 May the first-wave crews waited for the others to return. Shannon's did so until after 0700, hoping that the missing aircraft would somehow turn up. Wallis hung around the briefing room, too, until persuaded to go to bed in Gp Capt Whitworth's house. As he slept, several hardy spirits below consumed celebratory measures of alcohol. Meanwhile, others had expanded a similar occupation in the officers' mess into a spontaneous party, which protesting WAAFs were hauled from their beds to enliven. One casualty of these revels regained blurred consciousness in an armchair at 1300. By then the grim toll of lost aircraft and men from 617 Squadron had been counted.

9

Attack, Waves 2 and 3

SORPE, ENNEPE, LISTER AND DIEMEL DAMS

Aircraft of the second wave, briefed to attack the Sorpe Dam, left Scampton in advance of Gibson's nine Lancasters. They would fly the more northerly route over the North Sea and the Frisian island of Vlieland before turning south-east towards the Ijsselmeer to join the track of the first wave one mile south-west of Rees. An earlier departure was necessary because the operation order envisaged Gibson's leading flight of three and the first second-wave aircraft crossing the enemy coast 120 miles apart at the same time in an attempt to confuse defenders into believing that these were minor, intruder raids.

At 2128, therefore, the first aircraft to leave on Operation Chastise was AJ-E (ED927/G), piloted by Flt Lt Barlow. Unlike Lancasters of the first wave, those of the second departed singly. Nothing more was heard from AJ-E, which crashed 5km east of Rees near Haldern at 2350. Conflicting reports of its end have been recorded. A post-war British document held that it had been 'shot down'. One German account stated that the Lancaster had hit the high-tension wires which run north-west/south-east roughly parallel to the Rhine and main railway at this point, another that the aircraft tried to make a forced landing but exploded on impact, killing the crew. A combination of these reports could present the true picture: hit by flak, the aircraft then struck the wires and, realising that he had no chance of gaining sufficient height for his crew to bale out, Barlow tried to land the crippled machine. If this were so, the effort proved doubly unfortunate: the crew did not survive and the Germans recovered an Upkeep intact. Both German reports agree that the mine failed to explode. It did not detach itself from the aircraft, so the self-destructive mechanism was never fully armed, and evidently the aircraft did not come down with sufficient force for the mine to detonate on impact. Once the embers cooled, German officials examined the wreckage and Wallis's secret did not remain so for much longer.

One minute after Barlow, at 2129, Flt Lt Munro took off in AJ-W (ED921/G). For this crew the initial stages of the operation passed without incident. Compass and drift (recorded as 'nil') were checked over England, and the East Anglian coast was crossed on track at 2154, whereupon Munro 'increased speed a little'. At 2256, slightly behind schedule, AJ-W reached Vlieland and the mine was fused. Clay, the bomb-aimer, recorded: 'The sun had set when we reached the enemy coast but there was a little gloomy moonlight. I thought I saw someone to starboard skim the water and send up a plume of spray – it could have been Geoff Rice or Barlow or Byers.' Probably he saw Byers off track, about to cross Texel and pay the supreme penalty for his error. Officially AJ-W was 'damaged' by light flak crossing Vlieland at 2257. Apart from substituting 'Texel' for 'Vlieland' in error, Howarth, the front gunner, agreed: 'We had almost flown across the island of Texel when we were caught by light flak guns.' His pilot, Munro, also attributed their misfortune to land-based flak. Yet Clay, positioned close to Howarth in the nose of the aircraft, surprisingly reported events differently: 'Then we were over Vlieland in the Zuider Zee (Waddenzee) when suddenly a flak ship opened up. None of us in the aircraft saw this vessel although we had, as was customary, been keeping a sharp look out. We must have been a sitting target to the gunners below, a close target silhouetted against the sky.' Perhaps significantly, a detachment of 3/Marine Flak 246 stationed at the western end of Vlieland did report engaging 'several Lancaster bombers' between 2257 and 2340 on 16 May.

Nevertheless, whether caused by land-based guns or a flak ship, the damage to AJ-W was severe. Howarth wrote that the aircraft had been 'badly damaged . . . the intercom had been put out of action, also our VHF for communication with the other aircraft in the wave; the master unit for our compass was destroyed and . . . the tail turret pipes were damaged. This meant we could not speak to each other in the plane – essential for calling out height and speed and direction in case of fighter attack. We could not speak to the other planes in the wave, and were left with one rather unreliable compass, and very little defence against fighters. By the time the damage was assessed, we were well into the Zuider Zee, and our pilot Les Munro decided we had little chance of success if we went on, and decided to turn for home.' Clay reinforced and expanded this report: 'A hole was torn in the fuselage amidships, the master compass unit demolished and our intercom completely dead. Les kept on a south-easterly course for a while. Then Frank Appleby (the flight engineer) passed a short note down to me. It said as far as I remember: "Intercom U/S – should we go on?" No doubt Les had been considering the position. I wrote: "We'll be a menace to the rest." Had it been a high-level operation there would have been time to make up some sort of signals between Bomb Aimer, Flight Engineer and Pilot which may have worked. But on a quick-moving, low-level operation like this and with other aircraft in close proximity Les could neither give nor receive flying instructions from the navigator nor bombing instructions from the bomb aimer,' and the rear gunner would be completely isolated. 'A few minutes later we altered course for home [and] so ended W for William's effort in respect of this particular raid.' The pilot remarked years later: 'I was bitterly disappointed but I suppose that is why I am alive to-day.'

At 2306 AJ-W began to fly a reciprocal course for base, crossing the English coast at Mablethorpe at 0016 and touching down at Scampton once more with its mine still attached and fused 20 minutes later, the first Lancaster to return from Operation Chastise. With its means of communication shattered the crew was unaware that another early return was circling Scampton at the time, nor of the consternation that AJ-W caused by flying straight in as AJ-H prepared to land.

AJ-K (ED934/G), piloted by Plt Off Byers, took off one minute after Munro at 2130. Nothing more was heard from this aircraft, which was reported 'missing without trace'. Almost certainly this was the aircraft seen by Clay to starboard of the briefed track and heading for Texel, not Vlieland, for Byers was shot down by flak positioned on that island. According to a postwar Dutch report: 'During the night of 16/17 May 1943, Lancaster ED 934 K (for Kathy) was shot down by flak when it was flying on a level of 450 feet over the heavy [sic] defended isle of Texel instead of the isle of Vlieland, and crashed into the Waddenzee.' Crews had been warned that the fluctuating tides in the area could cause different profiles of the islands to those anticipated, but mistaking Texel for Vlieland could have been easily done in any case from low altitude and at speed. A post-war German report suggests that this aircraft fell victim to a 10.5cm heavy flak gun stationed on Texel, but a weapon of this calibre could not have been depressed to hit a low-flying aircraft, even had Byers crossed Texel at 450ft. AJ-K might have suffered the same fate as Young's aircraft in being hit by flak positioned behind it. Aware that he was off track and believing himself safe once clear of land, just as Gibson would do far to the south at about the same time and for the same reason, he climbed to identify landmarks. Then flak caught him and ED934/G vanished into the sea. Rice's crew reported an aircraft shot down by flak 'off

Texel' while flying at 300ft at 2257, and with evidence available that F/Sgt McDowell's body had been recovered from the Waddenzee off Harlingen, much later the British '. . . concluded that the aircraft and other crew members were lost at sea.' Shortly after the operation HQ 5 Group suggested that the aircraft might have flown high 'to get a coastal pinpoint' and had crossed Texel west of the briefed route either because it was 'south of the track from base or had altered course too soon from position 53°20' – 04°54'.' And German naval flak units 1 and 3/Marine Artillery 201 and 3/808 stationed on Texel have been officially credited with destroying Byers' Lancaster, which crashed into the Waddenzee at precisely 2257, eighteen miles west of Harlingen. Whatever the facts, 617 Squadron had indisputably lost its first aircraft on Chastise.

The fourth aircraft in the second wave was not shot down, but it suffered a bizarre experience. Like Munro, its pilot was forced to abort the operation. At 2131 Plt Off Rice left Scampton in AJ-H (ED936/G), also bound for the Sorpe Dam. Navigation presented a problem as, flying entirely alone, the crew found it easy to get off track. Rice admitted that 'at times you didn't really know where you were'. Conditions were perfect, however, and the Lancaster crossed the North Sea without trouble. MacFarlane, the navigator, took drifts at intervals by dropping flame floats which the rear gunner looked at through his reflector sight, confirming that drift was virtually nil. When two minutes short of Vlieland the crew recorded seeing the loss of an aircraft, probably Byers'. At low altitude, once the enemy coast had been identified Rice found the aircraft committed to its crossing point, and at 2259 AJ-H flew over the predicted narrow neck of Vlieland without having made the designated course adjustment at 53°20'N 04°54'E but with the mine fused at 2255. Rice was flying so low that he had to pull up over the sand dune, and once across the island he climbed to confirm his position, sank low again and turned south-east along the briefed track. By now Gee had failed and the navigator used another flame float to check drift. As AJ-H flew into the moon, height was difficult to judge, and just short of the Afsluitdijk the flight engineer noticed the altimeter registering zero. He was about to warn Rice, who later blamed himself for not using the spotlights to determine altitude, when a tremendous shudder shook the aircraft. Instinctively Rice pulled it up, and a second 'violent jolt' occurred almost immediately. The impact buckled panels of the main section of the fuselage and water hit the roof of the cabin and sprayed over the navigator's charts, to a plaintive 'Christ! It's wet at the back' from the rear turret and a terse 'You've lost the mine'. For when AJ-H struck the water, the mine had been torn off. Hitting the fixed tailwheel (the second impact), the mine drove it up through the main spar of the tailplane, shattering the Elsan toilet just forward of the rear turret. Meanwhile, as Rice put the aircraft into a sharp climb, water poured through the doorless bomb bay and down the fuselage. The rear gunner, Burns, up to his waist in disinfectant and salt water, might therefore be excused his mild expletive. AJ-H had cleared the polder (Afsluitdijk) and flew on into the Ijsselmeer before the full extent of its problem became apparent. Loss of the mine was verified as water drained out of the bomb bay once more and a damp rear gunner made himself marginally less uncomfortable.

With the mine gone, for this crew Operation Chastise had come to an abrupt halt. Turning back to the north-west at 2306, Rice flew over the polder once more and made an unorthodox exit between Texel and Vlieland ten minutes later. Alert defenders played searchlights across the gap and put up some flak, but AJ-H flew under this and set course for home. Approaching base, Rice sent the flight engineer to check the hydraulic system, and he reported that most of the fluid had been lost. The pilot therefore decided to use the emergency drill, under which an air bottle was used to lower the undercarriage. He feared however, from previous experience, that once the undercarriage had been locked down by this method, insufficient pressure would remain to operate the flaps fully. So the wireless operator warned ground control 'aircraft damaged – possibly no flaps' and requested maximum landing room. Rice circled at 1,000ft for 20 minutes while the emergency procedure was carried out. Then he ordered all but the flight engineer into their crash positions, with their backs to the main spar and facing aft, as he prepared to set AJ-H down on the long runway. As he did so another Lancaster flew in below him to land: without means of communication, Munro could not call up the tower and had simply gone straight in.

Eventually at 0047 Rice 'did a wheeler,' landing with the front wheels down and tail up. AJ-H crunched down on to its tail fins before turning off the runway. Rice switched off, scrambled out of the Lancaster and walked away 'very depressed'. Whitworth, who had driven out in his truck, found him, told him to shake out of his mood and gave him a lift to debriefing. Although embarrassed at having made 'a complete balls of things,' Rice stayed after debriefing to wait for the other crews. He noted when Gibson came in that the squadron commander's hair was plastered down with sweat, even though he had flown in shirtsleeves. And later, when he arrived from Grantham, learning the details of Rice's misfortunes, Harris commented: 'You're a very lucky young man.' There was, too, an interesting postscript which yet again illustrated the importance of accurate communication. Eaton's 'aircraft damaged – possibly no flaps' had caused consternation in the control tower.

'What did you mean "without a clutch"?,' a puzzled WAAF operator asked Rice.

The fate of the lost mine remained uncertain. To the crew's knowledge it did not explode. Most probably the hydrostatic fuses failed to work because the water was not deep enough to activate them, the area in which the mine dropped being exposed mud flats or water to the depth of only a few feet. Although some channels could have contained water over 30ft deep, a British official source later concluded: 'The chances are weighted fairly heavily in favour of it landing in shallow water.' But, armed at 2255, the self-destructive device ought to have worked, and it must therefore be concluded that the mechanism suffered damage during the mine's unorthodox departure from the aircraft.

Four of the second wave therefore failed to reach the Sorpe, and only Flt Lt McCarthy's crew remained to achieve success. Their experiences before take-off scarcely augured well: scheduled to leave first of all – even before Barlow – McCarthy eventually got away two minutes after the third flight of Gibson's first wave. During the final run-up AJ-Q (ED923/G), on which McCarthy 'had spent a lot of loving care,' 'turned sour' on him. A coolant leak occurred on the starboard outer (No 4) engine, and it rapidly became clear that the aircraft could not fly that night. One reserve aircraft was available: ED825/G, flown in by Bergel from Boscombe Down six hours earlier. Time had not allowed the fitting of the VHF radio or spotlights, but AJ-T had been bombed up and would fly. Terrified lest another crew having trouble with its aircraft should commandeer the reserve and so deny them a part in the operation, McCarthy and his crew frantically threw necessary movable equipment out of the cockpit window. In the process one parachute caught on a hook and 'blossomed all over McCarthy on the ground'. Undeterred, if rather vociferous, and having freed himself with difficulty, the pilot jumped into a nearby truck with the others and dashed off to claim the reserve aircraft.

There a further shock awaited them: there was no compass deviation card, which must have been mislaid in the confusion following Bergel's late arrival. Leaving his crew to complete pre-flight checks, McCarthy leapt into the truck once more and sped off to the flight offices. F/Sgt Powell brought some order to the threatened chaos by fetching the missing card from the instrument section and thrusting a replacement parachute through the window of the truck's door and into McCarthy's lap as he was about to dash off again. Eventually, at 2201 and some 34 minutes late, McCarthy's crew became airborne. Straining to make up for lost time by flying at 200 mph, trailing in the wake of the 13 other aircraft which he should have preceded and (erroneously) believing that his unpalatable task was to penetrate northern defences to distract enemy night fighters from the first wave, McCarthy missed minute geographical details in the early part of the flight, though he did note over the North Sea that 'in the slope of England the sun was just disappearing on the horizon'. In the bomb-aimer's compartment, by the subdued amber light Johnson was meanwhile checking the maps which he would use to ease the navigator's problems by establishing visual sightings of landmarks. After trying it in training, MacLean, the navigator, did not favour joining the maps together and mounting them on two rollers for continuity. This he considered 'dangerous,' because if the aircraft strayed off track to a wide degree the maps would become useless. And McCarthy did manage to make up some of the lost time: reaching Vlieland at 2313, he had cut the deficit to 21½ minutes.

Predictably, the defences were alert and unfriendly, although only two guns and one searchlight were positively identified. The pilot reported: 'Very hot reception from natives when crossed the coastline. They knew the track we were coming in on, so their guns were pretty well trained when they heard my motors. But, thank God, there were two large sand dunes right on the coast which I sank in between.' Once over the mainland, he used the shelter of hills and even trees to escape the attention of searchlights and flak guns. The enemy seemed 'baffled' by the low-flying tactic, especially the night fighters which McCarthy 'quite frequently could see . . . flying along at 1,000 feet above us,' oblivious of the Lancaster 900 feet below. 'I don't think they expected us down there at all.' The gunners, Rodger and Batson, nonetheless were not idle. Occasionally a searchlight could be doused, and, as the Lancaster hopped over hedges, flak gunners were given a frightful shock. On one occasion Rodger had a lively exchange with a light flak gun, both gunners 'pumping away' to no visible effect until out of range. On another Batson saw an 'innocent-looking train' looming up and asked McCarthy's permission to open up. Receiving it with a brief 'sure,' he began firing only to discover that it was heavily defended (possibly a special flak train for mobile defence). As a result AJ-T sustained its only damage on the operation, a cannon shell through the undercarriage nacelle which, unknown to the crew, burst the starboard tyre.

Like other crews, McCarthy's did not find navigation easy; pinpoints in the Netherlands were much simpler to identify than those in Germany. Shortly after 0015 McCarthy reached the vicinity of the Sorpe, having had difficulty in locating it due to thick mist. But in the immediate area of the dam perfect visibility illuminated the full extent of the problem which faced him. At least there were no defences. Circling over the village of Langscheid, he pondered

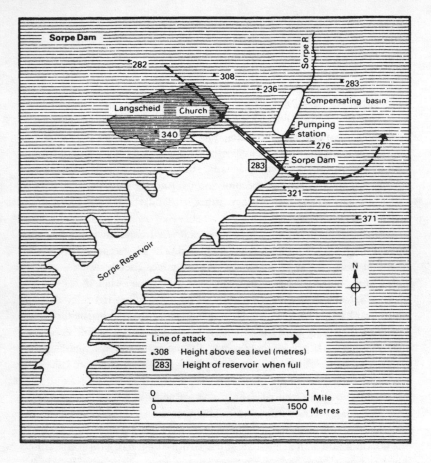

Sorpe Dam

Langscheid

Church

Sorpe R

Compensating basin

Pumping station

Sorpe Dam

Sorpe Reservoir

Line of attack - - - - ➤
•308 Height above sea level (metres)
283 Height of reservoir when full

N

0 _____ 1 Mile
0 _____ 1500 Metres

the special problem of avoiding the tall church spire, which stood below the
crest of the hill overlooking the dam, spontaneously observing: 'Jeez! How do
we get down there?' At length McCarthy realised that by flying over the
steeple he could actually line up his run with the dam. On the first run
Johnson, the bomb-aimer, was satisfied with neither line nor altitude and did
not release the Upkeep. The pilot pulled up over the hill at the end of the dam
and circled to port to try again. Nine times the aircraft carried out this
fruitless manoeuvre. The crew became restless, and Johnson gained the
distinct impression that most of the 'rather disparaging remarks' were
directed at him. Finally, at 0046 and ironically just as Rice brought AJ-H in
to land at Scampton after its abortive flight, Johnson was satisfied and
released the mine on the tenth run as close to the centre of the dam as he

could judge. AJ-H was flying on a course of 140°M (variation – 05°09′), at a ground speed of 170 mph and an estimated 30ft above the dam (as spotlights were not fitted) in 'perfect visibility – no cloud – bright moonlight'. The whiplash effect on the aircraft was pronounced as the mine fell and McCarthy pulled the Lancaster up over the hill. Rising swiftly to 1,000ft gave Rodger in the rear turret a severe shock, and he advised McCarthy 'to get the hell down' as they were 'a sitting duck at this height' for fighters. Behind there was a tremendous explosion and a plume of water reached upwards. As the aircraft flew back over the target the entire crew became 'really excited about crumbling along the top of the dam'; McCarthy became so vocal in his ecstasy that the navigator asked him pointedly and firmly to concentrate on flying the machine in the interests of their mutual safety. The bitter pill to swallow, however, was that the dam still held, even though the top had certainly crumbled over 15–20ft. Not until 0300, however, when was a mere 20 minutes from Scampton on the return flight, did HQ 5 Group record a W/T message from the aircraft: 'Goner 79C,' mine exploded in contact with the Sorpe Dam, causing a 'small breach'.

After a final look at the Sorpe in a vain hope that a belated collapse might occur, McCarthy's Lancaster had begun its journey home shortly before 0100. Flying back over the Mohne, Johnson saw only 'an inland sea' and concluded that there was 'no point in trying to map-read in that area'. Not long afterwards McCarthy was surprised to see what appeared to be a well defended town ahead, with searchlights and flak already climbing to greet them. In answer to his urgent and belligerent query, the navigator insisted that they were following the briefed track. Then the aircraft found itself over Hamm 'temporarily uncertain of position'. Several times it pounded through the famous marshalling yards at 50 feet. During one of these excursions the flight engineer remarked on a lull in the defensive fire, only for a Canadian voice to break in: 'Gee, at this height they don't need flak. All they need do is to switch points.' The reason for their meanderings became apparent: the aircraft had strayed off course, or as an official report noted, 'had trouble with compass'. Having extricated itself from this 'temporary difficulty,' the crew then floundered around trying to identify the lakes near Dülmen and at length decided to abandon any attempt to follow an official exit route in favour of back-tracking on the outward one, via the Ijsselmeer and Vlieland. In McCarthy's words, they simply 'set course as route out and headed for Zuider Zee.' Just short of the Ijsselmeer Rodger experienced 'the biggest scare of the whole trip' when one flak gunner managed to get their range even at minimum altitude. He felt that they were about to 'buy it,' but his pessimism was fortunately unfounded and at 0323 AJ-T landed safely at Scampton.

The homecoming did not pass without incident. As the aircraft touched down the right wing sank low and the flight engineer looked out to see a flat tyre to starboard. The bomb-aimer, who was uncomfortably close to the ground, observed that 'Joe controlled it [AJ-T] very well'. 5 Group later summarised the crew's experience: 'Compass slightly faulty having been swung with bomb load. Bullet hole through undercarriage which burst starboard tyre.' In his answer to the pilots' questionnaire McCarthy reported seeing everything at the target clearly, with the moon to starboard and visibility of five miles. After the explosion a 'half-circular swelling of water with wall of dam as diameter' was followed by 'a spout of water about 1,000ft. high.' Tracer, he felt, 'betrayed position of aircraft to searchlights and light flak en route' and therefore the 'pilot [was] not in favour of 100% tracer'. He concluded: 'Cannot say if a big breach in dam was made, but the raid seemed to be successful.'

In the meantime the five aircraft of the third and final (reserve) wave had taken off from Scampton. 'Each [was] detailed for one of the alternative targets and all [were] detailed to be prepared to attack the Möhne and Eder dams in the absence of any direct orders in the air to carry on to the alternative targets.' The operation order laid down that they would be controlled directly by HQ 5 group via a special W/T channel, so when the aircraft took off they were not certain of their ultimate destination. Like the second, and unlike the first, the reserve wave left Scampton singly two hours after McCarthy's departure to follow the southern entry route and scheduled to cross the enemy coast shortly after 0130. The first aircraft to depart was AJ-C (ED910/G) piloted by Plt Off Ottley, at 0009 on 17 May. Of this aircraft the 617 Squadron operations record book noted: 'Missing, acknowledged his diversion to the Lister Dam, no further trace'; and, in following the same line, HQ 5 Group's summary added: 'Believe Lister was not attacked.' Unwittingly, however, several aircrew engaged in Chastise witnessed Ottley's demise. 'About half an hour' after crossing the enemy coast, the pilot of a reserve-wave aircraft behind Ottley, Townsend, saw 'a hell of a flash' to starboard, and his navigator fairly accurately interpreted what he saw: 'Ahead and to starboard searchlights broke out and an aircraft was coned at something over a hundred feet; more searchlights and lots of flak and a terrific explosion in the sky. It was one of ours; probably a little too close to Hamm, a heavily defended rail centre, and too high.' Brown, pilot of another reserve-wave Lancaster, more explicitly described the crash. 'Ottley, on my right, was hit and pulled up, his tanks exploded then his bomb – the whole valley was lit up in a bright orange,' though Brown's bomb-aimer, Oancia, recalled only 'that the exploding aircraft was ahead of us'. Brown estimated the stricken aircraft's position as 4–5 miles north of Hamm and its height when hit as 500ft. The aeroplane which Gibson saw shot down in the area of Hamm was not a German fighter but AJ-C.

W/T messages between the aircraft and Grantham supplement the story to some extent. Once 5 Group had established that both the Möher and Eder dams had been breached and no aircraft of the first wave remained to attack the Sorpe, a decision had to be made about targets for reserve-wave aircraft. At 0230 5 Group called up AJ-C and a minute later sent 'Gilbert' (for this aircraft meaning 'attack Lister Dam'), which was acknowledged. The very next minute, 0232, however, a change of plan occurred, for 5 Group then sent 'Dinghy' ('Eder destroyed attack Sorpe') and repeated it at 0250. Neither message was acknowledged, suggesting that the aircraft was fatally damaged at about 0231. The crew of AJ-F, Brown's aircraft, reported that AJ-C hit the ground at 0235.

One member of Ottley's crew survived the crash, and confirmed the sequence of events reported by eyewitnesses. He also also explained a crucial error in 617 Squadron's operations record book which has been repeated by several printed works, including the Official History, for Sgt Tees flew that night in the rear, not front, turret. Had he not done so he would have died. Over the North Sea Tees and the navigator used flame floats to establish drift, but nothing untoward occurred until the coast, as they flew in over the Scheldt estuary. Here a few searchlights and the odd burst of flak scarcely disturbed them, and with Tees 'firing away' AJ-C quickly cleared small pockets of searchlights and flak over the Netherlands and Germany. At one point the aircraft was flying so low that he looked up and saw that it was below the height of a church steeple. When he felt that it was about 15 minutes away, Tees heard the wireless operator say over the intercom 'Möhne gone,' and almost immediately Ottley began 'We go to . . .,' when 'a hell of a commotion' occurred to interrupt him. The aircraft was suddenly bathed in searchlight and a tremendous barrage of flak struck it, mainly from the port side. Quickly Tees realised that the port inner engine had been immobilised, because he could get no power for his turret, and flames began to streak back past the perspex. Distinctly he heard Ottley say, 'I'm sorry boys we've had it,' and thereafter Tees' memory of events became blank. His parachute, like that of Burcher at the Möhne, was inside the fuselage and similarly he could not use the power mechanism to revolve his turret sufficiently to gain access to it. In any case, he thought, 'there's no future in baling out at nought feet with three engines on fire'. He regained consciousness on the ground, very badly burnt, and spent the remainder of the war either in hospital or in a prisoner-of-war camp. Squadron eyewitness reports suggest that two explosions took place: in the air (the tanks) and on the ground (the mine). It seems probable that in one of these – almost certainly the latter – Tees' turret was blown clear of the burning wreck for him miraculously to survive. The later report, attributing this sequence of events to Burcher at the Möhne, most likely referred rather to Tees near Hamm. The official 5 Group report of 7 June recorded that Ottley's aircraft had crashed at Hamm at 0235, seven miles off track. Assuming that the fatal damage occurred over Hamm, the report suggested that the aircraft must have turned some 2½ minutes short of Ahlen, so flying over Hamm rather than east of it. In reality, it crashed at Heessen, five miles north-east of Hamm, and was therefore probably hit west of the town. This would be consistent with its having turned too soon for the Ahlen-Möhne leg of the route.

AJ-S (ED865/G), piloted by Plt Off Burpee, left Scampton two minutes after Ottley at 0011 and suffered a similar fate, officially 'missing without trace'. Its loss was also seen by other crews. Flying at a height of 150ft in the area of Tilburg in the Netherlands, Brown's crew reported that at 0153 about ten miles ahead of it another aircraft exploded in mid-air and crashed in flames. At the time AJ-F was flying in longitude 05°06′E three miles south-east of Tilburg, and it was therefore calculated that the lost aircraft would have been at longitude 04°53′E and about 8½ miles west-south-west of the town. The bomb-aimer, Oancia, had a clear impression of what happened: 'The Lancaster ahead of us flew over a German airfield, was hit by ground fire, fuel tanks exploding and the ball of flame rising slowly – stopping, then dropping terminated by a huge ball of flame, as it hit the ground and the bomb exploded.' The pilot's view of these events was obscured, as he was making a course adjustment at that moment; for Burpee was 'just off our port wing ahead of us when he was shot down'. Brown had already noticed light flak to port 'but thought little of it' until he heard a casual voice over the intercom comment on 'one hell of an explosion'. Webb, front gunner in AJ-O, which was flying behind Brown, saw 'a bloody great ball of fire' ahead and to port.

Burpee had strayed from the briefed track at probably the most suicidal stretch of the route, where crews had been warned that they must fly between airfields at Gilze-Rijen and Eindhoven. A Dutch eyewitness saw AJ-S attempt a standard Luftwaffe practice by putting on the navigation lights, hoping to deceive defenders into believing it friendly. To no avail. A second Dutch eyewitness recorded its end: 'An aircraft approaches from the West at very low altitude and tries to break through the light-flak barrage between Molenschot and Gilze Rijen. It seems to be caught by searchlights. Then a fierce spreading red light becomes visible: the aircraft is on fire and crashes at the airfield amongst the buildings and hangars. A most terrific explosion follows. The explosion continues to burn quite fiercely for a time, much ammunition explodes time after time and a smokepile climbs to 1,000 feet.' Later, he added: 'We fear it is an Avro Lanc. According to reports from people of the airbase it was a four-engined aircraft.' From AJ-F's report it seems, too, that Burpee may have climbed just before this to establish his position, knowing that he was off track. Withering light flak devastated ED865/G and German records show that at 0200 it crashed on the edge of Gilze-Rijen airfield, six miles south-west of Tilburg. Its mine exploded on impact, demolishing kitchens, offices, ablutions and a large number of other buildings. Damage estimated at a cost of 1½ million guilders was done, so Burpee and his crew had not died in vain. Small wonder that 5 Group's attempts to divert AJ-S to the Sorpe at 0232 and 0233 went unacknowledged. Burpee may well have suffered because intruder sorties to Gilze-Rijen, designed to assist Chastise, had made flak units specially alert. For another Dutch eyewitness wrote in his diary: 'During the night [of 16–17 May] the activities were like mustard with the coffee in the moonlight. During the whole night British fighter bombers . . . were interfering with the airbase defences. One of the low flying aircraft found its end here.' He noted 'very strong' fire from light flak and machine guns and from heavy batteries at Klein-Tilburg and Nerhoven, backed by searchlights, at 2330 and 0030. At about 0130, minutes before Burpee's fatal error, another aircraft was fired on by light flak at Molenschot, which missed but damaged Dutch houses as it fell. Then, harassed by searchlights, this aircraft was engaged by the Nerhoven batteries. The reception committee had been well and truly warmed up.

The third reserve-wave aircraft, AJ-F (ED918/G), left Scampton at 0012. Its pilot, F/Sgt Brown, had a habit of smoking two cigarettes just before take-off, and on this occasion considered the ritual amply justified. Heaving the Lancaster off a grass runway, with a maximum all-up weight unevenly distributed, presented a nerve-racking experience for every pilot on Chastise. 'We had to use 2850 rpm and 9lbs. of boost to keep the old girl airborne, so we didn't have much more for take-off.' Rather like the battle of Waterloo, it was 'a damned close run thing' to clear the perimeter fence. And there was a stranger in AJ-F's crew that night: Sgt Buntaine had reported sick and one of Plt Off Divall's gunners, Sgt Allatson, took his place in the front turret.

Like Johnson in McCarthy's plane, bomb-aimer Oancia favoured maps on which pencilled entry and exit routes were marked to assist his identification of physical features in preference to the roller system: 'These maps were folded in an orderly fashion and enabled me to know at all times our ground position with respect to the proposed route. Any variations would be passed on to Dudley [Heal, the navigator] who would quickly recalculate the headings to place us back on course.' Oancia called out visual identifications to Heal, who made any necessary adjustments after plotting the position. Heal did not use the API aid. And due to the peculiar, low-level nature of this operation, Brown and Feneron, the flight engineer, decided to split responsibility for forward vision, with Feneron taking the starboard half of the windscreen and Brown the port. Occasionally during the flight over the North Sea another Lancaster could be seen, briefly illuminated in the bright moonlight. Quite unlike Hobday in Knight's aircraft, Heal found Gee transmissions jammed early in the flight. However, as with the first-wave aircraft, the crew of AJ-F found themselves off track at the Dutch coast, which was reached at 0130, and Brown needed to execute a sharp port turn, followed by another to starboard to correct the error. Heal then realised that a 5° error existed on the compass and thereafter made the necessary corrections to all calculations.

Over enemy territory AJ-F's flight was punctuated by the need to pull up over pylons and power lines and the unwelcome attention of enemy flak. Shortly after Burpee's crash a steam train travelling through meadowland from right to left was raked by Brown's gunners, who Feneron considered 'didn't do it any good'. Over Germany Brown put the nose of the aircraft down and once, when flying along a road, had the satisfaction of seeing enemy shells decapitate trees on either side without harming the Lancaster. During this stage of the flight only swift reactions prevented an unscheduled call on a local castle through the front door. Recovering from his shock, Brown mused that he would rather 'like to visit there some day' in more peaceful circumstances. The crew saw aircraft 'taking quite a beating on our port side' and thought that another Lancaster might have gone down, but this was probably AJ-O during one of the more traumatic stages of its journey. And it survived. At 0224, in plenty of time to prepare for that target, AJ-F received 'Dinghy' from 5 Group, acknowledged the message a minute later and set off to attack the Sorpe. Flying over the Möhne, the crew saw that it had been clearly breached between the towers, with water pouring through, but were disturbed to find that the defences on the dam were still active.

AJ-O (ED886/G), piloted by F/Sgt Townsend, took off from Scampton at 0014. The navigator, Howard, did not anticipate this exercise with relish: 'I had visions of the bumpy (grass) take-off causing the lights under the fuselage to be shaken loose so that instead of being 60ft. above the ground we would finish up 60ft underneath it.' But 'fortunately' his fears were not realised and 'we set course for Southwold on a beautiful full moon night'. Unknown to Howard, his pilot also had qualms about the take-off. There was little wind and the designated runway was not long. Very, very anxiously Townsend crawled over the boundary hedge – his impression was that the Lancaster actually went through it – semi-stalling as he 'just' got AJ-O into the air. Over the countryside of eastern England and again over the North Sea the spotlights were tested 'and found correct as far as we could judge,' though a nagging suspicion did linger that on take-off they might have become misaligned. From time to time another Lancaster was glimpsed skimming over the waves. Howard noted: 'There was no wind and the moon shining on the water made a beautiful picture, one which since that night I have not regarded as a romantic or even beautiful sight.' As the Lancaster approached the Dutch coast flak could be seen rising far away to port, signalling Burpee's demise. Turning correctly near the tip of Schouwen, Townsend flew over the enemy coast at 0131: 'The land below was clearly seen, peaceful with no sign of war.' That idyllic picture would soon change: even keeping to an altitude of 100ft would not save AJ-O from, in its pilot's words, a 'very, very nasty' flight.

At 0145 5 Group re-broadcast the warning of flak near Dülmen and almost immediately AJ-O was caught by searchlights and subjected to a cacophony of flak. Howard glanced down, clearly saw the enemy gunners and concluded that he would never see Perth again. But Townsend 'threw that heavily-laden Lancaster around like a Tiger Moth and we flew out of it'. How he avoided hitting the ground with one of the wings at that height Howard could never fathom, and despite the involuntary aerobatics, the aircraft found itself still dead on track for the next turning point, near Rees on the Rhine.

In his compartment Chalmers listened to news of the other aircraft even as he stood 'watching history from the astrodome, although everything happened so quickly (at 100ft.) that incidents came and went almost before the mind could appreciate them – flat meadows sped past as we thundered over Holland and Germany, a fiery glow, followed by the familiar black-streaked mushroom as aircraft fell to light "ack-ack".' Townsend recalled turning south for 30 seconds at one stage to avoid a flak concentration, and actually flying below the level of the trees through a fire-break in a forest to escape. His wireless operator confirmed this: 'We attracted some attention when we attempted to cross a canal, as suddenly ack-ack was turned on us. We did a quick about turn. Looking out I could see tree tops and realised we were circling a forest. Some debate took place about the best method of approach and the considered opinion was "head down, keep low and go on through". It worked and we were safely through with ack-ack all round us.' Away to starboard 'searchlights and lots of flak and a terrific explosion in the sky' indicated the end of Ottley close to Hamm and, near the Dülmen lakes,

AJ-O itself came under fierce bombardment. Then the aircraft reached Ahlen and turned towards the Möhne. Looking back, the rear gunner, Wilkinson, extinguished two searchlights which had briefly played on them. Chalmers had not picked up W/T messages announcing the breaching of the Möhne and Eder dams, but at 0222 5 Group signalled AJ-O to attack the Ennepe Dam, repeating the order four minutes later, whereupon Chalmers acknowledged. About 20 minutes afterwards the bomb-aimer reported a large lake below, only to receive a stern rebuke from his imperturbable navigator: 'Nonsense, there's no lake here.' Townsend went even lower to investigate and saw people clambering onto roofs to escape a widening flood. Howard, satisfied that his professional integrity had been unjustly impugned, joined in the loud and excited comment over the intercom, prompted by sight of 'a great stream of water rushing out of the breach in the dam and rolling down the valley below the wall'. At the same time, more soberly, he reflected that it represented 'a horrifying, frightening sight'. Flying south-west towards the Ennepe over 'wooded, valley-marked country with little or no features to map read,' the crew had great difficulty in locating their target, being frequently diverted from the dead-reckoning track by what appeared to be the moon shining on water. On investigation the 'water' turned out to be mist rising from a valley. During this final section of the flight, AJ-O flew close to the Sorpe, and may therefore have given rise to later conclusions that a second Lancaster was in the vicinity at the time that AJ-F carried out its attack there.

The fifth aircraft of the reserve wave and the final 617 Squadron Lancaster to set out on Operation Chastise, AJ-Y (ED924/G) piloted by F/Sgt Anderson, did so at 0015. It would be unsuccessful but would survive, officially 'unable to reach target, due to mist in the valleys'. Like other aircraft in this wave, AJ-Y flew the southern entry route. Its time of crossing the enemy coast (certainly later than 0131) and subsequent passage to the Rhine are not clear, but north of the Ruhr the aircraft encountered heavy flak, which forced it off track and created serious navigational problems. Malfunction of the rear guns also reduced its ability to deal with troublesome searchlights, and in addition mist-filled valleys hampered identification of landmarks. Anderson estimated that 'about five minutes before Dülmen we were forced off our track by searchlights'. At 0228 5 Group called up AJ-Y by W/T and a minute later passed, and received acknowledgement of, 'Dinghy,' which meant that Anderson would attack the Sorpe. However, two Air Ministry documents, without supporting evidence, indicate that the aircraft was ordered to attack the Diemel and diverted to the Sorpe. If so, as with Ottley's belated diversion from the Lister to the Sorpe, this had probably resulted from a reappraisal of the situation at Grantham. Off track, unable to establish his position, with the rear turret out of action, dawn rapidly approaching and still a long way from his target, Anderson decided at 0310 to turn back with his mine still aboard. Rather than risk getting lost trying to follow one of the briefed routes from an unrehearsed starting point, AJ-Y flew back the way it had come over the southern entry route and the Scheldt, becoming the only aircraft to do so on the operation. At 0530 Anderson touched down at Scampton in the second aircraft to return with its mine, the other being Munro's. At debriefing the only relevant comment he could make concerned use of tracer: 'Very satisfactory – no dazzle and continuous line very helpful and apparently scaring to enemy.' Another pilot surviving from the operation acidly scorned him for being 'in a hurry to get to bed,' but more sympathetic colleagues felt that in similar circumstances they might have made the same decision. Many pilots on other occasions believed that they had good reason to turn back for less pressing reasons. Anderson and his crew should not be condemned out of hand.

W/T messages to each aircraft at about 0230, while they were in the general area of Hamm, suggest that 5 Group initially planned for two (Brown and Burpee) to attack the Sorpe, and one each the Ennepe (Townsend), Diemel (Anderson) and Lister (Ottley). In that way at least one aircraft would have bombed each of the six dams on the operation order. Shortly afterwards, however, Anderson and Ottley were redirected to the Sorpe, for which three of the reserve wave were thus bound. The reason for this decision may have been that at 0230 no evidence existed that any second-wave aircraft had bombed the Sorpe – recognised by the Air Staff as the second most important Ruhr dam – as McCarthy's message that he had done so inexplicably did not come until a half an hour later. Such are the proverbial fortunes of war that only two reserve-wave aircraft reported attacking their designated targets. One was AJ-F.

By the time that Brown reached the Sorpe, the mist which had hampered McCarthy's passage to the dam had now thickened significantly. In Oancia's words: 'All low lying areas were covered with a fog or mist leaving only the tops of the hills exposed and thus making a determination of the exact ground location impossible.' The aircraft circled widely before the crew became satisfied that its original estimate of the position of the dam had been correct; for on completing a circuit, visibility had improved to show it nestling below and between its two hills. Like McCarthy before him, Brown did not welcome the additional hazard of a church spire or the need to pull up swiftly over the far hill. But likewise he appreciated the absence of defensive fire. Feneron, the flight engineer, like Rodger in AJ-T, particularly

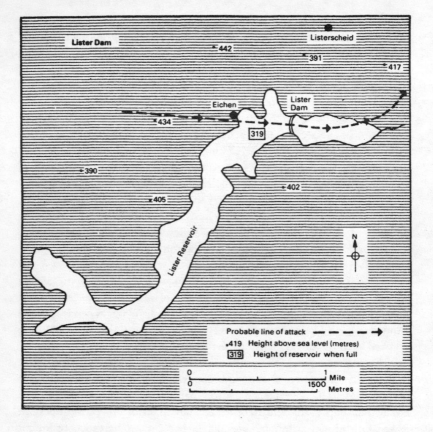

feared night fighters as the aircraft rose over that second hill. 'Several times' the Lancater attempted to carry out an attack, but as with McCarthy some 2½ hours before, the crew had difficulty in achieving the required line and altitude. After each abortive attempt Brown took the aircraft in a wide port sweep to come in again over Langscheid. On the third of these attempts, after turning from the dam, the aircraft flew into a deep mist-bound valley and very nearly came to grief. Brown therefore decided to mark out a circuit with the flares carried as navigational aids, which the wireless operator dropped on the pilot's command at predetermined intervals. Once facing a similar situation while trying to land at RAF Wigsley, Brown had carried out the same tactic successfully. Now at least the crew knew roughly where they were as they flew round to attack again. The galling aspect of this situation was that the immediate area of the dam was now clear and only the approach run presented a major problem. Eventually, with no cloud, in bright moonlight

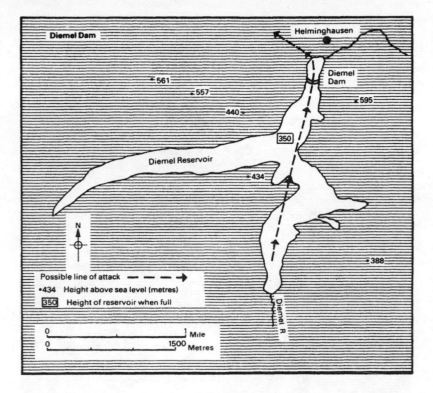

and with the spotlights on but the store not spinning AJ-F attacked once more. With Brown flying a course of 130°M at a groundspeed of 180 mph and at a height of 60ft, Oancia dropped the mine at 0314. Later a report showed that, as with McCarthy, this was the tenth attacking run. This was probably yet another typing error in an over-generous ration connected with Chastise, for the majority of the crew agreed that the final attack was the sixth attempt.

Justifiably, Brown remarked: 'We had stirred it [the Sorpe valley] up a bit'. The mine was dropped, like that of McCarthy, on the water side as close to the mid-point of the dam as possible, so that it would have to roll down the earth buttress before exploding. Brown had time to clear the end hill and bank to port before the explosion occurred: Oancia recorded 'after what seemed ages' seeing the large waterspout rising silhouetted against the moon, then slowly falling back into the lake. As the Lancaster circled back to examine the damage, 'crumbling' of the crown was seen over a much greater distance than that achieved by McCarthy. Nevertheless, at 0323 Sgt Hewstone transmitted: 'Goner 78C.' Upkeep exploded in contact with the Sorpe Dam, causing 'no apparent breach'.

The second reserve-wave aircraft to report attacking its target, and the last engaged in Chastise to do so, was AJ-O. Its short flight from the Möhne, like that of AJ-F, was complicated by thick mist rising from the valleys. Despite its distinctive shape of an irregular, inverted 'V,' the Ennepe reservoir therefore proved very difficult to find. When eventually it was located, Townsend circled the vicinity with caution. Mist drifting over the water and between the trees gave an eerie sensation in the silence. But, if meteorological conditions

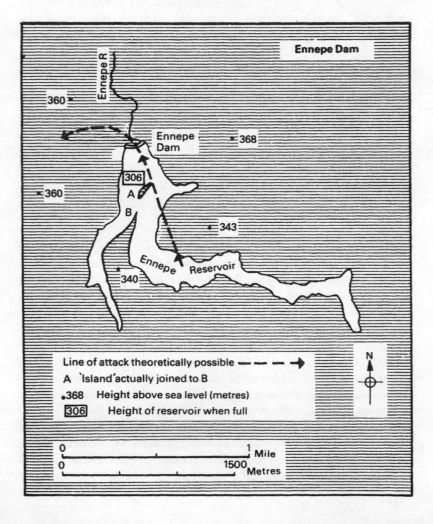

created a hazardous situation, at least there was no flak; some had been positioned to protect the dam at the outbreak of war but had since been withdrawn. Two difficulties did materialise. The target map had shown an island in the reservoir in front of the dam and about 300m from it; in reality it was joined to the bank by a narrow spit of land. The second difficulty was that in this aircraft when the mine began to spin it caused a definite shudder, resulting from a gyroscopic effect. Moreover, like the attackers at the Sorpe and Eder, Townsend could not get the necessary line and altitude immediately. Three times (in later official reports quaintly termed 'three diversionary runs') the bomb-aimer called a dummy run and Townsend circled to port for another try. Howard, the navigator, did not enjoy the exercise: 'With the aircraft shaking horribly with six tons of bomb revolving underneath I had to lean in the blister on the starboard side and guide Bill [Townsend] to the correct height with the two lights.' Of the terrain he could see little, but to starboard he glimpsed the outline of a large house on the skyline.

On the fourth run conditions were right for the attack on a bearing of 355°M (variation −06°02′) and at a groundspeed of 220 mph. At 0337 the Upkeep was dropped and after two bounces sank. AJ-O lifted high over the dam and the hill beyond. An estimated interval of 30 seconds elapsed before a huge spout of water and dirt rose into the air. When the aircraft flew round to inspect the damage, a circle on the water had spread outwards from the point of the explosion to strike the dam. Howard recorded: 'A mass of white water shot into the air: it settled, and we saw the dam wall intact.' The mine had exploded short, although the front gunner, Webb, felt immense relief that the job had been done, because crews were warned that an unsuccessful attack that night would require a return visit. Almost immediately dense mist closed in. The aircraft remained in the area for a few more minutes, its crew hoping in vain that others would arrive to complete their task. With dawn imminent, Townsend turned for home, and at 0411 'Goner 58E' – mine exploded 50 yards from the Ennepe with no apparent effect – was received by 5 Group. An official report would add to the sense of the transmission: 'Contact believed as ripples seen against dam.' This and other British sources would consistently refer to the dam as that of the 'Schwelme' and others, compounding a 617 Squadron typing error which gave the name as 'Ennerpe,' would render it as 'Enerpe' and even 'Ennipe'.

In the meantime Brown had completed his attack on the Sorpe Dam and started for home about half an hour before Townsend. Flying back over the Möhne, AJ-F's crew could scarcely believe their eyes. Heal, the navigator, was summoned urgently from his charts to witness the floods below. Alarmed by the absence of pinpoints to identify, he hurried back to his table to ensure that the aircraft stayed on track. The flight engineer reported water 'spitting' out of two distinct breaches in the dam, as the remaining flak gun on the dam opened up. Brown noted: 'He was not firing after our departure. Mac [MacDonald] our tail gunner really gave him hell.' Of the reservoir he observed that 'the water level had gone down considerably and there was a fast-flowing river below the dam'. Still worried about fighters, in Feneron's words, Brown 'got down quickly and opened up the taps'. Close to Hamm the aircraft ran into trouble. Brown wrote later: 'I had never known the Germans to put down low-level box flak as they did at Hamm. Two boxes were used, both were predicted on our track and airspeed and went off ahead of us.' AJ-F came through unscathed, and Brown could describe later 'great sport . . . dropping incendiaries on barges and other buildings we thought looked important'. Ahead lay potential death, however, for the crew feared fighters lurking in the Ijsselmeer area. If this particular peril did not materialise, AJ-F nevertheless almost perished at the coast. Crossing the Ijsselmeer before the short dash across the Helder peninsula via return route 1 and the comparative safety of the North Sea, Brown flew at 50ft on instruments, something which thereafter he vigorously advised others not to try. In the nose Oancia saw a welcoming display of searchlights and tracer shells coming up and through which the aircraft would have to fly. Fire from Allatson in the front turret caused the searchlights to waver momentarily. Seeing a land wall directly ahead, Brown lifted over it, diving down close to the surface of the water beyond and safety.

Heal recalled the incident a little differently. As dawn was breaking and just before the Helder, he realised that the aircraft was slightly off track. Before he could correct the error, searchlights crossed the aircraft from both sides, flooding the cockpit with light so that Heal could not understand how Brown could see to fly. Then flak opened up. The pilot's reaction was to put the nose even lower and pile on maximum boost; his navigator had not appreciated that a Lancaster could travel so fast. Everybody realised that the aircraft had been hit, although none of its crew were hurt, and flak followed it out to sea. Unlike Young, Brown kept his charge low and lived. Feneron confirmed Heal's impression. As Brown went lower he crouched down, hoping somehow to melt into the floor, with flak from each side pouring through the cockpit perspex. Peering up to his left he saw Brown, too, hunched over his instruments in those few, dreadful seconds.

With the immediate danger passed, the sky now quite light and the enemy coast behind, Feneron took over the controls and flew AJ-F back to the vicinity of Lincoln cathedral, where Brown reassumed charge for the landing at Scampton at 0533. The starboard side of the fuselage, where a shell had exploded and extensively perforated the skin with its shrapnel, resembled a sieve, and the top of the cockpit and fuselage was stitched with holes. Brown and Feneron had been wise to grovel. The flight engineer was so relieved to get back that he kissed the Lincolnshire earth. In the circumstances, the gesture was hardly extravagant. Baldly and unemotionally the damage would officially be described as 'cannon shell hole in fuselage starboard side' – a miserly exposition of structural confusion. In his report Brown noted that by the time AJ-F attacked the Sorpe the moon was on the starboard beam and visibility 500 yards: 'missile dropped about 10 feet away from the dam about $\frac{2}{3}$ of way across . . . semi-circular swelling of water against dam wall followed by spout of water almost 1,000 feet high crumbling of crown of dam for about distance of 300 feet.' About the tracer Brown seemed unenthusiastic: 'Very dazzling, ordinary night tracer preferred,' but quizzically appended: 'Appeared to have considerable effect on accuracy of searchlights.' His final remarks praised the routeing and he felt that his attack had been 'successful' despite the difficulties caused by hills and trees on both banks of the reservoir. However, his summary of the crew's observations at the Möhne were at variance with other reports. He confirmed that Feneron, supported by Oancia, had noted 'two large breaches close together between the two targets [sic] . . . [each] about a quarter width of space between the two towers' with water pouring out of the gaps and 'shooting well out before falling in two powerful jets.' He added: 'Front gunner reports a third breach beyond the tower on the north-west end of dam. Breach about half the size of other two. Water pouring through.' No subsequent photographs showed this, and it is likely that from above the crew actually saw water flowing around debris from the power station and dam wall, giving the impression of separate breaches. For by this time the two breaches caused by Young and Maltby would have undoubtedly fused due to the pressure of the escaping water.

Brown flew back over the Netherlands and North Sea in daylight, and Townsend trailed him by some 30 minutes. AJ-O, as briefed, also made for the Möhne, which the crew found great difficulty in identifying as a result of a 'sheet of water about 7 miles long and extending 4 miles wide up valley, with dam in middle.' Townsend noted that only the roofs of houses could be seen protruding above the fast-flowing water. Howard recorded: 'We turned for the Möhne – found it, and stared amazed at the drop in the water level on the banks of the lake – and still the water gushed in a white sheet down the valley.' Once more the pilot described the passage across enemy territory as 'very nasty,' but he put the Lancaster 'right on the deck'. He had never flown so low before, even in training, and from these minutes his memory retained only a hotchpotch of figures either waving or diving flat. As the crew flew over the

Dortmund-Ems canal, some members persuaded themselves that its water level had already been affected. With the moon paling in the west and the first rays of the sun piercing the eastern sky, AJ-O seemed naked to fighters and ground fire – a lonely minnow in a pool of hostility. In the strange mixture of dark and light, power lines, which seemed to proliferate in this corner of north-west Germany, were even harder to spot. As Townsend and his flight engineer, Powell, put on maximum power – estimates of speed varied between 240 and 270 mph – 'many a last minute jump' was necessary 'to get over the damn things'. Years afterwards Howard would write: 'I remember looking back at the country at this time – no doubt sure of our position for a few minutes – and seeing a miasma rising from the ground, looking to me after the events of the night like all the evil in the world manifesting itself.'

AJ-O planned to follow the second return route to the designated headland at 52°50'N 05°33'E, west of De Lemmer and south-east of Staveren ('Stavoren' in all Chastise papers), then, instead of crossing the Helder, 'sneak between the islands of Texel and Vlieland' like Rice earlier. Approaching Texel, as it flew over the calm water at minimum altitude the Lancaster was betrayed to enemy defences by the rising sun behind it. At extreme range its crew depressed a heavy flak gun on Texel – possibly the same one which allegedly accounted for Byers – and bounced shells off the water at the approaching aircraft. Perhaps they too had read about Nelson. Despite the similar use to which 617 Squadron had just put this technique, Howard thought the German behaviour 'hardly cricket'. Chalmers and Townsend both realised that some of the shells were skipping over the aircraft, and the wireless operator reflected: 'The fact that we were so low saved our bacon.' Unwilling to tempt fate further and seeing no healthy conclusion to this encounter, the pilot turned to starboard and flew back towards Germany before going to port once more and slipping out smartly, according to Howard, between Vlieland and Terschelling. Only then could the crew allow itself a mild sigh of relief. Of this dangerous episode Chalmers merely noted: 'I well recall the opposition we met at Texel, which forced us to turn back and sneak out higher up the Frisians,' though Townsend and Webb maintained that the aircraft had simply 'dodged Texel' by going between it and Vlieland, the route shown on records of AJ-O's exit that night. Officially enemy searchlights caused that diversion. Utterly confused by these gyrations, staff officers later concluded that the navigator had missed a turning point at Elburg (52°28'N 05°50'E); this was presumably an intermediate point not shown in surviving documents and designed by the squadron to take aircraft between Deventer and Apeldoorn and wide of Zwolle and Kampen.

The crew's troubles were not yet over. An oil gauge (later found to be

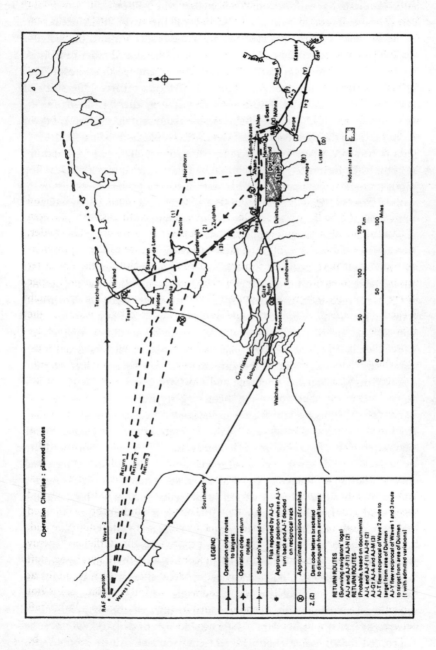

Operation Chastise : planned routes

LEGEND

Operation order routes to targets

Operation order return routes

Squadron's agreed variation

Flak reported by AJ-G

Approximate position where AJ-Y turn back and AJ-T decided on reciprocal track

Approximate position of crashes

Z, (2) Dam code letters bracketed to distinguish from aircraft letters

RETURN ROUTES
(Surviving navigators' logs)
AJ-J and AJ-P (1) AJ-N (2)
RETURN ROUTES
(Probable, based on documents)
AJ-C and AJ-F (1) AJ-O1 (2)
AJ-G1 AJ-A and AJ-M (3)
AJ-T flew reciprocal of Wave 2 route to target from area of Dulmen
AJ-Y flew reciprocal of Waves 1 and 3 route to target from area of Dulmen (it with admitted variations)

Industrial area

faulty) indicated a malfunction of one engine, which Powell shut down, and one crew member still holds that a 'Mayday' call then went out. More certain is the fact that Townsend stayed low over the North Sea and did not use his IFF equipment. Later he heard that this led shore-based radar to identify AJ-O as two Heinkels and cause Spitfires to be scrambled to intercept. This appears to be another fanciful distortion of fact, similar to the story of Harris's White House call. Two enemy aircraft were identified flying north-west over Lille at 0612, and four fighters were vainly sent up to intercept them as they crossed the Channel to orbit Deal. Meanwhile in broad daylight AJ-O approached base, where figures were crowding out of all manner of buildings to greet it. Unfortunately Townsend failed to distinguish himself before the motley throng, a result perhaps of his basic dislike for grass runways. At 0615, with oil from the front guns smearing the windscreen and forcing him to peer out of the quarterlight, he landed downwind into the sun on only three engines and succeeded in bumping 'an awful number of times – it seemed like twenty-four'. Nevertheless, he had safely brought back the last aircraft to survive Operation Chastise. But still his trial had not ended. At the bottom of the ladder leading down from the exit door he saw an eager gathering peering up at him expectantly. Exhausted by the strain of the operation, Townsend looked down with irritation. A much braided officer asked him how it had all gone. As he pushed past, Townsend told him to 'wait until debriefing'. Air Chief Marshal Sir Arthur Harris was not amused. Chalmers reacted less abrasively: 'I was first out of the aircraft to be met by Air Chief Marshal Harris, Air Vice-Marshal Cochrane and Gp Capt Charles [J. N. H.] Whitworth and at the shock of seeing them I nearly fell over in shaking their hands. They told us we were the last aircraft to land and congratulated me on my morse, which was easily read by them.' Webb, the front gunner, wrote years later of that night's drama: 'The fact is that if I had not "borrowed" an extra 1,000 rounds for each gun and rearmed while flying I would have had no ammunition for the return trip. The other fact is that if it had not been for the absolutely superb flying that Bill [Townsend] put in, simply by going lower and lower, we could not have survived. It is as simple as that. I still remember very vividly some of those power cables and pylons.'

On his report Townsend wrote that the Ennepe reservoir had been 'sighted by profile of hills' and that the attack had been executed 'running into moon in half-light reflected on mist and water' with visibility '¾ mile approx.'. He confirmed that a 'high column of dirt and water' had been thrown up by the exploding mine, and that it had detonated short of the dam for 'circle afterwards [seen] meeting dam'. There was 'no sign of damage'. Of tracer he concluded that it 'has a good deterrent effect on flak . . . no trouble with dazzle or stoppages and very encouraging to crew,' but he complained: 'The island in centre of lake on target map is actually joined to the spit.' 'Drifting mist and dazzle from moon' had made added difficulty at the target, and Townsend finished pungently: 'Considered timing too late as we were still over Germany in daylight.' Harris, Cochrane and Wallis all attended debriefing of his crew and Wallis asked: 'Did you notice the relative positions of the explosion and the wall of the dam?' Webb, who was in the best position to see when AJ-O flew over again, replied that the circle of disturbed water was bisected by the dam. That satisfied Wallis.

For a few hours yet these events remained a closely guarded secret outside the immediate operational circle. During the night of 16–17 May Lt A. R. Collins, camouflage officer of 4 Battalion, the Middlesex Home Guard, and in his daytime capacity the man who had carried out the tests for Wallis at the Road Research Laboratory and Nant-y-Gro, was on duty at Hatton Grange, later swallowed up in Heathrow Airport. Looking up at the beautiful moon in a clear sky he pondered: 'I wonder whether they've attacked the dams.'

10

Effect, Germany

COUNTING THE COST

Close to the Möhne the inhabitants of Günne heard an air-raid warning siren at about 2330 on 16 May. Some took refuge in their shelters, others did not. Not until almost a half-hour later were aircraft heard, and those who remained in their homes reported that the walls visibly shook as the mines exploded. One kilometre away beyond the dam wall, Max Schulze-Soelde saw Hopgood's burning machine edge its way over the nearby hill, heard an explosion and watched the mushroom of death rise. In the meantime Wilhelm Strotkamp, a police reservist on duty at the power station, having warned the engineer-in-charge, Klemens Köhler, of the air-raid alert, took refuge in a slit trench in the woods on the air side of the dam as the attacks began. Realising that they were developing from the reservoir side of the wall, he swiftly abandoned his refuge and scrambled higher up the bank. When the breach occurred, Strotkamp went to the guard hut to phone his superiors in Soest. Perilously close to the target, he had neither the opportunity nor the inclination to emulate a schoolboy in Günne who poked his small camera out of a window to snap the flak as it curled into the sky.

Chief of the police at Soest, Hilse, saw several aircraft flying north to south nearby and then heard flak firing from the direction of the Möhne reservoir. He immediately rang up the guard at Günne to be told that the dam was under attack, bombs had been dropped but, as yet, the dam held. Hilse then rang his superior, *Reg. Oberinspektor* Junghölter, and set out by car for the Möhne Dam, which he reached at 0108 to find it 'already damaged'. He discovered the guardroom at the Möhne in turmoil due to the effects of blast and its telephone out of action, so he established himself in the Hotel

Möhneterrassen. The entry in the guard book at the dam for this period read: '16–17 May 43. At about 0020 hrs. an enemy air-raid took place on the dam and the power station. The raid was executed by several enemy aircraft. The power station was completely destroyed, and the dam so heavily damaged between the two towers that the water poured out with a terrific force into the lower valley.'

Police reservist Hannermann observed the attacks from his flat in Körbecke, then went by motor cycle to the Möhne to give assistance. He recorded that the Möhne guard was warned of an impending air raid at 0010. But his account of what happened, although clearly written, is by no means accurate. Shortly after the warning, three aircraft attacked the flak positions on the dam, and 'at the same time the lock-house of the first tower was hit by a bomb'. While the gunners were engaging these aircraft a four-engined bomber flew over the water from the east at a height of ten metres and attacked the middle of the dam. All three guns on the dam turned their attention to this aircraft. 'Just before' the double torpedo net, which was 25m from the dam, 'the bomber dropped a special bomb' which produced 'a 10 metre high whirlpool,' dragging the net to the dam and exploding there. Blast blew the guns on both towers off their rests and put them out of action. The dam still held, although water was seeping through two fractures, as the bomber flew on westwards with smoke pouring from its tail to crash at Ostönnen. The other three aircraft then 'started a second raid': the power station got a direct hit and 'the electricity stored in the batteries was suddenly set free under a gigantic light reflex similar to lightning which probably doubled the effect of the explosion . . . It is to be supposed with all probability that at the same time a bomb had struck the dam in the middle for it broke.' Only one gun on the dam and three below it were still active at this stage. At 0230 'several aircraft' appeared and attacked the flak positions, which responded. Farmer Nettlebeck's barn was set alight by this 'second' group of aircraft, but the blaze was soon extinguished. He added: 'This time, too, one aircraft showed smoke and landed near Hamm.'

Another witness, Kleeschulte, reported that on this 'very clear moonlit' night, three to four aircraft orbited 'for a while' in the vicinity of the Möhne, then 'one aircraft which was brightly illuminated crossed directly above the Möhne Lake several times while the anti-aircraft artillery posted on the dam was firing at it. When after a few orbits the aircraft flew directly upon the dam the anti-aircraft suddenly stopped firing.' Kleeschulte maintained that he saw these events distinctly.

Alone in the power station, Köhler was told of an air-raid warning by 'the observers on the Bismarck Tower'. He was worried because the Möhne reservoir was a mere six cubic metres short of maximum capacity and any damage to the wall could lead to a catastrophic flood; for this reason he and other engineers at the power station had repeatedly called for reduction of the total volume of water in the reservoir to 80 million cubic metres. Hearing the approach of aircraft from the north, Köhler sensed that the dreaded attack was imminent and phoned his superiors in Niederensee and Neheim. His insistence that a serious threat existed was brushed aside. Bitterly he complained later that no warning was given to inhabitants in the valley.

His fruitless phone call over, Köhler went to the door of the building, which stood on the edge of the compensating basin, separated from the dam by a 50-yards-wide herbaceous border. Underneath the wall he could see nothing of events on the water side, although he heard heavy gunfire before AJ-G flew overhead through a blanket of shells. When Gibson's mine exploded he fled up the bank and threw himself down underneath a larch tree in a position high enough to see both towers and part of the reservoir beyond. From here he watched Hopgood's burning aircraft arch north-westwards to its doom and realised that the enemy had 'launched several bombs into the lake in front of the wall'. Köhler claimed that two gunners were blown off 'the towers' (almost certainly only the south tower) and lay wounded on the crown of the dam, although other flak guns on the wall and on the bank of the compensating basin near Günne continued 'firing like mad'. 'Now I saw the catastrophe coming without being able to do anything to help my cousins and nephews who lived near the sawmill on the lake below (all six were drowned), nor forester Wierleuke with his thirty paying guests on holiday, nor the people at Neheim, Niederensee and Himmelpforten . . . And down there in Neheim they had answered my warning with "Don't tell us any fairy tales!".'

An official 'secret' report by Dr Prüss, Superintendent of Works of the Ruhr Valley Dams Association (Ruhrtalsperrenverein), compiled from Luftwaffe documents, police records and interviews with military and civilian witnesses, was circulated to confidential addressees, including the Intelligence Branch of the Home Office (Civil Defence Department) in September 1943. It was at once more comprehensive and more specific than the observations of isolated individuals, but was by no means accurate. Noting a bright moon and good visibility, Prüss stated that '15–20 hostile aircraft circled at high altitude over the Düsseldorf-Essen-Duisburg area, obviously as a feint for the proposed attack on the dams'. As this manoeuvre (even more grossly exaggerated in the War Diary of the German Naval Staff) was carried out, two groups of four to five aircraft approached from Holland and shortly before midnight passed between Münster and Dortmund to the dam area. All aircraft flew at low altitude round the northern edge of the Ruhr defences, descending at times to 'tree top level' to avoid heavy anti-aircraft batteries. Prüss reported that the six 20mm guns at the Möhne opened up 'barrage fire' at the approach of the aircraft, having been alerted of their imminence by authorities at Hamm. The officer-in-charge of the 3/840 Möhne battery (Lt Widmann) reported that 'about twelve single attacks' were carried out and that bombs had not been dropped each time, thereby revealing that the flak gunners had indeed been bemused by the tactics of Gibson and Martin. Attacking aircraft kept to the right bank (the Möhne tongue of the reservoir) and 'suddenly appeared hedgehopping over the last wood clearing in front of the dam,' whence they pressed their attacks 'through the barrage and destructive fire of the anti-aircraft batteries with great determination'. Prüss added: 'Since then this wood clearing has been guarded by . . . guns.'

Prüss confirmed that 'according to observation by numerous people' Gibson's mine exploded in front of the protective torpedo netting short of the dam face. He explained that the netting was fixed about 25m from the wall to floating buoys 350m apart and comprised two nets six metres apart stretching 15m below the edge of the overflow. The upper rope of the nets extended across the lake, being fixed to each shore at its extremities. A heavy flat barrel was anchored in the middle of the net with a pulley fixed to it through which a rope ran to a cement weight to keep the net at a constant distance from the wall whatever the water level, which was further ensured by wooden fenders at both sluice towers. Damage to the left-hand floating fender indicated that the first mine (Gibson's) exploded on the shore side of the south tower.

Without the benefit of the pilots' operational reports, Prüss then confused both the number and order of the attacks. According to him the second mine exploded near the left-hand bank of the reservoir 80–100m from the face of the dam, possibly because the aircraft approached too close to the wall and released the weapon at an angle to it. Explosion of this mine, parts of which were later found when the reservoir was drained, caused the left bank to collapse over a significant distance. Prüss added that the giant upsurge of water which swelled over the southernmost part of the dam wall caused occupants of the left-hand tower to think that the dam had been broken. It is clear, however, that this described the third (Martin's), not the second, attack. Martin's mine may well have deviated from line for a number of reasons unconnected with those advanced by Prüss. The unscheduled release of the mine onto tarmac at Scampton during the morning could have affected its delicate balance or, possibly, the aircraft was not level at the moment of release at the Möhne. Wallis later explained to Glanville's assistant, Collins:

'The cylinder had a further *great* disadvantage in that while a slight degree of roll of the aircraft at the instant of release had no perceptible effect on the directional accuracy of the run, the result of roll on a cylinder was disastrous in that one end striking the water before the other, caused the cylinder to run on the arc of a circle. This unfortunate effect accounts for so many of the stores [sic] hitting the bank at the side of the reservoir.'

Prüss's third attack was in fact Hopgood's: accurate approach, mine dropped late, clearing the wall, destroying the power station, which 'blew up with a large sheet of flame,' immediately causing power failure 'over the whole valley area'. Prüss confirmed that the explosion from this mine severely damaged the roof of the left-hand sluice tower, immobilising the gun, and it seems reasonable to link this with Köhler's report that two gunners had been blown onto the crown of the dam. This damage, above the surface, far outweighed that caused by the explosion of the mines which were detonated underwater. Those succeeded merely in breaking a few windows in the Seehof Hotel on the northern shore. And faced with immobilisation of their weapons, the gun crew of the left-hand tower transferred unspent ammunition to the other tower along the undamaged road on top of the dam. Prüss reported that soon after this exercise had been completed a fourth aircraft attacked and released its mine 'a few metres from the centre of the wall': 'after a dull explosion which did not appear to be particularly heavy the wall between the two towers collapsed and water poured into the valley.' As Prüss described only four attacks, this one may well have been Young's, with Maltby's not added because the dam had already been breached. Prüss did however note that 'scout planes' appeared low over the Möhne Dam at 0245 and 0324. They engaged the anti-aircraft gun crews with machine guns and with incendiaries set fire to a barn in Günne.

This report in fact reflected the administrative chaos which 617 Squadron's attack caused at the time. Before and during the attack on the Möhne, night-fighter training continued from the military airfield at Werl, which had full runway lights switched on. The Luftwaffe authorities had neither reacted nor despatched aircraft to intercept the bombers even though Gibson's crews remained in the Möhne area for over half an hour. The only rational explanation for this is a breakdown in communication with the Möhne flak battery, which is borne out by Hilse. Surviving records also indicate that the battery commander did not report the breach in the dam and effective destruction of one tower and its gun to his superior until an hour after the attacks finished. Not until arrival of this message could the *Flakgruppe* commander order troops to the stricken area or commence the tedious but important task of informing a multitude of civilian, Nazi Party and military authorities from the Ruhr to Berlin of the disaster. Almost certainly night fighters did not fly to the Möhne, because none were requested. The rigid defensive system tied fighters to separate zones; activity elsewhere required extraordinary orders and specific authorisation. All local authorities agreed that most telephones in the Möhne area were out of action for at least an hour after the attacks.

Meanwhile, the whole panoply of regular and reserve military, police and paramilitary organisations on the ground had independently swung into action. The area of the dam was rapidly sealed off to the unauthorised, AJ-M's wreck investigated and a search mounted for those who might have escaped the holocaust. For Hopgood's bomb-aimer and rear gunner this resulted in a swift curtailment of liberty.

Quickly gathering his thoughts, Fraser set off away from the burning wreck. Unfortunately, as he emerged from a field east of Ostönnen he was seen and arrested. After preliminary questioning by the police, during which his captor recorded Fraser's nationality as 'Australian,' he was driven to Werl airfield and taken into Luftwaffe custody. At an interrogation centre – after seven days in solitary confinement and, as Fraser disarmingly noted, the Germans had 'found out where I'd come from' – an officer told him that the operation had 'accomplished as much as 100 normal air-raids'. That made him feel 'pretty damned good'. Fraser was physically unharmed during his escape from the aircraft. The rear gunner, Burcher, who had severely injured his back on the tailplane and been knocked out on hitting the ground, could not resist the soldiers who found him. Elsewhere, near Hamm, Ottley's rear gunner, Tees, had also been taken prisoner. After nearly two years in hospitals or prisoner-of-war camps, surviving severe burns, meningitis and forced marches in the process, he was eventually liberated by a jeepload of American soldiers. Arriving home, he discovered that his mother had been killed in the Chichester laundry where she worked by a stricken 'friendly' bomber returning from a mission and abandoned by its crew.

The operation in which Fraser, Burcher and Tees had taken part left havoc in its wake. The Chastise Lancasters tore a large gap in the Möhne Dam between the two sluice towers approximately 76m broad by 22m deep, for the force of escaping water had washed away masonry between the two original breaches, which had probably been narrowed in the first instance because Maltby's mine was drawn towards Young's breach by the flow of water. Torpedo nets from the reservoir were swept through the hole and stranded on the southern shore of the compensating basin, and a 20-ton turbine from the main power station was carried 100m downstream. Of the 132.2 million cubic metres of water in the reservoir, 116 million cubic metres poured out through the gap within 12 hours of the attack. The rapid fall in water level meant that water could not escape quickly enough from feeder ponds at Körbecke and Delecke above the dam, with the result that retaining dykes were severely damaged. The tidal wave flowed some ten metres high in the narrow Möhne valley, far higher than in the floods of 1890 which prompted construction of the dam. Buildings standing on the floor of the valley were destroyed up to a distance of 65km from the dam; so were bridges 50km away. Eyewitnesses agreed that before the bridges collapsed flood water rose to two metres above them. Within six hours floodwater had reached the junction of the Ruhr (into which the Möhne flowed) and, at the Rhine 148.5km from the dam, the water level remained four metres above normal 25½ hours after the breach.

Destruction in the valley was undoubtedly severe, with water and electricity supplies seriously affected. Authorities at Soest, in asking for one million Reichsmarks to carry out repairs, declared the damage 'catastrophic'. In their administrative area 9km of the Möhne and 12km of the Ruhr valleys had been devastated, and Günne, Niederensee, Lüttringen, Henningen, Waltringen and Wickede severely affected. At the Möhne the large generation station, with a capacity of 4,800kW, and the smaller one on the southern edge of the compensating basin, capable of 300kW, had been effectively demolished. Because the village of Günne lay largely on higher ground to the north, only eight houses (comprising twelve flats), two sawmills and the Schützenhalle were destroyed, and three houses and 'a few other buildings' heavily damaged. Thirty people died in Günne, but the flak detachment and police guard at the Möhne suffered no casualties. Himmelpforten-Niederensee in the direct path of the flood and 4km below the dam suffered more loss of property, although only eight deaths were officially recorded. At Himmelpforten, where many had remained in bed despite the warning, Father Berkenkopf rushed to ring the bell of the old monastery church, which had served the community as a parish church for a hundred years, and perished as the building collapsed. In Neheim-Hüsten, where the Möhne flowed into the Ruhr, extreme death and destruction were wrought: by 31 May 859 dead (147 Germans and 712 foreigners) had been recovered, but a further 34 Germans and 155 foreigners were listed missing, the bodies of some 30 being later recovered further downstream. The bulk of the foreigners killed (493) were Ukrainian women labourers, although the German authorities listed French POWs, Belgian POWs and Dutch male labourers among the dead as well. Shortly after the air-raid warning sounded, some 1,200 Ukrainians who worked in the town's factories were ordered into the shelters of their camp. No warning of impending disaster reached them, the police station at

Neheim receiving notification of danger from Arnsberg only as the flood struck the town. And in fact the camp commandant originally thought that the roar of the approaching flood-water was a train on the old Neheim-Möhne railway. He had no time to rectify his error when the torrent came in view, and almost half of the Ukrainians perished in their havens of supposed safety.

One of the Dutch workers in Neheim who survived, L. J. H. Hoesen, recalled the events of that night. With others he had been drafted to work in a factory. When the alarm sounded he left the top floor of the factory, where the labourers slept, and went outside to join a group standing on the reinforced bridge spanning a small river. It was a beautifully clear, moonlit night and Hoesen became fascinated by the distant display of military fireworks accompanied by the waspish tones of machine-guns and anti-aircraft defences 'having a go'. He saw too the extraordinary and inexplicable sight of low-flying planes with lights on. Suddenly Hoesen heard an 'appalling explosion' followed by 'a violent rushing sound'. For a moment he was puzzled before realising that the dam had been broken. Aware of 'a dark grey "something"' approaching at speed, he called out 'run, run up the hill' and began to sprint up the road leading away from the bridge. Only a Belgian named René followed. Pausing about 100m up the hill, Hoesen looked back: 'I saw that the water, with tremendous flood, had swept away the bridge with all the people on it. At the same moment there was a tremendous flash: the power station had also been washed away together with houses and streets.' Twelve factories in Neheim were involved in armaments manufacture, making shells, parts of aircraft and U-boats, small-arms ammunition and reinforcement materials for bunkers. Two were completely destroyed and the other ten damaged. When the floods receded, grass on second-storey window ledges bore silent witness to their depth. Other buildings which suffered damage were 30 'dwelling huts,' the slaughterhouse, an assembly hall, sports facilities, five footbridges, and an old iron bridge and a new concrete one over the Möhne, the latter probably being Hoesen's temporary vantage point. Köhler maintained that most of the foreign workers were either electrocuted or knocked senseless and then drowned when a power cable 200m from their camp was severed and the live ends fell into the water, and this may account for Hoesen's 'tremendous flash'.

Official reports stated that the tidal wave reached the outskirts of Neheim (some eight miles from the dam) 'at about 0055'. At the narrowest point between Neheim and Niederensee flood marks on trees later showed that the water had reached a height of 50ft, but in general the depth and speed of its passage through Neheim were estimated at 30ft and 15 mph. For some days the Totenberg district was so completely isolated from the main town that it was temporarily brought under the jurisdiction of Werl. And the Brokelmann aluminium factory was so heavily damaged by floodwater that its management described the effects as 'a great catastrophe'.

Relatively minor damage occurred in Bachum and Echthausen, but 10km below Neheim, beyond a broad bend in the river, Wickede suffered heavily. Official reports vary as to the full extent of the damage. One claimed that disaster struck at 'about 0100,' leaving the Ruhrwerk, Wickede Eisen and Stahlwerk factories and Rödinghausen iron foundry very badly damaged, the waterworks supplying Soest out of action with its chlorine equipment destroyed, and Wickede with neither gas nor electricity. Another stated that the police gave warning of impending danger at 0140, but with no aircraft in evidence most people had gone back to their homes. The only warning system available was that for fire, but when this was sounded many thought it was the all-clear and there was not enough time to get these people to safety on high ground. This report listed 22 houses destroyed, 35 heavily damaged and 104 slightly damaged, with four factories heavily and two slightly damaged. The Wickede-Vosswinkel railway bridge and Wickede-Menden road bridge were badly damaged. Surrounding farmland was strewn with trees, debris and furniture; clearly it would not be tilled for some time to come. The dead amounted to 117 (80 adults, 37 children), and the addition of 30 corpses from Neheim-Hüsten explains the higher figure of 147 dead for Wickede published elsewhere. The municipal authorities did not seem to exaggerate in describing all this as 'terrible chaos'.

The flood reached Fröndenberg, 25km below the dam, at 0300. On average the water flowed 3–4m higher than the previous maximum in 1890; at Hagen (65km from the Möhne) the level was 2m above the maximum and at the Baldeney Lake near Essen it was 0.5m above. Six hours after the breach the Ruhr valley south of Bachum was flooded to a depth of 6m for a distance of some 90km; here three bridges across the river were rendered impassable. Furniture stranded in tree tops would provide mute illustration of this phenomenon. As many pumping stations were flooded, these high levels ironically led to a serious water shortage, and towns like Hamm, Hagen, Bochum and Dortmund were without water. The important power station at Herdecke, with a capacity of 132,000kW, flooded to a depth of 2m, was also out of action.

The maximum rate of discharge from the Möhne reached 8,800m^3/sec shortly after the breach, declining to 2,000m^3/sec at 0600, 1,000m^3/sec three hours later, and coming to a virtual halt by 1200 on 17 May. The rate of flow of the swollen river reduced rapidly west of Essen, and to some extent this resulted from good fortune. Just south of Essen the Ruhr ran through three lakes: Baldeney (2.4km surface area and storage capacity of 9 million cubic metres), Harkort (1.4km², 3.3. million cubic metres' capacity) and Hengstey (1.6km², 2.8 million cubic metres' capacity). To prevent its being used as a navigational aid for Allied aircraft, the first had been completely drained, though when the attack occurred the other two were full. On receipt of the alarm these two were swiftly emptied, so that effectively three empty lakes with 15.1 million cubic storage storage capacity were available to siphon off a substantial amount of the floodwater. The pumping station at Hengstey was however flooded in the subsequent deluge. Contrary to the contention of those in Neheim, other authorities lower downstream found that the alarm system worked adequately. Those nearer the Möhne failed to react swiftly enough, refusing to believe the extent of the impending disaster. Nevertheless, despite the warning, the catalogue of destruction in the Möhne and Ruhr valleys was extensive.

As dawn broke on Monday 17 May, about three hours after breaching of the dam, gun crews at the Möhne began to remove rubble and restore some semblance of military order to their positions. In addition to the virtual destruction of the left-hand tower, the gun on the right-hand one had to be repaired, the roadway on the remaining section of the dam cleared, and the flak battery's living quarters and store, which had suffered extensively, reorganised. Within hours General Schmidt appeared from Air Zone (*Luftgau*) VI HQ at Münster to inspect the damage and issue orders for the rapid restoration of defensive arrangements. This was incomprehensible to those on the spot, who held that the enemy could hardly do more harm. Even at this early stage plans were afoot to fill the gap in the wall. Military disasters, like triumphs, attract high-ranking officers like bees to a honeypot: Schmidt was succeeded next day by General Weise, commander of the entire air defence of the Reich. In keeping with the practice of remote commanders, Weise praised the gun crews for their efforts, lauded their success in destroying one of the attackers and retired.

Such was the devastation in the Ruhr valley that German schoolchildren were brought in from the surrounding areas by bus to help in the cleansing process. At Niederensee one recalled seeing 'terrible things': old people sitting on top of their houses and waiting to be rescued with water lapping their shoes, dead cats and dogs, toys and domestic articles strewn about haphazardly. As the children helped to clear debris, soldiers and police concentrated on assisting stranded people. A massive rescue operation had been launched. Municipal authorities were reinforced by specialist Luftwaffe and Wehrmacht personnel, firemen, Red Cross workers, police and paramilitary units, plus an influx of Todt Organisation workers. Rehousing of the homeless was partly achieved by compulsory billeting within the area or, for non-essential people, evacuation; temporary labourers brought to the Möhne were accommodated in tents. Over 2,000 civilian and military helpers, diverted from their normal duties elsewhere, concentrated on Neheim and Wickede alone. The process of restoration did not prove simple. When Peter Theunissen, a conscript labourer, gained permission to travel back to the Netherlands on 5 June to visit his wife, who was dangerously ill, railway facilities in the area of Schwerte had still not been re-established, so that he had to make a lengthy detour. In fact, not until two days later did a single track begin to operate between Neheim and Hagen. On Thursday 20 May one inevitable sequel took place in a square in Neheim: a mass funeral service. Final official figures would show that below the Möhne 1,294 casualties were incurred: 476 German dead, 69 missing; 593 foreigners dead, 156 missing. Ninety-two houses were totally destroyed, 971 houses and 32 farms damaged. In all, eleven factories were totally destroyed and 114 damaged; 2,822 hectares of arable land, meadows and pasture were rendered useless and 1,221 damaged; the bodies of 6,316 cattle and pigs were found; 25 road and railway bridges were totally destroyed and 21 railway bridges damaged; and numerous power stations, pumping stations, and water and gas supply facilities were damaged or destroyed.

Much the same picture emerged near the Eder Dam. People in the vicinity were not unduly perturbed when they heard aircraft approaching shortly after 0100 on 17 May. As with the Möhne, the people expected the Allied aircraft to use the glistening surface of the reservoir as a navigational aid. Karl Albrecht, engineer-in-charge of the two power stations below the dam, was therefore totally surprised when the first mine exploded almost 30 minutes later, damaging the wall towards the northern end and Hemfurth I power station below it. Albrecht did not distinguish between the second and third attacks and seemed to assume that only two occurred. For he recalled being on the steps of Hemfurth II power station when he heard a dull thud (Knight's mine exploding under the water on the far side of the wall), and the ground trembled so violently that he thought the whole building would collapse. Irrationally, instead of fleeing into the open, he dashed into the threatened building to find everything in darkness. As masonry and water began to crash through the roof, he belatedly fled up the steps to the crown of the dam and saw the breach, which became wider even as he watched, and water from the reservoir gushing into the valley below. Another witness, an official of the Edersee dam authority, August Rubsam, found himself flung bodily several metres by the force of the explosion. Once he had recovered his composure he realised that his duty was to inform the responsible authority at Hannover-Münden of the disaster. But stranded north of the breach he was helpless to do so because all telegraph and telephone links had been cut in the immediate area. In Hemfurth below the dam people stood outside their houses early on 17 May and listened to the course of events without understanding what was happening. One farmer reported seeing a pilot poke his head out of the cockpit window as he flew beyond the dam, another that two explosions occurred close together about a half-hour after aircraft were first heard. The third decisive explosion, followed by 'an awful commotion,' took place at about 0200. In the Hemfurth I power station an engineer swept away by the ensuing tide and drowned became the first victim at the Eder. His body was found 20km away at Wabern.

Rescue services were once more organised swiftly as soon as the nature of the disaster had been fully understood. The duty official at the Bad Wildungen post office seven kilometres south-east of the Eder Dam heard the air-raid warning and then the sound of aircraft engines. Thinking that the Mauser small-arms factory on the Netze-Bühlen road east of Waldeck would be the target, he warned the flak position there, only to be told that the enemy had flown over. He went into the yard again and, like others in the area, listened to the unopposed aircraft circling without following the course of action or appreciating that the dam was under attack. 'I saw a high spiteful-green flame rise up and shortly afterwards an explosion, followed by a din like the distant, muffled sound of a railway engine.' Running into the post office he heard over the phone: 'Edersee here, the dam wall is broken, I . . .' The line went dead and all efforts to restore contact failed. So the postmaster at Bad Wildungen began to ring round other villages in the Eder valley. Affoldern, close to the dam, was contacted first, then within minutes every village as far as Fritzlar; the urgency of the situation was impressed on everybody. Arguably, this prompt action by Bad Wildungen post office saved many people's lives. Typical of the reaction to the warning was that of one resident in the valley: 'I immediately leapt into the cellar and called: "The dam is broken, everybody out of the cellar. The water is coming," grabbed my youngest child and ran outside to get to higher ground.' Scarcely had many scrambled to safety in this way than the raging torrent swept away everything in its path. At Hemfurth the iron suspension bridge disintegrated; in Affoldern the church, school and many dwellings were demolished.

The Eder Dam suffered from all three mines which exploded there. Shannon's caused damage in the area of the steps at the western end of the dam and also cracked the main wall. Eyewitnesses claimed that AJ-L's mine exploded just short of the dam wall near the right bank, Edersee village and Hemfurth II power station, damaging the parapet of the dam, the roadway and steps leading to the landing stage. Because most of the blast from its explosion went into the air, Maudslay's mine damaged only the pavement on the air side and part of the roadway above the tenth overflow outlet, together with the ashlar parapets on both sides of the road. Later German reports referred to this damage as 'cracks and loosened spots' and admitted that lengthy horizontal fissures were visible well beyond the area of the main breach. Knight had left a V-shaped breach slightly to the right (south) of centre; German reports mentioned 'a radius of 25m' or 'a semi-oval breach 70m wide and 22m deep.' At the bottom of the breach the wall was 18m thick and, in effect, some 30,000 tons of stone had been lanced from the structure.

At the time of the breach the lake contained 202.4 million cubic metres of water, of which 154.4 million cubic metres escaped. The initial outflow was 8,500m³/sec, slightly less than at the Möhne, where the breach was larger. This fact, plus the greater capacity of the Eder reservoir, meant that discharge continued for almost 48 hours. Even though an estimated wave 12m high and 8m wide was reported, the average depth and speed of the water were less than in the Möhne valley. For the Eder valley was broader, which allowed the flood to spread outwards more readily. At a point 75km downstream the maximum water level was below that of the highest known flood, in January 1941. At Interschede, near Bremen (425.6km from the Eder Dam), the flow of water was but 665m³/sec, and at Hannover-Münden (94.4km below the Eder) the wave flowed at approximately 2m/sec or some 5 mph, a third of the speed of the Möhne flood. Two-thirds of the water released from the Eder reservoir reached Interschede; that is, an estimated 58 million cubic metres of floodwater had spread across the valley before that point. Breaching of the Eder thus released a tidal wave which in some measure affected areas over 400km from the dam.

SS Colonel Burk, who organised troops for rescue operations in the area immediately below the dam, reported: 'The first impression of damage is devastating. The affected population have lost their houses. It is impossible to form any kind of picture of the casualties.' And in some ways the Eder attack was more far-reaching than that at the Möhne. Heavy flooding of valuable agricultural land and silting-up of irrigation, pumping and electricity supply facilities occurred and, moreover, the bed of the Eder river up to its meeting with Fulda was, in the words of a later German estimate, 'devastated'. In the Eder reservoir waves created by the explosions tossed small vessels high up the banks, shattering them, and as the water receded others were left helpless on the dry bed of the lake. In four places the sides of the reservoir had been affected by landslides and collapse of the banks as a result of the rapid lowering of the water level. For anglers, too, came the realisation that almost the entire stock of fish in the Eder reservoir had been lost. Below the wall holes with a volume of six cubic metres had been scoured by a combination of flood and blast. The cable conducting power between the two power stations and the connecting bridge had been destroyed. The additional equalising basin 3.3km in length below the dam between Hemfurth and Affoldern had disintegrated (only 500m remained unscathed), leading to heavy flooding in this area. The flood also immobilised four power stations close to the reservoir. A landslide one kilometre below the Eder Dam caused the road, which ran parallel to the river and on which Chastise crews saw the ill-fated car and its occupants swamped immediately after the attack, to subside up to two metres over a distance of 2km. With floods as high as seven metres recorded down to Hannover-Münden, few communities on the banks of the Eder, Fulda and Weser rivers between that town and the dam escaped heavy damage. Bergheim, whose flood defences proved very effective, suffered comparatively little, but houses at Mehlen and Giflitz were severely hit, the railway station at Giflitz was destroyed, and in Paul a large woodyard was swept away to the last stick. Although the inhabitants of Fritzlar had ample warning, to their cost many refused to believe that, even if the Eder Dam were broken, they could be troubled. The people of Kassel were warned of the approaching flood before dawn but were not affected until the afternoon of 17 May, when a flood nearly 2m deep inundated parts of the old town. Although dwelling houses and recreational facilities were swamped, the Henschel railway works and factories making aeroplane engines and military vehicles were not. Hemfurth and Affoldern were awash, as was a wide expanse of the region between Wabern and Falsburg. The runway at Fritzlar military airfield and buildings on the north-western edge of it were under water. Near Giflitz a railway bridge carrying the main line to Giessen and Frankfurt had been swept away. A German photographer summarised the problem when on 18 May he recorded the delivery of milk by rowing boat to inhabitants of Karlshafen, 139km below the Eder.

The effect of the floodwater was indeed extensive. Between Gunterhausen and Hannover-Münden the sluices of several small lakes were silted up and suffered structural damage. 30,000 cubic metres of earth had to be dredged from the Fulda and 5,000 cubic metres from the Weser beyond Hannover-Münden to restore navigable channels to normal. About 1,000 groynes were destroyed in the Weser, while there was serious damage to the banks of the Weser and Fulda; for the former some 5½km of bank had to be rebuilt. Apart from loss of life among people and cattle, some 50 hectares of land lost their valuable topsoil, and fertile fields were strewn with shingle and scree to a depth of two metres. The total damage could only be estimated at 'millions of Reichsmarks'.

In the administrative area of Waldeck, which included Affoldern, Bergheim, Giflitz and Hemfurth, 29 people (aged from one to 78) lost their lives; the overall figure for the Eder Valley was 47. In these places, together with Edersee, Mehlen and Anraff, 112 dwelling houses and 101 places of work were either totally destroyed or damaged. And those who strove to repair the damage produced an interesting negative fact. In the area of the Eder Dam no evidence of a crashed aircraft came to light, and a later theory that the wreckage of Maudslay's plane must have been swept away in the flood was effectively discounted when no remains were found downstream after the tide receded, nor on adjoining hills. Heinrich George, deputy director of the construction authority responsible for repair of the road network in the Eder valley, visited the dam on the morning after the raid and frequently travelled thereafter to construction sites in the area, and he heard no mention of a crash in the vicinity of the Eder at this time.

The attacks by McCarthy and Brown on the Sorpe, resulting as they did in no breaching of the dam, understandably created only minor interest in adjacent communities, while evoking positive official reaction. Seventeen months later the failure did prompt No 9 Squadron RAF to attack the dam, again unsuccessfully, with another of Wallis's brainwaves, his 12,000lb Tallboy. Prüss's official report on the Möhne also covered the Sorpe Dam, and once more its distorted details showed how confused both witnesses and authorities were by the attacks. The account of McCarthy's attack, 'at about 0045 . . . from an approximate height of 20 metres,' on the dam 'not protected by flak or balloon barrage or nets' was accurate. It agreed that the single aircraft flew across the dam 'several times' before dropping its mine on the tenth run. But, thereafter, Prüss forsook reality. Noting, correctly, that shortly after 0200 the Luftwaffe Air Zone reported the approach of between four and six aircraft from Holland along the same route as that used by the first wave, he claimed that two of these aircraft flew to the Sorpe, attempting 'to locate the damaged spot with their spotlights'. On its fifth run one of the aircraft dropped the second mine on the dam. It may be that on his way to the Ennepe Townsend flew close to the Sorpe or that one of the Brown's dummy runs (Prüss recorded that he made 'six or five' attacks) was confused with that of a second machine.

Theunissen, the Dutch conscript labourer who returned to the Netherlands early in June, was awakened at Hachen on the Röhr river below the Sorpe Dam in the early hours of 17 May 'by a tremendous din'. Looking out of the window he saw a four-engined aircraft apparently heading straight for the house. Sweeping low over the village, it banked sharp left and disappeared behind a hill, known to the workers as 'Angel Mountain'. Theunissen felt sure that it must have made a forced landing, but almost certainly he witnessed Brown on his third abortive attack, when AJ-F nearly crashed in a valley.

The dam was neither breached nor severely damaged, although the blast did cause some structural damage to the pumping station below at the side of the compensating basin and to houses in the vicinity. Prüss reported that two craters were discovered 30m apart 3m below the water level and that explosions had sent water 150–200m into the air, although their downward effect had been 'damped by the material of the rubble dam'. According to Prüss both craters were 'small,' but another German estimate made them 12m deep, and a third 8m in diameter by 4.5m deep. The dam essentially 'remained undamaged,' but the blast from the explosions had stripped the concrete wall on the water side 'to a depth of several metres'. Walking through maintenance tunnels at the base of the dam hours after the attacks, Ruhrtalsperrenverein inspection staff found no sign of seepage, but estimated that 70m of the crown had been torn away.

German sources raise a particular question mark about the Bever Dam, which no British document shows as being connected with Operation Chastise. The War Diary of the German Naval Staff (Operations Division) reported that the Bever Dam had been attacked without effect and Prüss wrote: 'At the same time as the Sorpe dam attack the Bever dam was attacked. Only one mine was dropped and fell about 800 metres from the dam wall in the middle of the reservoir and did no damage.' Subsequently the *Wupperverband* authority, responsible for the Bever Dam, recovered the remains of that mine close to the position of a dam which had been superseded following the enlargement of the Bever reservoir in 1935–9. Some post-operational British documents have further confused the issue by apparently referring to the Ennepe Dam as 'Schwelme', and 20 years later the German writer Hans Rumpf (perhaps attempting to make sense of British sources) claimed that two aircraft bombed the Schwelme Dam, which had 'an earth wall,' thus substituting 'Schwelme' for 'Sorpe'. No dam named 'Schwelme' existed in the area, and the only one of earthen construction other than the Sorpe was the Bever. There was, too, an eyewitness to an attack on the Bever Dam on 17 May 1943. Paul Keiser, a 19-year-old soldier on leave at his home close to the dam, awoke at about 0300 to the noise of an aircraft flying low over the dam wall. He dressed quickly and went outside: 'The aircraft made several approaches always from an easterly direction towards the west. It turned away over the dam to begin its attack profile in the same direction no higher than 100m in bright moonlight, dropped its weapon, there was a big

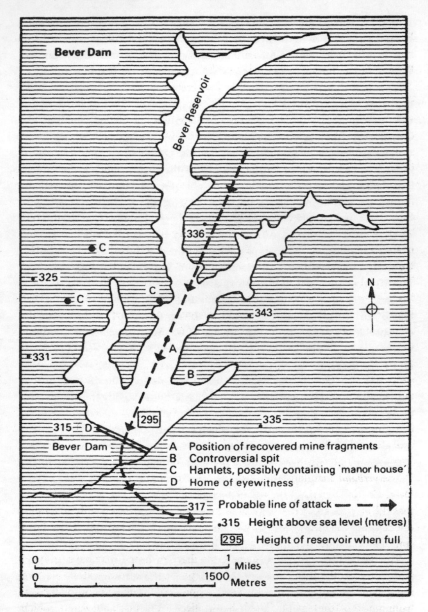

Bever Dam

Bever Reservoir

336

C

325

C

C

343

331

A

B

295

315 D

Bever Dam

335

A Position of recovered mine fragments
B Controversial spit
C Hamlets, possibly containing 'manor house'
D Home of eyewitness

317 Probable line of attack ━ ━ ━ ➤

315 Height above sea level (metres)

295 Height of reservoir when full

0   1
                        Miles
0   1500
                      Metres

explosion and a great pillar of flame in a column of water. The aircraft then
flew an identical pattern over the spot at which it dropped the weapon, lifted
over the dam wall and flew off in a westerly direction.'

Without having this evidence at his disposal, but evidently puzzled by Prüss's report, Wallis's biographer has stated that Townsend dropped his mine a half-mile short of the Ennepe Dam, thus effectively using 'Ennepe' for Prüss's 'Bever' and neatly solving the problem. However the *Ennepe-Wasserverband* authority is adamant that only a single bomb dropped near the Ennepe Dam during the entire war, some 350m short of the wall 'in the wood on the side of the dam,' and not in the water. This therefore apparently discounts Professor J. E. Morpurgo's conclusion, but also raises more searching queries about Townsend's attack. He reported dropping his mine in the water short of the dam, so that the spreading circle of disturbed water reached the dam wall after the explosion. And he admitted difficulty in finding the dam, which he eventually determined by 'profile of hills'. A German on the ground about 2,000m above the dam wall recalled an aircraft 'circling' the Ennepe reservoir 'for about ¾ hour' at approximately 0300, but heard no explosion. This may have been during the airborne conference, conducted by AJ-O's crew, to determine how to attack their target. For, as Townsend complained in his post-raid report, the map of the reservoir was inaccurate: there was no island, only a spit of land, in front of the dam. That is perfectly correct. Technically, with reference to the map and taking into account the magnetic variation at the Ennepe, it would be possible to attack the dam to the east of the 'island' on a bearing of 355°M as reported. But, in practice, aerial photographs and others taken from the centre of the dam show that the tree-covered 'island' or spit of land is directly in front of the two towers and only 300m from them. This would seem to eliminate any prospect of a briefed approach run and release of the weapon some 425 yards from the dam, so that the spreading circle of disturbed water reached the dam wall after the explosion. Independently the navigator, Howard, noted seeing a 'large manor house' to starboard during the approach run, but the *Ennepe-Wasserverband* maintains that no such building existed above the Ennepe Dam. Crucially, perhaps, one of Townsend's crew in a position to see holds that the aircraft attacked an 'earthen dam': the Bever Dam is only five miles due south of the Ennepe and very similar in layout to the Ennepe. It also has a spit of land to port of an ideal attack run.

The possibility must therefore be faced that Townsend may have, in good faith, attacked the Bever and not the Ennepe Dam. To some extent his own report and the comments of his crew support this view. He complained of 'running into [the] moon in half-light reflected on mist and water,' which was impossible if he attacked on 355°M. The moon's azimuth was 242° and altitude 16°05', which is consistent with an attack on the Bever Dam, not the Ennepe. Three of AJ-O's crew later stated quite independently that the moon had been on the starboard beam during the attack. Furthermore, a substantial building, which with the moon behind it may have resembled a 'manor house,' lay to starboard of an attacking run on the Bever Dam and about 1,200m from it. There were no towers on the Bever Dam. But approximately 500m apart at its extremities were two identical, small buildings used to store equipment, which in the conditions may have seemed like towers. If the bomb-aimer used the setting for the Ennepe Dam, he could have dropped his mine over 800m from the dam wall; and the data produced before the operation by Bullard, the Admiralty scientist, on the outward spread of waves from the point of an explosion in a reservoir would explain Webb's comment that the circle of disturbed water was bisected by the dam and the official report of 'ripples seen against the dam.' Townsend reported three runs, after which he carried out port circuits, and that he made another similar sweep after dropping his mine. This roughly fits Keiser's eyewitness account. However, Townsend firmly reported an attack on 355°M. If this were correct, AJ-O could not have attacked the Bever Dam. But it is the only available piece of evidence which rebuts that conclusion, and it may actually represent a staff officer's refusal to believe that AJ-O attacked on a bearing of about 210°M. He therefore treated that figure as a clerical error by the pilot or navigator (neither of whose original reports has survived) and substituted the briefed bearing in typed summaries of the operation.

On balance, therefore, German sources reinforce what Townsend, his navigator and his wireless operator unconsciously and separately revealed. Without realising it, the crew of AJ-O carried out a perfect attack on the Bever Dam. Unfortunately, they had no hope of success because the setting of the sight applied to the Ennepe. Moreover, the Bever had a concrete core supported by earth banks, demanding an attack of the type mounted against the Sorpe. And any pilot flying over the Ennepe reservoir would have been entitled to reject it as the target: attack with a bouncing mine there would have been literally impossible. It may be significant that neither on the radio nor in the British press was an attack on the Ennepe mentioned and that in post-operational reports the confusing designation 'Schwelme' was frequently – and perhaps deliberately – used. No river Schwelm flowed into any reservoir, but a small town of that name lay 6 miles north-west of the Ennepe and 10 miles north-north-west of the Bever. Claims to have attacked the shadowy 'Schwelme Dam', a description perhaps applicable to any dam geographically close to Schwelm, could not be readily refuted by the Germans.

Both the fact of the attacks and the implications of their success brought rapid reaction from German Government ministers. Albert Speer, as Minister

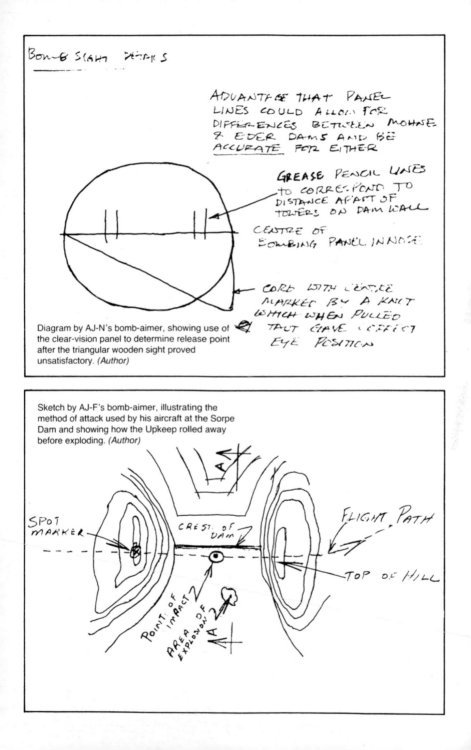

Bomb Sight Things

ADVANTAGE THAT PANEL
LINES COULD ALLOW FOR
DIFFERENCES BETWEEN MOHNE
& EDER DAMS AND BE
ACCURATE FOR EITHER

GREASE PENCIL LINES
TO CORRESPOND TO
DISTANCE APART OF
TOWERS ON DAM WALL

CENTRE OF
BOMBING PANEL IN NOSE

CORD WITH CENTRE
MARKED BY A KNOT
WHICH WHEN PULLED
TAUT GAVE CORRECT
EYE POSITION

Diagram by AJ-N's bomb-aimer, showing use of
the clear-vision panel to determine release point
after the triangular wooden sight proved
unsatisfactory. *(Author)*

Sketch by AJ-F's bomb-aimer, illustrating the
method of attack used by his aircraft at the Sorpe
Dam and showing how the Upkeep rolled away
before exploding. *(Author)*

SPOT
MARKER

CREST OF
DAM

FLIGHT PATH

TOP OF HILL

POINT OF IMPACT

AREA OF EXPLOSION

TIME	RQD. TRACK (T)	USED AND D.R. DRIFT	Course (T)	Course (M)	NAVIGATIONAL OBSERVATIONS (Pin-points, Fixes, Position Lines, Actual T.M.G., Actual Drift, G/S and W/V, Manoeuvres, etc.)	GENERAL OBSERVATIONS (Met. Conditions, Bombing, Intelligence, Enemy Action, etc.)	R.A.S.	HEIGHT & A. TEMP	T.A.S	D.R. G/S	DIST. TO RUN	D.R. TIME	E.
					WATCHES SYNCHRONISED — 1ST CHECKED	OK							
					Checks Away								
					Airborne BASE	IFF on							
	125		120	128	BASE s/c SOUTHWOLD		173	150'	182	184	117		
					WOODBRIDGE SPA								
					Cross River near Canal c/s 184	Test Searchlight with O/P							
					W/V 065/10 a/c								
					W/E Elsham								
					W/V 055/19 a/c								
					Fix 5238 0148								
					W/V 190/10 a/c				170				
	120		117	126	SOUTHWOLD a/c Posn C	Replace a/c	179	150'	180	170	99	35	
					W/V 165/9								
						1SS +55							
					Fix 5207 0208								
					W/V 090/10 a/c								
					Fix 5242 0232 TMG 190, a/s 180						174	54	
					W/V 000/28 a/c								
					Fix 5314 0208 c/s 190								
					W/V 254/15 a/c								
			090	095	Posn C a/c Posn D	Bomb Fused				135	85		
					W/V 060/16 a/c	Evasive Action							
										162	24	9	
			095	093	Posn D a/c Posn E	Leader turns back				168	51	18	
					W/V 060/101								
	065		065	072	Posn E a/c Posn F					155	37		
					W/V 060/10 a/c	GEE Jammed something chronic							
					P/P 5140 0610P c/s 169								
	082		082	088	Posn F a/c Posn G					165	36	13	
						Flak Spred at a/c Evasive							
					Cross Railway G/s 165	Taken							
					W/V 065/101 a/c								
	100		095	103	Posn G a/c Posn H	Identify Turning Point O.K.			180	170	31	9	
					W/V 060/10 a/c	Evasive action							
	155		151	159	Posn H s/c Target X	Switch on VHF			186	190	13		
					Target X	Contact S/L - Circling							
					W/V 060/10 a/c	Flak far too light							
						Receive OK. Flak.							
						Bomb Dropped Wizard							
						Send Message							
	188		343	349	Target X s/c Posn 4	Message Received O.K.		150'	320	219	19	5	
									204				
	260		278	284	Posn 4 a/c Posn G	Identify T/P			205	220	31		
	351		355	007	Posn G s/c Posn T	T/P							
					W/V 020/8 H/P	Evasive Action			205	200	45		
					P/P GUDSWOLD TMG 351								
					W/V 018/9 H/P								
	284		292	299	Posn T a/c Posn 4				205	205	47	14	
					a/c P/P PARKEBORGH a/s 302	TMG 289							
					W/V ML a/c								
	280		282	290	5203N 00048 a/c Posn 5				205	208	129	38	
			282	288	a/c								
					Cross Coast G/s 202	GEE still no dice							
						Flak North of Coast and							
						Searchlight							
					Fix 52 55½ 0200R TMG 280½ c/s 205								
					W/V NIL a/c	GEE Faint but workable							
						Change Colours of Day							
	278	NIL	282	287	D/R Fix 5230N 0240E a/c BASE					200	152	45½	
						Lowered a/c				196			
					Fix 5201 N 0222R	Rounding		1580	190	190	105	67	
					W/V 270/10 H/P	Down again Test Warning							
			210	300	VANTHLEY s/c BASE					187	39	12½	
					BASE W/V NIL a/c								
					Landed BASE	(10)							

Sgt W Nicolson.

Möhne Dam, showing the "double line boom with timber spreaders" supporting two underwater anti-torpedo nets, ornamental trees as ineffective camouflage on the dam wall, and two power stations. *(BAC)*

Gibson's signature in the Möhne breach, those of other Chastise crews on the shore of the drained reservoir. Note additional ornamental trees at left-hand end of dam, installed since pre-raid photograph (above) taken in April. *(BAC)*

Left: Navigator's log for Operation Chastise. Despite the peculiar operational conditions, it is a model record of AJ-J's flight to and from the Möhne Dam. *(617 Squadron)*

Möhne Dam the morning after. Note thickness of the shattered wall and continuing surge of water through the breach.
(Ruhrtalsperrenverein)

Möhne Dam later that day (May 17). The outflow has eased. Note size of breach and obliterated power station.
(Ruhrtalsperrenverein)

Another view of Möhne Dam, with rubble in foreground, anti-torpedo defences swept away, near-empty reservoir, and roof of tower prepared for flak gun.
(Ruhrtalsperrenverein)

May 17: submerged road, power station, bridges, railway coaches and sidings at Fröndenberg in Ruhr valley. *(IWM)*

Sorpe Dam, May 17. Note crumbling crest. Discoloration on slope and in compensating basin raised hopes of seepage. *(PRO)*

AJ-N's crew, who breached the Eder Dam. On a subsequent operation Plt Off Knight sacrificed his life, keeping his crippled Lancaster airborne so that the crew could successfully bale out. *(IWM)*

Eder Dam, with Waldeck Castle framed in the breach. *(Collins)*

Eder Dam, May 18. Water is still escaping through the breach, which is neatly silhouetted by the sun. *(IWM)*

May 18: swollen River Fulda and flooding in several areas of Kassel, 30 miles downstream from the Eder Dam. *(IWM)*

OPS HRS 101.35

Time carried forward :— 1788/05 1674.40

Date	Hour	Aircraft Type and No	Pilot	Duty	Remarks (Including results of bombing, gunnery, exercises, etc.)	Day	Night
13.5.43	1530	LANC L.929	F/L SHANNON	B/A	Y COUNTRY + BOMBING	1.20	
13.5.43	2105	LANC L.929	F/L SHANNON	B/A	NIGHT Y COUNTRY + BOMBING		2.30
14.5.43	1345	LANC D.703	F/L SHANNON	B/A	BASE - MANSTON - BASE	2.30	
14.5.43	2140	LANC L.929	F/L SHANNON	B/A	NIGHT EXERCISE.		1.30
16.5.43	2150	LANC L.923(R)	D.F. F/L SHANNON	BOMB AIMER	OP N°18. VIA HOLLAND TO THE		6.30
			F/S SUMPTER		HUN. SATISFACTORY ATTACK ON		
			F/O WALKER (N)	D.F.C.	EDER DAM 18 MILES WEST		
			F/O GOODALE (W/O)	D.F.C.	OF KASSEL. AVERAGE HT.		
			F/O BUCKLEY (2/E)		100 FEET.		
			SGT HENDERSON (F/E).				
			SGT JAGGER (F/G) (KILLED 20.9.44)				

SUMMARY FOR MAY 1943.
UNIT A.F. 617 SQDN. ... DAY 14.40 (1)
DATE 6.6.43 .... NIGHT 15.15 (2)
SIGNATURE .... (3)
O/C 617 SQDN ... TOTAL 29.55 (4)

TOTAL TIME... 1794.55 178. :10.

Extract from the logbook of F/Sgt L. J. Sumpter, showing two cross-country exercises, flight to Manston prior to Upkeep practice at Reculver, the final night rehearsal and Operation Chastise. *(Sumpter)*

Above: Gibson's crew entering AJ-G. Left to right: Trevor-Roper, Pulford, Deering, Spafford, Hutchison, Gibson, Taerum. Four were killed in September 1943, none survived the war. *(IWM)*

Below: Debriefing for Gibson's crew. Left to right: (sitting) intelligence officer, Spafford, Taerum, Trevor-Roper; Pulford and Deering partly hidden. Harris and Cochrane observe. *(IWM)*

Above left: Casualty telegram received shortly after noon on May 17, informing Mrs Tees that her son was missing. *(Tees)*

Above right: Sgt F. Tees, sole survivor of AJ-C's crash. *(Tees)*

Right: Letter from Gibson to Mrs Tees. Hope of survival is held out, but Sgt Tees is wrongly placed in the front turret. *(Tees)*

Telegram text:

PRIORITY MRS. E TEES 23 ST-JAMES ROAD CHICHESTER -

REGRET TO INFORM YOU THAT YOUR SON SGT F TEES IS MISSING AS A RESULT OF OPERATION ON NIGHT 16/17 TH MAY 43 LETTER FOLLOWS PLEASE ACCEPT MY PROFOUND SYMPATHY -

OC 617 SQUADRON

Reference :-
DD/6/43

No. 617 Squadron, RAF Station,
Scampton, Lincs.

20th. May, 1943.

My Dear Mrs Tees,

It is with deep regret that I write to confirm my telegram advising you that your son, Sergeant F. Tees, is missing as a result of operations on the night of May 16/17th., 1943.

Your son was Front Gunner of an aircraft detailed to carry out an attack against the Mohne Dam. Contact with this aircraft was lost after it took off, and nothing further was heard from it.

It is possible that the crew were able to abandon the aircraft and land safely in enemy territory, in which case news will reach you direct from the International Red Cross Committee within the next six weeks. The captain of your son's aircraft, Pilot Officer Ottley, was an experienced and able pilot, and would, I am sure, do everything possible to ensure the safety of his crew.

Please accept my sincere sympathy during this anxious period of waiting.

I have arranged for your son's personal effects to be taken care of by the Committee of Adjustment Officer at this Station, and these will be forwarded to you through normal channels in due course.

If there is any way in which I can help you, please let me know.

Yours Very Sincerely,
G. Gibson
Wing Commander,
Commanding, 617 Squadron, RAF.

Mrs. E. Tees,
23, St. James Rd.,
Chichester, Sussex.

Headquarters, No. 5 Group,
Royal Air Force,
St. Vincents,
Grantham, Lincs.

17th May, 1943.

BAC/DG/1/Air.

Dear Wallis,

Before reaching the end of this somewhat long but exciting day I feel I must write to tell you how much I admire the perseverance which brought you the astounding success which was achieved last night. Without your determination to ensure that a method which you knew to be technically sound was given a fair trial we should not have been able to deliver the blow which struck Germany last night.

2. I spoke to the Commander-in-Chief about your other project and is expressed the greatest interest. He asked if you would send him as soon as possible a copy of any papers bearing on the problem and when I suggested that you might come down in person to explain what you had in mind he said that this would be an excellent idea. I suggest, therefore, that you should get in touch either with him or with the Deputy Commander-in-Chief, Air Vice-Marshal R. H. M. Saundby, who also knows of the project.

3. If you want a trial there should be no difficulty in dropping the projectile which you have at Weybridge.

Yours sincerely

R. Cochrane

B. N. Wallis, Esq.,
c/o Messrs. Vickers Armstrong Co. Ltd.,
WEYBRIDGE.

P.S. Since writing this I have heard the result of the full photographic cover. What a dinster.

A.C.F.
W.A. DIVISION

R.A.F. Scampton.

May 20th

My Dear Mr Wallis,

Now that the floods are subsiding and the tumult dying down (Wait for the Surge) I'm at last found time to drop you a line. I'm afraid I've not much of a letter writer but I would like to say just this. The weeks that you gave up to deliver what like a dream - at you have earned the thanks of the civilized world.

All my fullest and I had the opportunity to represent the last [...] experiment in which two heard at your Heuston.

The [...], I wish you

Best Regards to [...] Staff and Hands

Yours Sincerely,
Guy Gibson

WRITE ON BOTH SIDES   IT'S A WARTIME ECONOMY.

Left: Cochrane's generous tribute to Wallis. Note Harris's willingness to consider a deep-penetration bomb now. *(Wallis)*

Examining the Möhne model during royal visit to Scampton, May 27. Left to right: Cochrane, Gibson, the King, Whitworth. *(IWM)*

Royal visit to Scampton. The King talks to the American McCarthy; background, Queen Elizabeth meets Shannon on his twenty-first birthday. *(IWM)*

Left: Gibson's personal letter to Wallis, written after completing 56 to next of kin. Note his hope that the Sorpe would yet collapse. *(Wallis)*

Group photograph during the royal visit. Their Majesties are flanked by Cochrane and Whitworth; Wallis is behind the King. *(Crown Copyright)*

Buckingham Palace, June 22. Chadwick (Avro Lancaster designer) and Gibson after receiving CBE and VC respectively. *(Sport & General)*

Right: Outside Buckingham Palace. Flt Lt D. J. Shannon and Sec Off A. Fowler, who met at Scampton before Operation Chastise and later married. *(Crown Copyright)*

Outside Buckingham Palace. Gibson, flanked by Martin and McCarthy, with others decorated for their part in Chastise. *(Sport & General)*

Illustration from a pamphlet dropped on Occupied France, showing anticipated damage to German industry through destruction of the Möhne Dam. *(Burton)*

Photographic proof. Reconnaissance photograph of the breached Möhne Dam with explanatory notes in French, included in the same pamphlet. *(Burton)*

REPERCUSSIONS SUR L'INDUSTRIE ALLEMANDE

Schéma illustrant les effets de la rupture du barrage de la Möhne, dont la génératrice fournissait l'énergie destinée à une chaîne de villes industrielles de la Ruhr.

Repairing the Möhne Dam. Loose masonry beyond and below the original breach is being removed. Note small steam engine under tower and debris beneath wall. *(Ruhrtalsperrenverein)*

Work under way at the Möhne Dam. Note balloon overhead and manned flak gun on tower, part of strengthened defences. *(Ruhrtalsperrenverein)*

Eder Dam with repairs almost finished. Note balloons at varying distances from the wall. *(Crown Copyright)*

Above: Warning notice on the Eder Dam. Anybody defacing the wall was threatened with a fine of RM1,000 or two years' imprisonment. *(Collins)*

Below: Post-war snapshot of the Eder Dam. Note that emergency sluices destroyed in the attack were not remade. *(Shannon)*

Menu card for the celebratory dinner on the evening of the Palace investiture. Note quaint spelling of "damn" and "Rhur", the second certainly inadvertent, and signatures of Gibson, Chadwick and stage personalities also dining at the Hungaria Restaurant. *(Sumpter)*

Below: Thirty-four years later. Menu card for Sir Barnes Wallis's ninetieth birthday dinner at a hotel near Effingham, with signatures of Chastise survivors. *(Author)*

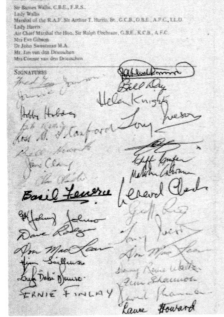

"DAMN BUSTERS"

Dinner to celebrate
the decoration
of members of
617 Squadron R.A.F.

following their gallant effort
on the Rhur Dams.

Given by A. V. ROE & Co Ltd.

THE HUNGARIA RESTAURANT
DORLAND HOUSE
14-16 REGENT STREET
LONDON · S·W·1

TUESDAY, 22nd JUNE 1943.

Our Guests

Sir Barnes Wallis, C.B.E., F.R.S.
Lady Wallis
Marshal of the R.A.F. Sir Arthur T. Harris, Bt., G.C.B., O.B.E., A.F.C., LL.D.
Lady Harris
Air Chief Marshal the Hon. Sir Ralph Cochrane, G.B.E., K.C.B., A.F.C.
Mrs Eve Gibson
Dr John Sweetman M.A.
Mr. Jan van den Driesschen
Mrs Connie van den Driesschen

SIGNATURES

"HE'S ALWAYS TRYING TO IMPRESS
EVERYBODY WITH HIS BARNES WALLIS
LANDINGS"

"Happy Birthday, Sir Barnes"
from the wartime aircrew of
617 Squadron, RAF, The Dam Busters.

of Armaments and Munitions, received 'most alarming [news] . . . in the early hours of the morning' that the Möhne was 'shattered,' its reservoir 'emptied' and that 'three other dams' had been attacked. He quickly made arrangements to visit the locality, flew over the Möhne, where 'the power plant at the foot of the shattered dam looked as if it had been erased, along with its heavy turbines,' and landed at Werl airfield shortly after dawn in a Fieseler Storch. He was in no doubt that the bombers had 'tried to strike at our whole armaments industry by destroying the hydroelectric plants of the Ruhr'. The black and white carcases of dead animals which speckled the countryside impressed him, but they were only of incidental interest. Surveying the destruction, he demanded flak guns for important German dams by that evening. For two days he inspected the area and consulted experts, concluding: '. . . the seemingly insignificant but grave consequence [of the Ruhr flood was] that the electrical installations at the pumping stations were soaked and immobilised, so that industry was brought to a standstill and the water supply of the population imperilled.' At Dortmund on 18 May, Speer met officials responsible for industrial, water, electricity and gas supplies, talked with Gauleiters Meyer, Schlessmann, Florian and Hoffmann, and sent a summary of his plans for action to Hitler. He then made priority arrangements to bring in electrical experts from all over Germany to get water and power supplies restored as quickly as possible and confiscated 'other motors of this [necessary] type from other factories, regardless of the consequences' to efficiency elsewhere. As a result he planned to have normal water supplies available 'within a few weeks'. Forty-eight hours after the raid, with Hitler's approval, 7,000 workers were on their way to help in the clearing-up process and to prepare for the necessary rebuilding in the administrative areas of the Möhne valley, Eder valley, Dortmund and Kassel, and a further 20,000 were to concentrate as soon as possible; many of these were withdrawn from the Atlantic Wall. Such was the gravity of the situation, Speer noted, that this was the only time that Todt Organisation labourers were employed within Germany rather than in occupied countries, and construction overseers were appointed to supervise the various repair projects. Worried about drinking water, Speer ordered preparation of a special report about the supply and distribution of domestic water supplies, which would take into account associated drainage as well.

On his return to Berlin on 20 May, after flying over the Eder Dam and Weser valley, Speer told Joseph Göbbels that the damage was not as serious as he had at first feared: by the beginning of the following week (22 May) he hoped to have the armaments industry in half-production again, in full working order at the end of that week. Goebbels commented in his diary:

'Speer is truly a management genius.' Neither Goebbels nor Speer noted that if these targets were to be achieved, by Speer's own admission, other factories and other projects (such as the Atlantic Wall) would suffer a haemorrhage of labour and equipment.

Speer recorded that when he reported in person to Hitler the attack made such a 'deep impression' on him that thereafter the Führer kept a close watch on associated events. Certainly the whole episode disturbed him. At a situation conference attended by Field-Marshal Keitel and Major-General Warlimont on 19 May, he referred to 'this disaster in the West'. Particularly worried about reduced production of self-propelled guns in the Ruhr, which was so necessary to balance losses in North Africa and on the Eastern Front, he brushed aside Warlimont's suggestion that the impact of the raid would not be severe: 'That may be so in the three summer months. If a dry year occurs, it will be "catastrophic". If we encounter a year when the Ruhr has no water, can we survive?' In his diary on 18 May Goebbels had already noted the Führer's less restrained instant reaction: according to Goebbels, Hitler was furious at the Luftwaffe's patent impotence in the affair.

Two days before Speer alleviated his worst fears, Goebbels wrote too: 'At the Möhne Dam the wall was ruptured by aerial torpedoes. The power station was washed away. As a result severe damage was caused to the drinking and industrial water supplies of the Ruhr area; this also caused a severe loss of electricity.' He went on to lament that 'many thousands' were believed dead, production must be severely affected and gauleiters, whose fiefs also contained dams, were already clamouring for better defences. The next day he had recovered enough nerve to ridicule Allied claims of 10,000 dead, and express relief that the final total would more likely be 1–2,000. In this figure he appeared, without specifically indicating it, to include the Eder casualties, for in the same entry he referred to 700 dead in the Ruhr, of which half were Russian POWs. He blamed the originator of an 'exaggerated' report of 17 May for giving him an unnecessary 'headache' and filching information from 'Radio London,' tartly adding: 'It's evident by this again how impracticable and irrational it is to broadcast wild stories of that nature to higher authorities.' However, he did admit: 'But for all that, considerable damage has occurred to our Rhine and Ruhr industry.' Unlike Hitler, Goebbels did not primarily blame the Luftwaffe for the disaster. For him its origin lurked in more muddy waters: 'Treachery was at work in the Reich . . . for the English were so precisely able to find their bearings and had after the attack such accurate knowledge of the damage they had caused, that it is hardly conceivable that they had discovered this through aerial reconnaissance alone.' And he was soon able to make unexpected capital out of a report, which appeared in an English newspaper and was repeated in the Swedish press, that the idea for such an operation had been fed to the RAF by a German Jewish refugee. Having condemned his own staff for panicking, he could thus write: 'Now it can be seen how dangerous the Jews are and how right we have been to take them into custody.' An unsavoury and completely unjust corollary to the operation had been fashioned. *Sicherheitsdienst* (Security Police) reports noted however that Goebbels's attempt to divert attention away from the poor German defences and onto Jewish responsibility for the dams attacks was 'a clumsy manoeuvre . . . sharply rejected by many'. Authorities in Halle-Merseburg and Mark Brandenburg reported 'general consternation' at the enemy's ability to hit the dams, and others in Kurhessen specifically revealed criticism of the lack of flak at the dams, with calls for punishment of the guilty.

German military sources sought on the one hand to minimise the entire matter, on the other to exaggerate the number of aircraft involved. The High Command of the Armed Forces (OKW) recorded on 17 May: 'Weak British flying formations entered the area of the Reich last night and dropped a few bombs in specially planned locations. Two reservoirs were damaged and due to the resulting escape of water heavy losses were caused among the civilian population. Eight of the attacking planes were shot down.' This report admitted that the Möhne and Eder dams had been 'badly damaged,' but maintained that the Sorpe had not been hit and that half the attackers did not reach their home base. The Naval Staff explained that 'seven' enemy aircraft had been shot down by anti-aircraft fire, but its account of the operation had barely a nodding acquaintance with fact. '180–190 planes' had operated over German-occupied territory during the night of 16–17 May, '70 of which flew over [the] Reich. Fifty aircraft in two waves attacked a number of valley dams. The Möhne dam and a section of the Eder dam were severely hit. The power plant at the Sorpe was damaged. The Bever dam remained undamaged.' Next day a supplementary report added: 'The raiders flew in in a low-level attack and were not detected either by plane reporting [*sic*] or night fighter controlling equipment [radar]. Only one of the attacked valley dams was protected by light anti-aircraft fire.'

McCarthy's observation that the night fighters were flying too high is borne out by German evidence. Kammhuber noted: 'The night-fighter force could not come to grips with the attackers since it was an attack at the lowest level, and the targets could not be picked up by radar, hence they offered no prey for the night fighters.' To some extent the rigid system of interception zones did not help. At 2359 on 16 May Sgt Kraft took off from Bergen in a Bf1 10 of IV/NJG 1, based at Leeuwarden, bound for the night-fighter zone

Hering in the area of the Helder peninsula, possibly as a late response to McCarthy's outward flight, and landed 105 minutes later. At 0510 the next morning he was 'specially scrambled' and ordered to the *Zander* zone at Zandvort at the neck of the Helder peninsula in pursuit of Townsend on his return flight, and this time he flew for 41 minutes. On neither occasion, despite excellent visibility, did he or his wireless operator Handke see an enemy aircraft, which was hardly surprising since their aircraft orbited at 6,000m. Later Handke learnt that Townsend had flown out 'north-west over Texel/Vlieland at low level'. With a tinge of regret he observed: 'The fact that this last aircraft was at low level and had changed its course from west to north-west probably saved it from being shot down.' Incidentally, this strengthens the argument that AJ-O flew back between Vlieland and Texel, not Terschelling.

The professional inquest in fact continued for some months, with still more versions of the attack circulating. At a Luftwaffe conference in Berlin chaired by Hermann Goering on 6 July, Colonel Dietrich Schwenke, from the Director of Air Armaments' Staff, stated: 'The first bomb made no impression on the dam, fell short of the dam and broke into pieces there. The flak crews had seen all of this imperfectly; they were very excited. The second bomb exploded. We don't know if at the net or the wall; at all events it didn't break the dam. The third bomb penetrated the wall. The fourth attacked, but when it saw that water was flowing out, it flew over the dam without dropping its bomb.' When others present pointed out that this version did not tally with other reports, Schwenke became indignant: 'There is no doubt . . . There were four aircraft, and altogether they made nine attacks. A bomb was not dropped on each attack: in all there were only three. That's absolutely certain.'

There was, too, another very interesting source of information on the operation: the Physical Institute of Göttingen University. Its earthquake observatory recorded seismographic readings of varying millimetres (mm) per second, which when matched with post-operational records confirm different attacks:

0027 0.6mm, 40.8sec	(Gibson, 0028)
0037 0.8mm, 14.9sec	(Martin, 0038)
0043 0.2mm, 02.6sec	(Young)
0049 0.8mm, 57.0sec	(Maltby, 0049)
0137 0.4mm, 34.0sec	(Shannon, 0139)
0150 0.2mm, 40.5sec	(Knight, 0152)
0337 not recorded	(Townsend, 0337)

This report noted that the movement recorded at 0337 was 180km west of Göttingen; that is, in the area of the Ennepe and Bever dams. The seismic disturbance recorded at 0043 would have been caused by Young's mine at the Möhne, but in compiling his report Prüss ascribed this to Hopgood because of the low reading obtained and its short duration (2.6sec). This may have led to his confusion about attacks at the Möhne: in attempting to present a logical marriage of two sets of data he made the unjustified assumptions that only four aircraft attacked and that Hopgood's must have been the third aircraft. An interesting possibility does emerge from the Göttingen figures, however. Knight is known to have breached the Eder with an explosion which recorded only 0.2mm; Young's mine at the Möhne registered precisely the same reading. Thus another strand may be added to the skein of evidence that Young created the initial breach in that dam.

Four known explosions are missing from the Göttingen list: Hopgood (about 0033, Möhne), McCarthy (0046, Sorpe), Maudslay (about 0145, Eder), Brown (0314, Sorpe). None of these mines detonated at a sufficient depth in the water to create a noticeable seismic disturbance. Hopgood's mine exploded above ground in demolishing the power station, and so did Maudslay's, which detonated on the crown of the Eder. The two Sorpe mines were activated on the sloping earth support, and damage to the top of the dam shows that the bulk of their blast went upwards. Thus the Göttingen observations provide an impartial confirmation of the 617 Squadron pilots' post-operational reports.

Dissemination of alleged Jewish involvement in Operation Chastise provided but one instance of the neutral press, in this case Swedish, acting as a two-way mirror. With little direct information emanating from enemy sources, the Allies relied heavily upon foreign countries for details of the operation's effectiveness. On 18 May the New York Times quoted 'a telegram from Berne' to report that the German public was now apprehensive about air raids, which could so easily cause floods, and that civil unrest had developed in certain areas due to the disaster. Morocco Radio reported rioting in Duisburg and Dortmund, where people feared flooding from the Ruhr river: 'Dortmund is threatened by complete inundation. The number of dead and homeless is growing each hour.' Bernard Valery, Reuter's special correspondent in Stockholm, estimated that the damage would take 'at least six months' to repair. During the ensuing week Reginald Langford, Reuter's special correspondent in Zürich, reported that the morale of the people of Kassel was at a low ebb, observing somewhat optimistically: 'Their only desire is that the war should end, whatever the result.' Langford added: ' "The danger was heavier than in the worst air raid," one informant said.' The

Handelstidningen in Gothenburg stated that work in Dortmund was at a standstill and revealed that the plan for the 'Niagara bomb' had been decided in Washington. *Allehanda* in Stockholm published an article by somebody who visited the Ruhr shortly after the raid. He reported that floods from the broken Möhne had 'created great havoc' and that in Dortmund streets were submerged, the only traffic was flat-bottomed boats and water had invaded furnaces, causing damaging explosions. Floodwater had reached Elberfeld, Barmen and Gelsenkirchen, in several places important railway lines were 'undermined' and two tunnels between Dortmund and Hagen had caved in. German authorities admitted 'heavy civilian casualties' but told Swedish correspondents in Berlin that comment was strictly forbidden. Allied metropolitan and provincial newspapers on both sides of the Atlantic eagerly seized upon these details to ice the cake of Air Ministry communiqués.

On the Continent, too, other factors connected with the crashed 617 Squadron aircraft were to emerge from people in the vicinity. A month later inhabitants on Texel reported a tremendous explosion south of the island. This may well have been Rice's mine, whose hydrostatic pistols had at length been activated by deep water, but no firm evidence supports this contention. The wreckage of Hopgood's aircraft, still smouldering, was quickly located just south of Ostönnen, close to the road to Volbringen and about 8km north-west of the Möhne Dam. Little apart from the tail section remained after the holocaust, and the four bodies recovered there (less Fraser, Burcher and Minchin) were taken to Soest. Some time later a civilian living near Marbeck gave his version of Astell's crash: the aircraft hit high-tension wires and exploded on hitting the ground. Something detached itself from the wreck and rolled some distance away before detonating with considerable force: the Upkeep's self-destructive fuse had worked. It is therefore possible that Astell's Lancaster, like AJ-E (Barlow's aircraft), was damaged by flak and then struck the overhead power lines.

It was from the remains of AJ-E near Haldern that the German authorities claimed their greatest prize. On 17 May the German Naval Staff noted: 'It is not known yet what type of explosive was employed (torpedo, mine, or bomb).' That ignorance did not long persist. Wallis realised this, for he later wrote: 'I knew that they had every detail of the bomb since MI5 quoted figures to me received from Germany immediately after the raid and asked if they did in fact refer to this special store, but I had always imagined that in this case the particulars were obtained from the Zuider Zee specimen' (Rice's mine, which Wallis thought the Germans had recovered). When he wrote his report Prüss stated: 'The nature of the bombs has been already established from an aircraft which crashed on the lower Rhine on its way in [and] there is, therefore, no need to refer to them again in this report.' By the first week of July a most detailed description of the Type 464 Provisioning Lancaster and Upkeep, its operation and installation in the aircraft, together with precise cutaway drawings, was available and circulated under the heading '*Britische Rotations-Wasserbombe* 3900 kg' ('British Revolving Depth Charge, 3,900kg'). The first set of diagrams and accompanying explanation was completed within ten days of the operation. Although some details were inaccurate – for example, the belt leading from the bottom of the starboard retaining arm to 'the special motor installed in the release mechanism' ran horizontally in the German diagrams – the analysis was remarkably accurate. It was realised that this motor fed off a power source usually employed to work the bomb-bay doors. This arrangement, and those of the supporting arms, retaining structure in the bomb bay, the weapon and all its accoutrements (pistols, nuts, endplates, etc.), were explained with specific measurements. Figures on the mine, which had been used for the analysis, were included: the interior of the centre section at the end carried the mark 'X 17,' its cover 'RA2/1832'; the head of one of the hydrostatic pistols showed 'Mark XIV 1729,' another part in the explanatory diagram 'Mark XIV 1723'. Knowledge that the Mark XIV was used in British depth charges therefore led the analysts to describe Upkeep as a revolving depth charge. In fact, this is probably the most accurate description of the weapon, which was termed a 'mine' in contemporary British documents and has since been more generally described as a 'bouncing bomb'. The Germans worked out correctly, too, that Upkeep contained three hydrostatic pistols (each with '1820g Tetryl'), and one other ('1255g Tetryl') in case the other three failed to function. The latter they decided would be activated about 15–30 seconds after release so that the attacking aircraft should not be imperilled by blast or debris. This and other points made in the analysis indicated that the Germans, at this stage, did not appreciate that the mine had bounced across the water. They did realise that it was 'dropped from a low-flying aircraft in advance of the target and set to explode at a predetermined depth.' The reports established that the weapon was cylindrical, 1,270mm in diameter and 1,530mm long, with an HE charge of 2,600kg, and that the bomb had backspin imparted to it, although Field-Marshal Milch is reported to have thought that Upkeep had forward spin. Ignorant of the bouncing characteristics, the Germans assumed that the spinning motion had been developed to give the unusually laden aircraft stability prior to release of the weapon. Cautious scientists set out to check the data and basic principles underlying the development of Upkeep and its peculiar method of delivery. This effectively retarded a German version by 18 months and it never therefore became an operational reality.

The fact remains, however, that despite British hopes and elaborate security arrangements, which forbade official disclosure of details for a further 19 years, Upkeep and the modified Lancaster III yielded their secrets on the banks of the Rhine and in a Berlin laboratory during May 1943. At that time the physical effects of their success were still very much in evidence below the Möhne and Eder dams. And the wider impact of the entire operation would reverberate around military and civilian circles in the Reich for a long time to come.

11

Aftermath, the Allies

NATIONAL AND INTERNATIONAL IMPACT

The scale of physical and psychological damage in evidence at RAF Scampton on Monday 17 May was far removed from that in the Ruhr and Eder valleys. Yet to the close-knit group of civilian and Service personnel intimately concerned with Operation Chastise it seemed no less disastrous. Serving in the officers' mess, LACW Edna Broxholme thought it 'a very sad sight to see the empty chairs . . . 617 Squadron were always a happy crowd.'

At 0800 LAC Munro and other maintenance personnel 'assembled at the hangar to pick up our equipment and fan out to the various aircraft. Quite frankly it struck us how quiet it seemed to be at their dispersal points. We finally discovered one or two in the north-east corner of the field next to the bomb-dump. It was as if these aircraft had managed to land and had their motors cut as soon as they reached the perimeter track. These same aircraft had flak holes through the fuselage of such a size that you could put your fist through them. The tractors were hitched on and these were hauled back to their hard standing.' At first Munro could scarcely grasp that these were all that remained of the force which had set off the previous evening. 'The vacuum in which we were operating soon was filled with the announcement that someone had heard on the radio about the raid.' For LAC Drury enlightenment came via the tannoy: 'To us at Scampton, it appeared to be the biggest thing the RAF had done.' Among the aircrew, Oancia was very aware that 13 fellow Canadians had not returned (though unknown to him Fraser had survived). Sumpter experienced a deep sense of anti-climax now that the training objective had been achieved 'in half a minute,' and Rodger balanced a reaction like Oancia's to the loss of so many friends with the realisation that in execution the operation had been 'a good show'. Arriving at his home near Manchester at 0700, after flying from Scampton, Chadwick told his daughter Margaret that 'it was a great success, but a great many young men died. Barnes Wallis was in tears when I left.'

When Herbert Jeffree woke up he remembered with alarm that aircraft with mines still aboard were potentially lethal, and incorrect handling might obliterate Scampton. Dashing towards the parked Lancasters, he agonised as to whether the armourers would know about the sophisticated fuse mechanism and a safe method of unloading Upkeep. A hundred yards away he saw men working on one of the weapons. He faced a sharp dilemma: to crouch ignominiously, retire rapidly or advance sedately. He reasoned that nothing could save him now and so opted to go on. Fortunately the armourers had the matter fully in hand, which allowed him to execute a dignified retreat and enjoy a leisurely breakfast before catching his train home.

Wallis left Scampton with less equanimity. The engineer in him rejoiced at Upkeep's success, but he could not come to terms with the loss of so many men for whom he felt direct responsibility. Cochrane found him 'quite inconsolable' on the subject and deaf to the argument that the 'percentage losses' were worthwhile; and Arthurton, the medical officer, found him equally distraught. Gently taxed about this aspect of the operation 20 years after, he abruptly replied: 'I don't want to talk about it.' During the morning he mingled with survivors and, after lunch, left with Kilner for the Vickers-Armstrongs factory at Castle Bromwich before going on to the Air Ministry at 2000, Weybridge an hour and a half later and eventually his Effingham home at 2230. Thus closed for him 48 hours which had been both physically and mentally harrowing.

Meanwhile, action had been taken on matters concerning publicity and discipline. At Scampton official photographers filmed groups of survivors together with Wallis and senior officers on that Monday morning; then Gibson concentrated his professional attention on the two early returns and one aborted sortie. The damage to Munro's aircraft and its inability to continue were plain. But after the last camera had clicked, Gibson and Rice sat down with their backs to the wall of the officers' mess and commanding officer quizzed pilot about his loss of Upkeep. After Rice had explained the circumstances, Gibson commented: 'Bad luck. I almost did the same. It could have happened to anybody.' Gibson was less satisfied with Anderson's explanation for returning with his mine. Officially the pilot and his crew were posted back to 49 Squadron on 3 June, but effectively they left Scampton forthwith.

Gibson then returned to the melancholy job of sending telegrams to the next of kin and following each with a personal letter; three days would elapse before this task was completed. In Chichester shortly after midday on 17 May Mrs Tees received a priority telegram: 'Regret to inform you that your son Sgt F. Tees is missing as a result of operation on night 16/17th May 43 letter follows please accept my profound sympathy = OC 617 Squadron.' Four days later one of the personal letters drafted by Gibson arrived. Like all official records it wrongly located Tees in the front turret of AJ-C. In expressing his 'sincere sympathy' and noting that Tees's personal effects would be forwarded 'through normal channels in due course,' Gibson tried to hold out some hope: 'It is possible that the crew were able to abandon the aircraft and land safely in enemy territory, in which case news will reach you direct from the International Red Cross Committee within the next six weeks. The captain of your son's aircraft, Pilot Officer Ottley, was an experienced and able pilot, and would, I am sure, do everything possible to ensure the safety of his crew.' On 1 June came a more formal communication from the Air Ministry Casualty Branch stating that 'enquiries have been set in hand through the Red Cross'. 'If any information regarding your son is received by you from any source you are requested to be kind enough to communicate it immediately to the Air Ministry. The Air Council desire me to convey to you their sympathy in your present anxiety.'

News of the operation spread quickly on 17 May. Ironically Collins, busy at Boscombe Down, must have been one of the last connected with the project to learn about it, late in the afternoon. His wife had already heard the wireless and was 'very excited they'd pulled it off'. For the press and radio had been busy all day publicising 617 Squadron's achievement; in the morning the BBC news, based upon an Air Ministry communiqué announcing that the Möhne, Sorpe and Eder dams had been attacked, broadcast the first details. That was how Wallis's wife discovered that the months of heartache and toil had been rewarded and how Eve Gibson learned of her husband's achievement. Metropolitan and provincial evening papers carried the story. The *Lincolnshire Echo* reported that according to the day's German communiqués 'two dams were damaged and heavy casualties were caused among the civilian population by the resulting floods'. It also repeated an Air Ministry statement: 'Last night aircraft of Bomber Command attacked targets in the Ruhr, in the Rhineland and at Berlin. Mines were also laid in enemy waters. Fighter Command aircraft carried out extensive intruder operations over enemy occupied territory. Nine bombers and one fighter are missing.' For, contrary to widespread belief then and later, 617 Squadron was not the only RAF unit operating over the Continent during the night of 16–17 May. Two

Mosquitoes bombed Berlin and another Kiel. Six others, two to each target, attacked Cologne, Düsseldorf and Münster between 0005 and 0018, when first-wave Lancasters of 617 Squadron were approaching the Möhne, probably causing the exaggerated estimate of Allied aircraft in that area. Elsewhere 54 Stirlings, Lancasters and Wellingtons dropped 'vegetables' (mines) in Heligoland Bay shortly after midnight, with 466 Squadron losing one Wellington. In addition ten Bomber Command aircraft flew 'special missions,' four dropped leaflets over Orléans, and Fighter Command was also active over the Netherlands and France. At intervals between 2250 and 0117 Mosquitoes took off to patrol Deelen, Venlo, Eindhoven, Soesterberg, Schiphol and Gilze-Rijen airfields. Listed as 'defensive,' that is primarily to deter or give early warning of enemy action against the United Kingdom, these patrols nevertheless served to confuse enemy defences, although perversely they might not have helped Burpee.

Official reaction to Chastise was swift and positive. At 0830 on 17 May Cochrane sent a lengthy personal message to Gibson: 'All ranks in 5 Group join me in congratulating you and all in 617 Squadron on a brilliantly conducted operation. The disaster which you have inflicted on the German war machine was a result of hard work, discipline and courage. The determination not to be beaten in the task and getting the bombs exactly on the aiming point in spite of opposition has set an example others will be proud to follow.' Later that day the Secretary of State for Air, Sir Archibald Sinclair, despatched a similar communication to Harris, which he followed with a more formal letter on behalf of the War Cabinet.

AOC-in-C Coastal Command sent a terse but no less expressive telegram: 'Well done Scampton. A magnificent night's work. Slessor.' From Portal in Washington came: 'Heartiest congratulations to you [Harris] and all Bomber Command on the outstanding recent successes against Germany. In particular please tell the special Lancaster unit of my intense admiration for their brilliant operation against German reservoirs last night.' And from Trenchard: 'Many congratulations on destruction of dams; it is splendid. Please congratulate Gibson and all concerned from me. Wonderful work of Bomber Command is being recognised by all now.'

Congratulations and thanks were not confined to service personnel. Cochrane wrote immediately, for example, to thank the Corby (Northants) and District Water Company for use of 'Corby Lake' (the Eyebrook reservoir), and Wallis naturally received recognition from a wide range of Service and civilian figures connected with the development of Highball and Upkeep. With typical thoroughness Cochrane did not forget the man whom he had already thanked verbally in the early hours of 17 May: 'Before reaching the end of this somewhat long but exciting day I felt I must write to tell you how much I admire the perseverance which brought you the astounding success which was achieved last night. Without your determination to ensure that a method which you knew to be technically sound was given a fair trial we should not have been able to deliver the blow which struck Germany last night.' He went on to say that he had spoken with Harris about Wallis's project for a big bomb and the AOC-in-C had shown sufficient enthusiasm to suggest early trials. In his own hand Cochrane added a postscript: 'Since writing this I have heard the result of the full photographic cover. What a disaster.' Harris himself telegrammed: 'We in Bomber Command in particular and the United Nations as a whole owe everything to you in the first place for the outstanding success achieved'; and Gibson wrote: 'All my pilots and I are honoured that we had the opportunity to take part in the last great experiment which has proved all your theories.'

Among the messages by letter, telegram and telephone from the Ordnance Board, MAP, RAE, Vickers-Armstrongs, National Physical Laboratory, Road Research Laboratory, Avro and individuals like Winterbotham and Pye which virtually showered White Hill House, two gave Wallis particular pleasure. Tizard wrote: 'Taking it all in all, from the first brilliant idea, through the model experiments and the full scale trials remembering also that when the sceptics were finally convinced you had to work at the highest pressure to get things done in time, I have no hesitation in saying that yours is the finest individual technical achievement of the war.' And a simple, moving telegram arrived from Wallis's elder daughter Mary, who had taken part in the early experiments with marbles on the terrace overlooking Effingham golf course, and who was at boarding school near Salisbury: 'Hooray Wonderful Daddy'. The marriage of professional approval and family ecstasy seemed apt. Then Chadwick appended a disarming and modest contribution on 25 May: 'It was a great pleasure for me to have helped you in some small measure and I shall always remember this particular operation as an example of how the Engineers of this country have contributed substantially towards the defeat of our enemies.'

Wallis answered every message, taking pains to give full credit to individuals and organisations, emphasise the team effort involved and, above all, praise 617 Squadron. Although to Linnell, former Controller of Research and Development at the MAP, he showed lingering irritation – 'I do hope that next time you will give us a little more time to do the job, as at the moment I feel as though I could not survive another effort at the same pressure' – two letters summarised the tone of them all. 'To you [Chadwick] personally, in a special degree, was given the making or breaking of this enterprise for if at that fateful meeting in CRD's office on the 26th. Feb. you had declared the task impossible of fulfilment in the given time, the powers of opposition were so great that I should never have got instructions to go ahead. Possibly you did not realise how much hung on your instantaneous reaction, but I can assure you that I very nearly had heart failure until you decided to join the great adventure. No-one believed that we should do it. You yourself said it would be a miracle if we did, and I think the whole thing is one of the most amazing examples of team work and co-operation in the whole history of war.' And in writing to Cochrane, he concentrated on the Service contributions to Chastise. 'It is impossible to find words adequately to express what one feels about the air crews. The gallantry with which they go into action is incomparable. While the older generation of Air Force officers may not be called upon to carry out actual attacks in person, the spirit of their juniors must proceed from their thought and training, and in praising your crews I would like to add the thanks which I feel are due to you as one of the senior officers of the Air Force, for the outstanding generation of pilots which your example and training has produced. Will you please accept the deepest sympathy of all of us on the losses which the Squadron has sustained. You will understand, I think, the tremendous strain which I felt at having been the cause of sending these crews on so perilous a mission, and the tense moments in the Operations Room when, after four attacks, I felt that I had failed to make good, were almost more than I could bear; and for me the subsequent success was almost completely blotted out by the sense of loss of those wonderful young lives. In the light of our subsequent knowledge I do hope that all those concerned will feel that the results achieved have not rendered their sacrifice in vain.'

On Tuesday 18 May, armed with the dramatic pictures which Cochrane had mentioned and furnished with comment from a variety of Service sources, including those who flew on the operation, the British press gave full rein to its enthusiasm. The *Daily Express*, with a rich mixture of fact and fiction, explained: 'Meanwhile Gibson flew up and down alongside the dam to draw the fire of the light anti-aircraft guns emplaced on it. Guns were poking artfully concealed out of the slots in the walls.' The *Daily Mail*, in common with other newspapers, reproduced a reconnaissance photograph showing the breach in the Möhne and another to depict the scene before 16–17 May with the caption: 'The Smash-Up: RAF Picture Testifies to Perfect Bombing.' It also printed two sketch maps with the heading 'Devastated – by Water.' One illustrated the area 'devastated' by breaching of the Möhne in a horizontal oblong from the dam to the Rhine river, optimistically including the bulk of the Ruhr industrial area from Hamm to Düsseldorf and Duisburg to Soest, and including 15 major industrial centres. The other traced the Eder, Fulda and Weser rivers from the Eder Dam to Bremerhaven and concentrated on the effects on navigation. It was explained that barges operated up to Kassel, then 'smaller craft' to Münden, but for the long Münden–Bremen stretch the Weser was navigable for 'boats up to 350 tons'; the final Bremen–Bremerhaven stretch had been dredged to a depth of 18 feet for larger vessels. No mention appeared, however, of the Mittelland Canal. Readers learned that 'two mighty walls of water were last night rolling irresistibly down the Ruhr and Eder valleys. Railway bridges, power stations, factories, whole villages and built-up areas were being swept away . . . No man-made defence can stand in their way.' A rollcall of doomed urban concentrations in the path of 'a tidal wave' followed: Dortmund, Bochum, Essen; below the Eder, Kassel. Colin Bednall, the paper's air correspondent, went on: 'It is quite impossible to predict where the damage will end . . . the devastation done to Germany's war machine has probably only just begun.'

Provincial newspapers were similarly enthusiastic, and interest did not slacken as more information and comment became available. Headlines such as 'Havoc spreads Hour by Hour' and 'Third Great Dam Now Tottering. May Burst at any Moment' kept up the momentum of expectation, and weekly magazines also gave the operation plenty of space. On 22 May the *Illustrated London News* produced a double-page spread, 'A Titanic Blow at Germany: RAF Smash Europe's Mightiest Dams', with appropriate photographs, a long article and an explanation based upon the Air Ministry cover story. A week later it produced another double-page spread with a large illustration 'drawn by our special artist . . . from information given by the Air Ministry'. *Punch* made two special contributions to the national celebrations. On 26 May a cartoon, 'The Song of the Ruhr,' depicted three sirens perched on rocks and armed with megaphones as floodwaters swirled about them, and a week later: 'It is suggested that any further leaflets dropped by the RAF on the Ruhr should be folded in the form of paper boats.' *Picture Post* used post-raid photographs of the Möhne Dam to explain the intricacies of photographic interpretation to its readers.

Those photographs and others released to the press came from RAF reconnaissance flights. A little over an hour after the last Chastise Lancaster touched down at Scampton on 17 May, a 542 Squadron Spitfire XI was airborne from RAF Benson on a reconnaissance sortie to the Möhne, Sorpe and Eder dams. The pilot, Fg Off F. G. Fray, clearly disenchanted with his lot, wrote in pencil on his report, 'that Damn Dam!,' but he brought back photographs which would soon be seen throughout the world. More flights followed that day and the next. The squadron continued to fly reconnaissance sorties over the Ruhr and Weser areas until the end of May, and its operations record book consequently noted: 'Letter received from SASO Bomber Command of their appreciation of the excellent reconnaissance recently carried out and the helpful and efficient manner in which all requirements were dealt with.'

A picture of widespread disaster was thus being built up in the United Kingdom, with the implication that a major – if not decisive – contribution to the war effort had been made. On 24 May the Assistant Chief of the Air Staff (Intelligence) published a full analysis of all reconnaissance photographs in a restricted document, 'Evidence in Camera'. Beneath a photograph of the Sorpe Dam, for example, damage to a stretch of 'almost 200ft.' of the crown was noted and 'water appears to have run down the face of the dam and carried earth from the dam into the Compensating Basin.' This was a realistic assessment which did not encourage wild speculation that seepage had started and would ultimately destroy the dam. Cover of the Eder reservoir on 18 May showed that the level had dropped by about 75ft, representing 'a loss of $\frac{7}{8}$ of the maximum capacity of the Lake'. Inundation of the villages of Affoldern and Bergheim, and collapse of 'at least 200 yards' of embankment on the main Waldeck–Bad Wildungen railway line near the latter, were noted. A photograph taken of the Eder 30 hours after the attack showed a breach 180ft wide through which water still poured. Apart from damage to the houses and bridges in Hemfurth, the Brinkhausen power station had been flooded, with the switch and transformer park silted up and the northern part washed away. Floodwater had broken the bank at Affoldern weir and power station, and apart from more damage to dwellings a road bridge had been broken in two places at Affoldern and the Mehlen-Bühlen road bridge destroyed. In the Ruhr valley Fröndenberg-Bösperde, 13 miles below the Möhne Dam, had suffered severe flooding, with the electricity works isolated, one road and one rail bridge destroyed, railway coaches wrecked and sidings submerged. Four miles lower down the valley, Dellwig also suffered heavy flooding, with the embankment of the road crossing the Ruhr breached in several places. The interpreters could not however estimate the effects of this damage, which left scope for exaggeration by more fertile imaginations. Nevertherless, about the Sorpe they were clear. On 26 May Bufton wrote to Wallis: 'It appears from the evidence . . . that no seepage was set up as a result of the attack.'

In his report to the War Cabinet on Chastise, described as 'the outstanding operation' and 'the great attack,' Sinclair contended that the 19 Lancasters set out 'to destroy the Möhne and Eder dams' – ignoring the fact that the five aircraft of the second wave were exclusively sent to the Sorpe – and that 'the less important dams of the Sorpe and Schwelme were also to be broken if enough weapons remained after the Möhne and Eder dams had burst'. This was a most unfortunate description of Operation Chastise which resulted in later inaccurate statements. Moreover, something he then said appears to have been overlooked. Acknowledging that the Möhne was attacked by five aircraft, three of which 'achieved no immediately visible result but undoubtedly loosened the masonry,' he stated most significantly: 'The fourth [Young] and fifth [Maltby] caused adjacent breaches estimated to cover 150 feet of the dam.' The Cabinet were not unnaturally enthusiastic about all of this, as was the King: two days after the operation he congratulated Harris at Buckingham Palace. Parliament also exhibited a lively interest in the affair. On 18 May Rear-Admiral Sir Murray Sueter, a First World War Royal Naval Air Service veteran, declared: 'We are . . . grateful to the Secretary of State for Air and the Under-Secretary and the Commander-in-Chief Bomber Command for organising the great air attack that resulted in our gallant pilots breaching the Ruhr dams, as we read in the Press to-day.' Eight days later another MP aspired to rival Mr Punch: 'Is it true that Herr Hitler is building an ark against the flood in the Ruhr?' And, although initially cautious, by early July the MEW gave cause for considerable optimism by stating that the Eder Dam could not be repaired before arrival of the autumn rains, which must cause severe flooding in the valley below.

Operation Chastise also had profound impact on the other side of the Atlantic. For Winston Churchill, facing American scepticism of British potential at the Trident conference, it proved timely. On 17 May, the Combined Chiefs of Staff officially 'took note' when Portal 'outlined Operation "Upkeep" [sic] and the results which it was hoped had been obtained,' and the following day 'Admiral Leahy, on behalf of the US Chiefs of Staff, offered Sir Charles Portal congratulations on the success of the RAF force in this operation'. In reply Portal noted that the success claimed by newspapers was borne out by aerial photographs.

The following day, quoting Reuter's correspondent in Berne, the *New York Times* exclaimed: 'The RAF has secured another triumph. With unexampled daring, skill and ingenuity it has blasted two of Germany's important water dams which are vital parts of the whole industrial and transportation system of West Germany and has thereby delivered the most devastating single blow dealt from the air.' 'All Americans will join with Sir Archibald Sinclair in congratulating Wing Commander G. P. Gibson on his feat and mourn with him the loss of the eight aircraft and their gallant crews in the enterprise.' On the same day an American radio announcer described Operation Chastise as 'one of the most daring and devastating raids of the war'. Reporting from

Berne, CBS commentator Howard Smith said that floods from the Möhne and Eder breaches had 'already inundated 54 towns and villages in the Ruhr, leaving some 50,000 families [sic] homeless'. An entire support division of 9,000 men had been assigned to rescue work, and the first packed refugee train had left that morning [18 May] 'for the protectorate of Bohemia'.

Then, on Wednesday 19 May, Winston Churchill addressed a joint session of Congress for 50 minutes. Afterwards a Reuter special correspondent in New York wrote: 'Mr Churchill's speech to the US Congress has been hailed as one of the most masterly and important of his career.' The British Prime Minister paid tribute to the achievements of United States forces and emphasised the increasing success of Allied efforts, particularly in recent weeks against U-boats. And he used Operation Chastise, in effect, to reiterate fundamental strategic bombing theory: 'The condition to which the great centres of German war industry, and particularly the Ruhr, are being reduced is one of unparalleled devastation. You have just read of the destruction of the great dams which feed the canals and provide the power to the enemy's munition works. That was a gallant operation, costing eight out of the nineteen Lancaster bombers employed, but it will play a very far-reaching part in reducing the German munition output . . . Wherever their centres [of war industry] exist or are developed, they will be destroyed.' He pledged British support for the United States, even if the European war should end before that in the Far East, in reducing Japanese munition centres and cities to ashes.

The RAF was not slow to exploit 617 Squadron's success on the Continent, dropping on occupied countries leaflets with fully annotated before and after photographs of the Möhne, diagrams showing the anticipated scale of damage and a lengthy explanation of the operation. Over France this appeared in the current edition of 'Le Courier de l'Air Illustré, apporté par vos amis de la RAF'. French readers learned that flooding of the Ruhr valley constituted 'one of the greatest successes of the RAF,' that Lancasters had dropped 'mines of more than 7,000 kilos on the dams, which served the war industries of the Ruhr'. Breaches of nearly 100m were claimed in the Möhne and Sorpe dams, with a similar one in the Eder. 'The attack, pressed home by determined men fully aware of the dangers which faced them, has resulted in material destruction of factories, which will be further increased by the loss of water when the floods abate.' These leaflets, with their clear evidence of a precision attack, were particularly significant because on 19 April and 10 May the War Cabinet had discussed complaints from French sources about the adverse effect of inaccurate bombing on pro-Allied opinion within France. On 22 May copies of De Vliegende Hollander dropped over the Netherlands headlined the bombing of the Ruhr dams and included similar photographs and information. In Holland there was also more tangible evidence of the operation: the bodies of Young's crew were washed ashore along the North Sea coast of the Helder peninsula at intervals during the last week of May. And on 22 June the only body recovered from Byers' aircraft, that of Sgt McDowell, was found floating in the Waddenzee in the Vliestrom channel south of Terschelling near buoy No 2. McDowell was buried next day in the Harlingen General Cemetery, Young's crew in Bergen General Cemetery. In the terse words of Dutch officialdom: 'The burials took place, as usual, without a German military mark of honour.' But 617 Squadron would find a special place in the hearts of Dutchmen. After the war an organisation would be formed exclusively to perpetuate its memory and at Bergen the carillon of a rebuilt church would be inscribed with the names of Young and his crew. Once a year it would be rung in celebration of Liberation Day. In 1975 617 Squadron Association paid a visit to the town, and the carillon played 'God Save the Queen'.

As their exploits were lauded at home and abroad, on 18 May Cochrane went to Scampton to congratulate the entire squadron before its personnel went on leave. Aircrew survivors were granted seven days from 18 May and the ground crew three days, with half going immediately and the remainder on their return. All squadron members were therefore due back at Scampton by Wednesday 26 May. Returning home from Scotland after three frustrating days working on the troublesome Highball, on 25 May Wallis found a letter from Cochrane dated two days previously which invited him to spend the following night at Grantham and added: 'Their Majesties are visiting Scampton on Thursday May 27th., and they have expressed a desire that you shall be present.' Such was Wallis's pressure of work that, having read the letter over breakfast following an overnight journey by train from Glasgow, he was at Weybridge by 1000 working on modifications to the Highball Mosquito and in the afternoon went to Burhill in connection with the design of the B.3/42 (Windsor) aircraft. Following a similiar programme at Weybridge and Burhill on 26 May, he left Effingham at 1615, an hour later was with Bufton at the Air Ministry, and he finally reached Cochrane's home near Grantham at 2000. Nevertheless he was in ample time for the royal visit. That could not be said of Plt Off Rice. Unaware of the occasion, Rice stayed overnight in Nottingham, reaching Scampton at 1100 on 27 May to discover 'a tremendous flap going on'. Gibson told his errant pilot, who had technically overstayed leave: 'Good job I'm in a good mood,' and Rice was relieved to discover that one of his crew had remembered to get him a lunch ticket. King George VI and Queen Elizabeth arrived at 1300. Painted on the turf were white lines behind which each crew had been drawn up, its captain in front with toes neatly brushing the whitewash. Countless photographers were let loose to record the happy scene during an inspection at which each pilot (in one instance, the navigator as his pilot was indisposed) introduced his crew to the King and Queen. Next day local and national papers printed full details of the occasion and pictures of King George VI in the officers' mess examining reconnaissance photographs of the damage. Readers learned that Gibson had used the briefing models to explain the operation and that the King had been asked to choose between two designs for 617 Squadron's crest: one depicted a hammer parting chains attached to a figure representing Europe, with the motto 'Alter the Map'; the other showed a broken dam with flash of lightning above and the words 'Après Moi le Déluge'. He selected the latter. Prominent in the published photographs was the huge figure of the American pilot, McCarthy, with his twin shoulder flashes, 'Canada' and 'USA'. Reporters noted, too, that 27 May was Shannon's twenty-first birthday and that the King had encouraged him to celebrate accordingly. The Queen also inspected a parade of WAAFs. Strangely, nobody seemed to realise that the chosen motto was a misquotation of Madame de Pompadour's alleged comment: 'Après nous le déluge,' which would have been equally appropriate. Later objections from heraldic authorities were parried with the retort that the King's approval had already been secured.

The royal visit 'to an air station in the north of England' had clearly been both a great success and a triumph of smooth organisation. Well, not quite. By some administrative quirk Wallis found himself included in the procession of people to whom members of the squadron had to be introduced. He and they found the experience amusing. Nor did their Majesties meet the crews together. King George VI, accompanied by Gibson, Whitworth and Cochrane, preceded Queen Elizabeth, who had an officer unfamiliar with the squadron as her guide. Clearly flustered, he contrived to get many of the names and background details wrong. Knight was presented as 'a newcomer' and was asked by the Queen if he were 'settling down nicely'. Munro refused to let an inaccurate introduction pass, retorting: 'Munro's my name'. No such difficulties apparently arose on 29 May, when the Secretary of State for Air inspected 617 Squadron with a marked absence of publicity.

Newspaper stories on 28 May about the royal visit also contained details of awards, headed by a Victoria Cross for Gibson. So the caption to the *Daily Telegraph*'s front-page story could read (strictly inaccurately) 'Gibson, VC, bombed both Dams,' while a photograph of the King, Gibson and Whitworth bore the legend: 'He [the King] is seen laughing with Wing Cmdr Gibson, who for his leadership has been awarded the VC.' Recommendations for awards had been forwarded from Scampton by Whitworth to HQ 5 Group on 20 May and been rapidly approved as they passed up the chain of command. Thus three days later Hobday and Sumpter were among those to receive congratulatory telegrams from Harris. When Sgt Webb received one he suspected an elaborate joke at his expense. But, having checked with Scampton, he found 'a shop round the corner' with a DFM ribbon and put it up. The 617 Squadron operations record book listed the awards on 24 May, and they were published in a supplement to the London Gazette the following day, which allowed Gibson and the others to wear their ribbons in advance of the more public announcement three days later. In his logbook, Gibson simply recorded: 'Awarded VC 23 May 1943'. In answering a letter of congratulations from the Warden of St Edward's School, he added: 'P.S. was awarded VC yesterday.' Thirty-four members of 617 Squadron, aged 20–32, received decorations: 19 RAF (including one Australian, Martin), seven RCAF (including the American, McCarthy), one RNZAF and seven RAAF. In all, five received the Distinguished Service Order (DSO), four a bar to the Distinguished Flying Cross (DFC), ten the DFC, two the Conspicuous Gallantry Medal (Flying), one a bar to the Distinguished Flying Medal (DFM) and eleven the DFM. Emphasising that the execution of the operation was 'fraught with danger and difficulty' and owed much to 'his inspiring leadership,' the citation accompanying the award of the VC rightly drew attention to Gibson's bravery in circling low over the Möhne Dam for 30 minutes after his own attack to draw enemy fire – an aspect underlined by Cochrane when he made the initial recommendation for a VC. It was appropriate, too, that five officers at HQ 5 Group and eight Servicemen (including the station commander, 617 Squadron's engineering and armament officers, four NCO fitters and an instrument-maker) should be commended for meritorious service.

However, cynics might be pardoned for suspecting that typists with two left hands had been foisted upon the operation, for errors appeared even in the London Gazette. Shannon's navigator was shown as Revil (not Revie) Walker, and for Webb omission of his first initial meant that his medal would be engraved 'E.,' not 'D. E.' Webb. MacLean suffered at the hands of administrative thrombosis: commissioned before 16 May, he should have been awarded the DFC, not the DFM. The adjutant, Humphries, offered to get the medal changed, to which MacLean replied pungently: 'Hell no'. Perhaps the most astounding hiccough involved Gibson's citation, which concluded with complete inaccuracy that he repeated at the Eder tactics employed over the Möhne 'and once more drew on himself the enemy fire so that the attack would be successfully developed.' There is no record of either sentry on the dam remaining to stage a shoot-out with attacking aircraft. Fortunately this piece of nonsense could in no way detract from Gibson's well deserved award.

The decorations were presented at Buckingham Palace on the morning of 22 June. Gibson received his award first, then other members of the squadron were decorated in alphabetical order irrespective of the medal. The ceremony took place in front of 240 other award recipients, including another VC, Lt Cdr R. B. Stannard, who was collecting a DSO. At the same ceremony Chadwick received his CBE. For the first time since Queen Victoria's reign a Queen had thus decorated a VC, for King George VI was in North Africa on 22 June, where among others he knighted Linnell, who had been CRD during initial Upkeep development. Sgt Webb reflected however that the Queen had been prevailed upon to take the Palace investiture because the authorities could not count on 'this lot' (617 Squadron) still being around when the King returned. But to many this special feature underlined the uniqueness of the occasion, which the Queen almost 40 years later would herself recall vividly, noting in particular how young and brave the recipients were and what 'a coup' Chastise had been. At this investiture Gibson received both his VC and a bar to the DSO, to become the most highly decorated man in the RAF. There followed the inevitable ritual of group and individual photographs inside the Palace courtyard and outside the gates for publication throughout the world and retention for private memory. The following day, for example, the *Daily Sketch* referred to the investiture of the 'dam-busters' with enthusiasm: 'Never before has a Queen Consort presented medals to British war heroes. It was a memorable scene as Queen Elizabeth stood alone on the dais in the Throne Room with the 34 airmen lined up in front of her.' The *Daily Mirror* quoted Gibson: 'I'm very glad to get that over though the Queen was most charming. She told me the King regretted that he could not be there.' On the other side of the Atlantic the *New York Times* printed a photograph of McCarthy with a special note of his part in Operation Chastise, while New Zealand, Australian and Canadian papers had group photographs of their nationals both at Scampton and Buckingham Palace.

On the evening of the Palace investiture, A. V. Roe & Co Ltd gave a dinner at the Hungaria Restaurant, Lower Regent Street, 'to celebrate decoration of members of 617 Squadron RAF'. The menu card was headed 'Damn Busters,' a splendid pun until reference to the 'Rhur Dams' lower down raised the spectre of another printing gremlin. Not all of those decorated attended, but Powell and Heveron, Whitworth and Humphries, Vickers-Armstrongs representatives including Wallis, Pierson and Kilner, and the test pilots Summers and Brown were there. Gibson was snapped signing his name on a photograph of the breach in the Möhne Dam, one of a before-and-after pair given to Wallis and brought by him to the dinner. After Gibson, other aircrew members signed. So on 24 June Wallis was able to write: 'The shores of the empty reservoir are now adorned by the signatures of the other members of the crews, and this picture will form a historical record of this outstanding accomplishment on the part of the RAF.' Both pictures would proudly decorate the wall of his study at Effingham in years to come.

Operation Chastise caught the imagination of public and Servicemen alike. Sec Off Ann Fowler noted that, if recognised, 617 Squadron personnel were wont to enjoy free taxi rides in London. Cochrane was 'very, very proud' of his association with 'a brilliant idea, brilliantly carried out by Guy Gibson,' whose training of the squadron 'in record time' had achieved 'the almost impossible'. Winterbotham, who had done so much to help Wallis in the initial stages, recorded 'utter jubilation' on learning of 617 Squadron's success. Flt Lt G. E. Pine, an intelligence officer who would later serve on the same station as Gibson, described the news as 'marvellous, terrific . . . a tonic like Winston Churchill's speeches'. Explaining that area bombing had not shown positive results, he added 'we did need it' and concluded that such a clear, sensational achievement would prove a valuable morale-booster. F/Sgt G. Allen, a flight engineer on 106 Squadron, which Gibson had so recently left, also emphasised the operation's moral effect. Sometimes crews would fly to Germany two or three nights in succession, 'worked to death' and hoping that they were causing heavy damage to the enemy. The station commander at Marston Moor, Gp Capt Leonard Cheshire, noted 'it certainly raised my morale'. For here was irrefutable, tangible evidence of success being achieved in the industrial Ruhr, and Allen believed that it must have done 'ten times more damage than a raid on Essen'. He did not know that Fraser's interrogator had multiplied that estimate by ten.

12

Significance

REFLECTION AND CONCLUSION

Writing to B. A. Duncan of Vickers-Armstrongs, Chester, five days after the operation, Wallis adopted the tone of optimism already assumed by Harris and Sinclair: 'I feel that a blow has been struck at Germany from which she cannot recover for several years.' A post-war Australian assessment agreed: 'All that had been anticipated came to pass. A tremendous blow had been struck at the German war industry,' and in 1955 a film critic referred to 'the mission that possibly did more than any other to win the war in the West'.

Others, though, have been less enthusiastic, some even caustically dismissive. A generation after Chastise, one British journalist wrote: 'The truth about the Dams Raid is that it was a conjuring trick, virtually devoid of military significance . . . The story of the raid is one of sloppy planning, narrow-minded enthusiasm and misdirected courage.' In *New Scientist* an academic scientist argued: 'The dams raid . . . had scant effect on German war production; the influence of the ricochet bomb on the imponderable sum of war was negligible.' At virtually the same time, in Germany, publishers of a book about the operation claimed that 617 Squadron's efforts '. . . were given publicity abroad far in excess of their significance – after the war an elaborate legend has been built upon them.' A separate German commentator maintained that the attack on the Möhne was 'not worth a single aeroplane to breach this dam for the effect it had on the German war effort'.

Critics of the operation have pointed to the temporary nature of the material damage. By mid-morning on 17 May the floods had subsided in Neheim and Wickede, and water supplies were completely restored in

Neheim and the surrounding area 'in a few days'. On 15 May the total water production in the Ruhr was one million cubic metres, a figure which dropped to a mere 260,000 two days later. But the original output had been restored by 27 June; specifically, the waterworks at Steele was out of action for just one hour, those at Horst, Witten and Langschede for less than four days. The water supply for Dortmund fell to 20 per cent immediately, yet was restored to 80 per cent in three days. The overall result, therefore, was temporary inconvenience, not permanent damage.

Nor did shortage of electricity apparently long embarrass the Germans: there was no need to rebuild the stations at the Möhne and the large Herdecke plant was out of action for only a fortnight. Alternative supplies could be obtained from generating stations relying upon water from the Alps. Throughout 1943 approximately 733,000kW capacity was permanently lost, but public power stations raised their capacity from 9.5 to 13.3 million kilowatts in 1940–4, and the parallel private sector increased its capacity by 20 per cent. Both systems contributed to the grid, which could thus make good local shortages. In total, during May 1943 390,000kW were lost through 'enemy action', and 345,000 in June. This was not serious, and repairs were soon made to necessary installations.

It has been easy, too, to refute claims of 3–4,000 dead in the Ruhr valley and to challenge estimates of 35 per cent dislocation in industrial production. The death roll, including unidentified bodies, has been confirmed as 1,294. Sceptics quote figures from Speer's Ministry which showed that output of aircraft, ammunition and weapons in the third quarter of 1943 exceeded that of the second and continued to rise in 1944, and the post-war United States Strategic Bombing Survey estimated only five per cent loss of armament output in the second half of the year. A slight hiccough occurred in June 1943, but by July production had equalled that of May and by September had exceeded it. Furthermore, even this temporary shortfall could not be solely attributed to Chastise, and steel production in Greater Germany and the occupied countries in 1943 exceeded that of 1942 by two and a half million tons.

However, this picture of negligible effect may be challenged. The waterworks at Fröndenberg and Echthausen (put out of action at 0200 and 0345 respectively on 17 May and important for north Westphalian coalfields) were not restored to full working order until 2 and 23 August respectively. And records of the *Hygienisches Institut des Ruhrgebeits* at Gelsenkirchen show that the waterworks supplying Neheim and parts of Hüsten, Soest and Herdecke were completely destroyed and that repair work concentrated on restoration only of essential services. A report of 1 July 1945, based upon these documents held that from May 1943 merely a 'tolerable' level of water supply was maintained. Moreover, the Ruhr did suffer an eight per cent loss of steel output in the latter part of 1943 and the whole of north-west Germany 1.9 million tons of crude steel during the year, but this was effectively masked because manufacturers held sufficient stocks to make up the loss. In north-west Germany (which included the Ruhr) during the second quarter of 1943 lost production of crude steel attributed to air raids increased by 60 per cent over the first quarter, virtually all of it due directly to damage. In May and June respectively, 304,000 and 300,000 metric tons were lost; only in four other months of the year did the loss exceed 100,000 and in the highest of these the figure reached 137,000. These post-Chastise losses, although not attributable entirely to the operation, were therefore significant; and Speer further admitted that air raids limited the increases in production which his rationalisation programme would otherwise have achieved.

The main assault by critics, however, had centred on the rapid rebuilding of the Möhne and Eder dams. By 23 September the gap had been closed in the Möhne, and on 2 October a celebration held there was attended by Speer and other Ministry officials who flew specially from Neuhardenberg to Werl for the event. Almost simultaneously similar work was completed at the Eder. Both dams were repaired in 'cyclopean rubble masonry of the same type as the original construction'; approximately 23,000 cubic yards (18,000m^3) were used at the Möhne, with all cracks sealed by the pressure grouting process. Because a deep hole on the air side scoured out by the water as it flowed through the breach was thought to have weakened the heel of the dam, a block of some 13,000 cubic yards (10,000m^3) was inserted to give additional support. At the Eder a light railway delivered materials to the foot of the dam and jib cranes hoisted them to the top, where they were distributed directly or by chute. In fact two steam locomotives, two excavators, 42 dumper vehicles and two compressors were used in this work, carried out by 858 workmen under the control of the construction company Philipp Holzmann of Frankfurt am Main. Overall responsibility for the repairs here and at the Möhne was in the hands of the Todt Organisation and ultimately Speer's Ministry. Loose masonry each side of the breach made by Knight's mine meant that a further 3,800m^3 had to be removed. The entire gap was then filled, the drainage system repaired (though not until June 1944, and two emergency sluices were not refashioned) and liquid cement inserted into special boreholes and cracks where weakness was feared. Nevertheless water did penetrate fissures. It was decided that the water level in the Eder reservoir must be a maximum 243.09m, or two metres below the top of the overflow, and repairs to allow full capacity again were not carried out until 1946–7.

Below the dam 100 foreign workers were used to repair 14km of roadway between Hemfurth and Geismar before the autumn, and temporary wooden bridges replaced those over the river destroyed at Hemfurth, Affoldern, Mehlen, Bergheim-Giflitz and Wega-Wellen, more permanent structures being built after the war. Although the damaged parapets on the Möhne and Eder dam walls were not replaced and some repairs were still incomplete or temporary, both reservoirs were thus able to hold water from the winter rains of 1943–4.

Rumpf and Speer are among those to criticise the RAF for not bombing the repair scaffolding from high-level. This would have required the unattainable degree of accuracy which led to the years of discussion before development of Upkeep and was even less feasible with the incendiaries which they proposed. And, whatever the long-term or national impact of the operation, local industrial disruption was not negligible: loss of water for coke works in the Ruhr valley meant that on 19 May major gas consumers had supplies reduced by 50–60 per cent. Nor did official Allied sources claim that Chastise caused 35 per cent interruption in enemy industrial output: that was an estimate of 10 June concerning the more general effect of bombing on German industry.

The level of water in the Möhne, Eder and Sorpe reservoirs was reduced, thus to some extent affecting their function, and German experts such as Dr Walter Rohland and Professor Dr-Ing Otto Kirschmer have agreed that the idea of attacking water supplies in the Ruhr did have merit. To some extent the attackers were unfortunate, for an emergency pumping system for the Ruhr industries using the Rhine had only recently been completed; thus an attack in 1942 would have been much more serious. But disruption of inland waterways below the Eder, upon which the important industrial centre of Kassel relied heavily, had been rightly emphasised from the Western Air Plans onwards and did occur for a number of months.

Chastise had an effect, too, upon agriculture and food supplies. Speer described the drowning of 'a few hundred cows' as 'unimportant,' and the loss of agricultural land as 'not serious'. But Heinrich George, deputy manager of the construction company responsible for repairing road damage in the area, held that floods in the Eder Valley carried away topsoil so that farmland could not be satisfactorily tilled for years to come, and much the same result was evident in the Möhne Valley. Of this Kleeschulte, the eyewitness at the dam, wrote in 1945: 'The fields in the valley below will yield no crops for many years owing to the inundation.' The loss of agricultural products could not be quickly made up from other regions due to the disruption of communications brought about by Allied air raids and the demands of fighting services now able to rely less upon countries outside Germany for sustenance. On 19 May Goebbels recorded in his diary: 'The reduction of the meat ration by 100 grammes had, after all, had a very serious psychological effect.' And the following month meat for 'normal consumers' was reduced again by 50 per cent as supplies of meat, fats and dairy products continued to decline. Already, due to a lack of the necessary imports of fodder, the numbers of pigs bred had been drastically reduced, and by mid-1943 the civilian fat ration was estimated at 50 per cent below average pre-war consumption. The general, unsatisfactory level of food supplies was exacerbated by poor potato crops in 1943–4, and as 90 per cent of German farmers still relied upon animals for draught, their loss became locally important. Thus, though the loss of agricultural land and more especially animals as a result of Chastise may not have appeared serious, the cumulative effect was significant. Dingle Foot, Parliamentary Secretary to the Ministry of Economic Warfare, noted in the Commons on 10 July 1943: 'The results of the bomber offensive have to be measured not only in the actual stoppage of production in certain factories but also in the vast amount of additional work which it makes necessary.' Chastise, whose spectacular achievements, according to Speer, caused 'concern' to the German government, bore out this contention.

The diversion of labour to deal with its effects was short-term, but the construction and manning of defences around dams liable to air attack constituted a more permanent drain on civilian and military resources. Measures were taken at vulnerable reservoirs, including those listed as Chastise targets and others like the Agger which were not. On 28 December 1943, a conference with Heinrich Butzer Company representatives about the Möhne, chaired by *Landesforstmeister* Bonse, looked at proposals to sink wooden fascines in the reservoir to protect the dam face, but doubts were expressed about the possibility of constructing a 500m-long sunken barrier by mid-March 1944. On 29 January 1944, a meeting chaired by Inspector Schmitz of the Luftwaffe Board of Works agreed on a series of a floating wooden deflectors instead, and Prüss, who had produced the report on Chastise, chaired a *Ruhrtalsperrenverein* conference about this on 1 February. Butzer insisted that the dams authority had set the maximum future water level in the Möhne reservoir at 208.50m and the firm had therefore planned a ceiling of 209m for the system. Prüss now insisted that the possible water level must be 212.30m: to lower it by three metres would mean loss of 47 million cubic metres of water. At length the conference agreed on 211m, with completion in four weeks, and that a third torpedo net would then be installed. Prüss told the meeting that in the meantime he had asked Air Zone VI to allocate special fighter defences to the dam. Next day Butzer complained, in view of the new requirements, of inadequate facilities and personnel, insisting that 520 specialists and labourers were needed and that a completion date of 10 May, not 9 April, was more realistic. On 9 March the firm revealed that 'higher authority' had agreed on 208.50m as the maximum height of water in the reservoir, accepting the penalty of lower capacity, but followed next day with a complaint that only 17 out of 30 promised carpenters had arrived at the Möhne and that the undertaking to provide security police to guard billets and other installations had been honoured for the flak detachments but not for the construction workers. Work on the system, which comprised 44 wooden deflectors and 398 buoys, continued for almost three months and was completed by an average of 280 men on 8 May.

Meanwhile, several firms had been contracted to provide 'round logs' for defensive purposes, and others to supply the torpedo netting. Thirty-six nets, each 18m by 18m, and six buoys were ordered and despatched in mid-May, and these constituted the third net, 400mm thick and some 650m long, which under the supervision of *Oberleutnant (W)* Odebrecht and *Korvettenkapitän* Wucherer, was finished by pioneers on 25 May and installed six metres from the existing double nets (each 100mm thick) between them and the dam wall. In theory, if a torpedo hit the first net the second would survive and the third remain in reserve. So at the Möhne passive defences included an aerial wire apron attached to steel pylons on each bank and stretched across the reservoir, a triple torpedo net in front of the dam, and anti-rocket or anti-bomb netting supported by struts jutting out from the face of the wall on the air side. In addition there were the closely spaced pieces of timber, supported at an angle of approximately 45° by floats anchored to the face of the dam and weighted by ballast, which acted as deflectors below the surface of the reservoir. The deflector system and torpedo nets needed only a few maintenance personnel, but the searchlights, balloons, anti-aircraft guns (including 88mm weapons) and smokescreen apparatus had sizeable detachments. At the Ennepe anti-aircraft guns, smoke canisters, balloons and a torpedo net were installed and, similar to the action taken on the Hevers Berg in front of the Möhne, the trees on the spit of land above the dam were cut down to allow a clear field of fire for the flak guns now positioned there. And within a few days of Chastise military transports delivered to the Sorpe Dam 'twenty-four barrage-balloons, torpedo nets and smoke dischargers,' the latter being activated 'by a light beam and thus, in the shortest time, visibility was virtually nil.'

Heavy defensive provisions were made at the Eder, too. During May 1943 balloon, flak and smokescreen equipment was brought up, and so nervous were the defenders that two RAF bombers shot down in the area the following month were thought, incorrectly, to be about to mount an attack on the dam. Twenty-four 20mm (some four-barrelled), four 37mm and eight 88mm flak guns were concentrated at the dam, together with six rocket-carrying vehicles, each with 24 dischargers, four 60cm and three 200cm searchlights, and 24 balloons capable of an altitude of 600m and another 24 capable of 1,200–2,000m. A local defence (*Landesschutz*) company of rifle-men was stationed nearby to cope with a paratroop landing, and there was a special company with 500 smokepots to produce a smokescreen. Altogether 1,300–1,500 men were therefore committed to active defence of the dam. In passive defence against low-level attack, 11 wooden stakes, each 10m × 20m, were attached to buoys and sunk immediately in front of the wall; 50m above the dam were three rows of buoys with torpedo nets three metres deep attached, and 200m higher up the reservoir a row of six mines was sunk. Three further rows of mines, 550m, 1,110m and 1,350m from the dam, were similarly installed; each 1,000kg mine would be electrically operated by the water turbulence set up by an aircraft flying at 80–100m, causing it to crash or be thrown off course. Paradoxically, these defences only succeeded in causing accidental damage to the wall. During the night 8–9 July, 1944, as a result of a heavy thunderstorm, the mines placed 250m and 550m from the dam exploded, damaging the face of the dam and the locking mechanism of the outlet pipe system, although the sum effect was more irritating than serious. Nevertheless, Harris and Button were justified in claiming that the troops diverted to defend the German dams in its wake constituted another practical achievement for Chastise. Quite apart from the equipment and weapons (not least balloons and flak guns), which could have been deployed around industrial targets, the defence of vulnerable dams involved over 10,000 regular troops in addition to reserve units. One operation had effectively deprived the enemy of a potential front-line division. Shortly after Chastise, on 30 May 1943, Hitler emphasised to Speer the importance of the German dams for industry, making him personally responsible for water supplies from them and, specifically, ordering him to arrange a satisfactory alarm system to ensure adequate defences. This perhaps, explains the flurry of activity which occurred prior to May 1944 as Speer strove to guard against a repetition of the operation on the original dams or on others.

There was also a direct consequence for the Luftwaffe. Emotionally committed to offensive action, Hitler was not in 1943 disposed towards a Service which urged commitment of great military effort and production capacity for defence. Inevitably, too, squabbles over the Luftwaffe impinged upon the political power struggle around Hitler. Goering's reputation, severely dented by his failure to subdue the United Kingdom in 1940–1, suffered further severe blows through the Luftwaffe's inability to defend such cities as Cologne, Lübeck and Rostock from devastating air raids or to fulfil its promises of aerial supply to the beleaguered Sixth Army at Stalingrad in 1942–43. In March 1943 Hitler openly scorned it for not protecting German citizens, ordered Milch to develop a high-speed, high-altitude bomber and pressed for 'intensification of the air war against Britain'. On the other hand, Milch and senior Luftwaffe officers like Adolf Galland urged greater fighter production. But Goering, anxious to regain Hitler's favour, blamed them for inadequate aerial defences and supported the idea of aerial aggression. On 8 May Hitler demanded that every new aircraft should be capable of carrying a bomb. Insofar as it reinforced Hitler's prejudice against the viability of aerial defence and his refusal to develop aircraft like the Me262 jet purely as a fighter, Chastise had a significant long-term impact on the broader air war over the Reich.

Its effect on civilian morale is more difficult to assess and in truth cannot be divorced from the general effect of air raids. Individuals in the Ruhr and Eder valleys who set about the task of repairing homes and property on 17 May exhibited an air of resignation and automatic reaction. Bombing was not new, and for those who survived the flood there was sure knowledge that, with the dams broken, the night's events could not be repeated. Hans Rumpf has argued that the morale effect upon the civilian population was the most serious result of Chastise, because defensive preparations were so obviously lacking that the competence of Luftwaffe authorities was called into question; Galland also believed that the operation had 'lasting effect'. It is doubtful if such a positive conclusion can be drawn, even though British sources made similar claims. Bufton considered the moral effect on the Germans 'very important' and Wynter-Morgan maintained that the operation made them 'thoroughly scared'. The undermining of civilian morale had been one of the justifications for attacking Chastise targets in Service papers since pre-war, and Allied 'black' propagandists actively used the raid in a curious way towards this end. They alleged that the dams had been destroyed not by the RAF but by an organisation of foreign workers whose impressive act would be only the beginning of their sabotage.

If the precise effect of Chastise on the German population cannot be gauged, that is not true of the Allies. In the words of a young civil servant, Caroline Rowett, then working on signal interception at Bletchley Park, the news was a 'tremendous uplift'. James Robertson, junior to Gibson at St Edwards and then a 19-year-old at pre-OCTU, used the same words: '. . . tremendous uplift after so many defeats and . . . we all thought that the Ruhr had been put out of action . . . on reflection I think that if nothing else the raid had a great psychological effect on people's morale'. Organisations such as the City of Birmingham Water Department, whose dam near Rhayader had earlier proved so valuable, recorded their pride that they had been fleetingly involved. The post-raid reports and dramatic photographs undoubtedly impressed citizens who had endured the Blitz, and Cochrane was right therefore to emphasise the 'very important' effect on civilian morale at home. The morale of another specific group of Allied Servicemen received a boost when news of 617 Squadron's attack filtered through to prisoner-of-war camps. Thirty-eight years later Gp Capt Sir Douglas Bader wrote: 'I well remember the destruction of the Möhne and Eder dams while I was in a prison camp. It had an enormous effect on Germans and the opposite effect, of course, on the prisoners-of-war.'

Britain's allies officially reacted favourably. On 18 March Field Marshal Sir John Dill had reported from Washington American doubts about concentrating aerial strength in Europe rather than the Far East, and at the Trident conference in May Churchill faced naval pressure to reduce priorities in the Atlantic and a more general challenge to his Mediterranean strategy. The Joint Chiefs of Staff's enthusiastic response to Chastise, although in no sense decisive, did draw attention to the possibility of clear aerial achievement in Europe and acknowledged a dramatic British success. The Russians, too, had through Stalin frequently expressed disquiet about the lack of military endeavour by their British ally in Europe. Chastise certainly impressed them. A cypher telegram from No 30 Mission to the USSR stated that Russian naval authorities wanted full information because 'they are showing great interest in this operation and are possibly contemplating something similar'. In London Pound demurred due to 'possible grave dangers to security,' but Evill, noting that 'the Germans know a good deal already,' pointed out that Upkeep was not Highball. On 7 June the Chiefs of Staff agreed in principle to send full details as requested. The final decision was taken on 11 August and that day, in advising No 30 Mission that details would indeed be despatched, the Air Ministry added: 'You should make greatest possible capital out of our handing over this important and highly secret information.' For General Martel had been pressing for release of the information in the context of improving Anglo-Soviet relations, pointing especially to the Russians' need for advice 'in aircraft matters' and the fact that information on Chastise would boost RAF prestige. Furthermore, when he temporarily halted the Arctic supply convoys at the end of March to permit a build-up of vessels in the Mediterranean for the invasion of Sicily, Churchill promised Stalin more effective bombing of Germany. Chastise graphically showed that he meant what he said.

The operation impressed not only civilians in the United States, as press and radio reaction showed, but also those in the occupied countries of Europe. In 1971 Mr H. van Soerewyn wrote to Wallis from Peabody, Massachusetts: 'Having lived for five long years under a harsh occupation of enemy forces, we are very grateful for the work you did during these years,' and the continuing high regard for 617 Squadron in the Netherlands underlines the sentiments of this letter. There was a strictly professional implication as well. Martin's flight engineer, Whittaker, remarked that the operation represented 'a great milestone in the standard it set,' a view supported by Rumpf, sometime Inspector-General of Fire Prevention in Germany, who pointed to the attacks on the dams as a 'most impressive success . . . carried out by precision bombing of a high order'. Significantly, Cochrane used 617 Squadron's achievement after hard training (2,288 practice bombs in six weeks) to urge all 5 Group crews towards greater accuracy on the range and over Germany: 'Unfortunately a number of bombs are still falling 2, 3 and 5 miles from the aiming point, and this is delaying victory.' For heavy bombers had now attacked targets with accuracy in the Ruhr, and Bufton maintained that this operation showed how the RAF had 'established a bridge-head over Europe,' making the same point as Trenchard in his post-Chastise reference to recognition of the achievements of Bomber Command. Evidence provided by the accurate execution of the operation also allowed wider criticism about Allied bombing to be deflected. On 27 May in the Commons R. R. Stokes asked if the Deputy Prime Minister were 'aware that there is an ever-growing volume of opinion in this country which considers the indiscriminate bombing of civilian centres both morally wrong and strategic lunacy'. Attlee replied: 'There is no indiscriminate bombing . . . [only] of those targets which are most effective from the military point of view.' Photographic evidence from the dams provided a valuable background for this retort and encouraged hope that the losses of Allied bombers in the first four months of 1943 – 295 in April alone, 699 since 1 January – would henceforth be reduced as a result of greater accuracy and achievement.

617 Squadron was seen as a symbol both of Bomber Command's efficiency and, through its mixture of crews from different countries, Allied co-operation. Wallis who in a sense was its founder, paid generous and lasting tribute throughout his life to the squadron's 'incredible bravery' and looked upon it as 'a beloved child'. Despite the assertion on its formation that Chastise would be only the first task, it is doubtful whether 617 could have survived as a specialist squadron – to carry out such successful attacks as those against *Tirpitz* and the Kembs barrage or to develop under Wg Cdr G. L. Cheshire the low-level marking technique which so effectively increased the

accuracy of night bombing – if its operation against the German dams had failed. But the creator, as well as the squadron, emerged from Chastise with an enhanced reputation, and this had important repercussions. Harris now described him as 'a wizard boffin' and Wallis wrote that 'it [Chastise] tended to establish in the minds of C-in-Cs such as Sir Arthur Harris and the CE [Chief Executive of the MAP] Sir Wilfrid Freeman an impression of the rightness of the lines on which I argued when writing my "Notes on means of Attacking"'. So Wallis gained military credibility and Upkeep was not forgotten. On 30 May Saundby recorded that Cochrane and Wallis had discussed breaking the bank of the Dortmund-Ems canal with it. A broader Air Staff appreciation, while drawing attention once more to the importance of hydroelectricity for the Italian war economy, recommended that Upkeep be used against four targets: the Rothensee Ship Lift between the Mittelland Canal and the River Elbe north of Magdeburg, so preventing ships from the Mittelland Canal passing to and from Berlin without 'an enormous diversion'; embankments at the southern end of the Dortmund-Ems Canal and branches of the Wesel-Datteln and Datteln-Hamm canals, which carried 'very heavy traffic' into and out of the Ruhr; banks of the Mittelland Canal just west of Minden, with the aim of seriously affecting east-west traffic; and embankments and locks of the Dortmund-Ems Canal just north of Bevergern and above its connection with the Mittelland Canal, to interrupt traffic to and from the north through both canals. But attacks of this nature could possibly involve dropping Upkeep on land. So on 2 June Shannon flew ED932/G (Gibson's aircraft on Chastise) to Farnborough for Vickers-Armstrongs staff to modify the spinning mechanism to allow Upkeep to be given forward, not backward, spin. Two days later, watched by Wallis, Gp Capt Dark, Wynter-Morgan and Wg Cdr Geoghegan, two 617 Lancasters dropped Upkeep, spinning at 500 rpm, from 100ft at a speed of 230 mph on the Ashley Walk Bombing Range in the New Forest near Fordingbridge. The initial bounce of each weapon was 30–40ft and their ranges 900 and 1,080 yards. 'Mr Wallis expressed himself as entirely satisfied at these tests', but both aircraft were 'peppered' by stones thrown up as the store hit the ground, and further experiments were carried out on 9 June from 200ft and 225 mph. The aircraft then went unscathed, but overall results were 'markedly inferior' to those of 4 June.

Meanwhile, on 8 June, Air Vice-Marshal Bottomley, as ACAS (Ops), chaired a meeting of Air Ministry, MAP and Bomber Command representatives plus Wallis to discuss operations with Upkeep subsequent to Chastise, and canals were especially considered. No more aircraft were to be modified for Upkeep, however, until specific operations had been settled, and Wallis undertook to investigate production of a 6,600lb version (with a 4,500lb charge) so that more fuel could be carried and greater flying range attained.

On 1 July Bufton chaired another meeting to discuss Upkeep attacks on canals and viaducts, and five days later Wallis pointed out to him that an attack on 'highly curved' Italian dams would require further experiments by the Road Research Laboratory, as the existing data were not appropriate. In the meantime, from the Air Ministry in a 'most secret' letter Wg Cdr A. P. Morley informed Wallis that Glanville was proceeding with experiments concerning possible use of Upkeep against Italian dams without waiting for written authority – strengthening the argument that in 1940 he did likewise for the Möhne when approached by Wallis. At the end of the month Wallis sent to Bufton a detailed appreciation of the Janisokoski Water Power Plant. Constantly referring to the preparation and execution of Chastise in his analysis, he recommended an attack 'directed at the centre line of the Power Station' and concluded: 'The vulnerable width is well within the degree of line accuracy attained in the practice attacks at Reculver and probably in the actual attacks on the Möhne and Eder dams themselves.' Thus on 12 August Rice, who had lost his mine in the Waddenzee on 16 May, found himself carrying out further trials with a forward-spinning Upkeep from Boscombe Down. But no Upkeep operation did in fact materialise: on 4 October Saundby noted that the weapon would be retained but the modified aircraft would now be used for training purposes, including fighter affiliation. Early the following year Wallis and Bufton again discussed using Upkeep against Italian dams without decision, and Wallis always believed that the refusal to attack some of the '100 Italian dams' which he listed 'threw away an early chance of victory'. 'If only Bert Harris had been a bit more flexible.' Hopes for future employment of Upkeep were never entirely abandoned. But eventually, after the war, remaining Upkeep mines were dumped in the Atlantic without further operational use and the Type 464 Provisioning Lancasters were unceremoniously scrapped. In Wallis's words, Upkeep had achieved only 'one wonderful feat'.

But the success of Chastise refocused attention on Wallis's earlier ideas. The morning after the operation, Cochrane revealed that Harris was prepared to reconsider the 'big bomb' concept. The meeting chaired by Bottomley on 8 June to discuss use of Upkeep against German canals also considered 'the deep penetration bomb producing a camouflet effect' to attack Ruhr coalmines (suggested in Wallis's 'Note'), and Cochrane thought that a 12,000lb bomb fitted with a delay fuse might be more suitable for canal work than Upkeep. Thus on 1 July Bufton chaired a meeting which noted that dropping trials with a 12,000lb blast bomb into 10–12ft of water from 300ft at 223–230 mph had been successful, although this was not the weapon of the same weight later developed by Wallis and called Tallboy. Nevertheless, the deep-penetration bomb had taken a great step towards reality. Highball was never used in anger, despite continued experiments and plans in the United States and Britain to deploy it against Japanese shipping in the Pacific as late as 1945, and Baseball similarly failed to reach operational status. However, Tallboy (12,000lb total weight, 45 per cent Torpex, 21ft long, 3ft 2in in diameter and capable of 100ft penetration from 20,000ft) and Grand Slam, its 'big brother' (22,000lb, 42 per cent Torpex, 25ft 5in by 3ft 10in) did contribute to the war effort. Tallboy was used to attack *Tirpitz*, the Kembs Dam and, interestingly, the Sorpe Dam, and Grand Slam was dropped on the railway viaduct at Bielefeld. But perhaps the most effective use of Tallboy was against V-1, V-2 and V-3 sites. Cochrane and Wallis independently maintained that these successes were major contributions to the Allied victory and more significant than Chastise. Without that operation and the recognition that Wallis consequently received, however, he would never have developed the deep-penetration weapons in time, if at all. For that alone Chastise was worthwhile.

Meanwhile the demonstration of Upkeep's capability on 16–17 May had prompted defensive measures at British dams similar to those taken in Germany. The vulnerability of water supplies to enemy attack, especially by airborne troops, had been recognised early in the war and reservoirs had been protected by police, Home Guard and military personnel, mainly through local arrangement. After Operation Chastise more elaborate precautions against aerial attack were implemented as a matter of national policy. On 27 May the Under-Secretary of State for Air, Capt H. H. Balfour, informed Sinclair and Evill that Mr Erskine Hill MP had complained of lack of protection for British dams, claiming that on the weekend after Chastise he had discovered 'several vital dams' to be vulnerable. Loch Ericht, with more water than the Möhne and if breached liable seriously to affect the Scottish Power Company's contribution to the national grid, was guarded by four policemen; and destruction of Laggan Dam would put British Aluminium 'out of operation'. But already the Ministry of Home Security had shown concern about this problem on 24 May and reported to the Chiefs of Staff the following day, and on 26 May the Anti-Aircraft Sub-Committee of the Chiefs of Staff had discussed deployment of searchlights and light anti-aircraft guns to eleven major dams, including Howden, Derwent, Laggan, Caban Coch (which had superseded the Nant-y-Gro near Rhayader) and Queen Mary, over which Wallis and Summers had initially spun the practice weapons. On

3 June Dr T. R. Merton chaired an *ad hoc* sub-committee for the Ministry of Home Security at Gwydyr House, attended by Cherwell among others, about possible enemy use of Upkeep, which noted: 'It is known that the enemy already have some information about "Upkeep". Although it is not improbable that all the projectiles reaching Germany exploded, yet it must be presumed that the enemy has pieced together much of the story by examining the Lancasters which were lost.' Defences such as minefields, possibly activated by light cables attached to small balloons, a barrage of balloons, various types of sloping, horizontal and vertical barriers to prevent the weapon striking a dam, searchlights and smoke were discussed without urgency as the meeting felt that the enemy had no aircraft large enough to carry Upkeep. Three days later the Director of Flying Operations (DF Ops) at the Air Ministry concluded that Loch Ericht needed no defence because it was too difficult to attack; and next day, 7 June, in observing that execution of Chastise would have been hampered by searchlights on the dams, Cochrane concluded that they should therefore be placed forthwith on all vulnerable British ones. The Chiefs of Staff referred to Merton's work and that of the Admiralty on protective minefields on 10 June, but noted that this fell within the scope of its own Anti-Aircraft Sub-Committee. Possibly as a result of a minute from the Prime Minister two days previously, also on 10 June DF Ops reported that the Admiralty was considering placing minefields 300–400 yards upstream from selected dams to deter low-flying aircraft, and revealed that 12 dams (not 11) were being considered for protection: for example, 'five Sheffield lakes' would together have 28 40mm anti-aircraft guns and 42 searchlights.

Another meeting at Gwydyr House on 23 June, which aimed at producing an inter-departmental report by 3 July for the Anti-Aircraft Sub-Committee, worked on the assumption that an Upkeep attack by the enemy must be anticipated 'within three months' of Chastise. Noting that 'immediate protection' had been given to 'important targets,' the meeting nevertheless agreed that 'permanent counter measures' were required, especially as it now appeared that the Heinkel He177 might be adapted to carry a full-size Upkeep. Minefields, balloon barrages and barriers were not now considered seriously, but a meeting of technical experts to discuss 'dazzle and smoke' was arranged for 1 July. An Admiralty proposal for floating masts was not supported, though the idea of a 'catenary' of heavy cable with secondary wires and attached explosive devices hanging down and slung between towers positioned on the banks of a reservoir was more readily accepted. 'The Derwent Valley Waterworks' were keen on this arrangement, and Dr R. E. Stradling of the Ministry of Home Security and Mr H. D. Morgan of W. T.

Halcrow & Partners were tasked with examining the project further. As a result some 5,000 men and women of 57 Anti-Aircraft Brigade were moved to cover the Howden, Derwent and other reservoirs in the Sheffield area, together with anti-aircraft guns, searchlight and smokescreen apparatus. As at the Möhne and Eder high steel towers were erected beside the reservoirs, with chains and hanging cables stretched between them to deter low-level attack. The smokescreen system, with '30,000 generation points built right up in the hills,' could allegedly obscure the valleys in five minutes, and an elaborate evacuation procedure, to be used in conjunction with a special 'dams breached' siren should the enemy succeed in penetrating defences, was worked out.

Two days after the second Gwydyr House meeting, on 25 June, from the Air Ministry Air Cdre S. E. Toomer sent Wallis details of enemy He177 dispositions and strength, adding that the Dornier Do217 might be modified to carry an 8,000lb mine. On 9 July Wallis wrote to Barratt at the MAP, clearly without effect, querying the validity of a catenary defence and arguing that this and boom defences would be easily identified by enemy reconnaissance aircraft. He held that 'the only effective form of defence is powerful dazzle with or without the addition of smoke'. 'Permanent dazzle lights installed in concrete emplacements with bullet-proof glass screens would be quite feasible, practically indestructible and brought into action at a moment's notice.' He suggested that 617 Squadron be asked to carry out an experiment to test the effectiveness of searchlights 'on a site such as the Staines reservoir or elsewhere,' though there is no evidence that this was done. In February 1944 the possibility of defensive barriers was again raised by the Air Ministry, but Wallis drew attention to the conclusions of the Gwydyr House meetings the previous year. Such a system had been discounted as the enemy might destroy the apron with an initial mine, leaving free access to the target. Thus almost a year after Chastise, its repercussions were still being felt in the United Kingdom.

The nervousness was understandable though unnecessary. The He177 (dismissed by Milch as a 'dead racehorse') suffered serious teething problems, never becoming an effective operational weapon, and the Do217 was not modified. The Germans did not actually develop Upkeep, although they carried out laboratory experiments in Stuttgart which were similar to those of Wallis at Teddington. But instead of adopting Wallis's weapon they worked on a type of sphere which used a different principle of ricochet, and this ultimately failed in November 1944.

Without pre-war recognition of the Möhne and Sorpe dams as bombing targets and the commitment of Portal and Bottomley to destruction of the

Möhne in 1940, it is unlikely that Upkeep would have been developed or Chastise planned, whatever the merits of Wallis's later arguments. Admiralty interest in Highball and its maritime application had some short-term influence, but Air Staff groundwork proved more important and undoubtedly the Air Ministry, not Vickers-Armstrongs, was the focal point for the operation. Both of Wallis's long papers relied to some extent upon Service information, which Beaverbrook authorised Tedder to reveal, and from mid-1940 onwards his files show that he did receive valuable material from MAP and Air Ministry sources. He did not therefore rely even in the early stages exclusively upon private research, and this explains why some of his figures, on measurements of the dams for example, do not coincide with those of any one published authority. Nor should it be forgotten that Road Research Laboratory staff controlled and conducted experiments at Harmondsworth and in Wales. Wallis was of course a crucial figure throughout the build-up to Chastise, and in his summary to Bomber Command on 7 June 1943, while concentrating on Service activity, Cochrane specifically mentioned his work. To a greater or lesser degree, civilian scientists were behind every military venture in the Second World War. To Chadwick on 20 May Wallis portrayed them in an even more decisive role: 'I do agree it is the engineers of this country who are going to win the war.'

In this context, it appears from Wallis's own sketches in his 'Air Attack on Dams' paper, photographic evidence from Reculver and a still photograph of the small-scale, experimental weapon that Upkeep was not conceived as a perfect sphere but had flattened ends. And the doubts that have been raised about Wallis's mathematical and scientific calculations concerning the final, cylindrical version are utterly groundless. When Wallis visited the Möhne Dam in May 1945 he carried on a bizarre conversation with the proprietor through the barred front door of the Seehof Hotel on the shore of the reservoir. Although Wallis admitted to a poor command of German, he gathered that two mines had hit the dam wall, which confirmed Maltby's observation at the time and all official post-operational reports. Undoubtedly Young, who would perish off the Dutch coast on the return flight, breached the Möhne Dam, and Maltby widened the gap. At the Eder, Shannon and Maudslay damaged the wall, but Knight broke it. It is clear from British and German sources that, apart from those of Young, Maltby and Knight, no other mine at the Möhne and Eder was dropped in the precise manner required by Wallis. When Young and Knight were able to do so, the dams were breached. But it must be re-stressed that none of the crews which failed to achieve the exact specifications should in any way be blamed. Reference to the conditions at the Möhne and Eder and the care taken by all captains at every dam to get maximum accuracy, even to the point of making several dummy runs, illustrates this.

Because Chastise broke two major dams – causing widespread flooding, interruption to industry, communications, gas, electricity and water supplies in varying degrees, re-deployment of troops and weapons, and diversion of labour to repair its ravages – this operation could well be termed 'a major disaster' for the enemy. Kammhuber wrote later: 'Measured against the frightful losses which the terror attacks caused in the German cities with their terrible destruction, the dam attacks were less significant; though this in no way detracts from their importance in other respects.' This was a post-war judgement based upon a review of the whole spectrum of bombing effort. On 21 May 1943, Goebbels recorded that 'recent damage, excepting that done to the dams, had been relatively small,' reinforcing the view that at the time the operation was indeed 'significant'. More broadly, the effect upon morale on both sides of the Channel and the Atlantic was substantial. In this, subsequent publicity, backed by the striking reconnaissance photographs, played a decisive part. Success in war depends upon maintaining the morale of one's own forces, population and allies, while undermining that of the enemy. Physical damage and battlefield triumph represent a means of achieving this, not an end in themselves. To concentrate on apparent imperfections in the material achievement of Chastise is to miss the point of its impact, although the question of whether the operation supports Trenchard's assertion after the First World War that the ratio of moral to physical effect of bombing is 20:1 must remain a moot point. Interestingly, Brig Hollis thought Portal very keen on 'propaganda,' and reports of the royal visit on 27 May were skilfully manipulated to suggest that 617 Squadron had been singled out for this distinction. The King and Queen were actually in the throes of a two-day tour of American and British bases in the area, and 57 Squadron was also inspected at Scampton on that day. An interesting commercial postscript concerned Vickers-Armstrongs' moves to secure patent rights for Wallis's work. Patent Specification No. 937,959, 'Improvements in Explosive Missiles and means for their Discharge', based upon the contents of 'Spherical Bomb – Surface Torpedo' and subsequent tests at Teddington, was registered on 11 August 1942. Patent Specification No. 937,960 fed from 'Air Attack on Dams', but covering all possible uses of the weapon across water and its different shapes, was registered on 10 July 1943. For security reasons, neither specification was published until 25 September 1963.

Benjamin Lockspeiser made perhaps the most succinct and apt assessment of Chastise by drawing attention to its 'tremendous psychological effect,' and in this context it may be linked with other single episodes of military achievement or heroism which have exercised moral influence far beyond the immediate confines of strategic or tactical gain. If, in the emotional aftermath of this unique operation, exaggerated claims were advanced for it, they should not obscure the reality of its short-term and long-term impact. In its execution 11 Lancasters attacked and two (Young's at the Möhne and Knight's at the Eder) effectively bombed a very significant number of installations below the breached dams which were listed as individual targets by the Air Ministry and destined otherwise for separate attack. That explains, perhaps, why Harris initially declared the results 'a major disaster' for the Germans and why F/Sgt Fraser's interrogator credited Chastise with a hundred times more impact than any other bombing raid.

For the British it proved politically timely, and ultimately it is difficult to dispute the conclusion of the *Annual Register* for 1943: 'The most spectacular air exploit of the month [May] and perhaps the war.' Furthermore, contrary to the claims of its latter-day critics, Operation Chastise was also eminently worthwhile.

APPENDICES

APPENDIX A. GLOSSARY AND ABBREVIATIONS

AAD	Aerial *or* Air Attack on Dams (Committee *or* Wallis's paper)
A&AEE	Aeroplane and Armament Experimental Establishment, Boscombe Down
ACAS (I)	Assistant Chief of the Air Staff (Intelligence)
ACAS (Ops)	Assistant Chief of the Air Staff (Operations)
ACAS (TR)	Assistant Chief of the Air Staff (Technical Requirements)
Adm	Admiralty
AI	Air Intelligence, Air Ministry
Air Cdre	air commodore
AJ	617 Squadron's code letters
Amatol	explosive
AOC	air officer commanding
AOC-in-C	air officer commanding-in-chief
AP	armour-piercing (bomb)
API	air position indicator
Avro	A. V. Roe & Co Ltd
Baseball	Version of bouncing mine intended for motor torpedo boat or motor gun boat
BC	Bomber Command
Brig	Brigadier
BRS	Building Research Station, Garston
Capt	captain
CAS	Chief of the Air Staff
CE	compound explosive
Chastise	codename for operation against German dams with Upkeep
CID	Committee of Imperial Defence

CIGS	Chief of the Imperial General Staff
CO	commanding officer
COps	Combined Operations
COS	Chiefs of Staff *or* Chiefs of Staff Committee
CRD	Controller of Research and Development, Ministry of Aircraft Production
CSRD	Chief Superintendent of the Research Department, Woolwich
D Arm D	Director *or* Directorate of Armament Development, initially Air Ministry then Ministry of Aircraft Production
DB Ops	Director or Directorate of Bomber Operations, Air Ministry
DCSRD	Deputy Chief Superintendent of the Research Department, Woolwich
D/CRD	Deputy Controller of Research and Development, Ministry of Aircraft Production
D/D Arm D	Deputy Director of Armament Development
DDB Ops	Deputy Director of Bomber Operations, Air Ministry
D/F	direction-finding
DMWD	Director *or* Directorate of Miscellaneous Weapon Development, Admiralty
D/R	dead reckoning
DSIR	Department of Scientific and Industrial Research, a Government supervisory body
DSD	Director *or* Directorate of Staff Duties, Air Ministry
DTD	Director *or* Directorate of Technical Development, Ministry of Aircraft Production
ETA	estimated time of arrival
Fg Off	flying officer
flak	German anti-aircraft guns
GCI	ground-controlled interception
Gee	navigational aid
glycol	coolant liquid
Golf Mine	codename for all bouncing mines/revolving depth charges
GP	general-purpose (bomb)
Gp Capt	group captain
HCU	heavy conversion unit
HE	high-explosive
Highball	codename for smaller bouncing mine or revolving depth charge for use in Mosquito
ICI	Imperial Chemical Industries Ltd
IFF	identification friend or foe
intercom	telephone system inside aircraft

km	kilometre
kW	kilowatt
Lt Cdr	lieutenant-commander
mag	magneto
Maj	major
MAP	Ministry of Aircraft Production
met	meteorological
MEW	Ministry of Economic Warfare
m^3/sec	cubic metres per second
mm	millimetre
mph	miles per hour
NPL	National Physical Laboratory
ORB	operations record book
OTU	operational training unit
PE	plastic explosive
Plt Off	pilot officer
PRU	photographic reconnaissance unit
RAAF	Royal Australian Air Force
RAE	Royal Aircraft Establishment, Farnborough
RAF	Royal Air Force
RCAF	Royal Canadian Air Force
RDF	radio direction-finding (radar)
RDX	Research Department Explosive
rev(s)	revolution(s)
rpm	revolutions per minute
RRL	Road Research Laboratory, Harmondsworth
R/T	radio-telephony
RNZAF	Royal New Zealand Air Force
SAP	semi-armour piercing (bomb)
SASO	senior air staff officer
Servant	codename for operation against *Tirpitz* with Highball
SOE	Special Operations Executive
store	bomb or aerial mine
Torpex	underwater explosive
Upkeep	codename for larger bouncing mine or revolving depth charge for use in Lancaster
U/S	unserviceable
USAAF	United States Army Air Force(s)

USSBS	United States Strategic Bombing Survey
VHF	very high frequency (radio)
VSG	variable-speed gear
WA	Western Air (Plans)
WAAF	Women's Auxiliary Air Force
Wg Cdr	wing commander
WO	War Office *or* warrant officer
W/T	wireless telegraphy

APPENDIX B. SIGNIFICANT DATES CONNECTED
WITH OPERATION CHASTISE

1937

September	AII(b) at the Air Ministry identifies German dams and reservoirs as potential targets.
1 October	Draft Western Air Plans, including projected attacks on the Ruhr industry, discussed in Air Ministry; leads to specific designation of Möhne and Sorpe dams as targets.

1938

26 July	Bombing Committee of the Air Ministry unenthusiastically considers torpedo or bombing attacks on the Möhne Dam.
28 July	AOC-in-C Bomber Command (Ludlow-Hewitt) expresses continued interest in destroying the Möhne Dam; attempts to develop a method of doing so proceed at the RAE.

1940

2 May	At the Ministry of Suppy research depot, Shrewsbury, Wg Cdr Finch-Noyes is instructed to re-examine all previous papers about attacking gravity dams.
3 July	AOC-in-C Bomber Command (Portal) presses Air Ministry to attack the Möhne Dam with Hampden bombers modified to carry torpedoes.
19 July	Wallis's first interview with Beaverbrook, Minister of Aircraft Production. It is clear that Wallis has been considering dams, among other targets connected with German industry, since 'autumn 1939'.
20 July	Wallis's second interview with Beaverbrook, at which he produces specifications for a six-engined bomber to carry a ten-ton, earth-penetration bomb and secures the Minister's promise of co-operation from his Deparment.
August	Aeronautical Research Committee agrees to Wallis using the wind tunnel at the National Physical Laboratory, Teddington, in connection with his big bomb.
2 September	Finch-Noyes' first paper outlining proposals for destroying gravity dams.
October	Tests instituted at Road Research Laboratory, Harmondsworth, on 1/50-scale model of Möhne Dam.
November	First Road Research report on gravity dam tests.

1941

9 January	Limited approval by Beaverbrook for continued work on the big bomb, provided other Vickers-Armstrongs projects do not suffer.
January	End of inconclusive tests on another 1/50-scale model of the Möhne Dam at the Building Research Station, Garston, in progress

	since November 1940; these and Road Research Laboratory tests witnessed by an *ad hoc* MAP committee under the DSR (Pye).
10 March	First meeting of Aerial Attack on Dams (AAD) Committee, a more formal body chaired by DSR.
March	Completion of Wallis's first major paper, 'A Note on a Method of Attacking the Axis Powers': ten-ton, deep-penetration bomb dropped by a six-engined (Victory) bomber.
2 April	Finch-Noyes' second paper, refining his proposals, forwarded to AOC-in-C Bomber Command (Peirse); subsequently discussed with him but not pursued.
11 April	Another committee of experts under DSR discusses Wallis's suggestion in connection with the destruction of underground oil storage tanks.
23 April	Professor Southwell's plan to destroy a dam with a mine attached to a parachute or drogue.
May	Air Staff rejects Wallis's big bomb, but more encouraging report from the Road Research Laboratory. Simultaneous attacks on the air and water faces of the Möhne Dam considered.
19 June	Second meeting of AAD Committee agrees that Wallis's work should continue.
10 December	Third meeting of AAD Committee marks return to previous ideas of high-level bombing and sympathetic detonation of mines.

1942

February-March	Further Road Research Laboratory tests, including unplanned success with contact explosion.
April	Wallis begins rudimentary experiments concerning bouncing technique, probably finalised in his mind during March.
22 April	Wallis meets Blackett at the Admiralty to explain his new idea, which Blackett refers to Tizard, who involves the Air Ministry.
25 April	Wallis given permission to carry out tests in a tank at the National Physical Laboratory at Teddington.
1 May	First Nant-y-Gro test: failure with proximity charge.
14 May	Distribution of paper, 'Spherical Bomb – Surface Torpedo,' which details the bouncing technique but not spinning of the weapon.
9 June	Tests commence at Teddington and continue at intervals until 22 September; Admiralty now closely involved.
29 September	Abortive meeting of Wallis with Cherwell.
30 September	Tizard expresses his written support for Wallis in an official minute.
12 October	Fourth meeting of the AAD Committee: rejection of sympathetic detonation of mines, but no specific encouragement to Wallis.
20 October	Spinning tests on the ground at Weybridge.
2 December	Spinning tests in the air over Queen Mary reservoir.
4 December	First dropping trial with practice spheres at Chesil Beach.
15 December	Second Chesil Beach trial.

1943

9 January	Wallis's second major paper, 'Air Attack on Dams,' circulated.
9–10 January	Third Chesil Beach trial.
23 January	Fourth Chesil Beach trial.
30 January	More tests at Teddington.
2 February	Cherwell less antagonistic in meeting with Wallis after receipt of 'Air Attack on Dams' paper.
5 February	Fifth Chesil Beach trial.
14 February	Harris reacts adversely to a minute by SASO Bomber Command, Saundby, summarising an Air Ministry meeting on 13 February about 'the spherical bomb'.
18 February	Personal letter by Harris to Portal, quoting CRD's support, shows opposition to Wallis's work.
19 February	Portal informs Harris that experiments are to continue and three Lancasters to be made available.
22 February	Wallis's visit to Harris at HQ Bomber Command, High Wycombe.
23 February	Linnell, CRD, tells Wallis to stop work on Upkeep; Wallis offers to resign from Vickers-Armstrongs.
26 February	Linnell reverses his decision; Upkeep work to proceed with all speed.
28 February	First full-scale drawings of Upkeep completed; frantic round of meetings, letters and telephone calls commences; Air Staff insists that Highball should not be used independently.
8 March	First conversion order signed for a Type 464 Provisioning Lancaster; Chiefs of Staff set up an *ad hoc* committee to monitor Upkeep and Highball progress.
15 March	Gibson posted to HQ 5 Group.
17 March	Squadron X formed.
19 March	Meeting at MAP, chaired by D/CRD, decides that 23 Lancasters are to be modified.
21 March	New squadron begins to gather at RAF Scampton.
24 March	617 Squadron RAF officially comes into existence.
27 March	617 Squadron commences intensive training with 10 borrowed Lancasters.
7 April	Spinning tests at Foxwarren; Wallis now satisfied that Upkeep will not leap out of retaining arms when spun at speed.
8 April	First Type 464 Provisioning Lancaster arrives at Scampton.
12 April	Chiefs of Staff agree to US observers at trials; Portal sends full details of Highball and Upkeep to RAF Delegation in Washington.
13 April	First Reculver trial with scaled-down practice spheres.
18 April	Second Reculver trial; decision to remove outer wooden casing and drop bare metal cylinder.
21 April	Third Reculver trial; Avro test pilot, Brown, drops first bare cylinder, possibly not yet full-size version.
24 April	Weybridge conference: Gibson agrees to height of release being lowered from 150 to 60ft.

29 April–1 May	Fourth Reculver trial: full-size Upkeep cylinder certainly dropped by Longbottom.
1 May	Gibson tells Wallis that he is confident of success.
5 May	Meeting at Air Ministry, chaired by ACAS(Ops), acknowledges 26 May as last date for Chastise (later changed to May 19).
6 May	More Reculver trials
9–10 May	Failure of Highball trials in Scotland.
10 May	SASO 5 Group, Satterly, sends draft operation order to Scampton for comment.
11–12 May	617 Squadron crews drop inert-filled Upkeep cylinders at Reculver.
12 May	Draft operation order returned to Satterly with Gibson's comments.
13 May	Only fully armed Upkeep dropped before the operation and bounced as intended off Broadstairs; more 617 Squadron crews practise at Reculver, where one modified Lancaster is irreparably damaged; twentieth Type 464 Provisioning Lancaster delivered to Scampton; Vice-Chiefs of Staff fail to agree that Upkeep should be used independently from Highball and that Chastise should go ahead, and signal to Chiefs of Staff in Washington for decision.
14 May	Portal signals from Washington that Chastise is to proceed; 617 Squadron crews again at Reculver; successful full rehearsal for Chastise at night.
15 May	Second live Upkeep dropped off Broadstairs without being spun; Air Ministry decision to mount Chastise as soon as possible; Cochrane warns Scampton; conference at HQ 5 Group, which probably modifies draft operation order; preliminary briefing of important personnel at Scampton.
16 May	Final decision to execute Chastise; series of pre-operational briefings; last-minute route adjustments; arrival of reserve Lancaster from Boscombe Down; mounting of Operation Chastise by 19 Lancasters, eight of which fail to return.
17 May	Möhne and Eder dams breached, Sorpe damaged and (probably) Bever attacked.
18 May	Press in United Kingdom and USA makes good use of dramatic post-operational photographs.
19 May	Winston Churchill addresses Congress in Washington, making specific reference to Chastise.
25 May	*London Gazette* publishes list of awards.
27 May	Royal visit to RAF Scampton.
22 June	Investiture at Buckingham Palace, followed by celebratory dinner given by Avro.
11 August	Chiefs of Staff agree to pass all information concerning Upkeep and Chastise to Moscow.

APPENDIX C. 617 SQUADRON CREWS ENGAGED
IN OPERATION CHASTISE, MAY 16/17, 1943

Aircraft (wave)	Times**	Pilot	Flight Engineer	Navigator
AJ-G (1) ED932/G	2139 0328	Wg Cdr G. P. Gibson DSO & Bar, DFC & Bar	Sgt J. Pulford	Plt Off H. T. Taerum RCAF
AJ-M (1) ED925/G	2139 0034	Flt Lt J. V. Hopgood DFC & Bar	Sgt C. Brennan	Fg Off K. Earnshaw RCAF
AJ-P (1) ED909/G	2139 0319	Flt Lt H. B. Martin DFC	Plt Off I. Whittaker	Flt Lt J. F. Leggo DFC, RAAF
AJ-A (1)* ED877/G	2147 0258	Sqn Ldr H. M. Young, DFC & Bar	Sgt D. T. Horsfall	F/Sgt C. W. Roberts
AJ-J (1) ED906/G	2147 0311	Flt Lt D. J. H. Maltby DFC	Sgt W. Hatton	Sgt V. Nicholson
AJ-L (1) ED929/G	2147 0406	Flt Lt D. J. Shannon DFC, RAAF	Sgt R. J. Henderson	Fg Off D. R. Walker DFC, RCAF
AJ-Z (1)* ED937/G	2159 0236	Sqn Ldr H. E. Maudslay DFC	Sgt J. Marriott DFM	Fg Off R. A. Urquhart DFC, RCAF
AJ-B (1)* ED864/G	2159 0015	Flt Lt W. Astell DFC	Sgt J. Kinnear	Plt Off F. A. Wile RCAF
AJ-N (1) ED912/G	2159 0420	Plt Off L. G. Knight RAAF	Sgt R. E. Grayston	Fg Off H. S. Hobday
AJ-E (2)* ED927/G	2128 2350	Flt Lt R. N. G. Barlow DFC, RAAF	Plt Off S. L. Whillis	Fg Off P. S. Burgess
AJ-W (2) ED921/G	2129 0036	Flt Lt J. L. Munro RNZAF	Sgt F. E. Appelby	Fg Off F. G. Rumbles
AJ-K (2)* ED934/G	2130 2257	Plt Off V. W. Byers RCAF	Sgt A. J. Taylor	Fg Off J. H. Warner
AJ-H (2) ED936/G	2131 0047	Plt Off G. Rice	Sgt E. C. Smith	Fg Off R. MacFarlane
AJ-T (2) ED825/G	2201 0323	Flt Lt J. C. McCarthy DFC, RCAF	Sgt W. G. Radcliffe RCAF	F/Sgt D. A. MacLean RCAF
AJ-C (3) ED910/G	0009 0235	Plt Off W. H. T. Ottley DFC	Sgt R. Marsden	Fg Off J. K. Barrett DFC
AJ-S (3)* ED865/G	0011 0200	Plt Off L. J. Burpee DFM, RCAF	Sgt G. Pegler	Sgt T. Jaye
AJ-F (3) ED918/G	0012 0533	F/Sgt K. W. Brown RCAF	Sgt H. B. Feneron	Sgt D. P. Heal
AJ-O (3) ED886/G	0014 0615	F/Sgt W. C. Townsend DFM	Sgt D. J. D. Powell	Plt Off C. L. Howard RAAF
AJ-Y (3) ED924/G	0015 0530	F/Sgt C. T. Anderson	Sgt R. C. Paterson	Sgt J. P. Nugent

* The positions of the two gunners in these aircraft cannot be confirmed.
**Times: Take-off, landing/approximate crash.

APPENDIX C. (CONTINUED)

Wireless	Bomb-aimer	Front gunner	Rear gunner
Flt Lt R. E. G. Hutchinson DFC	Plt Off F. M. Spafford DFM, RAAF	F/Sgt G. A. Deering RCAF	Flt Lt R. D. Trevor-Roper DFM
Sgt J. W. Minchin	F/Sgt J. W. Fraser RCAF	Plt Off G. H. F. G. Gregory DFM	Plt Off A. F. Burcher DFM, RAAF
Fg Off L. Chambers RNZAF	Flt Lt R. C. Hay DFC, RAAF	Plt Off B. T. Foxlee DFM, RAAF	F/Sgt T. D. Simpson RAAF
Sgt L. W. Nichols	Fg Off V. S. Mac-Causland RCAF	Sgt G. A. Yeo	Sgt W. Ibbotson
Sgt A. J. B. Stone	Plt Off J. Fort	Sgt V. Hill	Sgt H. T. Simmonds
Fg Off B. Goodale DFC	F/Sgt L. J. Sumpter	Sgt B. Jagger	Fg Off J. Buckley
WO A. P. Cottam	Plt Off M. J. D. Fuller	Fg Off W. J. Tytherleigh DFC	Sgt N. R. Burrows
WO A. A. Garshowitz RCAF	Fg Off D. Hopkinson	F/Sgt F. A. Garbas RCAF	Sgt R. Bolitho
F/Sgt R. G. T. Kellow RAAF	Fg Off E. C. Johnson	Sgt F. E. Sutherland RCAF	Sgt H. E. O'Brien RCAF
Fg Off C. R. Williams DFC, RAAF	Plt Off A. Gillespie DFM	Fg Off H. S. Glinz RCAF	Sgt J. R. G. Liddell
WO P. E. Pigeon RCAF	Sgt J. H. Clay	Sgt W. Howarth	F/Sgt H. A. Weeks RCAF
Sgt J. Wilkinson	Plt Off A. N. Whittaker	Sgt C. McA. Jarvie	F/Sgt J. McDowell RCAF
WO C. B. Gowrie RCAF	WO J. W. Thrasher RCAF	Sgt T. W. Maynard	Sgt S. Burns
F/Sgt L. Eaton	Sgt G. L. Johnson	Sgt R. Batson	Fg Off D. Rodger RCAF
Sgt J. Guterman DFM	F/Sgt T. B. Johnston	Sgt H. J. Strange	Sgt F. Tees
Plt Off L. G. Weller	F/Sgt J. L. Arthur RCAF	Sgt W. C. A. Long	WO J. G. Brady RCAF
Sgt H. J. Hewstone	Sgt S. Oancia RCAF	Sgt D. Allatson	F/Sgt G. S. MacDonald RCAF
F/Sgt G. A. Chalmers	Sgt C. E. Franklin DFM	Sgt D. E. Webb	Sgt R. Wilkinson
Sgt W. D. Bickle	Sgt G. J. Green	Sgt E. Ewan	Sgt A. W. Buck

All aircrew shown were RAF or RAF Volunteer Reserve unless otherwise indicated.

APPENDIX D. AWARDS TO MEMBERS OF NO 617
SQUADRON RAF FOLLOWING OPERATION CHASTISE

Victoria Cross
A/Wg Cdr G. P. Gibson DSO and Bar, DFC and Bar

Distinguished Service Order
Flt Lt J. C. McCarthy DFC
Flt Lt D. J. H. Maltby DFC
A/Flt Lt H. B. Martin DFC
A/Flt Lt D. J. Shannon DFC
Plt Off L. G. Knight

Conspicuous Gallantry Medal (Flying)
F/Sgt K. W. Brown
F/Sgt W. C. Townsend DFM†

Bar to Distinguished Flying Cross
A/Flt Lt R. C. Hay DFC
A/Flt Lt R. E. G. Hutchison DFC
A/Flt Lt J. F. Leggo DFC
Fg Off D. R. Walker DFC

Bar to Distinguished Flying Medal
Sgt C. E. Franklin DFM

Distinguished Flying Cross
A/Flt Lt R. D. Trevor-Roper DFM
Fg Off J. Buckley
Fg Off L. Chambers
Fg Off H. S. Hobday
Fg Off E. C. Johnson
Plt Off G. A. Deering*
Plt Off J. Fort
Plt Off C. L. Howard
Plt Off F. M. Spafford DFM
Plt Off H. T. Taerum

Distinguished Flying Medal
F/Sgt G. A. Chalmers
F/Sgt D. A. MacLean*
F/Sgt T. D. Simpson
F/Sgt L. J. Sumpter
Sgt D. P. Heal
Sgt G. L. Johnson
Sgt V. Nicholson
Sgt S. Oancia
Sgt J. Pulford
Sgt D. E. Webb
Sgt R. Wilkinson

* Both Deering and MacLean flew as F/Sgt on Chastise, with notification of their commissions appearing in 617 Squadron's operations record book on 18 May. Thus logically both should have received either the DFC or DFM.

† Draft recommendations showed 'Bar to DFM' for Townsend.

Notes
(i) All ranks, with the exception of that of Deering, are as at 16 May 1943.
(ii) Sources: *Supplement to the London Gazette*, 25 May 1943, which incorrectly shows Sgt E. Webb; App H to 'Report on Operation against the Ruhr and Weser Dams 16/17 May 1943' by AOC 5 Group, dated 7 June 1943, contained in PRO/Air 14/208.

APPENDIX E. ANALYSIS OF 617 SQUADRON CREW FLYING ON OPERATION CHASTISE

Casualties

	RAF or RAF(VR)	RCAF	RNZAF	RAAF	Totals
Engaged in operation	90	29	2	12	133
Killed	38	13	0	2	53
POW	1	1	0	1	3

Nationalities

	RAF or RAF (VR)	RCAF	RNZAF	RAAF	Totals
Pilots	11	4	1	3	19
Flight engineers	19	0	0	0	19
Navigators	11	6	0	2	19
Wireless operators	12	4	1	2	19
Bomb-aimers	12	5	0	2	19
Gunners	25	10	0	3	38
Totals	90	29	2	12	133

Previous Decorations

	DSO & Bar DFC & Bar	DFC & Bar	DFC	DFM	None
Pilots	1	2	8	2	6
Flight engineers	0	0	0	0	19
Navigators	0	0	4	0	15
Wireless operators	0	0	3	1	15
Bomb-aimers	0	0	1	3	15
Gunners	0	0	1	4	33
Totals	1	2	17	10	103

Sources

British Defence Liaison Staff, Canberra, Australia, letter dated 11 September 1977, BDLS/5530/3

Canadian Forces Records Centre, Ottawa, Canada, letter dated 20 June 1978, CFRC 1A

Commonwealth War Graves Commission, letter dated 15 June 1977, ENQ 2/5

Department of Defence (Air Force Office), Canberra, Australia, letter dated 27 October 1977, DGPS(R) 401899

Ministry of Defence, Defence Headquarters, Wellington, New Zealand, letter dated 5 August 1977, 54/4/16

Ministry of Defence, London, Dept AR8b(RAF): (i) letter dated 4 August 1977, 7557
(ii) separate, undated list of crews attached

Ministry of Defence, London, Dept AR9a(RAF): letter dated 12 August 1977, P404217/43

Programme of première of *The Dam Busters* film, 16 May 1955

Supplement to the *London Gazette*, 25 May 1943

617 Squadron's operations record book, PRO/Air 27/2128

617 Squadron Association's list of members

617 Squadron's navigators' logs from AJ-G (partial), AJ-J and AJ-N

Notes on sources

No two sources agree about ranks, initials or the spelling of names in every instance. 617 Squadron's operations record book is particularly unreliable, and the above summary has been based largely upon the other sources. The British Ministry of Defence's Airmen's Records Department is unable to verify any of the RAF or RAF(VR) non-commissioned ranks, initials or names, so errors may still exist in these.

Other points

(i) Records of the Commonwealth War Graves Commission and the Runnymede Air Force Memorial spell the name of AJ-K's bomb-aimer 'Whitaker'; AJ-G's rear gunner is sometimes shown as 'Trevor Roper'; Canadian records show AJ-G's navigator with a single Christian name, 'Torgerharlo,' rather than 'Harlo Torger'; with the exception of the pilot, the initials of the entire crew of AJ-Y ar. recorded differently in some documents; AJ-T's navigator frequently and incorrectly appears as 'McLean'.

(ii) Sgt F. Tees' position in the rear turret is shown in no document, but has been confirmed by him personally.

(iii) F/Sgt R. G. T. Kellow (March 11), F/Sgt C. T. Anderson (April 17), F/Sgt G. A. Deering and F/Sgt D. A. MacLean (both recorded in 617 Squadron's operations record book on 18 May) were commissioned before the operation without their knowledge; Plt Off H. T. Taerum (2 April) and F/Sgt J. L. Arthur (9 May) had similarly been promoted to Fg Off and WO II respectively.

Analysis of awards

All pilots, navigators and bomb-aimers of each of the eight aircraft (G, P, J, L, N, T, O, F) which attacked a dam and returned were decorated, together with three wireless operators (G, P, O), six gunners (both in G and O, the rear gunners of P and L) and one flight engineer (G). Thus 34 survivors were decorated, but only one complete crew (G), although six of the last aircraft to return (O) received an award.

Commendations for meritorious service

Headquarters 5 Group

Gp Capt H. V. Satterly DFC	Senior Air Staff Officer
Wg Cdr W. E. Dunn	Chief Signals Officer
Wg Cdr P. Brown	Engineering Officer
Sqn Ldr E. A. Goodwin	Armament Officer

RAF Scampton

Gp Capt J. N. H. Whitworth DSO, DFC	Station Commander
Flt Lt C. C. Caple	Engineering Officer
Plt Off H. Watson MBE	Armament Officer
WO W. H. Taylor	Fitter 1
F/Sgt A. T. Smith MBE	Fitter 1
F/Sgt H. Gover	Fitter 1
F/Sgt A. Campbell	Instrument Maker
Sgt A. Chambers	Fitter

A CONTEMPORARY
PERSPECTIVE

CONTINUING INTEREST, AND RENEWED CRITICISM

Almost sixty years on, the Dambusters Raid continues to fascinate. Crowds still flock to commemorative events, and media curiosity remains high. During 1997 and 1998, rumour that the last remaining scale-model of the Moehne Dam might be knocked down; recovery of four different versions of Barnes Wallis's unique weapon dropped during development trials off the north Kent coast; and demolition of water tanks at the National Physical Laboratory, used for experiments in 1942, attracted extensive press, television and radio cover, as did speculation that a new, American version of the commercial film might be imminent.

A marked feature of the past decade, however, has been a swathe of renewed criticisms about the operation, both in writing and on television, among the most provocative being 'elaborate legend' . . . 'more costly to England than Germany' . . . 'little more than a gimmick' . . . 'strategic failure'. The similarity, and in some cases disdainful ferocity, of these attacks must prompt careful evaluation, not simple, curt dismissal as colourful re-cycling of old, discredited material. Do they, in particular, invalidate the conclusions, reached nearly twenty years ago and set out in the closing section of the main text of this book?

Condemnation has been both general and specific, the Sorpe Dam providing one focal point. A 1993 TV programme 'revealed' that only days before the raid, planners 'realised that the Sorpe had no towers'. In reality, since 1937 its structure had been fully and frequently discussed, and in his widely-circulated 1942 *Air Attack on Dams* paper Wallis included an accurate diagram of it. Viewers of another documentary learnt that the Sorpe was 'a much larger dam . . . the most important target because it held far more water', a strange assertion given that its reservoir contained roughly half the volume of the Möhne and one-third that of the Eder. Evidently, too, 'scientists' warned that Upkeep would be useless against the Sorpe, 'but the men at the top were not listening. The advice was ignored'. Yet on 18 March 1943, Air Vice-Marshal N. H. Bottomley's *ad hoc* committee ruled the Sorpe 'unsuitable' for attack by Upkeep. It was eventually used there, after a quite different method of delivery had been devised, and according to Albert Speer (German Armaments and Munitions minister) came within 'just a few inches' of success.

The further contention, first put forward by Speer and Hans Rumpf (German Inspector-General of Fire Prevention), that it would have been 'very easy to destroy . . . with a few fire bombs' the rebuilding works at the Möhne and Eder has been resurrected by commentators like the German historian Dr Horst Boog. On 1 April 1943, Bottomley's committee correctly forecast that the Germans would swiftly take 'counter-measures' at the dams, so any follow-up would be 'completely ineffective'. The array of flak, smoke and other defensive weaponry deployed from 17 May frustrated another low-level attack, and a high-level one, especially with incendiaries, could never attain the necessary accuracy.

The main allegation, which has gathered special momentum, however, is that effects of the operation have been grossly, even wilfully, distorted, and specifically that it did not cause anywhere like the expected damage to armament factories. Therefore, 'was it worth it?' . . . 'was it really worthwhile?'

Undoubtedly, in May 1943, national and local newspapers – rapidly followed by periodicals and newsreels – did splash sensational headlines and pen highly imaginative articles of apocalyptic achievement. But they relied heavily on imaginative agency despatches from Switzerland and Sweden, possibly the most notorious of which proclaimed the people of Kassel so despondent that 'their only desire is that the war should end', closely followed by Morocco Radio's derivative account of rioting in the streets of the Ruhr's industrial cities. Press portrayals of such devastating effects did not reflect either Service expectations or post-operational assessment. The 1937 hopes, that breaching of the Möhne and Sorpe dams would paralyse the industrial Ruhr in a fortnight, had been severely modified six years later. Within a year of the optimistic pre-war forecast, the Air Ministry had warned that 'a not inconsiderable body of opinion' doubted industrial catastrophe if the dams were breached. In March 1943, the Chief of the Air Staff referred only to 'appreciable' damage through flooding in low-lying districts of the Ruhr. The following month, six weeks before the Dams Raid, he admitted that the outcome would be 'less far-reaching than had previously been estimated'. The Operation Order for 617 Squadron, while undoubtedly hoping for significant damage to hydro-electric generating stations and munitions output by rupturing the Möhne, nevertheless cautioned that any major effects would only be evident 'in the course of a few months' and that 'considerable local flooding . . . might (sic) cause havoc in the Ruhr valley'. In the Eder valley, flooding 'would probably (sic)' disrupt the inland waterways. Furthermore, Wallis's influential *Air Attack On Dams* paper was speckled with important qualifications, such as: floods '*might* . . . (cause) considerable damage' to the Ruhr valley's railway network . . . '*it is possible* that many of such (power) stations would be damaged or destroyed by flood waters consequent upon the breaching of the (Möhne) dam'.

Certainly, on 17 May when the aerial reconnaissance photos had been developed, Air Vice-Marshal the Hon R. A. Cochrane (AOC 5 Group) and Air Chief Marshal Sir Arthur Harris (AOC-in-C Bomber Command) declared the results 'a disaster' for the enemy, but 'disaster' meant a severe shock, not impending victory. In professional terms, Cochrane used the precision achieved by Gibson's Lancasters to urge greater accuracy among main force crews. Furthermore, at no time did Harris overstate the lasting impact of the raid, concluding immediately that 'in this memorable operation they have won a major victory in the Battle of the Ruhr', and in his post-war book, *Bomber Offensive*, repeating his belief that Operation Chastise was only one dramatic episode in that drawn-out campaign. Experienced operational analysts and photographic interpreters from the outset displayed caution, too.

That having been said, German sources do show that physical damage was not altogether negligible. Eyewitnesses, then and in retrospect, have emphasised the physical impact that local devastation had on communities. Writing in 1949, Dr Ing Otto Kirschmer reflected that, in spite of official denials, the densely-populated Ruhr had been 'very seriously affected', and damage below the Eder underestimated. Acknowledging that the attacks on the Möhne, Eder and Sorpe dams represented 'precision bombing of a high order', Hans Rumpf held that Germany only narrowly escaped 'a widespread stoppage of industrial production in the Ruhr', by implication admitting that substantial problems were indeed caused. Reflecting on growing fleets of British and American heavy bombers attacking industrial targets in autumn 1944, Albert Speer wrote: 'There had certainly been critical situations before this – the bombing of the Ruhr reservoirs, for instance'.

Distinct from damage assessment, the psychological impact on Germans cannot be ignored. Serious unease among inhabitants of the Ruhr valley was inadvertently exposed by exhortations to those living below the Möhne not to complain. Rather, they should imitate the stoicism of the people of Dortmund and Bochum, 'regular recipients' of Bomber Command's attentions. Rumpf later held that 'government cover-ups' were counter-productive: 'the fictional impression grew rapidly and discovered newer and newer totals of terror, of lives lost and damage to property'. Most significantly, postwar he concluded: 'Worse still than the direct damage . . . turned out to be the moral impression on the people', whose confidence in the Luftwaffe to defend them was severely dented. In March 1943, Speer recorded Hitler's fear that the morale of the German people had already been 'irreparably' undermined by Allied bombing. Twelve years after the Dambusters Raid, Adolf Galland, the fighter commander, acknowledged that it had 'lasting effect' on German opinion. Some critics accept that there was an impact on German morale, both military and civilian, but dismiss it as incidental and insignificant.

Emphatically, undermining morale was not an accidental by-product, fancifully seized upon by the publicity machine to conceal limited physical achievement – the allegation that 'like other follies, it was a public relations triumph'. In April 1943, Anthony Eden, the Foreign Secretary, told the War Cabinet that 'air attacks . . . have resulted in a sudden and in some cases severe decline in morale in the areas attacked and have induced a widespread sense of insecurity', a month later maintaining that 'progressive deterioration of German morale as a result of air attack has continued. In the Ruhr this has assumed grave proportions'. After the Dams Raid, the War Cabinet learnt from him that 'most important of the immediate consequences were that the success of the operation added very materially to the atmosphere of general disaster and panic in the Ruhr and helped to spread it over other parts of Germany'. A generous dose of wishful thinking lay behind these pronouncements, but they did illustrate that destroying enemy morale formed an integral part of bombing policy, not an optional extra. This was reinforced by documents directly associated with the planning of the Dams Raid. On 27 March 1943, the Chief of the Air Staff referred to 'serious repercussions on morale' of breaching the Möhne. In his lengthy memorandum on 2 April, Mr O. L. Lawrence from the MEW argued that 'the moral effects of the (ensuing) flood' would be heightened by 'alarmist rumours'. Because the area below the Eder was less densely populated, 'the total moral effect' would be 'inevitably smaller' than in the Ruhr. Nevertheless, it could confidently be expected.

Weakening enemy morale, therefore, constituted a primary wartime aim and a specific one for Operation Chastise. Conversely, raising that of the Allies, especially of civilians in Britain, was also crucial. Subject to stringent rationing of food, household goods and clothing, vulnerable to air attack and with family members in uniform daily in peril, they needed encouragement that the national struggle for survival was being won. The Dambusters Raid graphically illustrated this. That it was seized upon, especially the dramatic before and after pictures of the breached dams, for publicity purposes does not dilute its value in this respect. As Sgt D. E. Webb, front gunner of AJ-O, reflected: 'If we did nothing else, we gave people in this country a lift'. And the impact on the international community, especially in the United States and the Soviet Union, should not be forgotten, either.

The need to review information in the light of recent criticisms has incidentally led to clarification of some obscure points. Illness prevented Gibson's flight engineer from receiving his DFM at Buckingham Palace on 22 June, and he was decorated by the King on 16 November. Wallis's concept of a Victory bomber, linked to his plan to drop a 10-ton bomb close to the Möhne, undoubtedly owed much to his own 1938 idea for a large bomber, but this in turn 'was a revamp of Rex Pierson's project of 1937 for a six-engined aircraft', which Wallis acknowledged. The timings of the crew briefings at Scampton have not, though, been so easily agreed. Publications continue to maintain that the pilots were briefed on the previous day (Saturday 15 May) and some that all aircrew learnt their targets that day, presumably including those who did not eventually fly on the night. Such a meeting would have violated a formal instruction from 5 Group to restrict knowledge to the two flight commanders until receipt of the executive signal (despatched at 1645 on 16 May). Cochrane did allow the Squadron's navigation and bombing leaders together with Gibson's nominated deputy at the Möhne to be briefed with the flight commanders on the Saturday evening, but there is no reason to suspect any other dispensations on 15 May. Some further relaxation of the order did happen on the Sunday, however. Pilots and navigators were fully briefed in advance of the executive order, the bomb-aimers and wireless operators told about operational procedures affecting them. Nevertheless, the gunners, and probably all other aircrew apart from the pilots and navigators, did not learn their destinations until the main briefing at 1800, once the executive signal had been received at Scampton. In his post-operational report, Cochrane explained that briefing started early *on the day of the operation* because of the amount of material that had to be absorbed.

The use of the term 'spotlights' has exercised many a quill in the correspondence columns of aviation journals. Undoubtedly situated in the rear of the bomb bay and in the front camera slot, neither 'fitted beneath the Lancaster's wings' nor 'in the nose and tail', Avros has confirmed that they were 'modified Aldis lamps, about 6 ins. diameter and 4 ins. deep'. Maudslay's fate, too, can be settled. AJ-Z crashed at Klein Netterden, near Emmerich, at 0236 on 17 May, the bodies of the crew being initially buried in Dusseldorf North Cemetery, military section, then re-interred in the Reichswald Forest War Cemetery. Additional detailed information has emerged about the 1/50th scale model of the Möhne Dam, constructed at the Building Research Station, Garston, between 25 November 1940 and 21 January 1941. The model was not made of some 3 million miniature bricks individually bedded in mortar, as originally planned, but comprised 'four rows of blocks forming both the upstream and downstream faces, with the core filled with concrete. The rows of blocks on the downstream face were tilted back to simulate the coursing on the stone blocks in the real dam'. None of this made a significant difference to the nature of the tests nor their results.

In 1982, A. R. Collins, former scientific officer at the Road Research Laboratory, published a paper about the pre-raid experiments, in it pondering why the Möhne breach was 39% wider than forecast, that at the Eder only 11%. Subsequent discussion among engineering experts proved inconclusive, and Collins at length accepted that the bigger breach did result from two Upkeeps hitting the Möhne. Young should, therefore, unequivocally be credited with making the first breach in the dam, which Maltby widened. An unsigned and undated summary (possibly by Gibson) found in Squadron records confirms that 'Young had a good three bounces and contact'.

A ruling on 19 March 1943 laid down that Avros would modify the 20 Lancasters destined for the operation and deliver them to Farnborough for clearance by a Vickers pilot. The aircraft would then be taken to a destination nominated by the MAP (Scampton). It is now certain that, due to pressure of time, many – perhaps all – the Lancasters (not yet fully modified) were flown directly from Woodford to Scampton by ATA crews of No 14 Ferry Pool at Ringway. The recollections of one flight engineer, Lionel Dimery, involved in the transfer of three 464 Provisioning Lancasters is particularly interesting, and raises questions about where various modifications were carried out. No Lancaster left Woodford with its bomb-bay doors, but one delivered by Dimery 'had what appeared to be a large clamp underneath the fuselage, while inside was a revolution counter'. This was contrary to the decision on 2 March that the calliper arms would be fitted to all aircraft at Scampton for security reasons. As this attachment was on one of the last two, which Dimery delivered, it is reasonable to conclude that the fast-approaching deadline for

Operation Chastise dictated that modifications be carried out as and when possible at Woodford and Scampton.

Initial instructions that inert-filled Upkeeps should be painted grey, live-filled ones dark green, at the originating factory seem to have been varied, as well. Practice weapons recovered from the sea off Reculver at different times have been 'red ochre' in colour. A 617 flight mechanic, Victor Gill, recalls that the Upkeeps allocated to Young and Astell, whose Lancasters he serviced, were 'oxide red', though another Upkeep allocated to the flight had been green on arrival. Martin's crew is known to have painted its Upkeep black on 16 May, but whether it was previously dark green or red is unknown. German sources state that the weapon recovered from Barlow's crashed Lancaster was 'dark red'. It seems likely, therefore, that at the factory Upkeeps were coated with a red oxide primer but only early ones then completed in black or green, again due to fast-approaching deadlines.

Time has thus allowed clarification of many, though not all, surviving queries of detail. There remains much for the enthusiast and specialist to delve into, not least with respect to non-flying aspects of the operation at Scampton. Years after the event, Plt Off B. T. Foxlee, front gunner in AJ-P, penned a timely reminder: 'Don't forget the "penguins", who made the whole operation successful – the ground staff from ACH/GDs to Station Commander, and especially Rolls Royce – our Merlin engines never missed a beat.'

One fundamental question cannot be shelved: 'Was it worthwhile?' – posed by Wallis to Collins as late as 1972 in the context of such heavy loss (53) among 617 Squadron aircrew on the raid, and similarly raised in 1993 by F/Sgt K. Brown (pilot of AJ-F). No balanced answer to this should be attempted without reference to issues wider than the loss of Squadron members nor, critically, the war situation in May 1943, when ultimate Allied victory was by no means certain.

Undeniably, the physical damage was neither so widespread nor so devastating as press reports claimed, but this is a poor basis for reasoned judgement. By May 1943, planners did not expect the decisive results anticipated in 1937, though German sources confirm that damage was not insignificant. Undermining enemy morale represented a major objective for the operation, not an after-thought in justification, and the success of this aim, too, has been emphasised by German writers. Implicit in every military operation is the hope that success will have a direct effect on the prosecution of the war and provide a boost to morale on the home front. In this respect, Operation Chastise had unquestionable impact *at the time*, not least because the precision attack took place in the Ruhr against massive dams tucked away among inaccessible hills in the depths of the enemy's industrial heartland. Coupled with virtually-simultaneous triumph in North Africa, Operation Chastise held out promise of better things to come. At last, the tide had apparently turned.

The pithy retort of Flt Lt J. C. McCarthy (pilot of AJ-T), 'hey, you weren't there', to a latter-day inquisitor is apt. In the fourth year of war, British people needed hope, and that is what 617 Squadron gave them. The precise extent of the short-term damage or long-term industrial impact, while not negligible, is also not the most important aspect of the operation. Napoleon and, with specific reference to air power, Sir Hugh Trenchard in different centuries put the moral effect of military operations far in excess of physical damage. Operation Chastise heavily underscored this.

Closer inspection reveals the recent, flamboyant denunciations as eye-catching slogans, perched precariously on scant substance and failure to understand the social, political and military contexts in which the operation took place. On this evidence, there is no need to revise the conclusion that the Dambusters Raid was, indeed, a success.

John Sweetman
1999

POSTSCRIPT: ADDITIONAL
INFORMATION 2002

Despite the passage of years, more details are still being unearthed about Operation Chastise. Some clarify areas of uncertainty in the main text, but others raise further interesting issues.

When and by whom authorisation for the original model experiments was given, and the sequence of subsequent tests, has became clearer. In autumn 1949, Barnes Wallis approached Dr R. E. Stradling, chief scientific adviser to the Ministry of Home Security, for advice, knowing of the Ministry's Research and Experiments (R&E) Department's concern with an aerial threat to British dams. Stradling suggested that Wallis should contact Dr D. R. Pye, Director of Scientific Research (DSR) at the Ministry of Aircraft Production (MAP). On 22 October 1940, Pye informed Wallis that, following their meeting, he had contacted Dr E. Appleton of the Directorate of Scientific and Industrial Research (DSIR), who proved 'entirely sympathetic' to conducting experiments in connection with the destruction of enemy dams. On Appleton's recommendation, Pye suggested that Wallis approach the Road Research Laboratory (RRL) to 'hatch out a programme with Dr Glanville' (its director) for which Pye undertook to cover the costs. The MAP, therefore, accepted financial responsibility from the outset. Within a week tests had been arranged, and Appleton confirmed that the DSIR approved the programme 'on your (Pye's) representation of the national importance of the work'. On 31 October, Wallis warned Pye that, although he was confident that a method of dealing with multiple-arch dams would be ready in two months, there was 'no such certainty with the masonry type of dam'.

The report in November by A. R. Collins, the RRL scientific officer closely involved with them, about 'preliminary tests . . . on a roughly constructed 1:50 scale model of a masonry gravity dam', showed that the initial experiments took place at Harmondsworth. These prompted construction of a 'more carefully prepared model' at the Building Research Station (BRS), Garston. On 24 December 1940, Glanville recorded that Sir Henry Tizard (scientific adviser to the MAP) in discussion with Wallis had expressed doubts about successfully upscaling the results of the test with 2oz charges. Tizard, who thus became involved with Wallis's work much earlier that previously suspected, convened an ad hoc meeting of scientists including Wallis, who concluded it 'desirable to check the validity of tests on small models by a large scale test, if a suitable dam could be found'. Stradling, who was present, undertook to investigate. This is how the Nant-y-Gro dam in Wales came into the picture and, incidentally, another example of inter-departmental friction surfaced. On 3 January 1941, Stradling informed Tizard that he had 'secured a real live dam at Elan Valley and propose testing models of this in the laboratory and full scale tests in Wales'. No mention of the RRL. He asked Tizard: 'Will you back me in this by sending a letter expressing the interest of the MAP and stressing the importance from your side?' This he considered to be 'well inside my programme . . . (with) no necessity to get Treasury sanction'. But 'I must warn my financial people' that 'damage claims' might be lodged by the Birmingham City Water Department.

Recalling that 'some months ago' Wallis had approached him, Stradling wrote that 'following this' Pye had approached the DSIR 'direct asking for experimental work on models of dams'. 'The R&E Department was not aware of this until arrangements for the work were completed'. Quite what Stradling intended when he sent Wallis to the MAP is therefore obscure. In his letter of 3 January 1941 to Tizard, Stradling further muddied the waters of understanding by asserting that at Tizard's request, the R&E Department had 'again considered the problem and the results of experiments already carried out'. Four days later Tizard replied, acknowledging that the R&E Department was 'about to undertake experiments into the possibility of attacking gravity dams and that in this connection you have obtained permission for the use of Elan Valley for destructive tests'. 'Kindly keep us informed . . . (as) these tests will be of particular interest to the Ministry of Aircraft Production'. Two organisations, the Ministry of Home Security and RRL, were thus set to carry out tests in connection with gravity dams prompted by Wallis and sponsored by different sections of the MAP. Eventually, Stradling and Pye resolved the problem. On 26 February 1941, Pye confirmed that he would assume responsibility for the Nant-y-Gro experiments, which would ultimately be carried out by the RRL in 1942. None of this undermines Collins' feeling that Professor A. J. Sutton Pippard, who had been a consultant during the construction of the R100 airship, engineered Wallis's entrée to Stradling. Between November 1940 and April 1943, the BRS, RRL and Birmingham Water Department were reimbursed a total of £4317.16.0 (£4317.80) in connection with gravity dams tests.

The background to Collins' unofficial use of a contact charge on the damaged Möhne Dam model in February or March 1942, which substantially affected the chain of events culminating in Operation Chastise, warrants closer examination, too. Following the second meeting of the Air Attack on Dams (AAD) Committee on 1 July 1941, R. S. Capon from the MAP outlined the agenda for a meeting scheduled a week later at Harmondsworth. One question to be discussed was: 'How much evidence is there for charges required to do effective damage when they are in contact with the face?' Following that meeting, Capon wrote 'it is recommended that further consideration be given to attack on gravity dams by bombs designed for operation in contact with the face'. On 5 August, he explained that contact was envisaged by angling a bomb through water ('deviation of the water trajectory of bombs to increase the chance of hitting the face of the dam'). The idea of exploding a charge against the dam wall was therefore very much on the agenda from mid-1941, and on 3 October, W. H. Stephens, Secretary to the AAD Committee, mentioned to Capon possible contact tests with gravity dam models.

No such tests were conducted, as Collins' comprehensive series of reports to the MAP confirms. On 21 November 1941, Stephens virtually drew a line under this subject. 'As regards gravity dams, such as the Möhne dam in the Ruhr, the prospects are not promising'. The stumbling blocks were lack of a suitable bomb for contact purposes or a reliable method of delivery. In fact, during November, close attention was yet again given to use of aerial torpedoes; the following month, the 'sympathetic detonation' of a number of small charges by one large bomb. Both methods were still under active consideration in March 1942. On 3 February 1942, Capon outlined three theoretical ways of breaching gravity dams: a large bomb exploded within a specified distance of the face; a number of bombs 'detonated by the pressure wave from a trigger bomb'; detonation in contact with the dam wall. Collins, who attended many of the planning meetings, would have been aware of the latter option and perhaps unconsciously was seeking to prove its practicality when he blew up the Möhne model in early 1942.

Another aspect of the Möhne attack merits consideration. Critics have argued that the sluices should have been targeted. Hitting them directly was impossible. However, at the 10 December 1941 meeting of the AAD Committee, Wallis put forward the idea of a 'pressure wave set up by a very large bomb'; an indirect reminder, possibly, of his big bomb concept. Stephens, the committee secretary, discussed the prospect with the civil engineer who had written a report for the Air Ministry on the Möhne in December 1939. W. T. Halcrow maintained that the chance of success was 'very slight'. Except during maintenance the sluice valves were usually open so a pressure wave was unlikely to cause damage, an opinion which Capon conveyed to Wallis and Glanville on 22 December.

A further demonstration of the impact of the Dambusters Raid is presented by summaries of wireless traffic intercepted by the Government Code and Cypher School and passed to the Prime Minister. On 20 May 1943, the Japanese ambassador in Berlin sent a fanciful account of the raid to Tokyo supposedly based on an official German briefing. The attacks on the 'Eder dam and the Möhne dam' were accurate 'so as to break the walls of the dams . . . flying low . . . they used torpedoes such as are used for attacking ships'. The British success was achieved because 'both places were entirely lacking in air defences . . . a lamentable oversight in Germany's air defence'. This contrasted with the Sorpe dam where, 'owing to the presence of two anti-aircraft guns for the defence of nearby factories, six enemy planes were shot down' and no damage occurred. The disruption caused 'by the collapse of the (first two) dams was pretty considerable', though 'no damage to coal-mines and important factories' provided 'a bright spot in a bad business'. 'The heaviest blow was to the water supply', now denied to many areas. Floods were 'considerable', and 'it would take about two months to repair the breaches in the dams'.

Six days later, German Naval Headquarters in Berlin transmitted a more specific analysis to the Admiral Commanding Aegean Operations and presumably other similar commanders. 'In a successful attack on dams the British used 4-ton mine-bombs with 2.6 tons of explosive, hydrostatic and time fuze, dropped in low level flight. Effective even at a considerable distance (400 metres) from the object'. The admiral was warned that 'locks, moles etc.' were possible future targets 'especially in U-boat bases'. By 10 June, he must report on defensive measures already in place and intended to be deployed. Steps taken to protect thirteen of 'the most important dams in Upper Italy . . . against air attack' were demanded of Luftflotte 2 on 24 September, and Churchill asked whether any of these were feasible for an RAF operation. Air Chief Marshal Sir Charles Portal, Chief of the Air Staff, replied that only 'Suviana is thought to be worth destroying and tactically suitable for the use of the Upkeep weapon' though two others were under consideration. In the event, none were attacked with Upkeep, but the effect of 617 Squadron's operation in May 1943 evidently led to defences being strengthened not only around dams but perceived vulnerable military targets in Italy and the Aegean, as well as Germany.

The difficulty and, indeed, the danger of reaching conclusions based on sparse evidence is illustrated by the provision of dam models for crew briefings. In *Enemy Coast Ahead*, Gibson recalled being shown 'three models . . . perfect in every detail down to the smallest tree' on 29 March 1943. From references in other documents and knowing that only two models (Möhne and Sorpe) had been used, when writing this book I reasoned that he could only have seen those two, not three. Gibson's memory did fail him, but my analysis was also awry. Records of RAF Medmenham, where they were made, reveal that the Möhne model (M/328) was completed towards the end of March 1943, the Sorpe (M/347) not until 19 April and the Eder (M/371) on 17 May after the raid. Gibson could therefore only have seen the Möhne model on 29 March.

When R. S. Capon wrote to Wallis from the MAP on 1 December 1940, he referred to 'the effect of explosions on a model dam which you inspired', but reiterated that attempts to find a way of destroying gravity dams had been pursued 'from time to time' before and during the war. He thus confirmed that Wallis attacked the problem from a different angle, breathing new life into a lengthy quest. He found the way to breach gravity dams, which had eluded planners for six years. Crucially, though, not without their help and co-operation.

This wider dimension is starkly absent from *The Dambusters*, whose makers admitted selection and distortion in a search for entertainment. Greatly enhanced by stirring theme music, its celluloid images have become widely accepted as the definitive account of Operation Chastise, to the detriment of those excluded from its dramatic script.

John Sweetman
August 2002

BIBLIOGRAPHY

1. *Notes on Sources*

A variety of published and unpublished, contemporary and later written sources have been consulted and personal interviews conducted with Servicemen and civilians connected with Operation Chastise. Footnotes, however, have been omitted on the grounds that they deter the non-specialist and that references to 'The Barnes Wallis Papers' or private letters to the author are not in reality helpful to scholars. I have therefore settled for a detailed bibliography as a starting point for researchers and those seeking further information.

The danger of relying upon a single source, however official and seemingly authentic, should be very much borne in mind. For example, 617 Squadron's operations record book is such a trap for the unwary; many contemporary documents wrongly hold that McCarthy flew ED923/G to the Sorpe; and, due possibly to a typing error, Appendix E to AOC 5 Group's post-operational report (PRO/Air 14/840) put the time of AJ-W's take-off at 2139 (not 2129) and thus wrongly described the second wave's order of departure from Scampton. The operation order for Chastise provides another, particular instance of this problem. Both its draft and final versions are in PRO/Air 14/844, but only the final one in PRO/Air 14/2087. Examination of the second of these files alone would not reveal important overnight route changes. It is noteworthy, too, that some documents at Kew and casualty records held by the Ministry of Defence are still closed to public inspection.

The Official History must also be treated with caution. Compilers of such works have a difficult task, faced with a multitude of papers and being constrained to present the story as it emerges from official documents which may themselves be fallible. In this respect the crew list reproduced from the 617 Squadron operations record book and route map from AOC 5 Group's report of 7 June 1943, are especially relevant. It must be appreciated, too, that the writers of such volumes cannot devote inordinate time to the study of specific operations. And, furthermore, it should be noted that the captions of photographs in official archives may not always be correct.

Single sources are therefore doubtful if taken in isolation, and memory is an even more fickle basis for fact. Not only can false versions of events harden over the years, but genuine confusion can occur: two people – one Serviceman, one civilian – verbally described two separate instances connected with Operation Chastise in 1977 and four years later gave an entirely different account while denying the validity of the first. This overall difficulty arises, too, with many printed works which have leaned heavily on Wg Cdr Gibson's *Enemy Coast Ahead*, an excellent book for atmosphere but not always a reliable record of events and details.

2. *Collections of Papers*

(i) *Barnes Wallis Papers*

At the time of consultation these were in Sir Barnes' possession at White Hill House, Effingham, but have since been dispersed to locations such as the National Science Museum and Churchill College Cambridge. There was a mass of private and public, Service and civilian documents which were originally well organised but later suffered disruption and damage due to flooding in the Vickers works at Weybridge. As a result any attempt to identify a document other than by 'Barnes Wallis Papers' would be meaningless. Sir Barnes evidently received the minutes of most relevant Highball and Upkeep meetings, whether present himself or not, together with pre- and post-raid interpretation reports and a large number of other communications from ministries, firms and individuals. He retained a copy of all Collins' MAP papers, for example, a great volume of data concerning the construction and perceived economic importance of the dams. Sketches, drawings and copious notes in his own immaculate copperplate have survived, so too have a considerable number of official and eyewitness reports from Germany (some translated, some not). A translation of the report on 30 September 1943, by Dr Prüss, Superintendent of Works of the Ruhr Valley Dams Association (*Ruhrtalsperrenverein*), summarising the attacks and their effect is in one file, together with translated extracts from foreign newspapers and from Goebbels' diaries. A scrapbook of cuttings dealing with Operation

Chastise and several files of contemporary and later correspondence have survived also. Sir Barnes' personal diaries for 1940 and 1943 (though not 1941 and 1942) are among the collection of documents, and so are copies of his three major papers in connection with the destruction of German dams.

(ii) *Speer Collection, Imperial War Museum*
A few items refer: viz 3052/49, Interrogation of Albert Speer in 1945 and 3063/49, Reports 26 and 62 by Speer on Allied bombing of Germany.

(iii) *Milch Papers, Imperial War Museum*
Of marginal interest: eg Vol 20, f.5453, Quartermaster-General's development conference, 25 May 1943, discussed defensive measures to be taken after the Dams Raid; Vol 21, f.6065, conference of 1 June 1943, noted the General Staff's request for a report on the dam-busting aircraft which crashed (Barlow's).

(iv) *Cherwell Papers, Nuffield College, Oxford*
Of no specific importance, except that they demonstrate the breadth of Cherwell's interests and the number of wild schemes with which he had to deal. They contain copies of Wallis–Cherwell correspondence also in the Wallis Papers and PRO.

3. *Public Record Office, Kew*

The following documents were examined:

Air 2	4967	Citations and Awards
Air 4	37	Wg Cdr Gibson's logbook
Air 6	63	Air Council Memos Jan–Dec 1943
	67	Conclusions of Air Council Meetings, July 1940–December 1943
Air 8	1102	May–September 1943, protection of dams and reservoirs in the United Kingdom
	1234–6	February 1943–May 1945, possible use of Highball and Upkeep
	1237	March 1943–October 1944, Highball and Upkeep progress reports
	1238	March–April 1943, economic effects of destruction of German dams
	1239	July–August 1943, Russian request for Chastise information

	1458	Correspondence of Air Staff and Naval Staff, February 1943–March 1945
Air 9	96	1938–1940, War Plans
	102	Attacks on German War Industry (WA 5)
	214–6	Joint Planning Staff, 1941–3
Air 10	3395	Operational Numbers of Bomb Targets in Germany (SD 226)
Air 14	229	1938, Bombing Committee's Minutes
	595	Directly concerned with Chastise
	717	April 1943–October 1944, Operations of 617 Squadron
	790	June 1942–April 1945, Operational Research Committee
	817	July 1940–June 1941, attacks on German reservoirs and dams
	840	Directly concerned with Chastise
	842	Directly concerned with Chastise
	844	Directly concerned with Chastise
	1195	December 1941–July 1943, Bomber Command operations final report
	1385	January 1942–October 1943, analysis of night photographs
	2036	Directly concerned with Chastise
	2060–1	1943–5, further trials with Upkeep
	2062	April 1943, operational role of 617 Squadron
	2087–8	Directly concerned with Chastise
	2144	November 1942–October 1943, No 5 Group Intelligence Diary
Air 19	304	1941–3, publicity in the USA
	383	Attack on Ruhr Dams, including interpretation reports
Air 20	2617	Chiefs of Staff papers, Highball and Upkeep
Air 24	205	Bomber Command Operations and Administration, January–December 1943
	252–5	Bomber Command appendices to 205 with intelligence reports, February–May 1943
	579	Fighter Command Operations
Air 25	36	2 Group Operations Record Book
	52, 69	3 Group Operations Record Book
	93, 101	4 Group Operations Record Book
	119	5 Group Operations Record Book

	129, 135	6 Group Operations Record Book
	759, 761	92 Group Operations Record Book
Air 27	538	57 Squadron Operations Record Book
	2017	542 Squadron Operations Record Book
	2021	542 Squadron B Flight Operations Record Book
	2128	617 Squadron Operations Record Book
	9156	Citations and Awards
Air 28	682	RAF Scampton Operations Record Book
AVIA 15	384, 1001, 2340	Concerning the MAP
AVIA 18	715	A & AEE reports on ED 825/G
Cab 23	3, 13 16, 44B	War Cabinet minutes
Cab 65	34	Conclusions of War Cabinet meetings, 1 April–29 June 1943
	37–8	Confidential annexes to Cabinet minutes, 11 January–30 June 1943
Cab 66	36–7	War Cabinet memos, April–June 1943
Cab 69	2	War Cabinet Defence Committee (Ops) file, 1941
	5	War Cabinet Defence Committee (Ops) file, 1943
	8	War Cabinet Defence Committee (Ops), Secretary's Standard file
Cab 79	10–1	Chiefs of Staff Committee minutes, March–May 1941
	26–7	Chiefs of Staff Committee minutes, March–November 1943
	88	Chiefs of Staff Committee, Secretary's Standard file, 1943
Cab 80	27–8	Chiefs of Staff Committee memos, 30 March–26 June 1941
	39	Chiefs of Staff Committee memos, January–March 1943
Cab 99	22	Trident conference, May 1943, British Chiefs of Staff and Combined Chiefs of Staff meetings
DEFE	2	Investigations into the demolition of dams and Operation Cornet
W.O. 208	3262	Operation Cornet
W.O. 216	133	Mission No 30 at Moscow, May–December 1943

4. *Bundesarchiv-Militärarchiv, Freiburg, Federal Republic of Germany*

E 2024 and 204/1	Documents concerned with the interruption to water supplies following breaching of the Möhne Dam and their restoration; sectional and construction drawings of the Möhne Dam
RL 199/3 and 203/4	Progress of repair work on the Möhne Dam
RL 200/61	Effect of breaching the Möhne Dam on waterworks
RL 200/62–3	Details of defensive measures taken at the Möhne and other similar dams 1943–4
RM 122/v.M/1309/83077	Relevant flak records

Note: Microfilm copies of *Bundesarchiv-Militärarchiv* documents about damage sustained below the Möhne Dam are held in the Central Library, Royal Military Academy, Sandhurst; copies of Luftwaffe flak records are also held by the Ministry of Defence, The Hague, Netherlands.

5. *Wasser-und-Schiffahrtsamt, Hannover-Münden, Federal Republic of Germany*

This authority will answer no letters nor provide lists of material in its archives, but researchers may examine files if they make a personal visit. Transcripts of the following documents were obtained in this way, but no reference numbers are available.

Weekly reports of rebuilding at the Eder Dam, 17 July–30 November 1943

Report on repairs to electricity supplies, 27 July 1943

Report on 'The War Damage to the Eder Dam and its repairs,' January 1950, by the senior administrator and construction adviser to the *Wasser-und-Schiffahrtsamt*

Text of a lecture delivered at the *Technische Hochschule*, Hannover, on the damage and rebuilding of the Eder Dam.

6. *Department of Aviation Records, RAF Museum, Hendon*

B 689	Handwritten note by Dr Norman Davey, formerly of the Building Research Station, dated May 1980
DC 72/28	Instructions for the fitting of spotlights to Type 464 (Provisioning) Lancasters

DC 74/144   Various German eyewitness accounts and summaries of the
             course, damage and wider effects of the attack on the Möhne
             Dam

Drawings of the modifications required on a Lancaster III for this operation
and copies of German documents analysing Barlow's crashed aircraft and its
attached Upkeep, together with a copy of a cross-sectional drawing of the
Möhne Dam used by Wallis to brief 617 Squadron crews on 16 May 1943, are
also in this department.

7. *Other German archives*

The *Ennepe-Wasserverband*, Gevelsberg, *Ruhrverband und Ruhrtalsperre-
verein*, Essen, and *Wupperverband*, Wuppertal, Federal Republic of Germany,
hold records and certain eyewitness accounts, summaries of which may be
obtained on request.

8. *Miscellaneous Data*

Hansard, Parliamentary Debates   389 and 390 HC Debates Fifth Series
Albert F. Simpson Historical Research Center, Maxwell Air Force Base, USA
   HQ VIII Bomber Command, Narratives of Operations 15–17 May, 1943
   HQ VIII Fighter Command, Weekly Intelligence Summary, 16–22 May,
   1943

Navigators' logs from AJ-G (partial), AJ-H, AJ-J, AJ-N, AJ-P, and AJ-W
held by 617 Squadron, RAF Scampton
Office of Naval Intelligence, Washington, War Diary of the German Naval
Staff (Ops Division), translated 1948, Part A Vol 45
Speer's Office Diary (1943), pp 63–4, 99, 154–5 (supplied by the late Herr
Speer to author, but otherwise available)

9. *Published Books*

Note: published in London, unless stated

G. Aders   History of the German Night-Fighter Force 1917–
                  1943 (Eng trans 1978)
M. Balfour   Propaganda in War 1939–1945 (1979)
W. Baumbach   Broken Swastika: the Defeat of the Luftwaffe (Eng
                  trans 1960)
A. Boyle   No Passing Glory (1957)
R. Brett-Smith   Hitler's Generals (1976)

P. Brickhill	The Dam Busters (1952)
E. Burke	Guy Gibson VC (1961)
J. M. Burns	Roosevelt: the Soldier of Freedom 1940–1945 (1971)
L. Cheshire	Bomber Pilot (Mayflower ed, 1975)
R. W. Clark	Tizard (1965)
A. E. Clouston	The Dangerous Skies (1956)
C. Cruickshank	The Fourth Arm, Psychological Warfare 1938–1945 (1977)
L. Curtis	The Forgotten Pilots. Story of the Air Transport Auxiliary 1939–1945 (Henley-on-Thames, 1971)
C. Eade (ed)	The War Speeches of the Rt Hon W. S. Churchill, ii (1952)
H. Euler	*Als Deutschlands Dämme brachen* (Stuttgart, 1976)
S. Finn	Lincolnshire Air War 1939–1945 (Lincoln, 1973)
M. R. D. Foot and J. M. Langley (ed)	MI9 (1979)
A. Galland	The First and the Last (Eng trans 1955)
T. Gander and P. Chamberlain	Small Arms, Artillery and Special Weapons of the Third Reich (1978)
J. Garlinski	Hitler's Last Weapons (1978)
G. Gibson	Enemy Coast Ahead (Pan ed, 1955)
W. Green	Avro Lancaster (1959)
W. K. Hancock (ed)	Statistical Digest of the War (1951)
A. Harris	Bomber Offensive (1947)
H. Heiber (ed)	*Hitlers Lagebesprechungen* (Stuttgart 1962)
O. F. G. Hogg	The Royal Arsenal, ii (1963)
M. E. Howard	Grand Strategy, iv, August 1942–September 1943 (1972)
W. Hubatsch	*Kriegstagebuch des Oberkommandos der Wehrmacht* (Frankfurt-am-Main, 1963)
P. Huskinson	Vision Ahead (1949)
D. Irving	Hitler's War (1977)
D. Irving	The Rise and Fall of the Luftwaffe (1973)
R. V. Jones	Most Secret War: British Scientific Intelligence 1939–1945 (1978)
N. Kelen	*Gewichtsstaumauern und Massive Wehre* (Berlin 1933)

J. Killen	The Luftwaffe: A History (1967)
W. J. Lawrence	No 5 Bomber Group RAF 1939–1945 (1951)
J. Leasor	War at the Top (1954)
L. P. Lochner (ed)	The Goebbels Diaries 1942–3 (Westport, Connecticut 1970)
A. Ludin and F. Tolke	*Wasserkraft-anlager* (Berlin 1938)
K. Macksey	Kesselring: The Making of the Luftwaffe (1978)
W. Manchester	The Arms of Krupp 1587–1968 (1969)
W. N. Medlicott	The Economic Blockade, ii (1959)
J. E. Morpurgo	Barnes Wallis: a Biography (1972)
G. Pawle	The Secret War (Corgi ed, 1959)
M. M. Postan, D. Hay and J. D. Scott	Design and Development of Weapons (1964)
A. Price	Luftwaffe (1969)
D. Richards	Portal of Hungerford (1977)
B. Robertson	Lancaster – The Story of a Famous Bomber (1964)
S. Roskill	Hankey, Man of Secrets 1931–1963 (1974)
H. Rumpf	The Bombing of Germany (Eng trans 1975, pub Germany 1963)
J. D. Scott	Vickers – A History (1962)
A. Speer	Inside the Third Reich (Eng trans, Sphere books 1977)
A. Speer	Spandau Diaries (Eng trans 1976)
M. G. Steinert	Hitler's War and the Germans (Eng trans, Ohio University Press 1977)
United States Strategic Bombing Survey (Overseas Economic Effects Division)	The Effects of Strategic Bombing on the German War Economy (1945)
W. Warlimont	*Im Hauptquartier der deutschen Wehrmacht* 1939–1945 (Frankfurt-am-Main 1962)
C. Webster and N. Frankland	The Strategic Air Offensive against Germany 1939–1945 (the official history), i, ii and iv (1961)

10. *Articles and Pamphlets*

Anon	*Die Nacht als die Dämme brachen, TWS-Stimmen*, Jg 17, 1968

Anon	*Dokumentation: Möhnesee* (published Federal Republic of Germany)
Baker, Lord	William Henry Glanville, Biographical Memoirs of Fellows of the Royal Society, Vol 23, December 1977
British Intelligence Objectives Sub-Committee	German Experimental Work on the Attack of Reinforced Concrete by Explosives and Projectiles and Inspection of the Möhne and Eder Dams, September 1945 (unpublished)
A. R. Collins	Dam Busting: the 'uncivil engineering' behind the famous wartime raid, *New Civil Engineer*, May 1972
A. R. Collins	The Origins and Design of the Attack on the German Dams (draft article, unpublished in 1981)
Department of Scientific and Industrial Research	Building Research 1940–1945 (1948)
Department of Scientific and Industrial Research	Wartime Activities of the Road Research Laboratory (1949)
R. Gööck	*Als die (Eder) Sperrmauer Brach* (Korbach and Bad Wildingungen 1974)
I. Hutchings	Bouncing Bombs of the Second World War, *New Scientist*, 2 March 1978
G. Jones	Sir Barnes Wallis: inventor without a monument, *New Scientist*, 8 November 1979
O. Kirschmer	*Zerstörung und Schutz von Talsperren und Dämmen, Schweizerische Bauzeitung*, Jg. 67, nr. 21 (1949)
H. W. Koenig	*Instandsetzung der Sorpetalsperre zur Besichtigung von Kriegsschäden* (Hamburg 1961)
J. D. Lewin	German Dams Attacked Successfully, *Engineering News Record*, New York, 17 June 1943
Ministry of Information	Bomber Command (1941)
Ministry of Information	Over to You, broadcasts by the RAF (1943)
M. Piekalkiewicz	*Nach Uns die Sinflut*, an extract from *Spione, Agenten, Soldaten, Geheime Kommandos im 2. Weltkrieg* (published in Federal Republic of Germany)

A. Price — The Dams Raid and After, *Purnell's History of the Second World War*, Vol II, No 10

W. G. Ramsey — The Ruhr Dams Raid, *After the Battle*, No 3

S. E. Rigold — Reculver, Kent (1971)

H. Rumpf — *Die Luftangriffe auf die Möhne, Eder und Sorpe Talsperren 16/17 Mai 1943 und ihre Wikungen, Ziviler Luftschutz*, H.lc, 1954

B. N. Wallis — Dam Busting Weapon, *Air Clues*, May 1963

B. N. Wallis — The Man and His Bomb: the Dam-Busting Weapon, *Aerospace Historian*, 1973

F. W. Winterbotham — Dam Busting (unpublished draft chapter for a book)

11. *Newspapers and Periodicals*

Aerospace Historian
After the Battle
Air Clues
Aero Modeller
Annual Register
Daily Express
Daily Mail
Daily Mirror
Daily Sketch
Daily Telegraph
Express and Echo, Exeter
Evening News, Portsmouth
Evening Standard

Hampshire Telegraph and Post
Illustrated London News
Lincolnshire Echo
London Gazette
New Civil Engineer
New Scientist
New York Times
Observer
Picture Post
Star, Sheffield
Sunday Express
The Times
Western Telegraph

INDEX